Coins and the Archaeologist

Coins and the Archaeologist

Second edition

edited by
John Casey
&
Richard Reece

LONDON

First published in B.A.R.4, 1974
This edition first published 1988

Typeset by Enset (Photosetting)
Midsomer Norton, Bath, Avon
and printed and bound in Great Britain
by Biddles Ltd.,
for the publishers
B. A. Seaby Ltd.
8, Cavendish Square
London W1M OAJ

Distributed by
B. T. Batsford Ltd.
P. O. Box 4, Braintree, Essex CM7 7QY

Coins and the archaeologist. 2nd ed.
    1. Great Britain. Ancient Roman coins
    I. Casey, P.J. (Patrick John), 1935
    III. Reece, Richard
    737.4937

ISBN 1-85264-011-1

Foreword

This volume of thirteen papers is the result of a two day discussion on coins and archaeology held in the Institute of Archaeology, London in March 1973. The work of organising the discussion and forming the programme was done mainly by P.J.C., while the collection of papers afterwards was done mainly by R.R.

When collecting together the contributions of eleven workers, each of whom has a background of work in his or her chosen subject, there seems little point in attempting to impose an editorial policy. In the present case such imposition would have been an impertinence for the writers know better than the editors what they want to say. The policy has, therefore, been to collect together thirteen very different contributions, each with its individual style, in the belief that the well-knit subject of the volume – Coins and the Archaeologist – can only benefit from such diverse attentions. Several of the papers differ from the versions given in discussion, and three – on numerical aspects of coin hoards by R.R., on data for dating by J.R.C., and on monetary expansion and recession by D.M.M. – were not given in the original gathering.

Those who attended the discussion were mainly numismatists – though the proceedings were assisted by a number of archaeologists. We hope very much that the appearance of this volume will encourage the necessary cooperation between the two disciplines and give archaeologists and numismatists alike food for thought and incentive to further research.

John Casey, University of Durham
Richard Reece, Institute of Archaeology, London

Foreword to the second edition

That the papers in this volume have stood the test of time is a measure of the originality of numismatic and archaeological approach which the authors brought to their contributions. In responding to the demand of students for a reprint of the work, and with the opportunity presented by its appearance under the imprint of B. A. Seaby, revisions have been made to a number of the papers which amount to a radical replacement of material. Notable in this respect is the paper by G. C. Boon on counterfeits and copies in the Roman series. The new version of the paper takes into full account the enormous volume of research in this field which has taken place in the past fifteen years, research stimulated by a mass of new hoards and site finds from controlled excavations. Equally fruitful has been the work to advance knowledge in the English regal coinage from its inception to the reign of Henry VIII. Marion Archibald has extensively revised her paper both as regards new information and enhanced the bibliography even further than formerly; similar extensive revision has been made by D. M. Metcalf. In every case the authors of papers included in the volume have been given the opportunity to briefly review their work and to indicate the direction in which they see their aspect of numismatics developing. One entirely new paper has been added by Michael D. King on Roman Coins from Early Anglo-Saxon contexts. This paper extends the work of S. E. Rigold, bringing up to date the available information on Anglo-Saxon access to Roman coinage after more than a decade of excavation which shifted the balance from finds in burial contexts to those in domestic environments. It is a very sad task to record the deaths of two contributors to the original edition, Stuart Rigold and Michael Dolley. Both have left voids in the numismatic and archaeological worlds which have not yet been filled.

The editors readily acknowledge the kindness of their authors who willingly, and speedily, responded to the suggestion that a new edition be prepared.

John Casey
Richard Reece

Contents

			Page
	Abbreviations		ix
1	John Collis	A functionalist approach to pre-Roman coinage	1
2	Anne S. Robertson	Romano-British coin hoards: their numismatic, archaeological and historical significance	13
3	John Casey	The interpretation of Romano-British site finds	39
4	Peter Curnow	Coin lists: some problems of the smaller site	57
5	Richard Reece	Clustering of coin finds in Britain, France and Italy	73
6	Richard Reece	Numerical aspects of Roman coin hoards in Britain	86
7	George C. Boon	Counterfeit coins in Roman Britain	102
8	John Collis	Data for dating	189
9	J. P. C. Kent	Interpreting coin finds	201
10	S. E. Rigold	Coins found in Anglo-Saxon burials	218
11	Michael D. King	Roman coins from Early Anglo-Saxon contexts	224
12	D. M. Metcalf	Monetary expansion and recession: interpreting the distribution patterns of seventh and eighth-century coins	230
13	Michael Dolley	Some thoughts on the manner of publication of coins found in the course of archaeological excavations	254

14   Marion M. Archibald   English medieval coins as dating
evidence   264

Index   303

For the second edition the maps, charts and diagrams have been re-drawn by
Mr. Kevin Butcher.

Abbreviations

Arch Journ   Archaeological Journal
BMC   British Museum Catalogues
BNJ   British Numismatic Journal
JBAA   Journal of the British Archaeological Association
JRS   Journal of Roman Studies
NC   Numismatic Chronicle
Num Circ   Numismatic Circular (Spink's)
NNM   American Numismatic Society, Numismatic Notes and
              Monographs
RIC   Roman Imperial Coinage, Edd. Mattingly, Sydenham,
              Sutherland and Carson
RN   Revue Numismatique

1

A functionalist approach to pre-Roman coinage

John Collis

Summary

In this review of the achievements and potential of functional and geographical studies of pre-Roman British coinage, the group of British 'potin' coins is especially selected for study. It is suggested that there was a change in the status and value of potin coins during the first century BC, Class I coins being of relatively high value, similar to that of the contemporary gold and silver, while Class II shows rather the characteristics of the later bronze coinage of eastern England.

Traditional and functional interpretations

Firstly, I must make the disclaimer that I am an archaeologist and not a numismatist. My first hand experience of these coins is confined to the seven which I have either discovered myself, or which have turned up on my excavations. My data is therefore largely derived from coin-lists, notably those prepared by Mr. Derek Allen. In this paper I am using only the data published by him in his comprehensive lists published in 1961. I realise that there is now a great deal more data from recent finds, but this is only partly published, and to use it would be to introduce yet one more bias into the material, so I have decided to ignore it. The one exception is the potin coins where I have used Mr. Allen's more recent list (1972).

Numismatics is concerned with two major aspects of study. Firstly there is the classification and ordering of the coins chronologically, which the numismatist alone can do. Secondly there is the consideration and interpretation of the context of the coins, which is where the interest of the numismatist and archaeologist most overlaps. So far at least for pre-Roman coins interpretation has been along two major lines. Firstly they have been used for dating, but this has severe limitations as coins are generally rare on excavations, and also we know little about the time-span of use of specific types. Perhaps I am just a little embittered by my own experiences, whereby the earlier a numismatist would date a coin, the later is its stratigraphical position. Thus from Owslebury the earliest coin, a gold stater of Allen's Gallo-Beligic E, turned up in an unambiguous early Roman context.

The second approach is to study the context of the coins and to interpret the distribution of specific types. In the past this has been strictly framed in political or historical terms, whether it be the writing of a numismatist (e.g. Mack 1963), or an archaeologist (e.g. Frere 1966). Thus some types of early coins are seen as representing 'invasions' especially of Belgic groups from the continent, or the later inscribed types as documenting the spread of individual kingdoms. I have previously (1971) questioned some assumptions behind these interpretations, and I hope demonstrated that other explanations can explain these patterns as well, if not better. No one ever postulates invasion to explain the appearance of a new type of Roman coin in Britain, and there is no reason to assume we were so insular in the late Iron Age that two-way contacts across the Channel were not possible. The fact is, we know almost nothing about why and under what circumstances the various uninscribed coins were produced or what they were specifically used for, and it is very doubtful if we can argue back from the elaborate organisations of the Roman and Saxon periods with their highly centralized governments. We cannot assume that this early coinage was produced under centralized tribal or regal control, in fact the evidence of the coins' distributions and of classical authors such as Caesar would suggest it was not, and rather that anyone with the command of the necessary raw materials and technical skill was free to produce them.

My own approach has been from an economic and social view point. I have for instance attempted to identify market centres in which for the first time in Temperate Europe the small change retail market appears, itself a major economic revolution (Collis 1972). I have suggested that such centres can be identified by the occurrence of quantities of bronze coins, and that there is a contrast between sites which produce large quantities (major markets) and those that produce small quantities (minor markets), though in view of disparity of research and excavation on the sites, such a distinction must of necessity remain subjective. I was also able to contrast the distribution of bronze and gold coinage, the bronze being largely confined to the 'market centres' and their immediate neighbourhood, the gold being more widely distributed in peripheral areas, a fact which again urges caution in using coinage to define political boundaries.

Sometimes such an approach can lead to direct conflict with accepted numismatic views of the ordering and chronology of certain coin-types. For instance, I contrasted the distribution and function of the 'Durotrigian' silver and bronze coins and tentatively suggested that they might therefore be contemporary. The accepted view, however, states that the bronze are later and represent degenerate successors of the silver in terms of weight, silver content and typology. Whichever interpretation eventually proves correct, I hope that the setting up of alternative hypotheses can only prove stimulating in the field of numismatic studies.

The potin coins

General

The main theme of this paper is to consider a statement by Mr. Allen in his recent article on potin coins (1972):

'It was without question the first small change coinage in Britain, and hence the first evidence for the retail market of the kind of which there were so many in Gaul, a step incidentally in the direction of urbanisation'.

This completely out-flanks my own statement on this major economic revolution, as I had envisaged this happening at the *end* of the first century BC with the introduction of bronze coinage, rather than almost a century earlier with the appearance of potin, and on the archaeological evidence I would not wish to disagree with Mr. Allen's early dating of potin coinage in Britain and Gaul. In fact I find the whole statement is in direct conflict with my own views on the processes of market and urban development not only in Britain, but in Temperate Europe as a whole. On the continent it seems that urban centres were able to come into existence without the appearance of a small change retail economy, as at Altenburg bei Niedenstein (Hofmeister 1930), or Třísov (Břeň 1966), or Zemplín (Benadík 1965), and such evidence as we have suggests that small change coinage appears secondary to urban development.

If the potin coinage in Kent does represent small change, then the reverse is true of this area. In the early part of the first century BC when potin coinage seems to make its appearance in Kent, there is only one site in Britain at all comparable with the continental sites, at Henigstbury Head near Christchurch (Bushe Fox 1915), a long way from the main potin distribution. Even in the first half of the first century AD, when urban sites have appeared in eastern England, Kent, where potin coins have their main distribution, is peripheral to the main urban developments in Essex and Hertfordshire. There are no major 'oppida', and when I discussed the evidence for minor centres on the evidence of bronze coinage, I was only able to suggest one centre in Kent, at Canterbury.

This leads me on to question whether potin coinage is truly an equivalent to bronze coinage, or whether its status was similar to that of the small silver coins which could act in a dual role, both as bullion and as small change. Certainly in Gaul potin coins were used in large numbers on the post-Caesarian urban sites, as were also the small silver coins, but the occurrence for instance of a potin coin in a hoard of silver coins at Lattes, Hérault (Majural, Arnal and Prades 1967), might suggest that its original status was higher and that it functioned like gold and silver for wealth storage.

The evidence of the hoards

In Figure 1 I have constructed a pie-chart of the known hoards of pre-Roman coins according to the dominant metal type represented in each hoard. Silver and gold, perhaps not surprisingly, form over three quarters of the hoards. Bronze, however, is remarkable by its absence, especially compared with later Roman hoards. Even of those I have listed only one is of the small-change bronze of eastern England, from Colchester. The rest are of the ambiguous Durotrigian bronze coins, and two of these at least were deposited in Roman times. Bronze coins were not then usually buried in hoards.

HOARDS

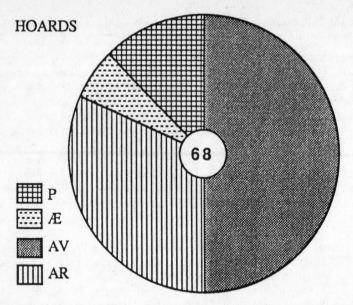

P

Æ

AV

AR

FIG. 1 Hoards of pre-Roman coins in Britain by dominant metal content

In contrast, several hoards of potin are known, some of them quite large. All the eight properly authenticated hoards belong to Class I of the potin coins, while only two dubious scattered hoards at Rochester and Canterbury are of Class II. It has been argued that all Class I hoards were deposited in response to a single historical event, such as Caesar's invasion, as all the hoards end with Allen's Group L. But some of the hoards, such as Snettisham, are well outside the main distribution and (pace Samuel Pepys) seem unlikely to be connected. Equally, the Claudian invasion failed to spark off a frenzy of burying bronze and potin hoards. The implication of the hoard evidence is that Class I potin was considered of sufficient value to hoard, but Class II was probably not.

Distribution on sites

In my 1971 paper I pointed out the association of the bronze coins with the major settlements such as Colchester and Verulamium, while gold was more common as single stray finds, presumably dating from farming settlements. In the 1972 paper I suggested it was possible to identify a number of minor sites with a relatively high number of bronze coins, sites which in this paper I shall term 'minor markets'. Using these sites as defined in that paper, it will obviously be of interest to see whether the distribution of the potin coins most closely resembles that of the bronze or gold coinage. In Figure 2 I have shown the two classes of potin coins compared as percentages on these different sites. I have also extracted Rochester which, on both the evidence of archaeology and of the high incidence of potin coins, might be

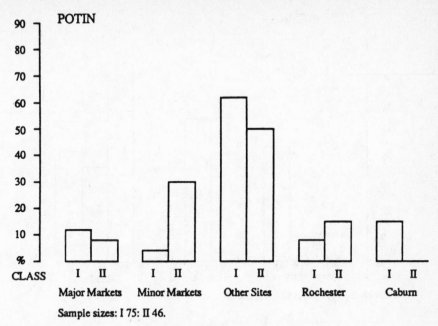

Sample sizes: I 75: II 46.

FIG. 2

suggested as a 'minor market centre', and likewise the Caburn, which has produced a number of coins both as stray finds and from the excavations. This is not strictly a statistical comparison, as distinctions must of necessity be subjective, and with sites like Hammersmith one is unsure whether one is dealing with another relatively important site or with a scattered hoard, or what. However, with these provisos, the incidence of potin coins on minor sites seems relatively high, especially Class I, but there is no statistically significant difference between the distributions of the two classes.

For comparative purposes I shall take the coinage of Cunobelin. The distribution of the gold coinage is quite straight forward, except that it is best to extract the plated forgeries, as these seem to have been recognized in antiquity, and are especially to be associated with the 'market' sites as shown in the bar charts on Figure 3. The silver coinage of Cunobelin is unfortunately rare, and the sample that we have is not of great significance. The bronze coinage is more complicated, as some types are almost entirely restricted to Colchester, whereas others are of more general distribution. I have therefore distinguished between three groups as follows:

1 Coin types with more than 50 per cent of known finds from Colchester.
   Mack 222, 225, 231, 250, 251, 253, 260a.
2 Less than 50 per cent of known finds at Colchester.
   Mack 221, 242, 246, 248.
3 Undiagnostic rare types with less than ten finds recorded.
   Mack 220, 223, 224, 226/9, 227, 228, 245, 261, Evans XII–11.

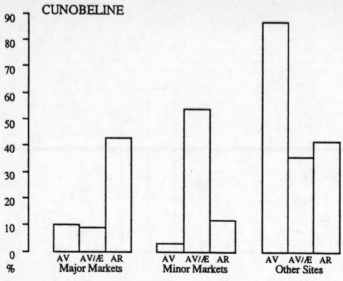

CUNOBELINE

Sample size: AV 92: AV/Æ 11: AR 25.

FIG. 3

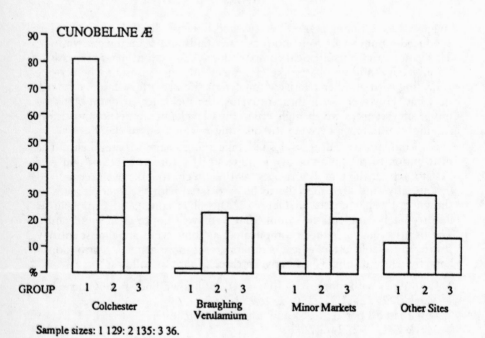

CUNOBELINE Æ

Sample sizes: 1 129: 2 135: 3 36.

FIG. 4

The division between groups 1 and 2 is in fact fairly clear, with only the small series Mack 222 (ten coins, five at Colchester) and 252 (twelve coins, seven at Colchester) at all ambiguous. These three groups have been expressed on Figure 4 as the percentage of each group that turns up on a certain category of site. As Colchester is so different from the other two major sites, Braughing and Verulamium, I have separated them in this diagram. As might be expected, Group 3 falls between the other two groups, and will be ignored in future discussion. The pattern of group 1, with majority of all known coins turning up on a major port site can perhaps be paralleled at both Hengistbury and Selsey, and as there is no similar site in Kent, it is unlikely that any of the potin coins will have similar distribution. It is group 2 which we should take as the norm. It is likely to have been minted at Verulamium, and is especially associated with the inland sites and the minor markets, though it does turn up at Colchester as well.

This data I have gathered together in Figure 5, taking the gold coinage of Cunobelin, and group 2 of his bronze coinage as defined above, and comparing it with Classes I and II of the potin series. Both fall in between the gold and the bronze distribution, Class I more closely resembling the gold, Class II the bronze, though as mentioned before the difference between the two classes of potin could be due to chance sampling errors. The expected lack of finds of potin on 'major markets' expected from the geographical considerations is compensated for a relatively high occurrence on the 'minor

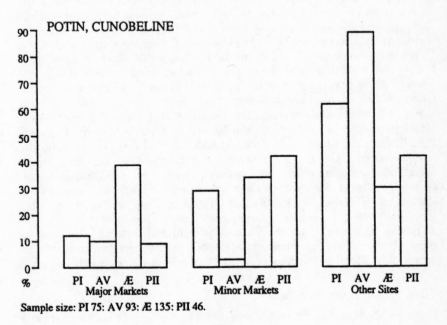

Sample size: PI 75: AV 93: Æ 135: PII 46.

FIG. 5

markets'. Using these results, I would suggest subjectively that there is evidence that the potin coinage at least initially enjoyed a higher status than bronze, but later became the equivalent in status to the bronze coinage of eastern England.

Conclusions

From the above data I would suggest the following interpretation, emphasising, however, that the case cannot be statistically proven:

1 Class I potin coins are of relatively high value, and functioned like silver coinage for both wealth storage and minor market transactions. The coins are most typical of the minor farming settlements and were used in hoards. Only one possible 'market site' can be assigned to this period, the Caburn in Sussex.
2 Class II potin coins was especially used for small change on 'market' sites, presumably for minor transactions, but was not usually hoarded. Its function is most similar to that of the contemporary bronze coinage.

If we accept Allen's dating, (Class I essentially belonging to the first half of the first century BC and Class II to the end of that century and the beginning of the first AD), it would suggest that there had been a downgrading of the status of potin around the middle of the first century BC, in fact the period when the 'market' sites were appearing in Hertfordshire and Essex. Looking at Allen's more detailed groupings A to L for Class I, and M to P for Class II, it appears that the break does in fact coincide with the change from I to II. Of the large group L, which belongs to the end of Class I, the majority come from single finds and they are well represented in hoards. It is, however, impossible to work out the precise statistics. Of Class II, the earliest groups M and N are both small with only four finds each, but in each case three finds come from 'market' sites. On this evidence it would appear that the distinction between Classes I and II is very real in terms of both function and typology.

It will be worthwhile saying a few words about Caburn. The finds come largely from the excavations by Pitt-Rivers (1881) and later the Curwens (1927), with one or two stray finds in addition, and this demonstrates the reappraisal of a site that excavation can produce. The occurrence of an occupation site using potin coins within an earlier defended enclosure can be closely paralleled by two sites in northern France both, from archaeological evidence, likely to be mainly pre-Caesarian. They are Fort Harrouard (Phillipe 1946–50), and Ste. Geneviève, Nancy (Beaupré 1910). A pre-Caesarian date would suit the Caburn as well, and these sites do seem to represent the initial developments towards full retail market, though they are much smaller than the classic 'oppida' that one encounters further south.

The future of functional studies

However sophisticated the techniques we may try to apply to our archaeological data, the results will not be worth the paper they are written on unless

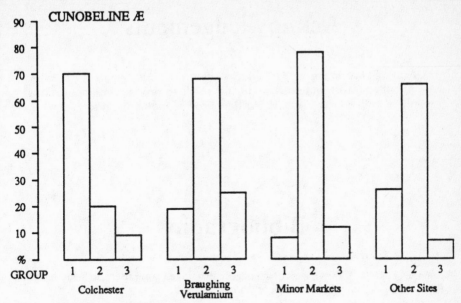

CUNOBELINE Æ

Sample sizes: C 148: B+V 34: MM 57: OS 61.

FIG. 6

the full limitations of the data on which they are based is taken into consideration. The suggestions outlined in all my papers are not facts but hypotheses which must be continually tested as more and better data becomes available. As mentioned in the introduction, I have deliberately not used the more recent and better data from excavations such as Verulamium, Harlow and Baldock, which may force a reconsideration of some of what I have written above, which is equally likely to allow more sophisticated techniques to be applied. On Figure 6 I have shown the different percentages that my different groups of bronze coins of Cunobelin form on different sites, again using the 1961 lists. It immediately stands out how similar to Braughing and Verulamium are the percentages of coins from the 'minor markets' in contrast with the finds from Colchester. But relationships were likely to have been much more complex than shown in this diagram, and one could suggest the application of more sophisticated 'similarity co-efficients', such as are being used experimentally in archaeology to compare assemblages of other sorts of artefacts (Hodson 1969). The results could be important for the development of both numismatics and archaeology. Simulation models of coin spread is another potential line of enquiry, which could be applied both in this country and on the continent.

Acknowledgements

As always I owe much to Mr. Derek Allen, not only from his published works, but also for numerous comments made in private communications. I would also like to thank Richard Reece for prodding me into action.

Bibliography

Allen, D. F. 1961: "The Origins of Coinage in Britain; a reappraisal", in S. Frere (ed.) *Problems of the Iron Age in Southern Britain*: 97–308.

Allen, D. F. 1972: "British Potin Coins: a Review", in D. Hill and M. Jesson (eds.) *The Iron Age and its Hill-Forts*: 127–194.

Beaupré, J. 1910: "L'Oppidum de Sainte Geneviève (Essey les Nancy)", in *Memoires de la Société d'Archéologie Lorraine*. 60: 265–29.

Benadik, B. 1965: "Die Spätlatènezeit Siedlung von Zemplin in der Slovakei", in *Germania*. 43: 63–91.

Břeň, J. 1966: *Třísov: a Celtic Oppidum in South Bohemia*.

Collis, J. R. 1971: "Functional and Theoretical Interpretations of British Coinage", in *World Archaeology*. 3: 71–84.

Collis, J. R. 1972: "Market and Money", in Hill and M. Jesson (eds.) *The Iron Age and its Hill-Forts*: 97–104.

Curwen, E. & Curwen, C. E. 1929: "Excavations in the Caburn near Lewes", in *Sussex Archaeological Collections*. 68: 1–56.

Frere, S. S. 1966: *Brittania*.

Hodson, F. R. 1969: "Searching for Structure within Multivariate Archaeological Data", in *World Archaeology*. 1: 90–105.

Hofmeister, H. 1930: *Die Chatten*. Band I: "Mattium, die Altenburgh bei Niedenstein".

Mack, R. P. 1963: *The Coinage of Ancient Britain*.

Majural, R., Arnal, J. & Prades, H. 1964: "Deux Nouveaux Trésors de Lattes, Hérault: Obols Massaliotes à la Croix", in *Ogam*. 19: 397–434.

Philippe, J. 1946–50: "Quelques Aspects du Fort Harrouard", in *Bulletin de la Société Normande*. 34: 72–80, 116–121. 35: 13–17, 46–49.

Pitt-Rivers (Lane-Fox), A. 1881: "Excavations at Mount Caburn Camp near Lewes", in *Archaeologia*. 46: 423–495.

A functionalist approach to pre-Roman coinage

This article is one of a number which I wrote in the early 1970s trying to re-orientate research into Iron Age coinage – it proved a more controversial matter than I had expected! The debate is adequately covered elsewhere (Collis 1981, Rodwell 1981, Roymans and van der Sanden 1980, Collis 1985). Though in detail some of my ideas have not stood the test of time, the basic approach is gaining in popularity and, I think, allowing new insights into the function of pre-Roman coinage in Britain and elsewhere. As far as the potin coinage goes, the most recent study is that of Colin Haselgrove (1986), in which he agrees with the basic thesis of a change of function of potin coinage, though using different evidence, that of the distribution of potin, which is similar in its characteristics to gold but different from that of bronze. Where he provides new evidence is firstly in the early dating of the end of the production of potin coinage, perhaps not even continuing as late as the beginning of the first century AD. The functional change he sees as post-dating the end of production, perhaps even being a post-conquest phenomenon.

Department of Archaeology and Prehistory, University of Sheffield

Bibliography

Collis, J. R. 1981: "Coinage, Oppida, and the Rise of Belgic Power: a reply", in B. W. Cunliffe "Coinage and Society in Britain and Gaul: some current problems", 53–55, *Council for British Archaeology* Research Report No. 38, London.

Collis, J. R. 1985: "Iron Age Coin-Moulds", in *Britannia* 16: 237–238.

Haselgrove, C. 1986: *Iron Age Coinage in South-East Britain: the archaeological context.* (Oxford).

Rodwell, W. 1981: "Iron Age Coinage: a counter reply", in B. W. Cunliffe "Coinage and Society in Britain and Gaul: some current problems", 56, *Council for British Archaeology* Research Report No. 38, London.

Roymans, N. & Van der Sanden, W. 1980: "Celtic Coins from the Netherlands and their Archaeological Context", in *Berichten van der Rijkdienst voor het Oudkeidung Bodemonderzoek*, 30: 173–254.

2
Romano-British coin hoards: their numismatic, archaeological and historical significance

Anne S. Robertson

The discovery of hoards of Roman coins in Britain

Over 1,600 hoards of Roman coins – and over 200 other finds of Roman coins which may have been hoards – have been recorded from Britain. There must, too, have been countless other such finds of which no record survives. Almost all the recorded hoards were discovered by chance, in the course of non-archaeological activities – either because someone who was ploughing, or draining, or ditching, or gardening, or cleaning out a well, or quarrying, or digging for gravel, or erecting a house, or other building, or cutting a canal, or constructing a railway, a road, a motorway or an airport, felt the tool he was using strike some obstacle which turned out to be a hoard of coins,[1] or because a dog scratching at a rabbit hole threw up a little shower of coins behind him, or because a cow caught her hoof in something which proved to be the narrow neck of a pot full of coins, or, in one instance, at Wingfield, Suffolk, because a ghostly lady glided, with a rustling of silk, before the astonished gaze of a cottager's wife and disappeared into the pig-sty where, on subsequent investigation, a hoard of coins was revealed.

Contemporary accounts of discoveries often have some particular interest of their own, which makes them worth preserving. There was, for example, the Okehampton, Devon hoard which, under the skilful handling of its recorder, became very probably 'the store of a beggar who sat beside the Roman road begging. . . . The beggar either died or could not find the place where he had deposited his collection'. The discovery of the Great Burstead, Essex, coins in the early nineteenth century weighed so heavily upon the finder that 'he was afraid to go to bed lest he should oversleep himself and be detected ere he could dispose of them'. There was the hoard found opportunely in a Roman villa at Bourton, Gloucestershire, c. 1895, the day before the Cotswold Field Club was due to visit the site, hastily covered up again, and then 'discovered' the next day before the assembled company. There was the hoard found at Farringford, Freshwater, Isle of Wight, in whose preservation Lord Tennyson took a lively interest. There was the hoard found in the early part of the seventeenth century at Minster in Thanet, Kent, solely because certain farm workers drove their plough much deeper than usual in a fury at being ordered to work on a holiday. There was the Wingfield, Suffolk, hoard with its supernatural antecedents and its strange sequel, compounded partly of good and partly of bad fortune. There was the hoard found at Leeds, Yorkshire, in 1909, part of which was re-buried by the finder in the saucer of a flower-pot. And there were at least two hoards of small brass Roman coins, one from Yatton, Somerset, and the other from Northallerton, Yorkshire, which, after discovery, circulated locally as farthings.

Significantly enough, only a small proportion of the known Romano-British hoards – less than one in ten – has come to light during the excavation of Romano-British occupied sites.

The concealment and loss of Roman coin hoards

The attempt, or aim, to save money was no doubt as widespread in Roman times as it is today. In Roman times, however, when banking was much less common than it is now, a thrifty householder had usually to make his own provision for the safekeeping of his money. The most convenient way of doing so would be to place the coins in some receptacle – a money-box or household vessel – and then deposit it in a safe place in his house, where he could conveniently add to it when circumstances allowed, and draw on it when need arose. A passage in Cicero's *Pro Cluentio* (*c.* 179) suggests that an *armarium* or money-chest was a familiar adjunct of a Roman household.

All Roman coin hoards, however, were not normal. One abnormal hoard provided the Roman playwright, Plautus, with the plot for a play, the *Aulularia*. In its prologue, the household god explains that a pot of money had been buried under the hearthstone by an old miser who could not endure the thought of his savings being spent by anyone, even his own son. In this case, and in others like it, money was withdrawn from circulation, and kept out of circulation by the miserliness, or meanness, of the owner. A much commoner motive for the deliberate concealment of money in ancient times must, however, have been fear.

For example, a wealthy man who was about to set out on a journey and who feared either the dishonesty of those he left at home, or the hazards of the road, might conceal his treasure in a safer hiding place than his house until he returned. In another play by Plautus, the *Trinummus*, a wealthy Athenian, Charmides, buried his riches in the earth before setting off on a journey, but took the precaution of disclosing the hiding place to a trusty friend. That was a wise, and surely, a usual precaution. Even if the owner never returned to enjoy his savings, they would not go unused.

Such fears, however, of dishonesty at home or of the dangers of a journey, must have affected only a few people and have caused the concealment of comparatively few hoards, most of which must have been recovered by their owners, or by others to whom the secret of the hiding place had been entrusted. There were, on the other hand, other fears in Roman times which must have affected great numbers of people. These were fears of brigandage, or warfare, or the ruthless suppression of an unofficial currency, when conditions became so disturbed that a man's life and property were endangered and his home ceased to be a safe hiding place for valuables. In the stress of such circumstances, many a householder must have removed his money-box or his pot of coins from his house, and concealed it in a safer place, always surely near some landmark, so that he would know where to find it again when the danger passed. Appian, in his *Historia Romana* (IV, 73), describes such a mass concealment of treasure at Rhodes in 42 BC, just before it was besieged by Cassius. After capturing the city, Cassius demanded the surrender of all private, as well as all public, treasure, and the reluctant citizens were in the end forced to hand over their hidden property, 'some digging it up from holes in the ground, others drawing it from the botton of wells, others again producing it from graves'. Concealment like that at Rhodes in 42 BC must have happened in almost any district which at any time suffered from the effects of war or other unsettlement.

It is probable, although we have absolutely no means of verifying this, that the majority of hoards concealed in times of violence or disturbance were recovered by their owners when settled conditions returned, and were put into circulation again like any normal coin hoard, unless of course the coins had been demonetised and rendered worthless. At least, we may be sure that the owner of a still valuable hoard amassed by thrift and self-denial would make every possible effort to recover it, either by his own hands or by the hands of another. The failure to reclaim buried treasure is always, in fact, an exceptional, abnormal circumstance for which some explanation must be sought either in the private life of the owner or, if a large number of hoards were lost at the same time, in contemporary events.

It has, of course, long been recognised that the widespread concealment and loss of coin hoards, at a particular period, in a particular country or district, was, in all probability, due to unsettled conditions in that country or district. It has also long ago been pointed out, notably by Sir George Macdonald,[2] by Dr. H. Mattingly,[3] by Mr. B. H. St. J. O'Neil[4] and by Dr. C. H. V. Sutherland,[5] that, in view of the probable connection between the loss of a large number of coin hoards and contemporary events, a study of the Roman coin hoards lost at various periods in Britain may be expected to throw light on contemporary Romano-British history, as well as, obviously, on contemporary Romano-British currency.[6]

A necessary preliminary to such a study is an inventory, as complete and as accurate as possible, of such records of the discoveries of Romano-British coin hoards as survive. The inventory now in process of completion has been formed by collecting and sifting the published references to discoveries of Roman coin hoards in Britain, and by examining hoards which are preserved in museums, particularly if they are unpublished or inadequately published.

It is inevitable, of course, that some hoards have escaped the net, either because they have never been published at all and have never reached a museum, or because they have only been mentioned briefly in some obscure, or out-of-print publication. The majority of recorded Romano-British coin hoards have probably, however, been included in the inventory, to which, now that it has been started, additions can be made periodically.

A find of coins is regarded as a true hoard, if there were any circumstances connected with the discovery which indicated that the coins had been deliberately collected together and deposited in one place, and could not have been dropped singly or accidentally through holes in ancient pockets. For example, a group of coins found in some kind of container is usually classed as a hoard. One exception to this rule is the Birdoswald (1949) find of twenty eight denarii contained in a bronze purse, which had been buried under the rampart backing of the fort at Birdoswald and which, it was decided at a coroner's inquest, had been accidentally lost rather than deliberately hidden.

The 'date' of Romano-British coin hoards

The latest coins in a hoard provide a *terminus post quem* for the date at which money ceased to be added to the hoard. A closer dating can often be arrived at by considering the condition of the latest coin or coins, and the general composition of the hoard. If the latest coins were unworn, and if the list of coins contained in the hoard formed an uninterrupted chronological series ending abruptly with the latest coins, then the hoard was probably closed only a few years after the date of the latest coins in it. On the other hand, if the latest coins in a hoard were very much worn, that is if they had been in circulation for some time before being added to the hoard, the hoard could not have been closed until some period after the date of issue of the latest coins. This is rendered all the more probable if there were gaps in the chronological series of coins in the hoard.

The date at which a hoard was closed, at which money ceased to be added to it, may or may not have been the date at which the owner laid away his treasure. The composition of a hoard once again provides a clue as to whether or not the two dates coincided. If the chronological list of coins in a hoard formed an unbroken series, stopping short suddenly with the latest coins, then the date at which saving or hoarding ceased was probably followed at once by the date of the deposit of the hoard. For an owner who had saved steadily and consistently was hardly likely to stop abruptly, unless the hoard was no longer within his reach. If, on the other hand, there were gaps in the chronological list of coins in a hoard, that is if the saving process appears to have been intermittent, then the date at which the saving process ceased may not have been followed at once by the concealment of the hoard.

Those hoards which have been completely examined are, in fact, for the most part made up of coins forming an uninterrupted chronological series. This suggests that, as a general rule, hoards were concealed soon after the saving process ceased. This is what one would expect, but of course absolute certainty on this point is impossible to attain, and speculation is fruitless. We can only determine, as accurately as the records allow, the date at which a hoard was closed and, in the absence of evidence to the contrary, assume that the date of concealment followed soon after. Thus a hoard ending with coins of Hadrian is 'dated' to Hadrian's reign and is assumed to have been concealed in that reign.

The numismatic significance of Romano-British coin hoards

The metals of which Romano-British coin hoards were composed

A survey of the metals hoarded in Britain at different periods shows that when coins of the previous metals, gold and, more commonly silver, were current in quantity, they were as a general rule hoarded in preference to copper, always provided of course the hoarder could afford to lay aside savings substantial enough to be translated into gold or silver. The hoarding of gold coins was in fact almost entirely restricted to the two periods mid-first to late-second centuries AD, and late fourth century AD or later. These were the periods when Roman imperial gold coins were not only issued in quantity but were also of a high quality.

During these two periods, gold coins were either hoarded alone or together with silver coins. All the gold *plus* silver hoards which have been fully examined have, whatever their date, proved to contain fewer gold coins than silver coins. The owners of these mixed gold and silver hoards may have aimed at changing their silver into gold in time, only to be halted by circumstances beyond their control before attaining their goal and their gold.

It is noticeable that in all the gold *plus* silver hoards of the period mid-first to late-second centuries AD, the latest gold coins were of an earlier date than the latest silver coins. Gold coins had a much longer circulation life than silver. On the other hand, in late-fourth century (or subsequent) gold *plus* silver hoards the latest gold coins were not always of an earlier date than the latest silver coins. After the reign of Honorius the flow of Roman coins into Britain shrank rapidly. So, as the years passed, the time-lag in the circulation life of gold coins behind that of silver coins would disappear.

Silver coins, when available, were hoarded throughout the whole period of the Roman occupation of Britain, in preference to copper coins, except in the reign of Claudius and again in the late fourth century AD or later. In the first years of conquest Roman bronze coins were apparently circulating in Britain in far larger quantities than Roman silver – presumably because the chief source of Roman currency was at that time the Roman army, whose pay included mainly bronze coinage.[7] For the period of the last days of the Roman occupation, hoards of gold or silver coins are very greatly outnumbered by hoards of copper coins, which steadily overtook the gold and silver as common currency.

During the third century AD the preference which the Romano-Briton had for hoarding silver (in preference to baser metal) manifested itself in his persistent devotion to the denarius, and dislike of the antoninianus. The antoninianus, introduced in AD 215, contained at first 50 per cent alloy, which by the reign of Gallienus (AD 260–268) had risen to 75–80 per cent. As late as the reign of Philip I and II, thirty years after the introduction of the antoninianus, denarii were still being hoarded alone. Where denarii and antoniniani were hoarded together, the denarii consistently outnumbered the antoniniani until the reign of Gallienus.

Thereafter bad money rapidly drove out good. Denarii became scarcer and scarcer in circulation as they were called in and melted down for their silver content. A few stray denarii, however, did survive in hoards as late as the end of the third century AD, to emphasise the persistence with which the Romano-Briton clung to good old silver when he could get it.

The size of Romano-British coin hoards

Of the 1,600 or more Roman coin hoards recorded from Britain, only about 1 in 12 contained more than 1,000 coins each. Of these all but a very few were composed either of debased antoniniani, or of antoniniani and fourth-century copper. The most famous of these is probably the hoard of about 30,000 antoniniani from Selborne (1873), ending with Constantius I, and regarded by some as a pay chest of part of the invading army which brought to an end the independent Romano-British empire of Carausius and Allectus.[8]

Hoards of gold were, as one would expect, usually of small size, although there is one (to Marcus) of 160 aurei from Corbridge (1911),[9] and another (to Constantine III) of 600 gold solidi from Eye.[10] Silver hoards seldom contained more than a few hundred coins, although a hoard of almost 2,000 (to Severus Alexander) was found at Falkirk in 1933,[11] and a composite hoard (to Honorius) from Cleeve Prior, Worcestershire, included 450–600 solidi and almost 3,000 silver coins.[12]

The general composition of Romano-British coin hoards

'Unless there is very strong evidence to the contrary it is probable that the coins composing a hoard were withdrawn from circulation within a very short space of time before the date at which the saving process ceased. For unless the owner of a hoard was a miser, he must have been constantly taking money out of his savings, and again putting money in, or even spending his whole hoard and then starting to save afresh. If then a hoard was fluid, and all or part of it had recently been withdrawn from circulation and was likely to be put into circulation again at any time the owner wished, the coins in the hoard must have been not obsolete but current, or at least acceptable as currency. They must, in fact, reflect or represent the contents of a man's pocket or purse at a given time, frozen (as it were) into immobility for our leisurely inspection. The contents of one man's pocket or purse, or of his hoard, would of course differ in composition from the contents of another's, although both were contemporary. Each would reflect not only the owner's financial position, but also his preference for certain metals or for certain types of coins. But even so, the coins in a man's hoard would all be coins acceptable as currency, for they were surely meant to be spent sooner or later and not hoarded up for ever. A group of hoards ending with coins of a certain emperor may then be expected to throw light on the currency in circulation in Roman Britain during his reign, unless there is evidence to prove that the hoards were all exceptional in composition. Moreover, if the obverse and reverse types of coins in such a group of hoards have been recorded, still more information can be obtained about the types of coins which reached Britain and about the approximate date of types whose date might otherwise be unknown.[13]

Peculiarities of composition

Although a group of contemporary coin hoards usually had the same general composition, yet there were included in some cases a number of rare, exceptional or unexpected coins. The most striking of these peculiarities are the persistent survival of certain types of coin, the apparently deliberate selection of coins for hoarding and the inclusion of sub-standard and barbarous coins.

(1) The survival of certain types of coin

Over a dozen Romano-British hoards included Greek imperial coins, usually silver drachmae of Lycia *in genere*, or of Caesarea Cappadociae, dating from Domitian to Trajan, Trajan's issues being the commonest. The hoards concerned were all hoards of denarii ranging in date from Faustina I to Severus Alexander. The drachmae may have been accepted as denarii.

A very much larger number of hoards contained Ancient British coins of varying metals and types, and with a varying proportion of Roman to ancient British coins. These hoards indicate the circulation life and powers of survival of different types of ancient British coins. One small area of Roman Britain, Hampshire, seems to have clung to its local native currency until the Antonine period.

Still more Romano-British hoards contained one or more denarii which were stated to be of the Roman Republic or of Julius Caesar, (although some so-called Republican denarii in inadequately recorded hoards now lost may really have been legionary denarii of Mark Antony). True Republican denarii were present in Romano-British hoards in large numbers until the reign of Hadrian. Until then the Republican denarius, of fine silver and substantial weight, evidently kept its place in the currency of Roman Britain, in spite of Nero's reduction in the weight of the denarius and the subsequent recall of heavier pre-Neronian denarii. In hoards of denarii later than Hadrian the number of Republican denarii shrank to a mere trickle. Thereafter, such denarii seem to have vanished almost completely from circulation, except for a very few sporadic survivors in hoards as late as Philip I and II.

At least ten of the Romano-British hoards containing Republican denarii came from Yorkshire alone, three from Scotland, six from Wales, ten from north England, and the remainder from the Midlands and south England. (At least five of these last also contained Ancient British coins.) In general, the Republican denarius seems to have been a particular favourite in north Britain and in the less romanised parts of the province, Wales and Scotland, whose inhabitants were so uncivilised as to prefer old-fashioned silver of a high quality to more recent but debased issues.

Over sixty Romano-British hoards contained one or more of the base legionary denarii of Mark Antony. Although Hadrian's reign saw the virtual disappearance of Republican denarii from the currency, legionary denarii of Mark Antony persisted in circulation until the reign of Postumus. They were particularly numerous in hoards of the reign of Severus and of Severus Alexander.

(2) The selection of coins for hoarding
The owner of a hoard had to compose his savings out of the coins which circulated in his area during the period covered by the saving process. Out of the total range of coins available, however, he might select those which for some reason or other appeared to him most desirable.

Just as gold and silver of high quality were preferred for hoarding when readily available, so the individual coins of which a hoard was made up often appear to have been specially selected, either for their fine condition, for their good quality or for some other reason. Many a Romano-British hoard, when examined in detail, has proved to include fine, unworn coins of all the emperors represented, from the earliest to the latest. It seems likely that the thrifty owner of a hoard selected for inclusion in his savings whatever well-preserved coins came his way, and no doubt tried to get rid of his more worn specimens.

A more subtle, but still recognisable, form of selection was that of choosing coins with certain reverse types for inclusion in a hoard. At least four Romano-British hoards are said to have been composed of coins all of which had different reverse types. The most famous of these is the Hadrianic hoard from Thorngrafton (1837) which consisted of three aurei and sixty denarii contained in a bronze arm-purse. 'The collection exactly filled the vessel and the coins were all different'.[14] The owner of the bronze purse must have selected for hoarding purposes, from all the coins that came his way, only those not already represented in his savings.

The selection of particular reverse types or of a variety of reverse types is easy to detect in a hoard like the Thorngrafton hoard. It is probable, however, that some kind of selection, less obvious but none the less effective, was exercised in many other hoards. Romano-British hoards have in fact produced very many variants on the types described in the standard coin catalogues, and many rare or even unique coins. The owners of hoards containing these variants or rarities may well have included them because they were different or rare. Such selective owners would, in fact, not only be saving money, they would also be collecting coins.

Several more than thirty Romano-British hoards are said to have been restricted to the coins of one emperor only: Claudius (AE), Tetrici, Carausius, Allectus, Constantine I, Constans, Valentinian I (gold), and Valens. The reason for the limitation of a hoard to the coins of one emperor can sometimes be detected. In the reign of Claudius, for example, Claudian bronze was almost the only bronze currency available in any quantity. Again, coins of Carausius and Allectus were minted in Britain, and hoards composed solely of coins of either of these emperors had probably come in bulk straight from the mint. In the case of the other emperors, their monopoly of hoards is not so readily explained. The owners of such hoards may somehow have acquired a supply of new coins in bulk, or have had a personal preference for the coins of a certain emperor.

(3) The inclusion of faulty or sub-standard coins
A directly opposite tendency to that of the careful selection of coins for hoarding is sometimes discernible in Romano-British hoards, namely the inclusion of faulty or sub-standard coins. Apart from the few plated silver coins, cast coins and metal blanks which found their way into hoards, there were two main groups of sub-standard coins: clipped silver siliquae and barbarous or irregular copies.

The clipping of siliquae resulted from an appreciation in the value of silver after the severance of Britain from the Roman Empire, when official Roman silver coins ceased to enter Britain in any quantity, and siliquae already in Britain were cut down to offset the growing scarcity of silver.[15] It is probable therefore that hoards in which the majority of siliquae were clipped were amassed later than those hoards which contained only a few clipped siliquae. For example, the Coleraine hoard which had almost all of its siliquae clipped contained coins of Constantine III dating after AD 407.

Barbarous or irregular copies found a place in hoards dating to periods at which they formed so high a proportion of the coins in normal circulation that they could hardly be excluded completely from a man's savings. For example, copies of bronze coins of Claudius were turned out in large numbers to make good a shortage of small change in the newly constituted Roman province, and they varied greatly in style and in quality, weight and fabric. Some of them at least may have been semi-official copies, but others were probably unofficial.[16]

Well over one hundred and forty Romano-British hoards of third-century date or later contained 'barbarous radiates', copies of antoniniani, which displayed more or less irregular or barbarous workmanship and which varied in diameter from that of official antoniniani to ¼ inch (6 mm) or less. Copies with a diameter of ½ inch (12 mm) or less have been classed as minims, but there are many borderline cases and a sharp distinction between small radiate copies and minims is difficult to maintain.

The inclusion of barbarous radiates in over ninety third-century hoards ranging in date from Claudius II to *c.* AD 300 proves that irregular or barbarous copies of radiate antoniniani were being produced as early as about AD 270. The evidence of third-century hoards also shows that even radiate copies of very small module ('minims') were being made before about AD 300.

Attempts have been made to identify regional centres for the production of radiate copies. The largest number of third-century hoards containing such copies has been found in East Anglia. This does suggest that one centre of manufacture was in East Anglia.

The reason for the manufacture of 'barbarous radiates' is thought to have been a desire to supplement the official currency, by the provision of an

even smaller denomination than the smallest official bronze coin. The life
of radiate copies, begun in the late-third century AD, did not in fact end in
that century. Between thirty and forty hoards of late fourth-century date or
later included such copies, associated in many cases with barbarous fourth-
century copies. There was, however, an interval between the close of the
third century and the end of the reign of Constantine I when, apparently,
'barbarous radiates' were not being hoarded. This interval seems hitherto
to have escaped notice. It presumably means that the currency of *c.* AD
300–337 was adequate in its range for those using it in Britain. Only later
did a lack of small change again make itself felt, resulting in the re-emergence
of 'barbarous radiates' along with some official antoniniani, and with fourth-
century or 'diademed copies'.

Around eighty Romano-British hoards included diademed copies, some
of them 'minims', and some even smaller, being 4 mm or less in diameter.
Diademed copies, large or small, imitated certain specific groups of official
coins, of which the 'Fallen horseman' type was the favourite. The evidence
of fourth-century hoards shows that diademed copies and 'minims' made
their first appearance almost as soon as their official prototype came into
circulation.[17]

The end of Roman currency in Britain

The evidence of hoards is conclusive that both radiate and diademed copies
and minims continued in circulation until the latest Romano-British coin
hoards were amassed, that is they were in use at least as long as Roman
coins remained current in Britain, however long that was. They must of
course have remained current in some districts much longer than in others.
It depended for example on how seriously life had been disrupted in a
particular district; how accustomed the inhabitants were to the regular use
of currency; how self-sufficient, or how dependent they were on trade with
others; how many coins were already available in that district; and on how
many finds of earlier coins turned up to provide an opportune, emergency
currency. The use of Roman coins from hoards found in modern times in
place of late eighteenth or nineteenth-century farthings or trade tokens must
have had many a parallel in the years following the Roman withdrawal.[18]

In any case there was not one end to Roman currency in Britain; there
were many ends. The end may have come in some districts even before the
Roman withdrawal, and in other districts long after it.

The archaeological significance of Romano-British coin hoards

A closely dated coin hoard provides a *terminus ante quem* for any objects
or structures found in association with it. These include the receptacles in
which the coins were stored or hidden, any other valuables concealed with
hoards, and the sites, military or civil or even pre-Roman, where they were
deposited.

The receptacles in which Romano-British hoards were contained

Throughout the whole span of the Roman occupation of Britain hoards of coins were most commonly stored in money bags, wooden money boxes and coarse-ware pots. The two former have rarely survived intact, but the pots have as always proved virtually indestructible.

(1) Coarse-ware pots
At least 500 Romano-British coin hoards are recorded as having been contained in one or more coarse-ware pots. These pots were, with a very few

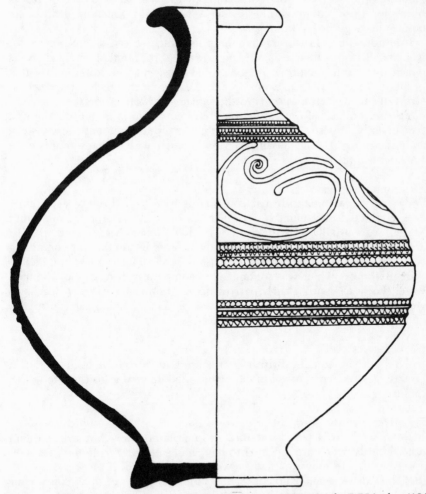

FIG. 1   Flask found at Ramsey, Huntingdonshire, *c.* 1890. Height 7.75 inches (195 mm). Container of coin hoard to Constantius II, Augustus.
The flask is of hard white ware with a black slip, decorated with a curvilinear pattern picked out in white paint and with bands of rouletting.

exceptions, flagons, jars or cooking pots, varying in size, according to the size of the hoards, but almost all having a narrow neck (Fig. 1). A few flagons or jars in fact had their necks stopped up and a slot cut in the side for the insertion of coins, after the manner of a modern 'piggy-bank'. Money is of course much more likely to stay saved if it is contained in a receptacle which makes the extraction of coins much more difficult than their insertion.

If a pot of a certain type was used as a container for a hoard of a certain date, then obviously that type of pot must have come into existence (or can be 'dated') before the date at which the hoard was closed. For example, a Hadrianic hoard from Southants contained in a 'coarse fumed' or black-burnished I pot, confirms other evidence for the introduction of this ware before the reign of Hadrian.

It is noticeable, however, that the pots which served as receptacles for Romano-British coin hoards were not always of the familiar, everyday types which turn up in quantities on excavated sites, but were often out-of-the-ordinary vessels (*see* for example Fig. 1). This fact, when interpreted in terms of human action, points to the satisfactory conclusion that the commonsense, practical Romano-Briton preferred not to immobilise a pot of a type in daily domestic use by turning it into a money box, but chose instead as a receptacle for his savings a vessel which was perhaps more of an ornament in his house.

(2) Samian vessels

Only a very few Romano-British coin hoards are recorded as having certainly been contained in Samian vessels. The reason was, no doubt, simply that Samian ware usually took the form of shallow platters, wide-mouthed cups, and open bowls, whose shapes made them quite unsuitable for containing coins safely. One of the exceptions was a hoard found at Kirkham, Lancashire (Balbinus), which was contained in a comparatively rare type of Samian vessel (Form 67) with a fairly narrow neck. Another hoard from Beachamwell, Cambridgeshire (Commodus), was stored in a Samian cup (Form 33), but had to be covered over by another vessel.

(3) Glass vessels

Only about six Romano-British hoards are known to have been contained in glass vessels. They range in date from the late second to the late fourth century AD.

(4) Silver, bronze, lead, tin or pewter vessels

At least six hoards were contained in one or more silver vessels. Certain other hoards which are reported to have had silver vessels found in association with them may originally have been concealed in those vessels. All these hoards were made up entirely, or almost entirely, of silver coins. Four ended with coins of Honorius of which one, from Fincham, Norfolk, was contained in a particularly beautiful silver flask.

Bronze vessels which served as receptacles for Romano-British hoards included arm-purses (the most appropriate of all containers), narrow-necked bronze jugs, paterae, bowls, a small bronze bell, a bronze bucket and other bronze vessels of unspecified type. Had they been found alone, some of the bronze jugs, with clover-leaf mouth, would have been given a somewhat earlier dating than that of the hoards which they did in fact contain. No doubt they had a long life as treasured ornaments. The most striking evidence from the list of bronze containers is that none has been found with a hoard certainly dated later than the end of the third century AD. Thereafter, pewter replaced bronze as a favoured metal for household plate.

Other hoards were stored in lead canisters or boxes, or in tin or pewter jugs, canisters or boxes. The tin or pewter vessels are only recorded for late third-century and fourth-century hoards.

(5) Miscellaneous containers

Some Romano-British hoards have been recorded as found in containers of unspecified metals; in stone urns, mortars or even in the central hole of a quern-stone; in a hollow bone; and in a 'hard lump' or 'round ball of earth' or in 'an earthen globe'. These last three had probably been originally in a leather bag or other perishable receptacle.

Objects found in association with Romano-British hoards

Since coin hoards represented the accumulated wealth of their owners, it is not to be wondered at that they often contained other valuables besides coins. Some impression of what constituted 'valuables' in Romano-British eyes may be gained by a survey of the objects found in association with Romano-British coin hoards. Also, as in the case of accompanying receptacles, a *terminus ante quem* for the date of manufacture of the associated valuables is provided by the date of the hoards with which they were found.

(1) Gold

Gold ornaments – most commonly finger rings, with a few armlets and chains – have been found with nearly twenty Romano-British hoards, which themselves were almost always of gold and silver coins. Gold ornaments seem to have been most plentiful at just those periods when gold coins were being hoarded in Britain, that is in the second century AD and in the late fourth century AD or later.

(2) Silver

Personal ornaments of silver were associated with more than thirty hoards, almost all of them hoards of silver coins. Most common among these ornaments were finger-rings. Bracelets, fibulae and silver chains were of rarer occurrence.

Silver plate – including paterae, cups and spoons – occurred in association with over ten recorded hoards. Some of the pieces of plate may actually have been used to contain the hoards. All but a few of these hoards dated to the very end of the fourth century AD (or possibly later). Silver plate was often present in such quantity that the hoards should more correctly perhaps be regarded as treasures of silver plate with coins in association, rather than as coin hoards.

Silver ingots were found in association with over ten hoards dating to the end of the Roman occupation. Miscellaneous articles of silver were associated with close on ten recorded hoards.

(3) Bronze

Personal ornaments of bronze were found with over twenty hoards, often composed of bronze coins and dating to all periods from the mid-first century AD to the late fourth century AD and later. It was evidently only as a material for household vessels that pewter replaced bronze in the fourth century AD, not as a material for personal ornaments.

On the other hand, bronze plate – bowls, a patera, a spoon, a lamp – were found in association with almost ten hoards, only one (the bronze lining of a pottery bowl) later than the late third century AD. Miscellaneous articles of bronze were associated with over a dozen hoards.

(4) Miscellaneous

A number of hoards are recorded as found in association with pewter vessels (all of the late fourth century AD), lead and iron objects, personal ornaments of ivory, glass vessels, beads of amber, jet, glass, clay figurines, a clay lamp and a sculptured slab. This, if genuinely associated with a hoard, may have marked the spot where the hoard was concealed.

The place of deposit of Romano-British coin hoards

The places of deposit were of three main classes: Roman sites (military or civil), native British sites, and natural landmarks.

(1) Roman military sites

Between sixty and seventy Romano-British hoards were found either in a legionary fortress, or in forts, milecastles and signal-stations. Where a record has survived of the exact location of the discovery, it almost always bears witness to an attempt at concealment on the part of the owner. Favourite hiding places were under or in the floor of a hut or barrack-block, in a hypocaust or cellar, in a pit, in a fort-ditch or rampart.

Losses of hoards were most common on Hadrian's wall in the second to early third centuries AD. All hoards found in the Yorkshire 'signal-stations', built about AD 370, dated to the end of the fourth century AD.

(2) Romano-British civil sites

About 120–140 coin hoards have been recorded as found in Romano-British towns, villas, temples and villages. The findspot usually indicated an attempt by the owner at concealment, for example under a floor or pavement, in the wall of a house, in a bath-house or hypocaust, in a pit, or even in a grave.

The loss of hoards appears, from the lists, to have been more likely to occur in towns and villages or other settlements during the late third and fourth centuries AD, in villas and villages only during the third and fourth centuries AD, and in temples towards the end of the Roman occupation.

(3) Native British sites

The recorded Romano-British hoards include more than seventy of varying periods, whose owners made their way to pre-Roman burial mounds or cairns, or scaled the ramparts of a pre-Roman hillfort or climbed down into a pre-Roman ditch, to find a hiding-place for their savings which would be at once secure and at the same time easily identifiable to themselves. Such native British sites must of course have been, in Roman times, even more prominent features of the landscape than they are today, and were often as far removed in time from the Romano-Briton as he is from us. They were, in fact, among the ancient monuments of Roman Britain.

(4) Natural landmarks

The largest number of Romano-British hoards were concealed away from, rather than in, inhabited sites, although not necessarily very far away from them and usually, we may be sure, near landmarks which would direct the owners back to their treasures again. Some recorded landmarks – caves, cliffs, rocks, hills, springs, rivers and seashores – are recognisable as such today. There must, however, have been many less permanent landmarks which have not survived for our recognition, for example a blasted oak, a tall pine tree or a clump of bushes.

The manner of deposit of Romano-British coin hoards

It was not only in the choice of a hiding place that owners of hoards showed concern for their savings. Some of them at least also took great care over the manner in which they arranged the coins in their receptacles, for example in rouleaux, and over the way in which they bestowed their hoards in the chosen hiding places. Several hoards were covered by a piece of stone, tile or brick, or were enclosed by tiles, stones or even by rough stone walling, or were covered by a wooden board or by a cloth or were packed round with clay. Hoards so deposited may be taken, fairly, as evidence of some threatened emergency which drove owners to conceal their savings, but yet allowed them enough time to arrange for their concealment in the safest possible manner.

The historical significance of Romano-British coin hoards

The number of hoards lost in Roman Britain during the reigns of different emperors was far from constant. The distribution of hoards over reigns is most evident from the accompanying diagram (Fig. 2). The most general, indisputable conclusion to be drawn from this distribution is that while the practice of saving or hoarding continued uninterrupted throughout the whole

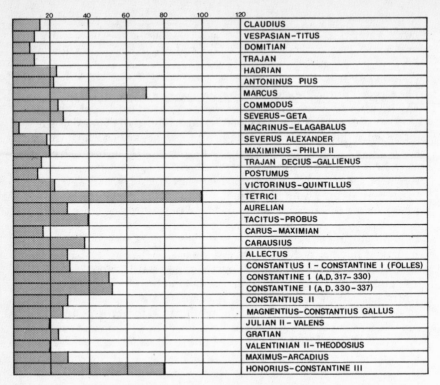

FIG. 2   The chronological distribution of Romano-British coin hoards
It would have been preferable to divide the diagram into equal yearly periods, e.g.
into periods of twenty years – AD 100–120 and the like – instead of according to
emperors who reigned for varying lengths of time. Since, however, the exact date
in years at which a coin hoard ended is usually difficult to determine, the diagram
had to be arranged according to the latest emperors represented in the hoards.

span of the Roman occupation of Britain, there were certain periods at
which more hoards were lost than at others, for example during the currency
of coins of Marcus and Verus and of the Tetrici, and in the last period of
Roman occupation – Honorius and later.

   If the numbers and the topographical distribution of the coin hoards lost
in Britain during each period are considered in conjunction with the literary
and archaeological evidence for contemporary disturbances, it becomes clear
that in general and allowing for some losses due to mere accident, the
evidence of the hoards tallies with evidence from other sources. The loss of
large numbers of hoards may then be accepted as a concomitant of unsettled
conditions and even as an index of them, particularly if there were large
concentrations of losses in certain areas and, in the absence of further
information, may even be admitted as evidence for unsettlement in Roman
Britain which would otherwise be lacking.

Three periods may be taken as examples: Marcus, the Tetrici, and Honorius and later.

(1) Marcus

More than sixty hoards ending with coins of Marcus or Faustina II have been recorded from Britain. Coins of Marcus, as Caesar, began to be issued from AD 140 onwards, though not in very large quantities, so that some of the hoards ending with coins of Marcus may actually have been lost before the end of Antoninus Pius' reign, possibly even as a result of the rising of about AD 155.[19] On the other hand, the thirty or more hoards ending with Lucius Verus or Lucilla were certainly lost after AD 161.

Taken together, the ninety or more hoards ending with coins of Marcus or Faustina II, or with Verus and Lucilla, make a startling total in comparison with the totals lost in previous reigns. A total so great at once demands an explanation. Significant also is the distribution of these hoards. They cluster thickest in Yorkshire, in Brigantian territory, with smaller groups on the line of the Antonine Wall, in the Midlands, in East Anglia, and in the neighbourhood of London, with as usual a few scattered outliers. On Hadrian's Wall only a few have been found (Fig. 3).

The high total and the distribution of these hoards confirm the literary evidence that there was trouble in Britain during the joint reign of Marcus and Verus, between AD 161 and 169, and possibly again after Marcus became sole emperor in AD 169.[20] The hoards in fact suggest a storm centre in Yorkshire, in Brigantian territory, rather than farther north, with ripples of disturbance spreading southwards to the innocent civil sites in the midlands, and possibly as far south as East Anglia and London and northwards to Hadrian's Wall and the Antonine Wall. Or it may be that the northern barbarians, encouraged by the initial success of their Brigantian kinsmen, joined in later on their own account, so adding to the general upheaval.

(2) The Tetrici

Tetricus I and II ruled the Gallic Empire, and presumably Britain, for three years from AD 270–273.[21] Well over one hundred hoards ending with the Tetrici have been recorded from Britain. They are distributed very widely over the whole of England, with a rather thicker concentration in East Anglia than elsewhere (Fig. 4).

The Tetrican hoards from Britain were almost all of very base copper antoniniani which, it has been suggested, may have served as a smaller denomination alongside the antoniniani of good billon, at least until about AD 300. If that was the case, then the Tetrican hoards of base copper antoniniani may not all have been saved up and buried during the three years of Tetricus' reign. Some, at least, of these modest savings may have been amassed later in the third century by those who preferred, or who were compelled, to express their thrift in this humble medium.

Since this possibility exists, it would not be justifiable to regard the sudden steep rise in the number of hoards from Britain to over one hundred ending

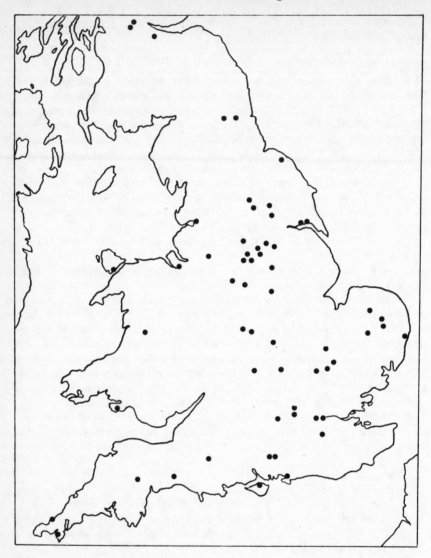

FIG. 3 Coin hoards ending with Marcus to Verus
Over seventy hoards are known from Britain ending with Marcus, Faustina II, Lucius Verus and Lucilla (*c.* AD 140–169).

with Tetricus I and II as proof of a cataclysmic upheaval in Britain between AD 270 and 273. The concentration of these hoards in East Anglia must not, of course, be ignored. It means, at least, that if the Tetrican hoards were lost over a period of many years after AD 270, the district in

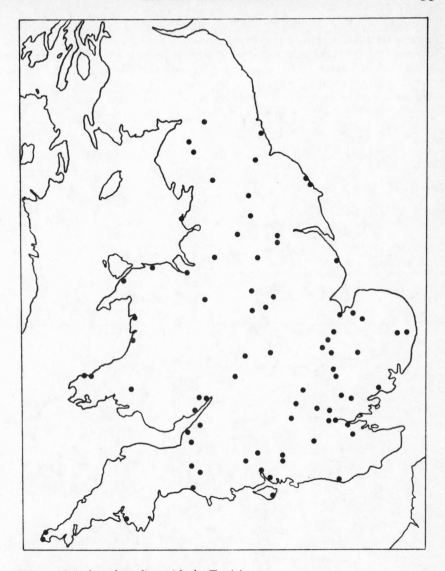

FIG. 4 Coin hoards ending with the Tetrici
Over one hundred hoards ending with coins of the Tetrici have been recorded from
Britain. They may have been lost any time between AD 270 and 300.

which the base copper antoniniani circulated in greatest abundance was
East Anglia.

An alternative explanation for the steep rise in the number of 'Tetrican'
hoards lost in Britain has recently been suggested by Prof. H. B. Mattingly.[22]

The emperor Probus, he submits 'was determined to enforce Aurelian's currency reform and drive the illegal moneyers out of business . . . Hoards of bad coinage went into the ground during his reign . . . doubtless to prevent their having to be surrendered at unfavourable rates, and in the vain hope of a change in government policy'. The failure to recover such hoards would be explained by their having become worthless.

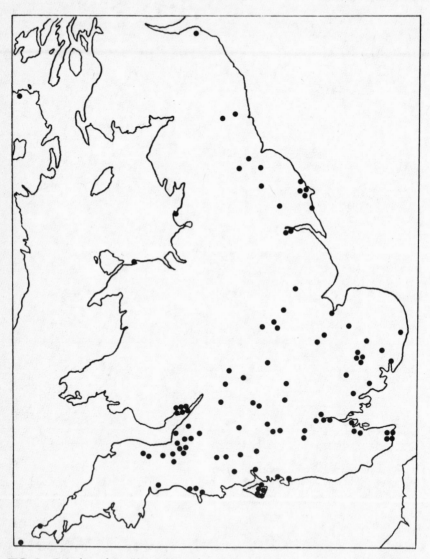

FIG. 5   Coin hoards to Honorius or later
About eight hoards are known from Britain ending with coins of Honorius, Constantine III or possibly Theodosius II. They may have been lost at any time after *c*. AD 393.

(3) Honorius and later (from AD 393 onwards)

Over one hundred hoards have been recovered from Britain which ended with coins of Honorius, or Constantine III. Over twenty others are listed under the less exact headings 'Theodosian', Minims ('Theodosian'?), 'End of Fourth Century', 'Barbarous Theodosian'. These hoards, making up a total of over one hundred and twenty, are the latest Romano-British Hoards. Apart from one in Scotland, one in Ireland, one in N. Wales and apparently one in Lancashire, they are concentrated in two areas, the coastal districts of west Yorkshire and north Lincolnshire, and in south-east Britain, south-east of a line from the Humber to the Severn, with thick clusters round the east and south coasts (Fig. 5).

Throughout the reign of Honorius, and during the years after it, while the Britons set their unpractised hands to defending and even ruling themselves, conditions in Britain were so unsettled and so insecure that life and property must have been in constant danger.[23] As a result, Roman coin hoards must have continued to be concealed and to be lost, as long as Roman coins remained current in Britain.

How long that was, it is, unfortunately, impossible to be certain. In about AD 395 the Gallic mints appear to have closed down and the flow of Roman coins from other mints into Britain shrank to a mere trickle. At the same time there was a growing scarcity of silver and copper. Coins of Honorius, in fact, were the latest coins to enter Britain in any quantity, so that the absence of coins of a later emperor than Honorius from a Romano-British hoard does not prove that it was lost in the reign of Honorius. It may have been lost at any time after AD 393.

Intensive studies of Romano-British hoards ending with Honorius have suggested certain clues, if not to the date at which they were lost, at least to their sequence.[24] Silver hoards, for example, which showed a preponderance of siliquae of Honorius over those of Arcadius, or which contained a high proportion of clipped coins, were probably later than hoards which did not display these characteristics. They were, in fact, probably lost after the usurpation of Constantine III in AD 407.[25] Both the characteristics in question were present in the Coleraine hoard, which included coins of Constantine III. By the time of his usurpation, the scarcity of silver had begun to make itself felt. One indication of this was the clipping of siliquae. Copper hoards too, in which coins of Honorius with the SALVS REIPVBLICAE reverse minted in Italy and the East outnumbered coins of Arcadius and other emperors with the same reverse, were probably later than copper hoards in which this was not the case.

Even, however, if there are certain hoards of silver and copper, ending with coins of Honorius, which for one reason or other seem of a later date than others, there still remains unsolved, perhaps insoluble, the problem of the date at which the very latest of these hoards were lost. They may have been lost at any time after the beginning of the reign of Honorius, as long as Roman coins remained current in Britain or, more correctly, in those parts of Britain in which the hoards were found, however long that was.

Whatever the date of loss of the hoards ending with Honorius or later, there is no doubt about the significance of their distribution in Britain. Clustered in west Yorkshire, in north Lincolnshire, round the Severn and in south-east England, they mark faithfully the districts where the money of Roman Britain was in its last days, and the districts where the money was lost. They reflect the havoc wrought on life and property by the Saxons landing on the southern and eastern coasts of England, by the Scots landing on the shores of the Severn and, possibly, by the Picts landing on the Yorkshire and Lincolnshire coasts. By itself, the distribution map of the latest Romano-British hoards establishes beyond doubt a connection between the widespread loss of treasure and contemporary warfare or other disturbance.

These latest Romano-British hoards even include two which may permit us to follow the disturbers of the peace back to their homes. One of these hoards, from Traprain Law, East Lothian, and the other, from Coleraine, County Londonderry, must have been taken there as loot from Britain, or possibly from Gaul. Each of these hoards contained silver plate as well as coins. They were hidden away and never recovered by the raiders, who seem themselves to have met a violent end.

Conclusion

Romano-British hoards represented the accumulated wealth or savings of their owners, composed in most cases of the most precious metals which were available in coined form, or which the owners could afford. The numbers of the coins included in the several hoards varied according to the metals used and the wealth of their owners. A hoard was for the most part made up of current coin, so that it could be spent at any time, but it sometimes included also a few exceptional coins which had been admitted either because of their high quality or because of the individual preference of the owner. Very often, too, a hoard shows unmistakable signs that the coins in it had been carefully selected, either for their fine condition or for their rarity or for other characteristics which attracted the owner. A few hoards even seem to owe their composition not only to the selective eye of the owner, but also to his collector's instinct. On the other hand, sub-standard or even barbarous coins found a place in hoards dating to periods at which these formed so high a proportion of the coins in normal circulation that they could hardly be excluded completely from a man's savings.

The owners of hoards usually stored their coins in vases or urns of pottery, which were in many cases extremely fine examples of the Romano-British potter's craft, or else in vessels of silver or bronze which were themselves of considerable value, or in wooden boxes or money bags. With their coins they often kept and concealed other valuables, most commonly of gold, silver or bronze, or other possessions which, though not of great intrinsic value, may have been treasured for personal reasons.

The careful selection of coins for hoarding, and the association with them of other treasures, are in themselves sufficient proof of the value which was set upon coin hoards by their owners. Additional proof is provided by the arrangements made for the safe concealment of hoards. Comparatively few hoards were deposited in inhabited sites, military or civil. The place of deposit was much more commonly a spot removed from habitation, but marked by some feature, natural or artificial, which would direct the owner of a hoard back to his treasure. Still further evidence of the care taken over the concealment of these hoards is the fact that many of them were buried deep in the earth and were deliberately surrounded with protective material.

In general, then, the composition of Romano-British coin hoards and the circumstances of their deposition or concealment leave no doubt that their owners thought them valuable, hid them away deliberately, and with care, and would make every possible effort to recover them when the reason for their concealment had passed. If they failed to reclaim them, that could only have been because they were prevented or discouraged from doing so by circumstances quite beyond their control. During periods of disturbance or of currency upheavals, more hoards than usual would be lost to their owners. Large numbers of Romano-British hoards were, in fact, lost at periods which are known from other evidence to have been unsettled for one reason or another.

Notes

1. In recent years, several hoards have been found through the use of metal detectors.

2. 'Coin Finds and How to Interpret Them', in *Proc. of Royal Phil. Soc. of Glasgow* (1903), 9ff.

3. *JRS*, XXII (1932), 88ff.

4. *Arch. Journ.*, XCII (1936), 64ff.

5. *Coinage and Currency in Roman Britain* (1937), 154ff.

6. Anne S. Robertson, 'The Numismatic Evidence of Romano-British Coin Hoards', in *Essays in Roman Coinage Presented to Harold Mattingly* (1956), 262ff.

7. Anne S. Robertson, in *NC* (1968), 61ff., *Proc. Soc. Ant. Scot.*, 113 (1983), 418ff.

8. Lord Selborne, in *NC* (1877), 90ff., R. Bland, *CHRB* III, BM Occas. Paper, 33 (1982).

9. H. H. E. Craster, in *Archaeologia Aeliana* (1912), 154, 210ff., G. Macdonald, in *JRS* II (1912), 1ff.

10. *NC* (1891), *Proc.*, 10.

11. G. Macdonald, in *NC* (1934), 1ff.; Anne S. Robertson, in *Studia Paulo Naster Oblata*, I (1982), 207ff.

12. B. H. St. J. O'Neil, in *NC* (1936), 314ff.

13. Anne S. Robertson, 'The Numismatic Evidence of Romano-British Coin Hoards', in *Essays in Roman Coinage Presented to Harold Mattingly* (1956), 268ff.

14. J. Collingwood Bruce, 'The Roman World', 2nd ed. (1853), 416; cp. E. Birley in *NC* (1963), 61ff.

15. J. W. E. Pearce, in *NC* (1933), 170ff.; A. M. Burnett, in *Britannia*, 15 (1984), 163ff.

16. C. H. V. Sutherland, 'Romano-British Imitations of Bronze Coins of Claudius I', *NNM*, 65 (1935).

17. Cp. the Poundbury hoard, Anne S. Robertson in *NC* (1953), 87ff.

18. See above, page 14.

19. Sir George Macdonald, *Roman Wall in Scotland*, 2nd ed. (1934), 9ff.

20. *Vita M. Antonini Phil.*, 8, 7 and 22, 1; cf. Dio Cassius LXXI, 16.

21. *Tyranni Triginta*, 24–25; cf. Aurelius Victor, XXXIII, 12 and Eutropius, IX, 9.

22. *N. Staffs. Journ. of Field Studies* (1963), 26.

23. Procopius I, 1–2; Zosimus VI, 1–6, 10; Sozomenos IX, 12; Orosius VII, 40.

24. Cp. F. S. Salisbury, in *NC* (1931), 14ff.

25. Cp. J. W. E. Pearce, in *NC* (1933), 170ff., and (1934), 61ff.; A. M. Burnett, in *Britannia*, 15 (1984), 163ff.

Romano-British coin hoards: a postscript

Since the publication of BAR 4 (1974), the number of hoards of Roman coins found in Britain has steadily increased: there are at this time about 1,600 hoards recorded and about 20 other coin finds which may have been hoards. By now, all of the 1,600 hoards have been reviewed, with the aim of preserving the original account of the circumstances of discovery and of confirming the coin attributions to Roman imperial personages and others. This most recent review has highlighted certain conclusions which were not so clearly defined in BAR 4.

1. Special interest attaches to the composite Romano-British coin hoards. A composite hoard may take the form of a pair of pots containing coins, for example from Edlington, Yorkshire (1935), to Gallienus, joint reign; of a bronze bowl, a bronze jug and a wooden keg, from Dorchester, Dorset (1936), of the same date; or of a cluster of three pots, at Gosbecks, Colchester, Essex (1983), to Aurelian and the Tetrici. In the last case, careful examination even established the chronological stratification of coins within the pots.

2. Attention has been focused not only on the distribution of coins of imperial personages and others, but also on reverse types and on mintmarks, for example in Constantinian hoards found in Britain. There also remain intriguing possibilities in studies of mint distribution in Romano-British hoards of Severan denarii and in the modest currency of the late fourth-century signal-stations on the Yorkshire coast.

3. Since 1974 a few spectacularly large coin hoards have been discovered, of which the greatest example is the Cunetio, Wiltshire (1978) hoard, with its nearly 55,000 antoniniani to Aurelian and the Tetrici. A question arises: should one try to separate Romano-British coin hoards into large 'official' hoards, and small 'private' hoards? Is there any relationship between such a dichotomy and the putative division into 'savings hoards' and 'currency hoards'? Do we know enough, or will we never know enough to justify such separations? Meanwhile, a suggestion that so-called official hoards might have come in bulk from a mint, group of mints or from a 'bank', calls for far more time-consuming searches for die identities in such hoards.

4. No numismatist can ignore the aids which modern technology offers, in the form of numerology, statistics, metrology, metallurgical analysis, computer studies and so on. The prime requirement is still that Roman coins (like any other coins) should be correctly identified, or re-identified, in the light of the most recent knowledge.

5. To the numismatic, archaeological and historical significance of Romano-British coin hoards, there should be added the antiquarian significance. The earlier (and not so much earlier) accounts of such finds are period pieces, redolent of the times in which the finders and recorders lived and worked. They have become antiquities themselves: and so will we.

Bearsden, Glasgow

3
The interpretation of Romano-British site finds

John Casey

The adaptation of systematic analytical methods to the study of site-finds of coins has been slowly gaining impetus over the last decade, though there is still some lag in the utilisation of these techniques as compared to some other branches of archaeology. This is partly because until recently the Roman coinage lacked systematic catalogues for the later imperial issues – material which is the most prolific in site coin lists. Fortunately, an acceleration in the production of corpora and catalogues has remedied this defect and the efforts of academic numismatists – and in this context I use the term academic to define the branch of numismatic studies which deals with the typology and chronological ordering of coins which contrasts with the applied numismatics with which the archaeologist is concerned – has made it possible to study the successive coin issues found in Roman Britain and, to a large extent, establish a regular pattern of occurrence. It is significant that almost all systematic work on Romano-British coin distribution post-dates the publication of *Late Roman Bronze Coinage*[1] which, for the first time, tabulated and dated the previously bewildering mass of fourth-century coinage. The near completion of the publication of *Roman Imperial Coinage* together with LRBC has made available to the applied numismatist the raw material for dating archaeological features by reference to individual coins in key deposits and to view the conspectus of the coinage as a whole; the tools now available render obsolete such unhelpful cataloguing as the notorious entry 'Coins with a post-Roman feeling' in the Richborough coin lists. [2]

Formalising the distribution of finds by means of visual displays in the form of histograms makes it clear that there is a strongly marked pattern in the coinage of Roman Britain. It is also clear from an analysis of the coins that make up the component parts of the pattern that it reflects factors other than the fate or status of individual sites. Arising from this observation comes the possibility of pointing to areas where coin evidence has been used in an inappropriate manner in the past and where, because finds from individual sites have been analysed without reference to the overall coin distribution pattern of the province, general phenomena have been interpreted as individual characteristics and the dating of structural features and the assessment of economic and social status of sites may have been affected. However, it is not the purpose of this paper to reconsider specific sites so much as to outline general principles which, it is hoped, will make clear in which areas or periods reassessment might be profitable.

At the outset it is important to define the nature of the material with which one is dealing. Coins comprise a class of evidence which presents peculiar problems not found in the general range of dating material used by the archaeologist. By and large that material is literally rubbish – broken pottery being overwhelmingly the most common dating artefact. Coins, however, are most emphatically not rubbish; they are a store of wealth, they represent security, food, shelter, diversion and all the other basics of existence. They are not usually deliberately thrown away and they are certainly not deposited with an eye to their convenience to archaeologists. What is more, the life of the individual coin may be very long, it may disappear into a hoard only to emerge in pristine state many years later or be reinvested with currency value long after its initial date of issue. Coins also have subsidiary functions, for instance as jewellery or as small weights, and these functions may keep coins in a non-monetary circulation for considerable periods. There are thus very obvious limitations on the deductions that can be drawn from coin evidence and any such deductions must always take account of the most important factor of all – human nature. This unquantifiable factor, so often ignored in archaeological thinking, is profoundly important when dealing with coins. There can be no doubt that, in general, the coin material available for study from site finds will represent what the original owners could best afford to lose. One must expect that coins of high value will always have been the subject of intensive search when lost, very much more so than small value coins (witness, for instance, the fate of the wretched new halfpenny); that larger coins will have been more easily recoverable than small coins and that losses in a domestic environment will have been more easily recovered than those in the public place, especially if the latter were ill-tended. It should also be borne in mind that only a very small proportion of the available currency of a large site will come to the hands of the archaeologist and that even on sites that produce many coins these represent very little in monetary terms. Few sites, indeed, produce the hundred sestertii which would make up a single gold aureus.

We can illustrate the actual paucity of material by constructing a coin population model for a well documented site. Corbridge has produced 1,387 coins of the first and second centuries (counting hoards as one coin) which are the equivalent of twenty six aurei, representing one hundred and twenty years of military activity on the site. Over this period the garrison varied in its composition[3] but for the purposes of calculation we can take the effect of occupation by a quingenary cohort and accept a scale of four aurei a year as being the basic pay of an auxilliary soldier.[4]On this basis we can calculate that the 1,387 coins represent a potential coin population of 240,000 aurei or 24,000,000 sestertii. It should be emphasised that this is a minimal-view model, making no allowance for officers' or centurions' pay, for soldiers on enhanced pay scales, for differences in pay that may have existed between cavalry units and infantry units or for the possible effect of the payment of accession donatives. What we cannot add is the extent to which the same coin circulated from generation to generation but with the attested rapid changes of garrison this is a minor factor. In any event the small proportion of surviving coin is dramatically evident.

Whilst the factors outlined above must be borne in mind when attempting any general interpretation of coin finds, the fact that it is possible to construct a general pattern on the basis of the material available shows that whatever factors affected coin losses in antiquity operated uniformly, and we may assume that the loss from the original coin population will always have been roughly constant in relation to the numbers in which the coins were issued and circulated. Equally, we may assume that, for sites with long coin lists, a cross sample has been recovered which is representative of the original coin population, though generally of the lowest denominations of that population. With these provisos in mind we may turn to the visual evidence of a series of histograms representative of the coin found on a number of very productive sites. Two sites have been selected for attention as representing the general pattern of coinage, Silchester and Caerwent (Figures 1 and 2). Both are major towns of the Roman era that have been explored over a long period. Both have produced an abundance of coins – Silchester 8,870 and Caerwent 3,751 (hoards being counted as a single coin) – and both provide a sample of coinage from what may reasonably be assumed to have been a numerically stable population of inhabitants. That is to say that these civil sites will not be affected by the sort of factors which arise when considering the coin losses on military sites, where troop movements can be expected to affect the volume of coinage to be found at various periods, as can the actual composition of individual units, and where problems such as the operation of the *annona militaris* will provide complicating factors. It is evident that virtually all well-explored urban sites produce similar coin distribution patterns and such variations as occur from site to site can be attributed to such things as differing dates of establishment, early military activity on the site (as at Wroxeter, Lincoln or Corbridge) or selectivity in areas of excavation.[5] But even in these cases the succession of peaks and troughs in the site histograms in the post-military phases are similar to other civil sites and the relative frequency of coins is preserved, though necessarily statistically depressed by the rather heavy representation of early material (Figure 3).

$$\frac{\text{COINS PER REIGN}}{\text{LENGTH OF REIGN}} \times \frac{1,000}{\text{TOTAL FOR SITE}}$$

This formula is an extension of that established by Dr. Ravetz in her study of the fourth-century coinage and has found general acceptance as a uniform working method.[6] The application of this method not only allows for uniformity as a factor frequently overlooked in the interpretation of coin finds. Coin volume clearly fluctuates from reign to reign not merely for monetary reasons but because some reigns are longer than others so that, all things being equal, a longer reign will be better represented than a short reign. That such an elementary concept should have escaped the grasp of archaeologists in so many publications where sheer coin volume has been

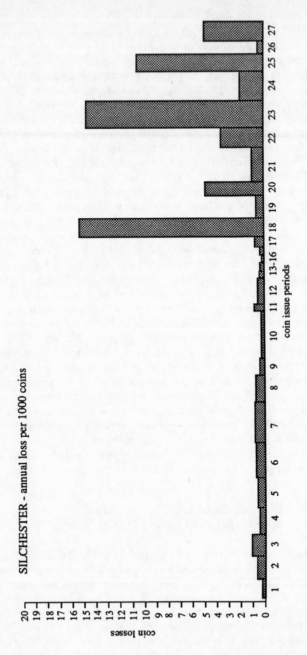

FIG. 1

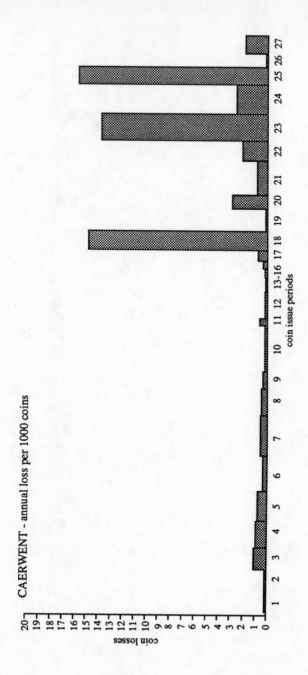

CAERWENT - annual loss per 1000 coins

FIG. 2

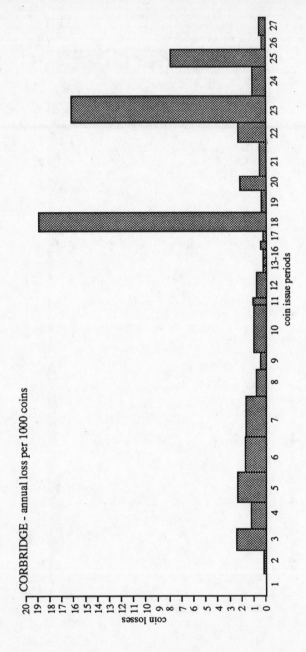

FIG. 3

used to illustrate density of occupation or economic status is a sad commentary on the general level of archaeological reasoning. The presentation of finds is, however, complicated by periods in which there is a multiplicity of rulers and others in which it is not the issuer who is important so much as the module and metallic content of the coinage. This is especially so in the third and fourth centuries when coin issues reflect rapid changes in the physical composition of the currency which are more important than the identity of the actual issuing dynast.

The coin issue period divisions used in this study are as follows:

1.	Claudian	AD 43–54
2.	Neronian	54–68
3.	Flavian I	68–81
4.	Flavian II	81–96
5.	Trajanic	96–117
6.	Hadrianic	117–138
7.	Antonine I	138–161
8.	Antonine II	161–180
9.	Antonine III	180–192
10.	Severan I	193–217
11–17.	Severan II	217–260
18.	Gallic Empire	260–273
19.	Aurelianic	273–286
20.	Carausian	286–296
21.	Diocletianic	296–317
22.	Constantinian I	317–330
23.	Constantinian II	330–348
24.	Constantinian III	348–364
25.	Valentinianic	364–378
26.	Theodosian I	378–388
27.	Theodosian II	388–402

(In the present survey pre-Claudian coinage has been omitted as well as all copies except Claudian, which are treated as Neronian issues. Reference to the function of copies will be made at the appropriate point in the commentary.)

Reference to Figures 1, 2 and 3 makes it clear, at once, that there are periods in which coinage is very abundant and others in which it is virtually unrepresented and this on sites where there is no reason to postulate either periodic abandonment or a serious decline in population. It follows that there are reasons for the fluctuations that are inherent in the nature of the coins themselves or are the result of generally operating factors. On the whole the fluctuations will be seen to be the result of internal changes in the currency itself, though there are occasions when political factors play a part in determining the presence or absence of coins in the province. This is especially so at periods when Britain was severed from the central empire.

Early currency is not well represented, both because of the inevitable slow initial economic growth of the sites and because early levels are less well

explored than upper levels. Supplies, too, were very restricted with very
little Claudian copper or bronze being issued after about AD 46 and no
Neronian base metal currency at all for the first ten years of the fourteen-year
reign. Nevertheless, coin up to Period 8 seems to have been supplied in a
steady stream, but a general decline is visible in the succeeding phases up
to Period 16, though all sites show a modest upswing of currency in the
reign of Severus Alexander in Period 11. The reasons for the decline in the
numbers of surviving coins may be sought in the nature of the composition
of the currency. A shift in the emphasis of individual denominations issued
can be traced from the first century with the As giving way to the dupondius
and sestertius by the time of Trajan, whilst by the end of the second century
the silver denarius seems to have been the common coin of maximum utility.
Obviously the same sort of inflationary pressures operated on the currency
as can be seen in our own day. Looking back over the currency of the
present century we can see a movement towards ever higher value coins
and whereas the penny was the most common coin at the start of the century,
it had been supplanted by the sixpence in the late 1950s which has, in turn,
yielded place to the ten new pence (two shillings) piece in the present currency
mixture. The change in pattern of issue away from an essentially base metal
currency to a silver one, albeit of a very debased nature, means in archaeological terms that representative material of the later period will be scarce.
Single denarius will represent the purchasing power of four sestertii or
sixteen asses and proportionally less currency units will have been available
to be lost. Furthermore, the higher value coin will have been the more
eagerly sought when dropped.

Early silver of the third century is marginally more common than that of
the middle of the century when the coin of commerce was once again
changed, from the denarius to the so-called antoninianus, or double denarius.
Contemporary copper and bronze coin is virtually absent from Britain,
though it does appear in other provinces. This may be an indication of
generally high prices prevailing at the time in Britain, though large amounts
of earlier base metal currency continued to circulate. In these circumstances
few deductions can be made relevant to the economic status of individual
sites, and the postulated decline in the prosperity of villas in the early third
century,[7] for instance, may be nothing more than the observed effect of the
decline in the coinage pattern of the province. The interpretive error is
compounded if the vast quantity of coin of Period 18 is seen as evidence of
prosperity or, as was attempted recently,[8] the sudden abundance of coin is
used to postulate a change in ownership or social habits. The coin finds of
this period consist entirely of the base double denarii of the Gallic Empire
and its central rival, coins having as little as a one per cent silver content,
the result of a catastrophic collapse in the Roman currency system. The
decline of the empire's currency is plotted not merely by the number of
coins of Gallienus, Postumus, Victorinus and Tetricus found on Romano-
British sites, but also by the opening of a number of new mints to produce
the coinage and the increase in *officinae* in pre-existing establishments.
Reference to modern inflations indicates than an increase in the number of

units of currency in circulation does not indicate an increase in prosperity – indeed, the contrary situation pertains since the larger volume of currency is needed to purchase an unchanged amount of goods and services.

From the third quarter of the third century the pattern shows the effects of a series of reforms and depreciations of the currency. Period 19 is ill-represented, consisting as it does of the reformed coins of Aurelian and his successors, who sought to stabilise the empire's monetary structure after the debacle of the previous period. The transition between the apparently unsuccessful Aurelianic reform and the comprehensive reform of Diocletian (Period 21) is interrupted in Britain by the large injection of coin occasioned by the advent of the usurper Carausius, whose not uncommon coins must represent a calculated political gesture. Perhaps more important is that many of the Carausian coins are overstruck on the issues of the Gallic Empire and this may indicate that this currency's life as a circulating medium terminated at this time, though examples occur occasionally in later hoards. Both Aurelianic and Diocletianic coins are rare as site finds, but this is only to be expected since both are high value units and the latter issues are substantial silvered coins of 10 grammes weight, coins of a value and module that made recovery of lost specimens both desirable and relatively easy. Such Diocletianic coins as are present are almost without exception issues from the end of the period when the follis had declined to a mere 4.5 grammes with a corresponding diminution in module. Further weight reductions in the follis, and an increase in production rates, can be traced in the last years of the reign of Constantine I (Period 23). The decline is foreshadowed in the previous period, but the 2.5 gramme and, later, 2.0 gramme coins issued between AD 330 and 348 are among the most common of finds. The minor value of these pieces is emphasised both by their survival rate and by the attempt to provide a more stable small change system with a wide ranging reform in AD 348. A relative scarcity of finds in Period 24 is represented numismatically by a return to the Diocletianic standard of a 10 gramme silvered coin, with fractional supporting pieces, bearing the legend FEL TEMP REPARATIO. The supply of this currency was interpreted by the revolt of Magnentius (AD 350–353) and only a trickle of coin datable to the post-Magnentian period reached Britain. Most of the material represented in the histograms precedes AD 353 and in the absence of sufficient supplies of small change between that date and 364, or more probably AD 369, large-scale copying of the Fel Temp Reparatio issues was undertaken, in a variety of modules and of varying fidelity to the original type.

Bulk supplies of the 2.5 gramme coppers of the House of Valentinian provide the penultimate peak in the finds graphs (Period 25) whilst material that can be dated to Period 26 (AD 378–388) is very rare indeed and almost certainly this void reflects the separation of Britain from the central empire during the usurpation of Magnus Maximus and his withdrawal of troops from the diocese for his continental adventure. Certainly the resumption of modest coin deposits in Period 27 exactly coincides with his defeat and presumably represents the resumption of payments to the administration of Britain from imperial revenue. These payments seem to have ceased in AD

409[9] perhaps because the shipment of coin was interrupted by the invasions of Italy, from which Britain was supplied after the closure of the Gallic mints in AD 395, by Alaric in 401 and in 405 by Radagaisus. If this is so, the sense of isolation engendered in Britain must have been a powerful factor in the events which led to the army mutiny which raised Constantine II to the purple in 406.

It is clear from the foregoing that there are periods of high coin deposit and periods of low coin deposit which are the product of factors other than population movements or individual economic events impinging on individual sites. Rather we have the reflection of a complex combination of factors, provincial as well as empire-wide. Some of these factors are political, others economic and somewhere buried in the overall pattern are those elements specific to individual sites. On the present evidence, however, as far as the towns are concerned the effect of the non-specific factors overwhelms the individual events. Smaller sites with intermittent occupation, however, can be studied against the full numismatic background of the major sites. After the third quarter of the third century the swift changes in coin types and in the weight and alloy of individual issues, under the influence of inflationary pressures, allow confident predictions to be made as to the probability of the appearance or non-appearance of coins in site lists. With the exception of Period 25 (AD 378–388) the phases in which coins tend not to appear correspond with changes in the currency which are always in the direction of raising the value of the individual currency unit. Thus we have seen the trend towards a silver currency in the Severan period, the Aurelianic reform, the Diocletianic reform and the issue of the Fel Temp Reparatio coinage providing the low points in the coin distribution pattern. At these periods not only are people more careful with their money but that money is available for loss in a diminished volume since the high value coin is doing the economic work of several smaller units. At these periods site activity may not have diminished but the chance of finding coins to indicate, or date, that activity certainly will have diminished. Conversely, large deposits of coins coincide with periods when the coins themselves are of little intrinsic value and the absence of coins of these periods must be regarded as evidence for the cessation of site activity or of declining prosperity since the chances of finding coins of these periods is so very high. In practice, because every high deposit period is preceded by a low deposit period it is only possible to date the cessation of activity in a time bracket embracing the whole of the low deposit period through to some notional point at which the succeeding currency would have become well established. Obviously the full range of coin of any period will only be completely established in the following period and in sparse lists smaller peaks will themselves assume the status of low coin deposit periods relative to the list as a whole. In lists from sites that terminate in low deposit periods a further phenomenon may be observed. Since the low deposit periods are followed by periods which are high deposit as a result of a proliferation of currency accompanied by reductions in standards, it is in these periods that intrinsically valuable coins of the previous period will have been withdrawn from circulation either by the state or by individuals by the operation of Gresham's Law, and certainly hoard evidence substantiates this observation. In consequence, the greater the count of high value coins in the terminal phases of the list the more likely is site activity to have ceased in the low deposit period itself, or very early in the succeeding period.

Within the individual component elements of the overall coin pattern there are internal variations and close attention to dated issues of the first and second centuries, and to mint marks and sequence symbols in the later coinage, allows for the establishment of sub-patterns. An important sub-pattern has already been mentioned in connection with the coinage of Period 24 (Fel Temp Reparatio issues). Analysis of finds indicates that more than two-thirds of the material of this period relates to the years pre-353, thus two-thirds of all finds of the period relate to the first six years and the residue to the remaining twelve years. In consequence there is very much less than a one in three chance of finding a coin dating to AD 353 to 364, and this in a period when coin finds are scarce anyway, though there is supplementary material in the form of contemporary copies. In practical terms the dating of sites is clearly difficult and no doubt sites of this period have on occasion been dated too early on the basis of the presence of the prolific coinage of the preceeding Period 23. But a further problem arises from this internal sub-pattern. Dr. Webster has recently drawn attention to a group of villas with coin lists terminating with issues of Magnentius which, he suggests, represent estates confiscated to the imperial purse by Paul the Notary.[10] As we have seen, the period pattern almost precludes the appearance of coins later than Magnentius – what is significant is the non-appearance of the prolific coins of the following period. Here, indeed, we may have not a group of Magnentian villas but a group that suffered in AD 367 and which, in consequence, did not receive Valentinianic coins. This is, of course, merely a speculation but it serves to illustrate some of the dangers inherent in drawing rigid frames around the coin periods without considering internal developments. Equally important is the realisation that the domino-like columns of the histograms need, in reality, to be pushed over sideways, for in daily use the coinage of one period would considerably overlap the next period whilst some individual denominations might persist in use through several periods. To some extent the study of hoard evidence allows for some calculation as to the life of individual coins, but hoards themselves are of such a varied nature that generalisation is impossible beyond observing that coins in hoards tend to consist of the high value issues of low deposit periods, when they are not the demonetised issues of the Gallic Empire. Attempts to establish circulation life of coins by observation of the degrees of wear which they exhibit have not achieved general acceptance, but observation of finds from northern military sites of known foundation date, especially *vici*, indicate that large numbers of second-century sestertii circulated till the middle of the third century. These coins may have recirculated under the impact of Postumus' brief attempt to foster the use of the double sestertius, a coin produced by overstriking earlier sestertius issues. No doubt the prospect of doubling the value of one's obsolete currency acted as a powerful stimulus to bringing it back into circulation.

It remains, finally, to briefly examine the problems arising when dealing with the coinage derived from military sites. Because of imperial coin production policy early military sites are notoriously short of coin finds and this situation is not ameliorated until the Flavian period. With the establishment of permanent military stations in the north provision seems to have been made for the regular supply of coin for troop payments. We have already alluded to some of the problems that arise from consideration of the military coin deposits. Most important is the uncertainty as to the nature of the unit from period to period. Larger units might be expected to deposit larger numbers of coins, but in periods of troop movements, for instance during the move from Hadrian's Wall to the Antonine Wall line, coin deposits should be expected to drop. Unfortunately, it is not possible to be certain that the attested move of a fort garrison is followed by a period of non-occupation of its original station. There is enough evidence from Wall forts to suggest that in the absence of auxilliary garrisons some installations were occupied by legionaries. There are thus variable factors that make a general interpretation of military coin finds hazardous. Figure 4 shows the coin distribution histogram for the Hadrian's Wall fort at Housesteads based on a site total of 364 coins. On archaeological and epigraphic evidence we know that the garrison of Housesteads was numerically very stable throughout the fort's existence, so that it allows for a reasonable comparison with a town site.[11] Housesteads was probably occupied by a military cohort in the second century while the thousand strong Cohortis Primae Tungrorum is attested as being in occupation throughout the third and fourth centuries. This garrison was supplemented by two units of unknown size, and for unknown duration, during the third century – the *Cuneus Frisiorum Ver(covicium)* and the *Numerus Hnaudifridi*. The status of the site during the occupation of the Antonine Wall is not known but, on analogy with other Wall forts, it may have been occupied by legionaries. In any event, the picture is one of occupation over a long period by units of similar numerical strength and the expectation might be that the coin distribution pattern would be similar to that of a civil site. Comparison between the histogram for Housesteads and that for the nearby garrison town of Corbridge (Figure 3) shows that this expectation is not fulfilled. The disparity is very great and the fall off of coin finds at Housesteads in the fourth century is very marked, although where coin is present it is represented in the same relative frequency between period and period as is found in fuller civil lists. This reinforces the observation that the coin itself is the dominating factor in producing the peaks and troughs of the overall pattern. The explanation for the discrepancy between the two classes of sites lies in the operation of the *annona militaris*, the system of paying troops largely in ration allowances and equipment rather than in cash. The operation of the system, and the date of its introduction, are obscure but the incidence of coins down to the Gallic Empire (Period 18) at Housesteads strongly suggests

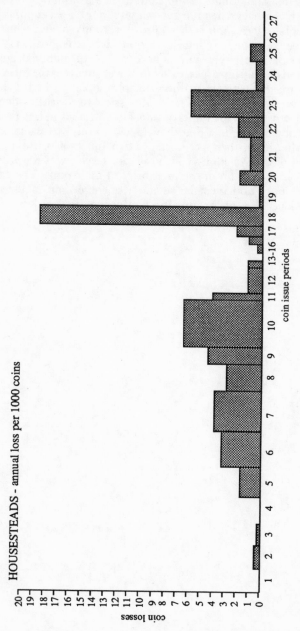

HOUSESTEADS – annual loss per 1000 coins

coin losses

coin issue periods

FIG. 4

that the *annona* did not function until after that period and seems to confirm the Diocletianic date usually assigned to it. The continuous deposit of coins in the fourth century, when the *annona* was in full operation, is the residue of the vestigial *stipendium* still paid to the troops, a sum which was little more than pocket money. What is not found archaeologically is the evidence for the considerable payments made to troops on imperial anniversaries, birthdays and consulships. These *donativa* were made in the form of precious metal and are thus subject to the principles affecting high value coins in general. In these circumstances it is not possible to use the evidence of coins to define, for instance, the military status of garrisons in late periods on the northern frontier. The fact that they appear to receive less coin, of smaller intrinsic value, than their predecessors is a function of the nature of the coinage and of the system by which military service was rewarded, it is not necessarily an indication of the inferiority of the troops. The confirmation of such a supposition must be sought elsewhere than in the coinage, as should evidence for occupation or non-occupation at low coin deposit periods.

Notes

1. Carson, R. A. G., and others, *Late Roman Bronze Coinage*, (1960).

2. Bushe-Fox, J. P., *Fourth Report on the Excavations of the Roman Fort at Richborough, Kent*, (1949), p. 304, items nos. 25560–25580.

3. Gillam, J. & Tait, J., 'The Investigation of the Commandant's House . . . Corbridge', in *Arch. Aeliana*, 4th ser., XLIX, (1971), 1–29.

4. Watson, G. R., *The Roman Soldier*, (1969).

5. Curnow, P. in Stead, I., 'Verulamium, 1966–1968', in *Antiquity*, XLIII, (1969), 51–52.

6. Ravetz, A., 'Fourth Century Inflation and Romano-British Coin Finds', in *Num. Chronicle*, 7th ser., 15, (1965).

7. Rivet, A. L. F. (ed.), *The Roman Villa in Britain*, (1969), Chapter V.

8. Brodribb, A. C. C. and others, *Excavations at Shakenoak* 11, (1971).

9. Kent, J. P. C., 'Coin Evidence for the Abandonment of a Frontier Province Graz', in *Carnuntina*, (1960).

10. Webster, G. 'The Future of Villa Studies', in Rivet, A. L. F. (ed.), *The Roman Villa in Britain*, (1969).

11. The argument deployed here assumes that there was no dramatic reduction in the fort garrison in the fourth century. A contrary view is expressed by J. Wilkes in 'Excavations in Housesteads Fort' (1960), *Arch. Aeliana*, 4th ser. XXIX, (1961), 279–319. During these excavations it was revealed that in the Constantinian period one at least of the barracks was rebuilt as a series of individual 'chalets', so that ten *contubernia* were replaced by six large single rooms. The nett reduction in floor space was ten per cent and if this reflects the factor by which the garrison was reduced it would be nugatory in terms of coin-loss representation. If, on the other hand, a change from ten double rooms to six chalets represents a reduction of forty per cent in the garrison, the effect should be seen in the coin losses. We can calculate the possible result of such an effect relative to the coin-loss graph by expressing the coinage of Housesteads and Corbridge as percentages for the third and fourth centuries' coin totals. These percentages should be similar if the sites were similarly occupied and coin flowed equally to both.

	Third Century	Fourth Century
Corbridge	42%	58%
Housesteads	75%	25%

If we correct the Housesteads figure for an assumed maximum reduction in unit size of forty per cent by adding that factor to the site's fourth-century coinage, we get:

	Third Century	Fourth Century
Housesteads	64%	36%

These figures are still sufficiently disparate from the 'full occupation' figures for Corbridge to indicate the operation of a factor which can be equated with the *annona militaris*. In fact, the uncorrected figure is closer to the order of magnitude to be expected for a full strength unit operating under the system expressed by   the rescript of Valentinian I (*Codex Theodosianus*, 7.4.14, presumably bringing *riparienses* into line with other *limitanei*), which tells us that troops received cash payments for only three months of the year. If we recalculate on this basis, i.e. that the Housesteads coins represent payment for a quarter of a year, and increase the total by seventy five per cent, we find that the relative proportions are now:

	Third Century	Fourth Century
Corbridge	42%	58%
Housesteads	42%	58%

It would seem in these circumstances that on the coin evidence there is no confirmation of reduction in unit size at Housesteads in the fourth century.

Interpretation of Romano-British site finds

The accumulation of further site records has confirmed the overall pattern of coin distribution in Britain as it was outlined, on small data base, in this paper. As far as urban sites, both large and small, are concerned for the present the situation remains that the strong pattern of deposition imposed by the cyclical nature of coin debasement from the second half of the second century, still obscures regional or heirarchical economic differences which must have existed in the real economy of Roman Britain.

New analyses of individual coin issues, their volume and distribution, are now being made and further sub-divisions of the supply pattern and its frequency will allow a more refined perception of the factors which contribute to coin pool in the first century (Walker, 1988). In the sphere of deposits on military sites the systematic collection of very large coin lists from hitherto neglected sites suggests that any equation of low, late deposit rates with the operation of the *annona militaris* may need to be modified. It seems clear that there were well-favoured and less well-favoured units in the garrison of late Roman Britain and that the status of a unit is, to an extent, reflected in the coin deposits associated with its fort site. For instance, troops on Hadrian's Wall, at sites such as Housesteads, do not seem to have had access to the prestige coin denominations available to the garrison of a major hinterland fort such as Piercebridge, County Durham, who were an elite force functioning as a strategic reserve to the less formidable units policing the actual frontier line itself. Work on this aspect of regional coin distribution is proceeding but is in its formative phase (Casey, forthcoming).

It is also apparent that temples and religious sites present specific numismatic problems which arise from the nature of the votive and ritual deposits made by worshippers. These problems arise from the fact that votive coins are deliberately deposited and are not a random selection of coinage lost from a changing coin pool over a period of time. Temple assemblages often show a high incidence of coins which are quite scarce on urban sites, representing issues or denominations which were withdrawn because of their premium value during the cycle of coin use which produces the periodic frequencies displayed by urban sites. It follows that coins of premium quality from religious sites are more likely to have been deposited closer to the date of their issue than individual coins from other sites.

University of Durham

Bibliography

Casey, P. J. 'The coins from the fort at Piercebridge, Co. Durham', in P. Scott *Excavations at Piercebridge* (forthcoming).

Walker, D. 'The coins from the temple at Bath', in B. Cunliffe *Excavations at Bath*. Vol. III.

4
Coin lists: some problems of the smaller site

Peter Curnow

'Numismatic Hack' is the phrase Bryan O'Neil uses for himself and those like him who identify and report on coins for archaeologists in his article 'Coins and Archaeology in Britain' in 1935[1]. He then enumerates the use of coins to the archaeologist. It is obvious that the stratified coin is the major requirement of the archaeologist – it is a closely dated document – but care should be taken not to place upon it more evidential value than in fact it will bear and this itself will vary with the type of coin found. Thus a couple of coins of the Tetrici with an assemblage of miscellaneous pottery variously dated is not going to help a great deal. But the presence of a good condition denarius of Augustus in a context of Claudio-Neronian pottery would assist an excavator in suggesting that this assemblage was indeed pre-Vespasianic. The addition of a Claudian As in good condition would clinch the matter. This may not seem a very surprising conclusion, but in view of the doubts which frequently attend groups of pottery which are in fact residual from earlier periods, sometimes long past, the presence in certain cases of even the single coin does give us a little more to go on. Although the residual factor normally applies with even more force to coins than pottery, especially single examples, in the case of pre-Neronian reform silver, several factors are present which differentiate it from the 'average coin find'. Thus on Nero's Reform it immediately became an undervalued piece of silver and as such was unlikely to survive in circulation for any length of time.

The two examples above may serve to indicate that while all coins are equal, being dated objects some are more equal than others for a variety of numismatic and historic reasons. The use of a single coin by itself is of course limited to giving us its *terminus ante quem,* which may mean either that the Romans were there or that a passing numismatist between then and now dropped a coin. The context in which the coin was found and the association with other evidential objects begin to fill out the picture. Thus it is that the single denarius found with the Claudio-Neronian pottery begins to assume credibility as evidence.

Dr. Kent has stated succinctly that numismatics is neither more nor less than the study of one species of evidence to be used in the service of archaeology which itself is one of the Rooms in the Mansion of History. For the evidence to be effective in the Roman period there is no substitute – at least in the post-Samian period – for a good half dozen coins to be sealed in each level. In these days of uncertainty over pottery, coins in quantity are the archaeologist's best friend. It is nevertheless a fact of life that on many small sites firm dating evidence in the form of coins is too scarce to permit of valid conclusions.

Any archaeologist with good eyesight and a modicum of patience can identify most coins in time, and since these comments are directed towards the problem of the smaller site many excavators will wish to deal with the relatively small number of coins from sites themselves. However, in this era of 'mass archaeology' when new excavators pour into the field, it should be stated that the excavator making his own coin list and interpreting it would do well to have at least a nodding acquaintance with one or two other and perhaps very different site lists and be aware of the differing patterns of coins which occur sometimes on neighbouring sites. On many sites those coins found stratified will be in a minority and in any event will probably be inadequate in number to provide a general picture. It is the total coin list which gives the overall numismatic history of the site and O'Neil pointed out the value of unstratified coins. It is the total list with which I am now concerned. The whole reason for these differing patterns is not known to me and is probably unknowable, but a differential rate of coin loss as between periods on otherwise comparable sites is often striking and must be taken account of. Mrs. Ravetz, in her article[2], brought out the distinctive peaks to be found on fourth-century AD sites, i.e. Constantinian, the House of Valentinian I and the House of Theodosius I, by means of graphs.

The archaeologist can and surely should attempt a coherent history of his site, but a tame numismatist, if the excavator has no pretensions here, is best consulted to provide advice on the evidence which the coin list affords. It may be that the two views do not coincide – both are in any case more or less subjective – but none the worse for that.

Sites are not uncommon where coin evidence pointing to one date is accompanied by a total absence of pottery of that date. For example, parts of the Gadebridge Villa complex contained ample mid-second-century pottery but accompanied by ample Constantinian coinage. Even on a small site producing relatively few coins it is desirable for the coin list to be accompanied by a report, albeit limited to a few comments, by the person dealing with the coins – at the very least these might indicate the reliability or otherwise of the numismatist. Peaks of coin loss, anomalies in the coin list or numismatic oddities can be drawn to the attention of the non-numismatic reader by this means even if some aspects of these points are dealt with by the archaeologist in the main text. There should in fact be discussion between excavator and numismatist at all times. The excavator will of course have the last word in that the excavation report embodies his interpretation of the evidence but the coins must be allowed to speak for themselves as clearly as they can. Evaluation not mere numerology is required.

Following on from the above there arises the question of the form which the coin list should take. This may seem obvious but it is of importance if its use is not to be limited solely to the site for which it was prepared. The ability to compare the information from various sites reasonably quickly and accurately should suggest that the format of lists should be more or less uniform. Mr. Dolley has dealt with this problem in detail, but it is worthwhile drawing attention to the fact that on many small sites, perhaps dealt with by a small and possibly inadequate local organisation, coin lists are woefully inadequate as regards both identification and presentation. This does not happen on large sites where specialist reports are dealt with by specialists, but occasionally shortage of space as a result of the need to deal with a mass of coinage means a maximum of abbreviation and a loss of clarity in the format of the main list. When perusing a list, the obverse, especially pre-AD 296, and for the fourth century the reverse type are essential, as is, in my view, the denomination for the former and the mint for the latter. Variants and irregularities should also be ascertainable. The fact that the reference number, R.I.C. (or sometimes B.M.C.) or Late Roman Bronze Coinage, is given where possible still leaves the problem that as with any other specialist report it is there to be read intelligibly as part of the total evidence and ought to be assimilable by the non-specialist. Esoteric break-downs, graphs and the like may well follow in a large report. There some-times seems to be a tendency for the specialist reports, even on a small site producing only meagre relevant evidence, to swamp the main report of the excavator and to be written only for the specialist, thus in my view meriting the smallest of type reflecting the number of potential readers. The coins, like some of the pottery, brooches and other objects used as prime dating evidence, should be dealt with clearly and intelligibly. In the 1930s O'Neil and T. V. Wheeler were amongst the pioneers in presenting coin lists in tabular form, as for example in the earlier Verulamium volume[3]. This is by far the clearest method, although of course the earlier Richborough and Malton reports were models of their kind providing full information at a time when there were inadequate reference works and which, at least in the former case, produced evidence for their compilation. The tabular form seems generally acceptable in archaeological reports, although less so in numismatic publications. The Great Casterton lists and reports are good examples of providing maximum information in a minimum of space. It is arguable that on the rare sites producing the sort of numbers found at Richborough, and at the other extreme those sites with less than about a dozen coins, this tabular method is wasteful of space.

The relevance of including the excavators site reference and also the degree of wear will vary from site to site. Both are relevant if there is a separate list or lists dealing with stratified coins and/or specific groups of coins. For most purposes stratified coins can be discussed in the main text where the degree of wear can be mentioned and the coin referred by numbers to the total coin list. Since the degree of wear is incapable of yielding a truly objective conclusion, depending as it does on the weight and metal of the coin, the length of its currency and its velocity of circulation, to say nothing of the difficulties encountered due to the vagueness of striking and the incidence of corrosion, care must be exercised in assessing the evidential value of wear, and even more of the lack of wear.

On the smaller site, which might yield from one to ten pre-Hadrianic pieces in a total list of about a hundred, it may be tempting to look for proof of first-century activity in the presence of an unstratified assemblage composed of a Claudian As and three or four Vespasianic pieces, all worn. In the absence of pottery, especially Samian, however, no such conclusion is warranted, and a second-century date for the deposition of those pieces would tend to be confirmed by the presence in the coin list of pieces of Trajan, Hadrian and the Antonine emperors, preferably in decreasing degrees of wear. Certainly in this case wear is a consistent and therefore a considerable factor in interpretation and should be indicated in the text or an additional list. Despite this, for the great majority of coins in the list the degree of wear will be relatively unimportant, as for example in the radiate issues or those of the House of Constantine. To indicate the degree of wear of a normal series of Fel Temp Reparatio imitations would be of limited archaeological and numismatic significance but would begin to both impair the clarity of the coin list and severely reduce the space available.

For the final coin series on a site the importance of the degree of wear is obvious, and many a postulation of mid-fifth century activity has been made on the basis of the condition of the issues of the Theodosian Victoria Auggg and Salus Reipublicae types. It is certainly true that many of these pieces exhibit a considerable degree of wear and generally speaking Theodosian Æ 4 issues, even allowing for the poor striking, show more wear than the run of Constantinian issues. But pushing activity too far into the fifth century on the basis of perhaps half a dozen imperfectly identifiable Æ 4s which might have been in active circulation before AD 390 should be eschewed.

Our knowledge of the precise behaviour of various coinages is of course even now limited, but acquaintance with Keynsian theory, for example with relevance to the velocity of circulation, is as valid for past coinages as it is today. Of considerable importance when evaluating even a small list is the length of currency of a coin rather than the date brackets of its issue. As suggested above this is especially relevant as for example in the case of first and second-century *aes*, notably sestertii, which could be retained as currency up to the middle of the third century – Postumus (AD 259–68) struck sestertii, sometimes over-striking earlier pieces. The evidence for the currency of issues must largely be derived from major site collections, but the extent to which various coinages exhibit wide divergences in their lengths of currency must be read alongside the degree of wear, and obviously applies to sites large and small. The significance of this when applied to one or two stratified coins used for dating a building is equally obvious and should be made explicit in the text of a report.

The pattern or make-up of coin lists is probably best expressed visually in what can best be called pseudo-histograms. These need not be true histograms, in which the horizontal scale should represent periods expressed according to the number of years each contains, but mere block diagrams. The simplest form may merely take an agreed number of periods shown as of equal width and with the number of coins to each period indicated on the vertical scale. For the histogram to be of use the chronological scale should show numismatically significant divisions, and for comparative purposes it is obvious that these should be generally accepted. Dr. Richard Reece and the author proposed an agreed chronological division[4] whereby the periods were in some cases subdivisible so that they were adaptable to both small and large sites.

Whilst the writers made no claim to originality in the concept, it was felt necessary to press for uniformity of format so that different histograms could be immediately and validly compared. At this level they present an immediate block picture of the coinage, devoid of percentages, annual averages or any other sophisticated statistical devices which may be suitable for particular purposes or where large numbers of specimens are available. The danger of getting too far away from the actual number of coins should be avoided as far as possible on small sites where numbers are inadequate for generalised conclusions extrapolated from single groups. Comparisons between sites can often be very clearly demonstrated by this means however, and on a large site histograms are the simplest and most economical way of revealing divergences in the weight of coin evidence of different dates in different parts of the site.

The site discussed in the main part of the article, of which the appendix has already been cited[4], affords an excellent example of how a relatively small series can be of the greatest archaeological value. The excavation of the King Harry Lane site[4] immediately outside the Silchester Gate of Verulamium produced a series of coins which, one or two strays apart, ended rather unusually with an As of Macrinus (AD 238) (Figure 2c). No apology is made for the element of interpretation embodied in this statement. The very thin scatter of one or two late radiates and late Constantinian issues are the least that could be expected to be found in the vicinity of a road or in almost any field surrounding the city. The contrast with other parts of Verulamium is striking (Figures 1 and 2) and its relevance to the date of the construction of the city wall can hardly be ignored. The pottery at this date cannot really be expected to give such an unequivocal answer. Pottery, if securely dated, remains the principal source of evidence on Romano-British sites and for the first century of the Roman occupation the presence of Samian, together with distinctive native-derived types and early Roman coarse ware, provides a secure basis for many sites. However, coins and the lack of certain issues can lend weight and precision. For the later periods, however, despite the existence of distinct and dated products of certain potteries, (for example, Castor, New Forest, Calcite Gritted Wares and others), there is often at best an imperfectly defined date-bracket in which they may be confined, and this applies with even greater force to many general types which may be regionally or locally produced at widely differing dates. One of the problems certainly applicable to the smaller site is that in the last two-thirds of the third century precise dating by means of pottery, coins, brooches or small finds is equally difficult. The coins are obviously the best dated objects, but on some sites their very quantity should engender caution. The base antoniniani issued from the reign of Gallienus to the reform of Diocletian thus remained current over a period of half a century and on their demonetization represented a vast bulk of coinage which is

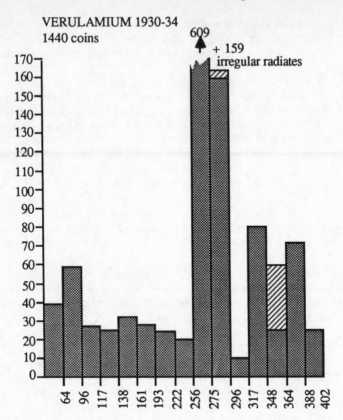

FIG. 1a

frequently found in Constantinian contexts. That demonetization was effective is now generally accepted, but apart from the many coins still about at the turn of the century large numbers of the poorer issues, especially those of the Gallic Empire, found their way into large or small hoards which, if dispersed, may appear unrecognised in many site lists. These residual effects should be borne in mind but the presence of the coinage of the mid-third century does not deserve to be glossed over. With the provisos mentioned above it still remains the best evidence for third-century activity.

A vast quantity of radiate coinage was one of the features of the coin list of the Verulamium Excavations of 1930–33 (Figure 1a). Subsequent sites, both in the later 1930s and more recently, have not uniformly confirmed this (Figures 1b and 2a). Whilst this note is concerned principally with the smaller site, it nevertheless seems worthwhile to draw attention to the very different patterns of coinage which exist in various parts of a large site. The various insulae and buildings which have been subject to separate excavations and reports reveal wide divergences in coin distribution. It is sometimes

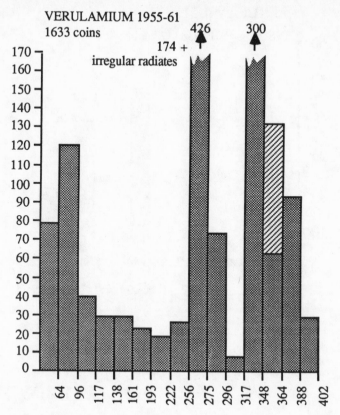

VERULAMIUM 1955-61
1633 coins
174 + irregular radiates

FIG. 1b

difficult to read the pattern clearly in a large excavation covering many buildings, where the stratified coins may well appeaar in the total list. No doubt the excavation report will emphasise the periods of activity of the various buildings, but the histograms for the total coin finds already cited (Figure 1) do make their point quite clearly. Another site which has produced widely divergent patterns is the substantial but scattered town of Baldock, set at an important cross route on the Icknield Way and of pre-Roman origin. Here, excavations carried out in the 1930s on Walls Field[5], north-east of the present town, produced a large cemetery mainly second century in date and a wide chronological spread of coins. The miscellaneous coin finds from Baldock in the Letchworth Museum also show a general run through the Roman period. In recent years Baldock has been the subject of several limited area rescue excavations in the north-east part of the town, notably Brewery Field by Mr. J. Moss Eckhardt in 1967 and the Tene site a short distance to the east which yielded a rich late Iron Age 'Chieftain' burial giving rise to the excavation by Dr. I. M. Stead. This only occupied a small

VERULAMIUM

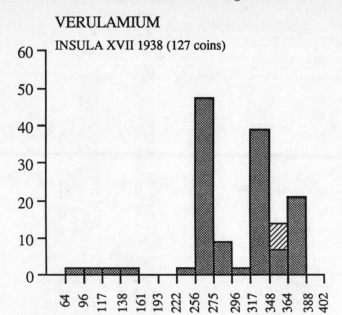

FIG. 2a

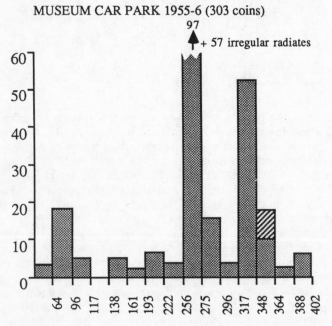

FIG. 2b

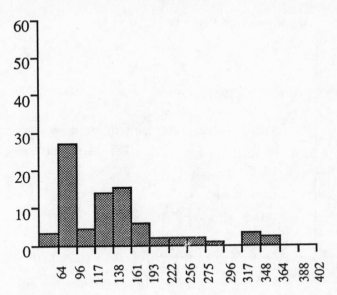

KING HARRY 1966-7 (80 coins)

FIG. 2c

part of the site which was excavated subsequently. Following these, a major and still continuing campaign was directed at the extensive sixty-acre site immediately to the north-east of Walls Field.

Although the excavation of the main site is not yet complete and work on the coins is likewise incomplete, it is clear that the areas of the township show widely differing occupation patterns. Brewery Field (Figure 3c) showed substantial weighting in favour of the mid-fourth century, (out of 103 coins, 61 = 59.2 per cent AD 330–364), while only a short distance away at the Tene site the later fourth century was extensively represented, contrasting both with Brewery Field and the main site where the series ran through from an extensive Belgic coinage to the fourth century, although without the peaks shown by the other two sites. It must be obvious that the proportion of the total site excavated and the various areas chosen can produce very different results. On the larger sites mentioned above valid conclusions can be reached with respect to particular areas of a settlement, and in any event the complete excavation of a large site is a rarity.

Similarly, on villa sites in the past the excavation was all too often limited to the actual main dwelling. This can produce misleading results. At Great Weldon[6] the site list was dominated by Constantinian issues, notably the two victories type of AD 341–8, and the coin series was reduced to a trickle after Magnentius – both Magnentius and the immediately preceding Fel Temp-Phoenix type are represented by a single specimen. There is then a

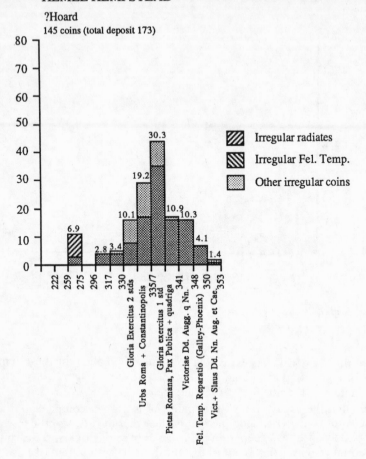

FIG. 3a

gap, with not a single irregular Fel Temp fallen horseman, until the Valentinianic period represented by only three coins. For the final period, had
the villa alone been excavated, the total of six Theodosian coins would have
been drastically reduced. Only one was found more or less stratified in the
upper debris levels, but at least three were from the general area of the
forecourt which had been largely stripped during the excavation. This pointer
to a late fourth-century presence on the site which does not seem to include
occupation of the villa may be paralleled elsewhere. Thus at Gadebridge,
where more or less complete excavation of a villa complex which included
Baths, ancillary buildings, yards and other features has been achieved, several
points of similarity with Great Weldon appear. Firstly, the relative gap in

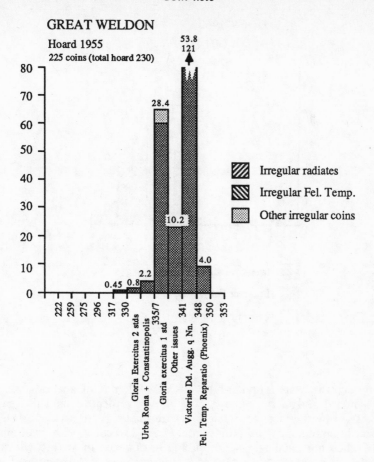

FIG. 3b

the fourth-century series following the earlier Fel Temp and the Magnentian issues seems to be a real gap and not just the falling-off in the coin supply and/or coin loss noted by Mrs. Ravetz.[2] As a feature of certain sites this phenomenon would bear a closer examination, both from the historical and economic point of view as well as from the purely numismatic standpoint. Whilst the histogram for Hemel Hempstead (Gadebridge) site shows, even without the use of Mrs. Ravetz's formula, that it falls into her class A, the period divisions cannot reasonably be reduced to distinguish between the pre-AD 358 Fel Temp coinage and the subsequent 'fallen horseman' type, unless detailed analyses are provided as Mrs. Ravetz does for certain sites. Normally reference to the list itself will have to be made.

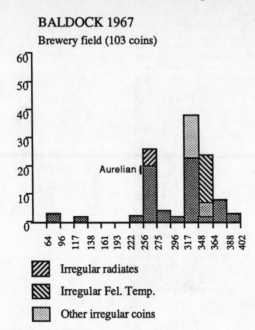

BALDOCK 1967

FIG. 3c

Coin deposits were found at both Great Weldon and Gadebridge, in one case a hoard and in the other a possible votive deposit, and this gap is emphasised by the fact that while both are made up almost exclusively of Constantinian coinage and both number over 150 coins neither contains a single fallen horseman, the series ending in one case in AD 350 with nine Phoenix types and the other in AD 353 with two types of Magnentius (Figure 3a and b).

The immediately subsequent histories of the sites are not identical in that non-numismatic evidence seems to suggest general activity in the Valentinianic Period in one case, whereas at Gadebridge later activity seems to have centred on minor structures beyond the villa. The second point of comparison which, as noted, depended on complete area excavation, is the significance of the find spots of the relatively few Theodosian Æ 4s at Gadebridge. As at Weldon these clearly indicated that such limited activity as there was excluded the villa and probably the other buildings as well.

The comparison above is between sites showing conformity in several respects although widely separated geographically. There is nothing surprising in this, but the comparative study of further sites should lead to the building up of a picture of villa sites with similar histories. Conversely neighbouring sites, for example Gadebridge and Boxmoor,[8] can yield strongly contrasting peaks of coin loss. Again this is a truism, but I think it is true that relatively little time or effort has been given to gathering and collating the coin evidence from a large series of smaller sites. Allowing for the facts already mentioned that there should be enough coins to form some sort of opinion, and that we must accept that much is unknowable of the historical circumstances determining the individual patterns of coin loss, it should nevertheless be possible to discern certain patterns of coinage perhaps reflecting types of occupation. Thus, of two neighbouring sites one may be complementary to the other for the simple reason that one villa or farm may replace another as the centre of an estate.

It may well be that further light can also be thrown on the relationship of various sites which may be linked by virtue of economic or administrative function. It has been postulated that a relationship existed between the East Yorkshire signal stations at Malton and the villa at Langton, Langton possibly providing primary food stuffs and Malton being the marketing centre with the auxilliaries at the signal stations being the consumers. The coinage at Langton, which shows a vast Theodosian preponderance, contrasts with that at Malton but is similar in some respects to that found on the signal stations. The story does not seem quite consistent with the facts and further work on this important and interesting group of sites, to which must be added the villa at Beadlam which produced a coin list comparable to Langton, is in hand and may suggest that there was a different economic organisation. The ability to compare and contrast sites, as in this case, has depended on the availability of reliable coin lists and the cumulative evidence which can be deduced provides one of the strongest arguments for a consistent, clear and adequate record of the coins which must be interpreted against the remainder of the archaeological evidence. In the case of the Yorkshire sites, it is the coins which appear to me to be decisive.

Notes

1. O'Neil, B. H. St. J., 'Coins and Archaeology in Britain, 1936', in *Arch J.*, XCII, (1935).

2. Ravetz, A., 'Fourth Century Inflation and Romano-British Coin Finds', in *Num. Chronicle*, 7th ser., 15, (1965).

3. Wheeler, T. V. and R. E. M., 'Verulamium: A Belgic and Two Roman Cities', in *Soc. Antiq. Res. Rep.*, XI, (1936).

4. Stead, I. M., 'Verulamium 1966–1968', in *Antiquity*, XLIII, 45, (1969), and Appendix to the above by P. E. Curnow and R. M. Reece.

5. Westell, W. P. 'The Romano-British Cemetery at Baldock, Hertfordshire', in *Arch. J.*, LXXXVIII, (1931), 247–301.

6. *J. R. S.*, 44, (1954) 93, 95; 45, (1955), 135; 46, (1956), 133–34; 47, (1957), 213–14.

7. Neal, D. S., 1963–68. *Soc. Antiq. Res. Rep.*, XXXI. I would like to thank the author for allowing me to discuss this site.

8. Interim Report, *Britannia*, II, (1971), 270.

A postscript

Since contributing the above, rather basic comments on some of the problems attending the production and use of coin lists from the smaller Roman site, 'archaeological numismatics' has made great strides especially in terms of statistical analysis. Both in BAR 4 and elsewhere the editors and other contributors have subjected a considerable bulk of coin evidence, both old and new, to new methods of interpretation and presentation. While the larger site will have most to gain, the smaller site with a limited coin sample must profit from varied analytical techniques, especially when an increasing number of good site reports are becoming available to be treated comparatively.

Since this is a reprint only, one or two comments and minor modifications are called for. Thus it is considered that the chronological periods used in the pseudo-histograms (Figures 1–3) still remain valid for the smaller British site and it is proposed to continue to use them. However, the refinements used by Richard Reece which are intended to improve and extend their potential for analysis may be more suitable in relation to the larger and/or European site.

Richard Reece has thus extended the number of major periods from fifteen to sixteen. Period I running to AD 64 (the date of Nero's drastic tinkering with the coinage) and period II AD 64–96 are replaced by three periods: I to AD 41, II a and b AD 41–69, III AD 69–96. These divisions will obviously be useful when dealing with old coin lists merely identifying emperors and, on pre-Flavian sites, producing substantial numbers of coins. The only other marginal alteration is to the period which Reece ends in AD 294 (Diocletian's reform) rather than 296 (i.e. including Allectus). For the British sites it is clearly more realistic to include the coinage of Allectus. On the single, smaller site producing fifty to three hundred coins I remain in favour of the simple block bar chart (*see* page 61 paragraph 2) despite its great troughs and peaks which may mislead the unwary. Also, despite the relatively complicated type-setting, the tabulated list still seems to provide the maximum of information within a reasonable compass. Where more than one site is dealt with for comparative purposes, tables as used by Reece in his survey of fourteen Romano-British sites (*Britannia* pp. 269–276) may be more economical of space and true histograms and other techniques will be required to illuminate particular aspects. It is hoped to produce comparative material in the forthcoming coin report on the Gorhambury Villa, but generally the aim on the smaller site must remain that of producing clear and comprehensive lists of coins, enabling any comments to be checked against the evidence which can be used by others without recourse to the coins themselves.

Since 1974 there have been considerable advances in the identification of Romano-British pottery but there are still areas and periods where coins must perforce fill gaps. Imperial coins are the same whether found on the

Welsh marches or in the south-east, and despite the pitfalls pointed out by this and other authors in BAR 4, notably Dr. Kent, the coins must be allowed to speak for themselves, even if only to say goodbye!

5

Clustering of coin finds in Britain, France and Italy

Richard Reece

Between 1965 and 1969 I gathered together information on Roman coins found at sites in France and Italy and added this to a growing body of archaeological coin reports from Britain. The work could not be done in the library, and this still remains the case, because so few excavations outside Britain have been published with full coin reports in the Mediterranean area; the coins found on sites remain in museums, mainly unpublished, and the only way to obtain the information is to collect it in person. In Germany, Austria and Luxembourg site finds have been published, so that this work could be extended in certain areas but, for France and Italy, there is not a great deal of information to add to that gathered in the 1960s. Future work will be able to take account of the publication of many rescue excavations of the 1970s when I hope this work will be useful as a first study. The idea behind it is to throw the information, collected by geographical areas, into a general analysis to see what groupings arise from the coins themselves rather than from our geographical and historical preconceptions. The grouping which does appear in this work can be tested and refined, or rejected as more information becomes available.

A suitable starting point is Figure 1, already published in *Britannia*, but repeated here, slightly altered, for ease of reference. The coins from my four regions have been drawn in four columns, each of which is divided into four phases. Phase A contains all coins up to AD 259, Phase B coins from 259 to 294, Phase C coins from 294 to 330, and Phase D coins from 330 to the end of mass production in about 402. Each block of the diagram represents the average percentage of coins in that region which falls into that phase. It has been suggested that the pattern shown in Figure 1 is warped by the under-representation of phase A in Britain. Figure 2 therefore shows the pattern which emerges if phase A is removed from the reckoning

Table 1

Phase	Britain	N. France (percentages)	S. France	N. Italy
A	14	51	60	63
B	28	21	20	14
C	5	12	8	10
D	53	16	12	13

but, although phases B, C and D are now more evenly represented in all four groups, the British floruit in phase D remains the most obvious point of the diagram. Tables 1 and 2 give the numerical values expressed in Figures 1 and 2.

Table 2

Phase	Britain	N. France (percentages)	S. France	N. Italy
B	32.5	43	50	38
C	6	24.5	20	27
D	61.5	32.5	30	35

The next step is to use the phases to explore clusterings of sites within each region. Thus, if we consider the relationship of the coins in phase A at each site in Britain to the coins in phase B we might find that some sites are close to one another, are related in one way, while a second cluster of sites are related in another way. With luck, all sites in Britain might fall easily into one cluster or the other – and the way would be clear for the suggestion of two categories of sites within a single region. Table 3 gives the information necessary for this analysis in Britain. The coins in each

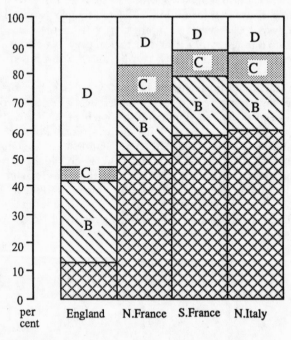

FIG. 1

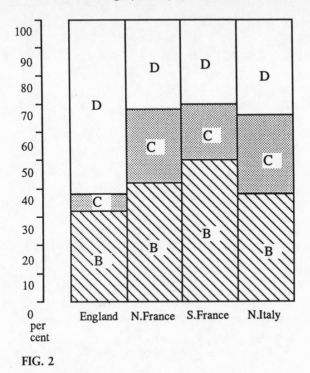

FIG. 2

group have been expressed as percentages in Phases A, B, C and D. Thus at Canterbury (2) phase A contained 9.9 per cent of the coins, B – 41 per cent, C – 3.3 per cent and D – 44.8 per cent. The coin groups and the numbers by which they are identified on tables and diagrams are given in Table 4.

Before expressing the figures on Table 3 on a diagram it is convenient to construct another table which shows how each value deviates from the regional mean – thus Canterbury is 3.9 per cent below the British average in Phase A, 13.3 per cent above in Phase B, 1.9 per cent below in Phase C and 7.7 per cent below in Phase D. To avoid a congestion of figures which would deter a majority of readers all subsequent tables have been omitted. They can all be presented from the figures printed in *Britannia* vol. iv by a simple process of addition and subtraction; the only values which involve any major calculations are the means which are given in Table 3.

We now have four values for each group and can plot a diagram. If we use the two axes of graph paper we can plot two values at once and show the relationship of coins of Phase A to coins of Phase B at all sites. Figure 3a shows this diagram which is constructed by plotting the deviation from the mean in Phase A against the deviation from the mean of Phase B. On purely subjective inspection the groups fall into two clusters: both clusters are around the mean of Phase A but one cluster is above the mean in Phase

Table 3. British Groups

Phase	1	2	3	4	5	6	7	8	9	10	11	Mean for all regions
A	4.7	9.9	5.7	20.1	4.9	10.2	24.4	12.1	12.0	63.6	0.3	45.7
B	17.1	41.0	9.6	63.0	29.8	35.0	39.0	39.0	14.3	32.0	16.8	20.6
C	2.3	3.3	10.6	1.8	5.4	4.3	3.4	3.7	1.5	1.4	27.0	8.4
D	78.4	44.8	70.3	15.5	58.6	45.4	33.2	39.0	68.6	1.6	54.0	23.5

Phase	12	13	14	15	16	17	18	19	Mean for Britain
A	5.4	8.3	17.0	15.0	2.4	5.8	5.0	25.2	13.8
B	46.0	23.0	19.8	7.7	21.8	14.4	42.0	14.6	27.7
C	4.6	5.1	7.6	4.0	2.6	2.6	2.4	5.0	5.2
D	41.6	65.7	56.6	65.9	75.3	76.8	51.4	54.9	52.5

Table 4. Site numbers used in diagrams and tables

BRITAIN

1. Richborough
2. Canterbury
3. Lullingstone
4. Verulamium Wheeler
5. Verulamium Theatre
6. Wheeler/Theatre
7. Verulamium Frere
8. Verulamium Verulam
9. Thistleton
10. Fishbourne
11. Portchester
12. Winchester
13. Wanborough
14. Cirencester Museum
15. Cirencester Excavations
16. Chedworth
17. Nettleton
18. Henley Wood
19. Sea Mills
(Britannia iii, 269–76)

N. FRANCE AND THE RHINE

20. Mainz
21. Speyer
22. Rheinzabern
23. Haguenau
24. Pachten
25. Sélestat
26. Rhine Valley
27. Belfort
28. Langres A
29. Langres B
30. Langres C
31. Autun
32. Avallon
33. Auxerre
34. Châtillon-sur-Seine
35. Sens A
36. Sens M
37. Verdun
38. Condé-sur-Aisne
39. Soissons

S. FRANCE

40. Dijon
41. Bourges
42. Poitiers
43. Toulouse
44. Foix
45. Perpignan
46. Montpellier
47. Nimes A
48. Nimes B
49. Arles
50. Glanum
51. Aix-en-Provence
52. Banon
53. L'Escale
54. Vienne Museum
55. Vienne Theatre

N. ITALY

56. Pavia
57. Verona
58. Cividale
59. Udine
60. Aquileia
61. Portogruaro
62. Venezia
63. Adria
64. Padova
65. Este
66. Bologna Civic
67. Bologna University
68. Ravenna
69. Faenza
70. Arezzo
71. Cortona
72. Tiber I
73. Tiber II
74. Ostia

Coins and the archaeologist

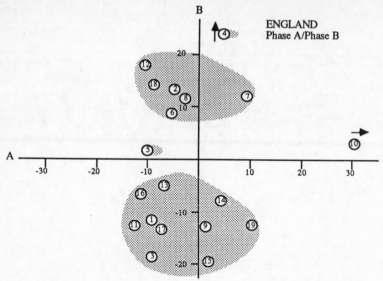

FIG. 3a

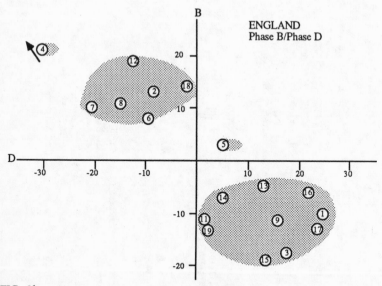

FIG. 3b

B and the other is below. Fishbourne (10) is an obvious outlier, and Verulamium Wheeler (4) and Verulamium Theatre (5) lie outside the obvious cluster which includes Verulamium Frere (7) and Verulamium Verulam (8). The composite group Wheeler+Theatre (6) reconciles these opposites.

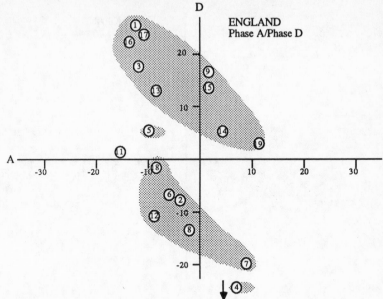

FIG. 4a

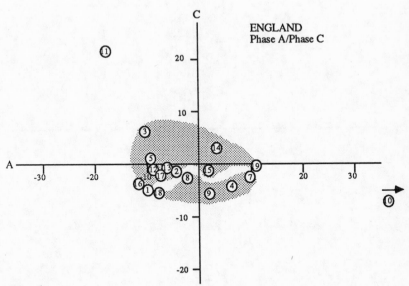

FIG. 4b

Because there are four phases, and we can only plot two at once, we can draw six diagrams viz. AB, AC, AD, BC, BD and CD. These are shown in Figures 3, 4 and 5. In every case except AC (Figure 4b) the groups of coins fall into two well defined clusters with Fishbourne as a constant erratic,

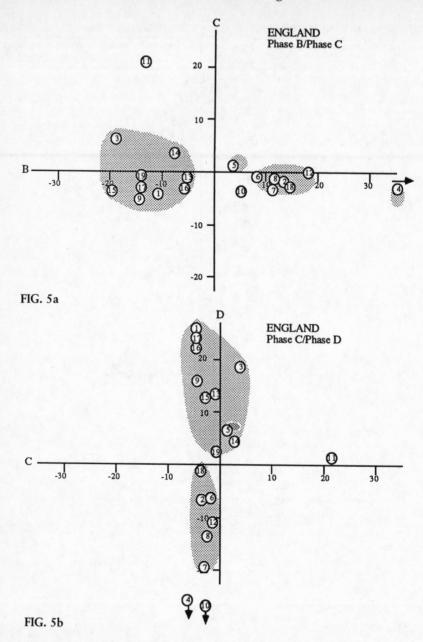

FIG. 5a

FIG. 5b

Verulamium Wheeler and Theatre constantly balancing each other, and Portchester erratic in Phase C.

Exactly the same procedure may be followed for the North of France and the Rhine. Figure 6a shows diagram BD – phase C as in Britain confuses

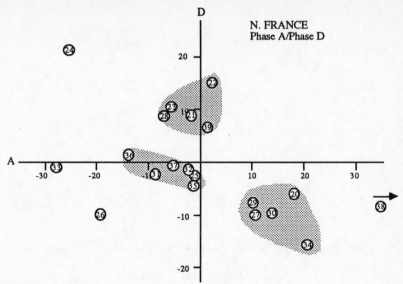

FIG. 6a

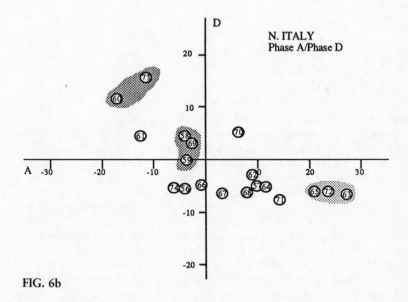

FIG. 6b

the picture. The same three clusters and four outliers appear in all diagrams
except AC. For the South of France four clusters and two outliers are
consistently represented, as in Figure 7, which shows the typical diagram
AB. Finally, in Italy there are the two small clusters which can be seen on

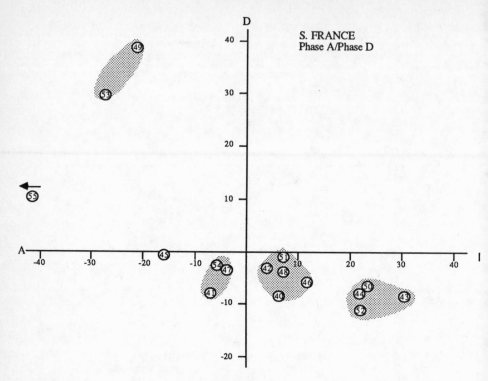

FIG. 7

Figure 6b – diagram AB – with the majority of coin groups forming a fairly uniform central spread.

Armed with the warning that regions may carry within them particular clusters of coin groups it is possible to ignore the regional boundaries and plot all four areas on a single diagram. Six diagrams, as before, can be plotted but only one is shown here – Figure 8 – Phase A against Phase D. The dotted lines represent a human attempt at clustering based on the results of the 24 group diagrams (e.g. Figures 3 to 7) and all six complete diagrams. Groups shown clustered do therefore hang together on all diagrams and, whatever the explanation, the phenomenon is real rather than imaginary.

Many points spring out from Figure 8, some of which can be explained, others which need considerably more work to be understood. Not only do the two British clusters (XI and XII) remain separate entities but they also keep well away from all continental clusters. One pair of sites from Southern France, Arles and L'Escale (49 and 53, XIII), always strain towards the British clusters and the next cluster, XIV, has several N. France groups together with Aquileia (60) and Tiber II from Italy. Then follow clusters XV, XVI and XVII which are often difficult to tell apart and the diagram ends with a miscellaneous cluster, XVIII, whose main aim seems to be

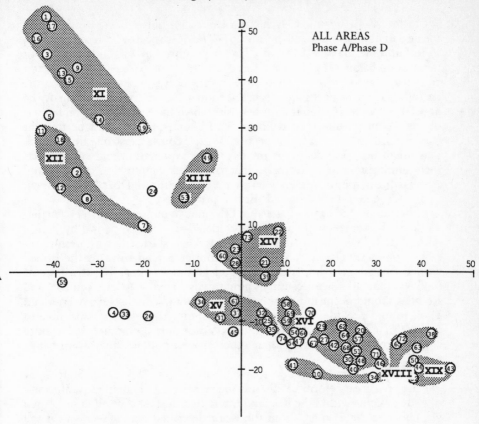

FIG. 8

centrifugal. Within cluster XVIII there is a concentration of S. France groups, XIX.

Apart from clusters there are constant outliers and it is easiest to start explanations with these. Pachten (24) floats uneasily near the British clusters and thus presumably reflects the similarity of a crossroad settlement set well back from the Rhine frontier to a British commercial site in a rather military province. Vienne Theatre (55), Verulamium Wheeler (4), Auxerre (33) and the Rhine Valley (26) always float together outside the continental clusters. Rhine Valley should be discounted for this is a purely synthetic group made up from finds over a large area. Vienne Theatre and Auxerre hang well together for they are medium-sized collections marred by hoards of radiate coins which were noticed when they were being listed. This means that severe doubt is cast on the authenticity of Verulamium Wheeler which will shortly be investigated in the current work on all Verulamium coins. I would predict the existence of a scattered hoard of radiate coins which were too widely dispersed to be obvious to the excavators but which, with hindsight, might be isolated by careful search.

Cluster XVIII is almost a cluster of outliers, but it has a very definite theme running through all its groups. The histories of Fishbourne (10), Vertilium (34), Banon (53) and Glanum (50) are known, and each one of these sites belongs to the first three centuries AD. Coins at Banon stop completely at AD 270 and at the other sites decrease sharply, giving little encouragement to postulate a fourth-century occupation. Condé-sur-Aisne and Tiber I are very similar river deposits which have a large preponderance of early coins; while their deposition and composition might be thought similar with only a cursory inspection of their coins, the strong links which bind them on these diagrams invite careful explanation and suggest that their similarities are more than fortuitous. This conjunction of Tiber and Aisne is thrown into further relief by the behaviour of Tiber II (73) which, as already noted, tends towards British properties.

Little can be said at this stage about the main continental clusters. Further work of the same sort in which more detailed analysis, period by period within each phase, is possible has already been started but the results are still incomplete. Five groups from the continent tend towards the British clusters: Pachten, Arles, L'Escale, Aquileia and Rome (Tiber II). It seems unlikely that all fourth-century mint towns listed – Arles, Aquileia and Rome – should occur in this zone by accident and coin lists from Trier and Lyon should provide a test for this suggestion. At present it is possible to suggest that groups in clusters XI to XIV not only used and lost far more coins in the fourth century than other groups but that they were better supplied with such coins.

A final word must be devoted to Phase C (AD 294–330). Starting at Diocletian's great reform of 294 it is the first period of complete uniformity of issue of coins within the Roman Empire; for the first time all mints struck virtually the same coins. From the work described here it seems as if the phase is also one of uniformity in use and loss of coinage. This suggestion comes from the fact, already noted for Britain, that Phase C in all areas makes nonsense of the clustering. This happens because in Phase C there are no special clusterings and all sites seem evenly scattered round an area close to the mean. The absence of the usual clustering must presumably indicate a surprising uniformity in coin use and loss in Phase C. Further analysis of the periods in and immediately around Phase C should pinpoint the anomalous coins and suggest an explanation.

In conclusion, it seems reasonable to suggest that a new method has been developed for the analysis of groups of coins – new, that is, as applied to coins. Even at the crude and simple level outlined above, which needed only pencil, graph paper, and the ability to add, subtract, multiply and divide, many new ideas have been raised. Further work may lead, for convenience, into the maw of a computer but the basic idea is extremely simple and I hope this gentle introduction will give my arithmophobic colleagues courage to follow me so that I may have the benefit of their continued help and criticism.

Afterword

Work since the first publication has concentrated on finds within Britain because the material has come easily to hand as reports have been completed on coins from the growing number of rescue excavations. The two British groups defined with only some 19 lots of coins have stood up to further analysis, and the addition of far more information, though the picture which emerges when 140 sites are used instead of 19 is far less simple and clearly cut. The town group remains a definite cluster on any graphical method that is used to plot this information, with the exception of Cirencester and Caerwent which stray out into the non-town area of the diagrams. Use of the term non-town may seem imprecise, yet the sites which are outside the town grouping are, as in this study, very varied. Temples, with the exception of Henley Wood already seen in this study, villas, villages, small towns, forts and rural settlements intermingle in the second group and no method so far has separated out these different classes of site. The conclusion must be that there is, in Britain, an urban type of coin-use and a rural type, characterized by use of many coins of the fourth century, so that at this rather crude and simple level of analysis further distinctions in coin use are unlikely. The way forward will be to look in greater detail at short periods of coin-use within the outline of Roman Britain and to work on from there. For a summary of recent work I would refer the reader to my book on *Coinage in Roman Britain* (Seaby, 1987).

Institute of Archaeology
London

6

Numerical aspects of Roman coin hoards in Britain

Richard Reece

This paper results from a brief study of a sample of coin hoards deposited in Britain in the Roman period. The composition of many hoards was analysed numerically but only in a few cases were any results obtained which are useful to archaeology. Three examples have been chosen to illustrate the method and the area of useful conclusions. Hoards of silver denarii from the conquest of AD 43 to the mid-third century may be able to tell us something about the composition of the coinage and the way in which money went into circulation, hoards of bronze coins up to about 250, though fewer in number can help us on the problem of survival of coinage of low intrinsic value, and hoards of copper coins from the end of the fourth century have their own special characteristics. These examples tread a little of the same ground as Dr. Robertson (*see* page 13) and Dr. Kent (*see* page 201) but lack Dr. Robertson's encyclopaedic knowledge of Romano-British coin hoards and Dr. Kent's wide-ranging knowledge of hoards in general. They have been included because they sometimes reach similar conclusions by different methods and provide some numerical examples on which the reader may base his own calculations.

Early silver hoards

There are two ways of analysing material in hoards of denarii and examples of each will be given. The first method is to examine the composition of several hoards deposited within a few years of one another. The examples chosen from the whole range which has been examined is that group of hoards which have no coins later than the death of Septimius Severus in AD 211, though they are firmly dated, at the earliest to his reign, by some percentage of his coins. These hoards are:

Name	County	Reference	Number of coins
Silchester	Hants.	*Archaeologia*, LIV, p. 473	253
Portmoak	Scotland	*Proc. Soc. Ant. Scot.* LII, p. 265	103
Carrawburgh	Cumbs.	*Numismatic Chronicle*, 1937, p. 146	66
Bristol	Glos.	*Numismatic Chronicle*, 1938, p. 86	1,481
Handley	Dorset	*Numismatic Chronicle*, 1950, p. 312	441
Owston Ferry	Lincs.	*Numismatic Chronicle*, 1953, p. 139	4
Abergele	N. Wales	*Bull. of the Board of Celtic Studies*, 1936, p. 188	350

Table A numbers

	Silchester	Portmoak	Carrawburgh	Bristol	Handley	Owston Ferry	Abergele
Republic	9	—	5	60	14	1	24
Nero	4	1	—	10	2	—	2
Otho/Galba/Vit	5	4	2	13	7	—	5
Vespasian	38	6	3	162	39	—	95
Titus/Domitian	16	5	—	54	32	—	27
Nerva	—	1	—	9	15	—	3
Trajan	27	10	—	103	41	—	36
Hadrian	50	18	3	145	61	—	46
A. Pius	48	27	—	200	96	1	65
M. Aurelius	40	22	5	181	98	—	32
Commodus	14	7	—	64	34	—	9
S. Severus	2	2	48	480	2	2	6

Table B percentages

	Silchester	Portmoak	Carrawburgh	Bristol	Handley	Owston Ferry	Abergele
Republic	3.6	—	7.6	4.2	3.2	25.0	6.8
Nero	1.6	1.0	—	0.7	0.5	—	0.6
Otho/Galba/Vit	2.0	3.8	3.0	0.9	1.6	—	1.4
Vespasian	15.0	5.7	4.5	11.0	8.8	—	27.0
Titus/Domitian	6.4	4.8	—	3.6	7.2	—	7.8
Nerva	—	1.0	—	0.6	3.4	—	0.9
Trajan	10.8	9.7	—	7.1	9.3	—	10.3
Hadrian	20.0	17.5	—	10.0	14.0	—	13.0
A. Pius	19.0	26.2	4.5	14.0	22.0	25.0	17.0
M. Aurelius	16.0	21.3	—	13.0	22.0	—	9.1
Commodus	5.6	6.7	7.6	4.4	7.7	—	2.6
S. Severus	0.8	1.9	73.0	33.0	0.5	50.0	1.7

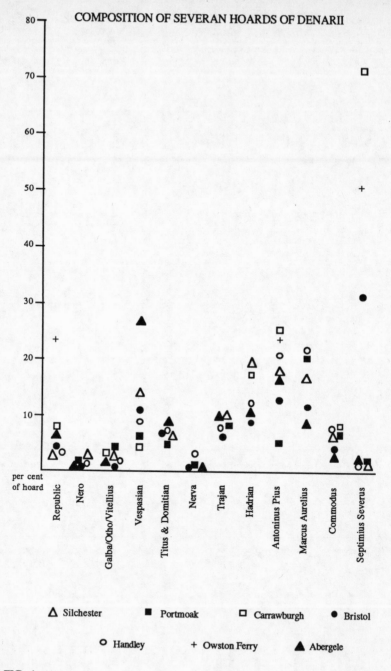

FIG. 1

The composition of these hoards by emperors expressed first as numbers, then as percentages is given in Tables A and B. The percentages in Table B are plotted in Figure 1.

A diagram similar to Figure 1 could be constructed for the hoards deposited in any reign. This Severan example has been illustrated because it puts forward all the necessary points in the clearest form, but the points to be drawn from it might be drawn from any or all of the other possible diagrams.

 (i) The tables and the diagram make it quite clear that there is such a thing as a 'normal' Severan silver hoard.

 (ii) While it may be conceded that it is possible to define the typical Severan (or Hadrianic, Claudian or Tetrican) hoard, first by a simple diagram, and then in numerical terms, it may be pointed out that there are exceptions and that at all periods these exceptions show up most clearly in the period in which the hoard is presumed to have been buried. Thus in Figure 1 the hoards from Carrawburgh, Owston Ferry and Abergele have varied and high percentages of coins of Severus. This accords well with the suggestion that most hoards contain current coin and suggests some of the possible mechanisms of commerce. In an economic area close to the incoming batches of coin intended presumably for military and administrative pay, and state debts and projects, payments might be in coin already in circulation or in new coin being put into circulation. We have no hoards of silver coins in our sample in this, or any other period before AD 250 comprising only newly minted coins, but what we do have is a succession of hoards in which such coins are progressively diluted by the standard circulating coinage. Thus Carrawburgh has 48 (73 per cent) Severan coins and 18 (27 per cent) 'general' coins, Bristol has 480 (33 per cent) Severan coins and Handley has only 2 (0.5 per cent). Numerically speaking Carrawburgh is 'near' to a batch of newly-minted coins, Bristol represents Carrawburgh when the new coins have changed hands several times more with the inevitable additions and subtractions, and Handley represents the general coinage into which Severan coins slowly percolated.

In our present state of ignorance any more 'social' explanation must be strongly resisted. Thus Carrawburgh invites a link with military pay, and on similar reasoning Bristol should represent administrative pay. Beyond the point already made, that the Bristol hoard may have been several times diluted since leaving any official coffers, it must be emphasised that we need far more objective hoard analyses before we can put forward any sound ideas on the speed and distance of movement of Roman coins during their monetary lives. Bristol might equally originate from a detachment sent out from York to buy in the South-West during a winter of the Severan campaigns or a local villa owner who had just sold part of his estate to a retired London merchant one of whose wealthy customers was high on the staff of the provincial governor. The examples are not intended for discussion but to point out the infinite variations on any attempt to explain the composition of a hoard and the pointless nature of such attempts when our knowledge is not even well enough developed to prefer one explanation to another.

(iii) If our sample of Severan hoards does reflect the general coinage in circulation at a moment in time, and if it is agreed that the hoards with high and varied representation of coins of Severus show new coins on their way into the general pool of coinage, then some important if qualified conclusions may be drawn on the coins most likely to be lost at any given period. At the accession of Severus the general pool of circulating coins would have no coins of the new emperor. Within a year troops would have been paid in new coin, sums of money containing new coins would have been accumulated, and Severan coins would have come into general circulation. By the end of Severus' reign all the coins to be struck in his name would have left the mint and within perhaps one year they would all have left official hands for the first time. The proportion of Severan coins in the pool would therefore rise through Severus' reign and continue to rise well into the reign of his successors as bulk sums of money, such as the Bristol hoard passed into and out of circulation and became diluted by the pool – at the same time enriching the pool in recent coins. The inevitable result is that the coins of a given emperor will never stand at their highest proportion in the general coinage until well after that emperor's death – perhaps some twenty or thirty years later. This theoretical model is borne out by the Severan diagram and its fellows which are not illustrated – thus Vespasian reaches a peak under Trajan (fifteen to forty per cent of each hoard), Trajan is at his highest values (twenty to fifty per cent of each hoard) under Hadrian and Antoninus Pius, and Severus is consistently more common (twenty to fifty per cent of each hoard) than his successors up to 238. The vital point here is *not* survival – this depends on the relative volume of coinage struck in a sequence of reigns, but inception, and both from the theoretical and practical side the general picture shows that a coin will only be at its most common some time after its issue has ceased.

There is a second method of analysing early silver hoards which can give further information on the process of use, loss and wastage of coins; here the coins of one date are examined throughout the hoards in which they occur. Thus coins of Antoninus Pius occur in hoards deposited between AD 138 and 268. The percentage of coins of Pius in hoards buried in his reign or that of Commodus or Severus Alexander can be found and plotted in a diagram such as Figure 2. In the sample of hoards that has been studied there were twelve hoards deposited under Antoninus Pius, twenty one under Marcus Aurelius, four under Commodus, seven under Severus, three from 211 to 222, nine under Severus Alexander of which three had no coins of Pius, three from 235 to 238, seven from 238 to 253 of which five had no coins of Pius, four under Gallienus and Valerian, and three under Postumus – both groups having two hoards which had no coin of Pius.

Figure 2a strongly supports the conclusions drawn from the sample of Severan hoards. Again, the coins of Antoninus Pius have been taken as a clear example, but similar diagrams result from the study of all other coins, except those of the Republic, and similar conclusions may be drawn from the diagrams. The two points which emerge from Figure 2a are the peak of Antonine coins only in hoards of Marcus Aurelius, not, in general, in

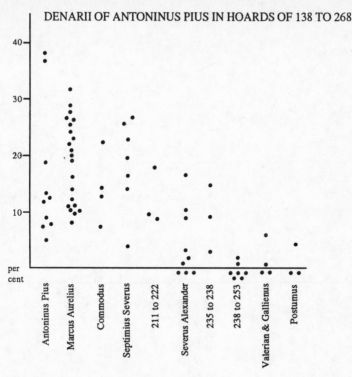

FIG. 2a

hoards of Antoninus' own reign, and the gradual dropping off of Antonine coins from AD 180 onwards. It has so far been tacitly assumed that after reaching a maximum representation sometime after the end of their period of issue all coins would slowly drop out of circulation by loss, continued dilution by new coins, hoarding, and other natural hazards. The possibility of determined withdrawal has not been considered and any comment is best left until the diagram of the representation of coins of the Republic in later hoards has been examined.

The first person to look quantitatively at the occurrence of coins of the Roman Republic in hoards buried during the Roman Empire was Bolin in his highly stimulating, but much maligned work on the fiscal and economic aspects of Roman coins. While Bolin's errors and flights of fancy have drawn unnecessarily harsh comment his positive contributions, such as his evidence for a change in silver standard under Trajan, and his concept (if not his application) of over-valuation, have been adopted into the orthodox canon of numismatics without comment. Bolin found, from a study of silver hoards in Europe, that coins of the Republic occur commonly up to the reign of Trajan but are rare thereafter. The few issues which survive the reign of Trajan to be incorporated in later hoards are predominantly coins of Mark

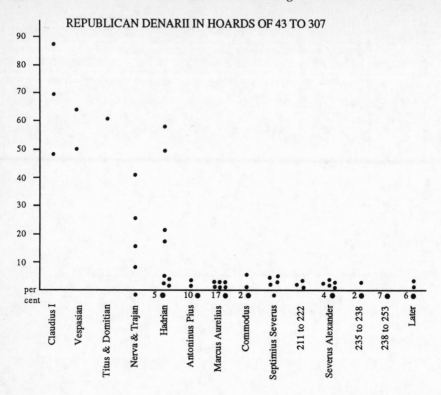

FIG. 2b

Antony's legionary issue of 32 BC. Using the rather uninformative phrases in Dio that Trajan called in the worn coinage and reminted it, adding to it the knowledge obtained from hoards and the interesting fact that when the Republican issues disappear under Trajan a token set of 'restored' Republican coins were issued, Bolin made out a case for a lowering of the silver standard to a point which made it profitable to withdraw most Republican issues which contained over ninety per cent of silver but not those of Mark Antony which Pliny (and perhaps others) had erroneously regarded as very base.

Figure 2b shows the results obtained from a larger sample of hoards than Bolin used, but in this case all from Britain. The contrast with the gradual disapperance of coins of Antoninus Pius is remarkable, and the case for withdrawal of these coins under Trajan seems unanswerable. Even here there is a further point worth study, for the Hadrianic hoards seem to fall into three groups – five hoards without Republican coins, four hoards with the low percentage of Republican coins characteristic of later hoards, and four hoards with the high percentage of Republican coins characteristic of earlier hoards. The hoards with their reference and details are (opposite):

Name	County	Reference	Rep. Coins	Total coins
Dewsbury	Yorks.	*Journal of Roman Studies*, 1925, p. 227	—	24
Mallerstang	Cumbs.	*Trans. Cumb. and West. Arch. Soc.*, XXVII, p. 205	—	139
Great Chesters	Cumbs.	*Archaeologia Aeliena*, 1902, p. 62	—	9
Corbridge	Northumbs.	*Archaeologia Aelinea*[3], VIII, p. 234	—	7
Brecon	Mon.	*Excavations at Brecon Gaer*, p. 101	—	9
Swaby	Lincs.	*Numismatic Chronicle*, 1934, p. 216	6	178
Southsea(?)	Hants.	*Numismatic Chronicle*, 1911, p. 42	13	677
Wroxeter I	Salop.	*Wroxeter Excavations*, 1914, III, p. 71	1	23
Wroxeter II	Salop.	*Wroxeter Excavations* 1914, III, p. 71	1	20
Thorngrafton	Northumbs.	*Numismatic Chronicle*, 1872, p. 63	11	60
Birdoswald	Cumbs.	*Trans. Cumb. and West Arch. Soc.*, XXXI, p. 130	17	29
Verulamium	Herts.	*Verulamium Report.*, p. 17	20	41
Ormskirk	Lancs.	*Numismatic Chronicle*, 1948, p. 232	28	119

The last four hoards with their high percentages of Republican coins could be explained away as sums of money put together before Trajan's call for such coins and not subject to examination prior to final burial in the reign of Hadrian. But such detailed explanations need to be based on detailed evidence, such as the condition of the different coins in each hoard, which is not available, and it is far better simply to allow that while the overall continental evidence quoted by Bolin demonstrates a withdrawal of coinage, such a measure had not filtered all Republican coins out of circulation in Britain until some thirty years had passed.

Now that we know what picture withdrawal seems to present in our hoard analysis it seems accurate to say that since the hoards of no other period show sharp changes in composition of hoards, there is strong evidence against any further withdrawals unknown from historical sources.

Early bronze hoards

As already mentioned above, the sample of hoards consisting mainly of Roman bronze coins struck before AD 300 has one particularly interesting group. Out of the sample of twenty hoards no fewer than eight were deposited after AD 240 – these will be further examined. The other twelve hoards are spaced out through the first and second centuries, giving at most three hoards (Claudius I) to any one reign. Since there are not enough hoards to form any reasoned conclusion about the composition of bronze coinage at any one moment the only possible conclusion is the suggestion that up to the end of the second century new bronze coinage reached Britain with little delay. Thus, hoards of which the latest coins were struck under Marcus Aurelius have full sequence stretching back to Claudius I (e.g. Whitchurch, *V.C.H. Oxfordshire*, pp. 325 ff) and the same is true for hoards reaching to the reign of Severus (e.g. Owston Ferry, *Numismatic Chronicle* 1953 p. 139). In the absence of any signs to the contrary it is therefore reasonable to assume that bronze coinage was entering Britain throughout the first and second centuries, being used there, lost and hoarded.

Hoards deposited after AD 240:

Name	County	Reference	Number of coins
Ilchester	Somerset	*Numismatic Chronicle*, 1886, p. 96	293
Ham Hill	Somerset	*Numismatic Chronicle*, 1949, p. 173	772
Alcester	Warwicks.	*Numismatic Chronicle*, 1969, p. 123	50 (plus 95 Ant)
Gare	Cornwall	*Numismatic Chronicle*, 1970, p. 181	1,018 (plus 47 AR)
Leysdown	Kent	*Numismatic Chronicle*, 1970, p. 189	498

Name	County	Reference	Number of coins
Ramsgate	Kent	*Numismatic Chronicle,* 1970, p. 199	27
Bamburgh	Northumbs.	*Archaeologia Aeliana,* II, 1958, p. 14	22
Peterborough	Northants.	*British Numism. Journal,* 1904, p. 351	11

	Ilchester	Ham Hill	Alcester	Gare	Leysdown	Ramsgate	Bamburgh	Peterborough
Vespasian and Titus	—	5	—	5	7	—	—	—
Domitian	10	13	—	18	12	—	—	—
Nerva and Trajan	44	66	4	65	41	—	—	—
Hadrian	136	210	6	162	132	3	1	1
Antoninus Pius	53	198	14	230	94	6	2	3
Marcus Aurelius	46	202	14	366	155	7	5	4
Commodus	3	46	9	124	43	9	2	—
Septimius Severus	—	8	—	23	6	—	2	—
Severus Alexander	—	14	1	15	4	1	—	1
235–253	1	7	—	6	2	—	—	—
Postumus	—	3	2	4	2	1	—	—
Others (Radiate Billon)	—	—	—	—	—	—	9 Gallienus, 1 Aurelian	1 Claudius II 1 Carausius

The pattern of coinage shows through the figures in a very obvious way, for all these hoards were deposited around the year AD 260, yet none of them has as much as ten per cent of its total made up of bronze coins struck between 200 and 260. The likelihood is that bronze coinage in third-century Britain was made up of a majority of old and worn coins and it is very difficult to account for this by any explanation other than a serious fault in the supply of newly minted coins from the mainland of Europe.

It has already been argued (*see* page 90) that hoard evidence shows a greater proportional volume of coinage of any emperor in the general circulation pool of his successor (e.g. Antoninus Pius reaches his highest percentage volume of the coinage in the reign of Marcus Aurelius). The eight hoards analysed above show that a considerable number of, say, worn sestertii of Hadrian were still in circulation circa 250; they seem to have formed from ten to thirty per cent of the bronze coinage of that date. If the coins of Hadrian deposited at various times in our sample of twenty hoards are added together, then 146 were deposited before AD 220 and 711 after. While it is not permissible to draw numerical conclusions on the probability of *site* losses from *hoard* material, there does seem to be a very strong likelihood that a majority of worn sestertii of Hadrian were lost in the mid-third century rather than at any earlier date. This factor must obviously be borne in mind when interpreting the coin loss on any specific site.

Late bronze hoards

Although hoards of bronze coins were deposited periodically throughout the fourth century, the only occasion from which enough hoards which have been well published are known is the last period of Roman coinage in the Western Empire, i.e. after AD 388. From the sample of hoards collected only a small number, seventeen, are available in enough detail for analysis. Other known hoards such as Hoards I and II of *Richborough* V give categories such as 'Constantius II' – a span of 48 years – which prevent any further numerical investigation. But the seventeen hoards rescued from published sources are only a fraction of the late bronze hoards which have been encountered in excavations in Britain. At Richborough, as already mentioned, a number of Theodosian hoards were recognised, but it seems very likely from the common find-spots of the late coins that many scattered Theodosian hoards were not recognised by the workers in clearing the topsoil. In excavations such as Canterbury, five fourth-century hoards were found, and three of those are used in this section; at Dorchester on Thames, two, both used; at Dorchester, Dorset, two; at Cirencester, six; at Winchester, three; and the list could be expanded without difficulty. Careful examination of the find-spots of late coins on many late Roman sites often shows very strange concentrations which are most easily explained as remains of a hoard scattered in or since antiquity. In summary, it seems very likely that the hoard of copper coins lost, rejected or deposited after about AD 400 is the hoard most commonly encountered on Roman sites in Britain, (n.b. radiate hoards are far less commonly found *on sites*), and may eventually prove to be the most common type of Roman hoard. This would scarcely be surprising for it is the most obvious time when money might have been considered useless, hidden for 'the time being', and never recovered.

The seventeen hoards supplemented with five from excavations are:

Hoard	Reference	Number of coins
Kiddington	*Oxoniensia*, I, p. 75	1007
Weymouth	*Dorset Archaeological Society Transactions*, LI, p. 158	4177
Filey A	*Archaeological Journal*, LXXXIX, p. 251	92
Filey B	*Archaeological Journal*, LXXXIX, p. 251	17
Scarborough	*Archaeological Journal*, LXXXIX, p. 251	49
Northants	*Archaeological Journal*, XC, p. 286	759
Little Langford	*Numismatic Chronicle*, VI, 1906 p. 330	299
Icklingham	*Numismatic Chronicle*, 1929, p. 319	1023
Cirencester	*Numismatic Chronicle*, 1929, p. 332	595

Hoard	Reference	Number of coins
Wroxall	*Numismatic Chronicle*, 1933, p. 220	462
Woodbridge	*Numismatic Chronicle*, 1935, p. 49	498
Laxton	*Numismatic Chronicle*, 1936, p. 156	335
Warle	*Numismatic Chronicle*, 1946, p. 154	224
Redenhall	*Numismatic Chronicle*, 1946, p. 157	122
Wiveliscombe	*Numismatic Chronicle*, 1946, p. 163	1107
Bermondsey	*Numismatic Chronicle*, 1946, p. 167	297
Brindle	*Numismatic Chronicle*, 1946, p. 216	21
Canterbury 4	Excavations of Prof. S. S. Frere	19
Canterbury 5	Excavations of Prof. S. S. Frere	84
Canterbury 6	Excavations of Prof. S. S. Frere	21
Dorchester on Thames A	Excavations of Prof. S. S. Frere	31
Dorchester on Thames B	Excavations of Prof. S. S. Frere	496

Table C gives the composition of the hoards, in percentages, broken down into divisions in which all coins have roughly the same module, e.g. AD 317–330 – AE 3 of roughly 18 mm diameter, AD 345–348 – AE 4 of roughly 14 mm diameter.

Some remarks which can be drawn from Table C have already been made in the content of early silver hoards and therefore only need be made briefly. Thus, although each hoard may be expected to have a unique history, the 'normal' Theodosian hoard can be defined within fairly close limits and the abnormal hoards can then be seen in contrast. The 'normal' Theodosian hoard has a heavy preponderance of coins struck after 388 – between eighty three and ninety five per cent of its total, between one and eight per cent of its coins were struck between 364 and 378, between one and five per cent between 348 and 355, and between one and four per cent of the hoard always represents the coinage of 330 to 341. Regular radiates of Gallienus and Claudius II often occur, as do coins of the Gallic Empire; reformed radiates struck after 274 are almost unknown; and Carausius and Allectus are rare. Folles are unknown at full size, very rare at their second size (307–317) and sparse at their smaller size (317–30).

Against this background of 'normality' a few hoards stand out – the most obvious ones being Little Langford, Warle, Redenhall and Wiveliscombe. These have high values of earlier coins because they lack Theodosian coins, and this can very easily be explained if the hoards were deposited soon after 388, before Theodosian coins reached their peak in everyday coinage.

On analogy with the early silver hoards Theodosian bronze coins should reach a peak only after the last issue had reached Britain. If this is so we have only those few truly Theodosian hoards – buried before 402 – and the majority, or the 'normal' late hoard, represent deposits made sometime after that date. The third hoard at Auxerre (*NC*, 1972, 162) was a hoard of just this type, and contained a single coin of Valentinian III (*Late Roman Bronze Coinage*, Part II, no: 2606) to be dated 425–50. This evidence, though slight, shows that the coinage of 388 to 402 was still available for,

Coins and the archaeologist

	Kid	Wey	Fil A	Fil B	Scar	Nort	Litt Lang	Ickl	Cir	Wrox	Wood
Before 253	—	—	—	—	—	0.1	—	—	0.2	—	—
253–270	0.1	0.1	—	—	—	0.3	—	0.3	0.3	—	—
Gallic Empire	0.9	0.7	—	—	—	0.5	—	1.7	—	0.1	1.0
270–94	—	—	—	—	—	—	—	0.2	—	—	—
British Empire	—	0.1	—	—	—	0.1	—	0.1	—	—	—
Folles 294–307	—	—	—	—	—	—	—	—	—	—	—
307–317	—	0.1	—	—	—	—	—	0.1	—	—	—
317–330	—	0.1	—	—	—	0.1	—	—	—	—	—
330–341	2.4	2.5	3.0	6.0	4.0	3.0	6.7	2.1	2.0	1.3	2.0
345–348	1.3	1.8	—	—	—	1.0	—	1.6	2.3	—	0.6
348–355	1.3	2.3	2.0	—	—	2.0	—	1.8	3.3	—	2.0
Magnentius etc.	—	0.1	—	—	—	0.3	—	0.4	—	—	—
355–364	0.4	0.1	—	6.0	—	0.8	1.7	0.9	0.2	—	1.8
364–378	2.0	2.7	41.0	36.0	2.0	5.0	39.0	6.9	5.2	3.3	2.0
378–388	4.0	0.5	—	—	2.0	0.8	43.0	2.0	1.3	—	0.2
388–402	92.0	87.0	53.0	53.0	92.0	86.0	10.0	84.0	85.0	95.0	90.0

	Lax	War	Red	Wiv	Ber	Bri	Can 4	Can 5	Can 6	Dor A	Dor B
Before 253	—	—	—	—	—	—	—	—	—	—	—
253–270	0.6	1.2	8.1	—	—	—	—	—	—	—	—
Gallic Empire	0.3	—	17.0	0.9	1.0	—	—	1.2	—	3.0	3.0
270–94	—	—	—	—	—	—	11.0	4.8	—	—	—
British Empire	—	—	—	—	—	—	—	—	—	—	—
Folles 294–307	—	0.5	—	—	—	—	—	—	—	—	—
307–317	—	—	—	—	0.3	—	—	—	—	—	0.2
317–330	—	—	—	—	5.2	—	—	—	—	—	—
330–341	1.2	29.0	24.0	3.5	0.7	—	5.0	2.4	10.0	3.0	3.4
345–348	—	16.0	5.7	3.6	1.7	—	5.0	1.2	—	—	1.8
348–355	1.8	26.0	16.0	4.5	—	1.4	—	3.6	10.0	—	2.2
Magnentius etc.	—	3.6	5.8	0.7	0.3	—	—	1.2	—	—	—
355–364	—	—	—	0.4	3.0	—	—	—	—	—	—
364–378	3.3	22.0	15.0	78.0	2.3	1.0	—	—	48.0	9.6	0.4
378–388	—	1.2	0.8	2.5	—	0.5	—	1.2	—	—	5.4
388–402	93.0	2.3	7.4	6.5	85.0	72.0	79.0	84.0	33.0	84.0	83.0

and thought worth, hoarding in the second quarter of the fifth century. Without raising a spectre of indiscriminate coin use in the fifth century a balanced view which took cognizance of the pattern of other hoards would probably put the era of hoarding which produced British late bronze hoards within the first half of the century, but not necessarily the first quarter. It must be emphasised that hoarding, the use of numbers of coins rather than individual coins, may have lasted longer than simple use of single coins, but a date for the end of widespread single coin use in Britain which both agrees with the hoard evidence, satisfies the archaeological picture and avoids stretching credulity is probably to be put circa 425.

The recognition of a post-coin phase in Romano-British archaeology is as yet in its infancy, but after such heavy coin use well into the fifth century phases which continue Roman occupation and produce typical Roman artefacts, but no coins, must be dated in the second quarter of the century.

The 'tail' of earlier coins on the nucleus of Theodosian coins is a phenomenon which has already received comment. In this particular case, however, it has important lessons for the archaeologist. Of the coins hoarded in the fifth century about eighty per cent were minted in 388–402, but 2.5 per cent were minted in 330–45. Thus out of every hundred coins lost in the fifth century two or three belong to a very much earlier period. The finding of a single coin of 330–45 is therefore of very doubtful value, for there is a reasonable chance that it was dropped at anything up to one hundred years after it was minted. Two coins of this date are far more diagnostic, and five, all of 330–45 and none of 388–402, have very little chance of showing a true fifth-century date. This is an obvious point, but it needs to be made because the archaeologist tends to use his dating material to its limit and he needs to know when he transgresses that limit.

Finally, late bronze hoards stress the importance of the module of any coin in its loss or survival. Folles, large bronzes of 348–50, of Magnentius or of Julian are unknown in late fourth-century hoards. As the follis declines in size it is represented in such hoards, but it has to pass the point at which it is regularly known as a follis (330) before it is commonly represented. Even after this date it is only the small faulty or copied flans of 14–16 mm diameter which survive – never the good flans of 330–333 of 18 mm. The only issues of 348–55 which survive are small copies, and this is true for Magnentius. Even coins of 364–78, regularly struck at *c*. 18 mm, are represented by worn examples with 'frayed' edges. The overwhelming visual impression given by these hoards is one of dismal uniformity soon reinforced on closer inspection by an aura of heavy wear and sparsely legible detail. It is hardly surprising that such unprepossessing hoards have been little studied except by that giant of practical numismatics, B. H. St. J. O'Neil. The lesson, that large coins disappeared quickly from circulation when their successors were smaller, is pointed by the remarkable survival rate of the small coins struck from 356 to 361 with the legend SPES REIPVBLICAE. As site finds in English excavations or in continental museums they are rare, often not represented, yet they survive in these hoards at a reasonable rate and are usually present even in small hoards. The only point in their favour is their size for they are almost indistinguishable from the module in use from 388–402.

After these positive aspects of the analyses of hoards it is only fair to end on a negative note. Roman coin hoards in general are highly selective and can therefore give little or no information on the composition of the coinage when new denominations appear, old ones die out, or an extreme change occurs. Thus, after the first appearance of the radiate billon coin in 214, hoards tend to be either of denarii or of radiates and the battle of the denominations leaves only tantalizing traces in the hoard record. Diocletian's reform of 294 set out to reform the coinage completely and it would be fascinating to know how far, and how quickly it succeeded, but hoards give us very little information. In Britain, radiate hoards containing coins up to 296 are numerous, hoards of folles struck from 294 to 310 are fairly common, but these two coins – radiates and folles – are different denominations, and just as few second-century hoards contain denarii and sestertii, so hoards with radiates and folles are far to seek. This picture continues throughout the fourth century – hoards of 324–330 contain few folles, hoards of 330–41 contain few earlier coins, and so on.

Unfortunately, we may not draw any conclusions from the composition of these hoards and apply them to the composition of money in circulation. A final example may be taken by returning to the hoards of *c.* 400. Hoards of the House of Valentinian, 364–78, contain very few coins of any earlier date. But we have already seen that hoards of 400 *do* contain reasonable numbers of these earlier coins. If we assumed from the Valentinianic hoard that earlier coins had died out we should be wrong; similar assumptions at other dates are also likely to be wrong. What we see is probably hoarding of AE 3 seized coins from 364–378 and, later, the hoarding of the only remaining smaller denominations.

Like all archaeological evidence coin hoards have their opportunities and their pitfalls and detailed study is usually needed to exploit the one and avoid the other.

Afterword

There is only one point at which it is possible to add anything to this study which is in effect a little island created by applying certain methods to certain information. If either aspects were changed the results would of course be different, but it is difficult to see how this piece of work could change on its own terms. The point of progress has resulted from throwing all the hoards studied into a general group, regardless of date or metal or denomination, in order to examine the variability of hoards according to the number of coins in each hoard. This work has been published in more detail in C. Carcassonne and Ed. T. Hackens, *Numismatique et Statistique*, (Pact 5, 299–308, 1981). The number of coins in a hoard is simple; the variability of each hoard is only little more complicated. For example it could be taken at the level of the number of emperors represented; a hoard with three coins can only have three emperors, a larger hoard will have more emperors up to a certain level. It could be taken at the level of coin reverses, and this would give much higher numbers. The interesting result from these studies is that once the variability of each hoard has been defined it bears a fairly simple relationship to the number of coins in the hoard, as common sense would suggest, within certain limits. This is not the vital discovery; the important point is that in the hoards discussed in this paper there are no eccentric hoards, they are all alike. The really eccentric hoard, such as that from Falkirk, stands out very prominently. The implication is that all hoards were drawn instantly from circulation, and only those which can be proved to be erratic may act as a basis for an historical novel.

Institute of Archaeology
London

7

Counterfeit coins in Roman Britain

George C. Boon

PART ONE
Introductory survey

One day, about the year AD 250, the young Paul of Thebes fled from per-
secution into the mountains of Egypt, where he came upon the entrance to
a cave blocked by a stone and overshadowed by the roots of an ancient
palm growing beside a rill. Rolling it aside, he discerned a chamber with
cabins beyond, as in the Peak Cavern of Derbyshire, but here containing
the remains of equipment for coining. Jerome, who tells this tale of the first
hermit, adds that documents identified the spot as a clandestine mint of the
time of Antony and Cleopatra[1]. Nefarious practices demanded concealment,
especially when the police force was a platoon of foreign soldiers;[2] and
picturesque though the details are, we may detect in them the effect of a
raid which left the outer chamber blocked. At Coygan in south-west Wales,
at White Woman's Hole on Mendip, at Draethen lead-mine near Caerleon,
and at Sprotborough near Doncaster, remote spots all, the evidence of
coining was hastily concealed. But not all false-moneyers preferred to operate
from the depths of the countryside; others depended on the anonymity of
the myriad metal-working premises in the towns. In Britain alone, Colchester, Dorchester, Lincoln, London and Silchester have provided traces, and
in Gaul the quantities of coiners' moulds from the heart of ancient Lyons
(**17**), where an important branch of the Roman mint was established, have
been so great that early commentators took them for legitimate equipment.

Ancient writers abound in allusions to false coin. Herodotus, as far back
as the fifth century BC, recounts a tale of Polycrates, King of Samos, who
about a hundred years before had bought off the Spartans with coins made
of gilt lead; and such coins are known today.[3] But at no period has the
forger been so active as the Imperial Roman. Forgeries enter into the composition of hoards, designedly perhaps when what may have been produced
as a base counterfeit turned out with the passage of time to be substantially
more valuable than the latest debased official issue. Forgery was thus endemic, and false coins appear in every site-series – many no doubt discarded
rather than lost as a comparison of the proportions in hoards, where they
were strained out to some extent, suggests[4]. At times, however, 'epidemics'
of counterfeiting can be followed, and these give our subject its chief interest
today.

Counterfeiting and the law

The penalties for counterfeiting or diminishing the coinage were severe in

102

the case of gold and silver. The Imperial law was an updating of the provisions of 'one of those great constructive pieces of legislation dating from the late Republic and early Principate', the *Lex Cornelia testamentaria nummaria*, Sulla's law of *c.* 81 BC commonly called the *Lex Cornelia de falsis* – concerning fraud. Banishment or, for the lower classes and slaves the mines, the arena or crucifixion, were the punishments enjoined – eventually, when treason or sacrilege had usurped the concept of mere fraud in coinage, burning. However, there was no specific reference to *aes*, the brass, bronze or copper subsidiary coinage, which was not precisely covered until 371.[5] Here a caveat may be entered, for from about 270 the alloy of the silver coinage was so poor that we tend to regard the antoniniani of that period, and the Constantinian nummi which followed, as 'bronze', especially as specimens are common and ubiquitous. But they were issued with a slight silver or silvery coating to show that they belonged to the silver component of the coinage, and would therefore have been covered by the law at an earlier date. Savage as these penalties were – and they were no more or less savage than other nations at other times have inflicted for coining – they were ineffective. Always there are those who will take their chance.

The money supply

The tellers of the aurei depicted on a famous Neumagen relief of Severan date would seldom have been deceived by false coin,[6] for scrutiny of gold would always have been very careful.[7] In these pages, however, we are little concerned with gold. Indeed, little was seen in everyday transactions:[8] at Pompeii – not one of the great commercial centres such as Ostia, where financing by loan and repayment from profits would have kept large sums in gold tied up,[9] but with a bustling financial life nevertheless – aurei accounted for a bare 4 per cent of finds.[10] The Roman world suffered from the extreme feebleness of its money supply, and in the first and last analysis from the State's attitude to the coinage as a medium of financing its own requirements first and foremost, and only incidentally those of its peoples.[11] In Cicero's time an actual shortage of coin might very well depress the prices of real estate, because there was no satisfactory mode of payment which avoided the intermediacy of hard cash.[12] Among the specific consequences of this state of affairs was an uneven, inadequate and sometimes an interrupted supply of coin to the periphery of the Empire, thus encouraging the forger and stimulating the epidemics. These are chiefly phenomena of the north-west provinces and from time to time of the Balkan provinces also, for, in the east, small change continued to be provided by the many city-mints whose western counterparts, never so numerous, had been suppressed by the middle of the first century AD.

Validation: marks and countermarks

The ubiquity of false coin imposed a heavy burden of inspection (*spectatio*) on the money-changers or *nummularii* (*mensarii*) based in the larger towns.

Through their hands passed, sooner or later, most of the coin in local circulation, for ordinary goods in the marketplace were cheap,[13] and there was a continual need for small-change. The *nummularius* might buy denarii say for fifteen rather than the nominal sixteen asses, and sell them for seventeen, so providing an income for himself, if he was free, or his master – he would often have been employed by a capitalist banker (*argentarius*) or by a public authority, as it might be a town or a provincial government.[14] Recourse was also to him when the coins for some important transaction needed authentication, and in that case another charge (*cerarium*) was due for re-sealing the bag.[15] Tested and counted sums on deposit were kept in sealed bags bearing bone or ivory labels giving his name and that of his master, and the date (*see* Figure 1). Parchment labels may have been used for bags of coins attested for the public.[16] We may imagine the *nummularius* in his booth or his lock-up premises in the forum, his hands already soiled by his first business of the day, a dark green cloth spread on his stout, panelled wooden counter to rest his eyes, and an indifferent portrait of the Emperor hanging behind.[17] Poor fellow; if he succumbed to temptation, his fate was exemplary.[18]

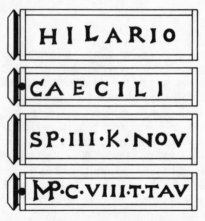

FIG. 1 Ivory label naming Hilario, slave *nummularius* of Caecilius, dated third day before the kalends of November (30th October) in the consulships of Imperator Caesar for the eighth time and T. (Statilius) Taurus (26 BC). After Herzog. In the second and fourth sides a piercing for string will be seen near the left-hand end.

The *nummularius* had neither time nor need for elaborate tests:[19] the appearance, feel, weight, ring and even the smell of coins were the basis of a judgement which with practice must have become subliminal.[20] Well might Trimalchio, a freedman himself, claim that the work of 'spotting the copper through the silver' was as difficult as that of another professional often of servile status or origin – the doctor.[21] A few coins illustrate these remarks. The fine aureus of Titus from Caerleon (**1**) bears a rapidly-engraved M, and sometimes tiny letters or symbols are found stamped or cut on gold and silver coins (*see* Figure 2). These are the private marks of *nummularii*, and

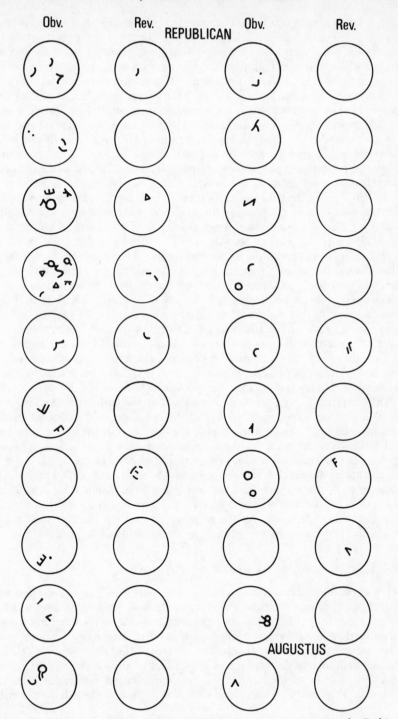

FIG. 2 Bankers' marks on denarii, Republican down to Augustus, in the Dobîrca hoard, Romania. After Chirilă. Full size.

were applied less to test for false, plated coins (though they would in most cases have revealed them)[22] than to denote approval, particularly of good weight and condition: *nummi asperi*, 'sharp' or unworn coins which would command an unofficial premium.[23] On *aes*, such markings are naturally much rarer: the As of Nero from Exeter (2) bears a stamped R, and parallels are known.[24] By what authority such letters were stamped, and what they meant, cannot be determined; but *spectatio* is manifestly indicated, even if the action was private. For official stamping, we have countermarks of quite a different and often easily interpretable kind (33), and other instances are given below. The peckmarks on the robe of the Victory on the reverse of 2 represent a test for a plated core of iron or lead (p. 112);[25] and the studiedly 'casual' abrasions defacing the portraits of Claudius on the sestertii from Ham Hill,[26] Silchester and Lower Germany (3–5) were probably also applied surreptitiously as tests, because the imperial portrait always commanded *prima facie* acceptance,[27] and these copies are of good style. Doubtless, as much difficulty was experienced then, as now by the numismatist, in distinguishing such material from the orthodox. The battered sestertius of Claudius (4) is one of a pair from Silchester with the countermark PROB (*probatus*, 'tested'), until recently thought very possibly to be British. Indeed, Mr. Robert Kenyon has traced some thirty examples (more than half site-provenanced) in this country, compared with a total lack in the Rhineland, where most of the countermarked western *aes* otherwise occurs, admittedly much of it pre-Claudian. However, numerous specimens come from the bed of the Tiber, and the metropolitan origin of the mark cannot now well be disputed. A consignment of validated coins may have been sent by sea to Britain for military pay, before the provincial *fiscus* was fully operative.[28]

The sestertius (5) is of special interest among the countermarked material from Lower Germany. First, we notice the chisel-cut at the edge to test the coin for plating. Then on the obverse are the carefully-spaced stamps IMP and PRO which accepted the doubtful piece into the imperial series; finally, DVP on the reverse indicated a value reduced to half because of the severely worn state of the piece. Unlike PROB, which occurs only on Claudius' first issue of 41,[29] these marks cannot well have been applied for very many years. Other sestertii carry the same cut and same stamps similarly arranged, and go to show how careful the scrutiny of coin for the *stipendia* was – prudently, given the chronic grumbling of the soldiers.[30]

Demonetisation; further marks and countermarks

Thus, countermarks were intended at least partly to guarantee coins for further circulation when otherwise they might have been demonetised (33).[31] Indeed, despite the difficulties of obtaining the vast amounts of *aes* for the *stipendia* three times yearly, demonetisation overtook the small-change more than once, and it was thought worthy of remark that the Emperor Vitellius did *not* demonetise the coinage of Nero, Galba and Otho[32] – perhaps, as Governor of Germania Inferior, he had experienced difficulties over the *stipendia*. Vespasian, his successful rival, did his best to abolish the beautiful and abundant *aes* of Nero, scarcely five years old;[33] no wonder that survivors such as (5) had to be retained, and Neronian pieces such as 7, countermarked VESPAS, made to serve another turn.[34] The defacement of 6 may have had political overtones: in publishing it some years ago, I compared it with a sou of Louis XVI similarly cut, only to dismiss the comparison as superficial; but coins of Nero seem to have become the especial butt of the anonymous carver, examples being known whereon his florid mass of curls – blond on the man – have been removed; but this facilitated circulation under Galba or Vespasian, both 'thin on top'.[35] Countermarked coins are rare in Romano-British contexts, and would form an interesting, though brief and limited, list. With reference to yet another aspect of the *aes* coinage in the troubled times at the close of Nero's reign, in the 1974 version of this paper I illustrated an As from Burghfield, near Reading, with the stamp SPQR, applied by the rebels under Vindex in Gaul.[36] Kraay has shown the limited areas over which the various classes of countermarked coins are found along the Rhine, and it may be observed that legionary countermarks were never allowed there in Julio-Claudian times, indeed nowhere in Europe except very briefly in Spain and on the Danube in the same fateful year of 69;[37] in the east, curiously enough, *aes* bearing legionary numbers or symbols continued down to the 160s. The reason is that the imperial authorities had striven to suppress the local *aes* of the west, notably in Spain and Provence, by the time of Claudius in order to generalise the medium of the currency, and end its local focus; but in the east it was allowed to continue, indeed was augmented in many cases by issues in the names of the emperors from cities which had not had their own bronze coinage before.[38] In the west, however, the abundant *aes* issues of the late first and second centuries, and the stability of the régime, combined to do away with the practice of countermarking. Counterfeiting was at the endemic level, and even when new *aes* again became scarce north of the Alps in the third century, the checking of coin was not resumed; the older coin was now eked out with very poor counterfeit material, the 'lightweights' (11–12). The reason seems clear: the army was again being paid in silver (alloyed by 50 per cent or so as it now was) and much more easily transportable – an important point, now that the legionary stipend had been increased from 300 denarii under Domitian to 450 (?) under Severus, and then to 675 (?) under Caracalla, the latter figure three times the pay under Claudius. Even then, however, there had been difficulties in meeting the requirements of the *stipendia* in decent coin, and these we shall encounter in studying the first of the great epidemics (*see* page 118).

PART TWO
Endemic counterfeits

Practical details – casts

The multiplication of coins by casting in moulds taken from originals is the simplest method; and if casts themselves come to be used as the models, then the sequence of shrinkages – of the clay mould on being fired, and of the cast metal on cooling – not only degrades the quality of the imprint, but results in a diminution in size. The 'lightweight' asses of Antonine (**11–12**) represent two such generations: **12** was cast from one of the same batch as **11** (cf. page 124), with the spaces between the standing figure's legs cleared out;[39] the heavily leaded bronze used for such pieces facilitated the thin casting.[40] False denarii may be cast in an alloy totally lacking in silver, such as three of Severus from Caerleon which proved on recent analysis to be composed of a high-tin bronze (25 per cent); the appearance of the polished metal was far different from the greyish-green that meets the eye, a warm colour within, resembling quite closely silver such as the alloy of the originals, which would have been little more than 50 per cent fine.[41] Others again may be cast in base metal, and plated.[42]

Be the alloy what it may, however, casts usually stand out in a site-series by their different appearance or colour; their surfaces may feel a little 'greasy' (**13, 65**, cf. the sharply struck **64**) as the result of the air trapped between metal and mould preventing a really close contact, and the edges may show the line of junction between the two halves of the mould, or a point where the jet or flash has been trimmed off. A sharp, filed edge contrasting with smooth or worn-looking surfaces is an infallible guide to a false cast, and one may also be wise – as indeed the ancient *nummularii* must have been advised – to check the alignment of the reverse to the obverse, the standing figure or other type being at 360° or 180° to the portrait on regular issues, or a close approximation thereto. Casts were made either in two-piece slab-moulds (*see* Figure 3) or else in pile-moulds (**17–19, 57**) which were sometimes keyed (Figure 4, **17**) to ensure a correct alignment; it was easy otherwise to combine the moulds wrongly and thus produce 'hybrids'.[43] But

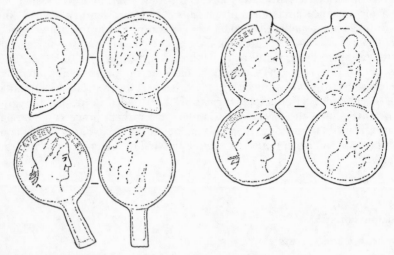

FIG. 3   *Limesfalsa:* lightweight casts, from two-piece moulds, of sestertii of Severus Alexander. Carnuntum (after Kubitschek). Reduced.

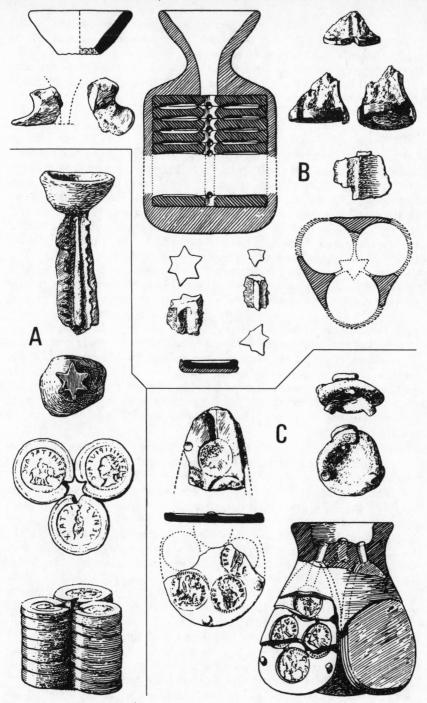

FIG. 4 Coin-moulds (after Behrens). A is from Damery, Marne; B and C from Cologne. Reduced.

although the impression has been given of crudeness, of poor and easily-distinguished material, the skill of the ancient metalworker should not be underestimated. Not only could he produce a surface to which gold itself was a stranger; he could cast denarii of such perfection that 'they can only be described as horrifying . . . sharp enough to be almost indistinguishable from the real thing'.[44]

Die-struck

Dies might also be produced by casting from original coins, the need for an intermediate positive resulting in a shrinkage of up to about 2 per cent in the case of a wax model and anything up to 25 per cent for clay. A series of struck copies from cast dies has been studied by P.-H. Mitard, who found that the original radiate bronze of Postumus was just over 11 per cent larger than the first-stage cast from it, and the second stage cast was a further 16.6 per cent smaller again.[45] The only dies found in Britain are for denarii of Hadrian (20) and Crispina, their iron sleeves lost; they are unquestionably false; one was found at Verulamium.[46] The preference, however, was for engraved dies, of very variable competence: 14–15 are respectively regular and counterfeit antoniniani of Philip I, the latter displaying a degree of coarseness and linearity foreign to the rather smooth product of the Roman mint. The weights of the two are interesting: the orthodox coin is at the bottom of the officially-acceptable range, 2.8 grammes; the counterfeit, at 4.2 grammes, is well up to the orthodox average. No doubt another coin from the same false pair of dies would have been much lighter. Given the overvaluation of the antoninianus in circulation, the profit from the false coins would have been considerable, for the silver is at a glance scarcely different, but only 25.1 per cent fine against an orthodox 43 per cent is revealed by analysis.[47]

From silver to *aes*; and here the example is a small die-linked and stylistically identifiable series of dupondii, two from Caerleon and single examples from Camarthen, Caerwent, Wroxeter, Ffrith near Wrexham, and Chichester.[48] Three die-pairs are known, one of which links Caerleon, Wroxeter and Ffrith (25–27). The weights range from 13.4 down to 10.7 grammes, the heaviest being up to the orthodox average; the metal is a good *orichalcum* (brass), straight from the coinage itself, but economising in metal to the extent of one dupondius in every eight. Were scrap-metal added to the melt for such products, the profit was naturally increased, and made it an attractive possibility to sell to the merchants and travellers who would each take his gain before passing safely on his way. These coins share the peculiarity of an early portrait of Trajan allied with the name and titulature of his predecessor, Nerva: the reverses are Nervian, or of Trajan's later SPQR OPTIMO PRINCIPI type cut by mistake so as to appear retrograde on the product. Confusion of this kind is not uncommon, as we shall see (page 128). In this case it seems unlikely that the early portrait of Trajan would have been reproduced once the very different later portrait was known from a large series of coins; the group may therefore be dated to the period immediately after the introduction of the *SPQR Optimo Principi* coinage in 103, but before it had become widespread or common. The Chichester specimen, if indeed it belongs to the group, makes a definite answer to the question of origin somewhat imprudent. A similar puzzle often arises: in no acuter form, perhaps, than the case of two early unorthodox coins of Carausius (p. 00) markedly different in weight – 9.55 and 2.28 grammes – from the north and south extremity of Wales respectively in the Little Orme, Llandudno and Penard (Gower) hoards. There were few, if any, internal die-links in the Little Orme hoard, but the Penard hoard had several; one may perhaps deduce payment originating in some common source, of coin arriving in somewhat less mixed condition in South, than in North Wales.[49]

Plated

Plated coins retain the appearance of a full-sized original of good metal. It has been calculated that a single antoninianus of Gordian III would supply enough silver to plate ten counterfeits.[50] Our examples include a serrate Republican denarius (28), a denarius of Nero (29) and a siliqua of Valentinian I to illustrate the recrudescence of the problem of plated coins when a sound silver coinage had reappeared after the third-century crash (32). It is an obvious deduction that the serrated edge of the plated copper denarius (28) was intended to show that the coin was of solid silver; but manifestly *serrati* could be counterfeited (probably by fusing silver granules on the surface of the already-serrated blanks), and the same issue occurs on both serrated and plain flans. Serration was a passing fashion, as elsewhere.[51]

Plated coins are known of nearly every Republican moneyer between 124 and 37 BC, but there is no reason to believe that they were fabricated over this entire period; and the 30,000 plated pieces calculated to exist would sink with little trace in the sea of 40,000,000 denarii estimated to have been current by that date.[52] Crawford has unequivocally denounced all plated Republican denarii as false, and is correct in doing so;[53] even if it could be demonstrated that the same dies were used (as has been claimed) to strike both genuine and plated pieces, occasional fraud by mint-personnel misusing dies which had just gone out of use (and should have been destroyed) is the best explanation.[54] Most plated coins, however, are of an inferior and easily recognisable quality. A London hoard proves that plated Republican coins, with cores of iron[55] as well as copper, were being produced as late as AD 52, perhaps 64, when Nero debased the denarius for the first time and so imparted a premium to those of earlier striking. Among the die-linked sequences in this hoard are examples (30–31) of a denarius of Antony and Octavian from false dies moulded from an authentic original, as indicated above: on Antony's neck appears a *nummularius'* mark much in the form of an R, which had been present on the worn original.[56] The weak point of plated coins is always their edge, and the denarius of Nero from Norfolk (29) is constructed in an ingenious way to defeat edge-nicking: it has an extra medial disc of silver which is thickened around the rim, enclosing the silver skin of either face as the setting of a ring encloses a gem.[57] The

Silchester siliqua (**32**) has been cut in half, demonetised by the chisel in
the proper way.[58]

Another method is the reverse of that discussed. An original coin is placed
in a fold of silver-foil and that between two plates of lead. A heavy blow
causes the foil to take up an exact impression of the coin, the lead acting
as a cushion. The original is removed, a channel cut for the flow of metal,
the foil replaced, and an alloy of suitably low melting point is poured in.[59]
The Silchester specimen (**21**), for an antoninianus of Tetricus II, is a late
instance, the official coinage then being plated far more thinly – a matter
of a few microns – than the thinnest foil;[60] but well-silvered struck counterfeits of the period are also known (**69**), and with the products of these
so-called *cliché* moulds they go to show that the official coin must have
been very heavily overvalued. Abroad, a mould from Mandeure (Doubs)
for denarii of Trajan and Hadrian still retains the bronze binding which
would have been tightened with wedges to keep the two halves of the mould
closely in contact.[61] The most elaborate example, being forty-four impressions of a denarius of Nero, was found at Arlon (Belgium); it measures
some 28 by 12 cm and is so made that one valve fits neatly inside the other.[62]

Plated *aes* (page 106) occurs with lead cores, produced by the same cliché
process[63] or, mostly, with iron cores hot-dipped.[64] Plated *aes* was especially
common at two periods – the Julio-Claudian, when testing official or unofficial was usual, and the Severan: the dupondius (**16**) is most probably of
the latter date, though Lucilla's coinage belongs to the 160s. Plated *aes*
seems to the modern mind an exercise in misplaced ingenuity, for although
coined metal was no doubt more valuable than uncoined, Romano-British

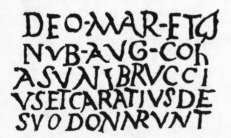

FIG. 5   Inscription on two sides of the base of a statue of Mars from the Foss Dyke,
near Lincoln (British Museum). *Deo Mar(ti) et Nu(mini)b(us) Aug(ustorum). Colasuni, Bruccius et Caratius, de suo dona(ve)runt ad sester(tios) n(umero) c(entum).
Celatus aerarius fecit et aeramenti lib(ram) donavit, factam (denariis) III* – 'To the
God Mars and the Divine Powers of the Emperors. The Colasuni, Bruccius and
Caratius, presented (this statuette) at their own expense at the cost of sestertii, one
hundred in number. Celatus the bronzesmith made it, and gave a pound of bronze
made for three denarii.' *RIB*, no. 274. The two men, Bruccius and Caratius, were
presumably brothers sharing the family-name Colasunius, made up on the extension
of the citizenship to all freeborn in the early third century. After *Archaeologia* XIV,
1803, by courtesy of the Society of Antiquaries. Full size.

sites abound even today in fragments of bronze and in *aes* coins, so that the metal itself could never have been scarce or particularly valuable. 100 to 1 seems to have been the normal ratio of copper to silver;[65] but scrap bronze was nevertheless treasured up,[66] and therefore its value has to be considered as being superior to that of lead or iron. The Romano-British bronzesmith Celatus who 'made' a pound of bronze, and contributed it to the five *librae* needed for a statuette of Mars found in Lincolnshire (Figure 5),[67] affords us a glimpse into actual costs, for it was valued at three denarii. A *libra* was the nominal weight of twelve sestertii (the equivalent of three denarii), and we need look no farther for the source of the 'made' libra. At least a hundred *subferrati* could have been produced from a dozen sestertii abstracted from circulation, given a little scrap-iron for the cores.

PART THREE
The epidemics

General considerations

The conditions of an epidemic of forgery are foreign to our own experience. In this section we try, therefore, to set the phenomenon in perspective. What is true of one epidemic is very largely true of the others, so our examples will be drawn from them all. The mere designation of the coins produced as false, or else as 'money of necessity', has occasioned much dispute. But before dealing with this point, other considerations may be allowed to supervene.

The origin of the epidemics is recognised to be a shortage of coin, and this was brought about in three several ways. First, the demonetisation of the coinage of Caligula and the closure of the Rome mint led to the production of copies of Claudian *aes*, which naturally dominate the earliest Roman circulation in this country; second, the almost total debasement of the silver coinage in the third century exacerbated a price-inflation which was duly serviced by floods of 'barbarous radiates' imitative of the overvalued antoniniani (or double-denarii, worth only 1½) which were the chief coins in general circulation; and third, the reforms of the petty coinage in the fourth century generated artificial shortages, of which the most notable produced the 'falling horsemen' of *c.* 354–64. However, the extent to which counterfeit coin entered 'good' circulation in the third and fourth centuries is well shown by hoards such as that from Llanbethery (Barry), 56 in a total of 814, 7 per cent.

Barbarous workmanship and declining size

The acceptability of counterfeits, demonstrable from the great distances over which coins from the same dies might travel (Figure 10), is curious in the light of their often barbarous, even bizarre execution, which casts doubt not only on the literacy, but also on the awareness of the makers where even the greatest public events of their time were concerned, notably the root-and-branch changes in the government during the third and fourth centuries. Though the majority of the pieces are more or less closely copied from the commonest coins of the day, as would be expected, the occasional apposition of inappropriate types is significant only of political isolation, unawareness, and innocency. If the counterfeits both endemic and epidemic arose for the most part from the lowest level of market trader and petty manufacturer, we may understand and excuse their solecisms and hapless barbarities; but when their execution is competent, their vagaries are less easily comprehended: an excellent coin of Tetricus I, published by Giard, not only has a Rome reverse of the Emperor Probus, but the legend incorporates Probus' name. Either an excellent capacity for die-sinking was not allied with a basic literacy which would fend off such a mistake, or else somewhere an obverse of Probus and a reverse of Tetricus I remain to be identified and linked with this piece. However, it is not alone; and furthermore, if we turn to the material from White Woman's Hole, at the eastern extremity of the Mendip Hills, we find that a 'reformed' antoninianus of Tacitus suffered exactly the same fate as coins of the Gallic Empire and of large 'barbarous radiates' in being quartered to provide flans for minims (9–10) (page 129).[68] It is possible, therefore, to make more of inconcinnate hybrids than they merit. They remain curiosities, and attest the carelessness with which the inhabitants of the Roman Empire were apt to regard the details of their coinage. The remoteness of many rural communities is, perhaps, partly to blame for an ignorance of current affairs.

E   F

FIG. 6   Examples of 'minimissimi' from the Lydney II hoard, arranged within 18 mm circles (the size of the prototype) and compared with a modern 2p piece.

Often coupled with barbarous execution is a decline in size, carried to astonishing extreme: the celebrated Lydney 'minimissimi' (Figure 6) average less than 3 mm across, but their descent from 18 mm originals is perfectly traceable.[69] Almost the same extreme attends the 'barbarous radiates'; and even among the Claudian copies, examples of only 2 grammes or so compare with the 11 grammes or so of the originals. The mechanism was throughout identical: *profit*, by striking more pieces from a given amount of metal than it had produced before. Over the score of years during which the Claudian copies circulated, or the dozen years of the 'barbarous radiates' and the 'falling horsemen', copies would have been made more and more from the metal available in the form of earlier copies, so that what seems to us a ridiculous decline would not have appeared so at the time. The Coygan finds demonstrate the melting of larger to make smaller copies very well.[70] There is no question of smaller denominations, merely of smaller coins.

The small size of some of the material has, however, prompted commentators to propose that such pieces did represent smaller denominations than the designs might suggest: for example, Daphne Nash has pointed to an apparent correspondence between the weight of small Claudian copies and the weight of Gaulish native bronze, still circulating in Julio-Claudian times, and found with cut fractions of asses or dupondii in the early military stations of the Rhine.[71] There was indeed a demand for fractional coin: the Nîmes as (8) is filed ready for cutting into two;[72] but this view takes no account of the *chain* of declining weight (page 129) or of the wide weight-range of coins issuing from the same die-pair, which sometimes differ by as much as half or a third.[73] A copy that is a simulacrum of an As is best regarded as its simulacrum in value too; not only do counterfeits hoarded together vary considerably in size – the Lydney Hoard II was by no means solely composed of 'minimissimi' – but minims made from quarters of orthodox coins must have been worth more than a quarter of their originals, for otherwise there was no incentive to cut them up (9–10). That is far from proving that they were of identical value with the originals, but such is the implication; and if it is difficult to accept, the further point may be made that the value of the originals may well have been declining also.

The end of epidemics

In every case there was a sudden and radical end to the epidemics, brought about by the appearance of decent new official coin. The Roman forts of Wales, for instance, yield few Claudian copies if their history does not go back beyond *c.* 64, when the Neronian *aes* began to appear.[74] As to 'barbarous radiates', the latest originals imitated are those of Probus or Carus, there being no true copies of Carausian coins of minim size – say 12 mm or below: the rural coiners' dens mentioned above (page 102) were almost certainly destroyed at the same time by government action which, under Carinus, had the promotion, delayed as it was, of a decent new antoninianus as its object.[75] Gone are the days when numismatists argued for an extremely

FIG. 7 Radiate minims from Wroxeter fancied to have 'fourth-century' reverses. (After Wright, *Uriconium*, 1872). Full size of the woodcuts.

late fifth, indeed sixth century – persistence of 'barbarous radiates' and
'falling horseman', some of the former with 'fourth-century reverse types'
so barbarous as to be almost anything (Figure 7) (**164**);[76] as regards 'radiate
minims', the discovery of the sealed Verulamium Theatre hoard dating to
c. 300 was a salutary shock,[77] and the virtually exclusive distribution of the
Valentinianic coinage at Brean Down temple in Somerset made plain the
fact that even the smallest of the 'falling horsemen' were obsolete by the
mid 360s.[78] All else is a chimaera, as Bryan O'Neil began to realise, and
John Kent took pains to enunicate over thirty years ago.[79] A Dark Age
coinage will not delay us here, for there was none.[80]

The status of epidemic imitations

Where the same dies were used to strike both solid copper and specious
plating, both coins must obviously be false: to name only one instance, there
is a subaerate Claudian copy, found at Richborough (**55**), from the same
dies as a piece in solid copper from Colchester, as Mr. Robert Kenyon
discovered; J.-B. Giard has noted a similar pairing.[81] These coins are very
barbarous; but what of other imitations, which are not (**48–51**)? It was
Sutherland's contention, in setting the imitative series in order over fifty
years ago and devising his celebrated grading system (I-II literate, III barbarous, IV part or all of the designs reversed), that the best imitations were
not only the product of literate communities, as was obvious, but originated
'in the military towns' as an 'official method of supplementing the military
chest' – 'semi-official copies . . . executed either by camp-moneyers or by
native British craftsmen'.[82] Thither it seems impossible to follow him. There
seems to be very little sign in the published material from the great Rhenish
military stations, or those of Britain, of the clustering of die-duplicates, such
as would be expected to remain in the vicinity of local mints. Indeed, imitations are remarkably diffused throughout Gaul north of the Loire as well
as the Two Germanies, as is shown by the quantities cast as votive offerings
into river crossings at or near local capitals – into the Vilaine at Rennes,
the Mayenne at Saint-Léonard a few kilometres along the highway from
the capital of the Diablintes at Jublains, the Yonne at its confluence with
the Seine at Montereau, and the Aisne at Condé-sur-Aisne near Soissons.[83]
  Among these masses of coin, of all Sutherlandian grades, are numerous
die-duplicates and some links further afield (page 120). Perhaps these finds
in their occurrence so near the tribal capitals tell of the location of the
monetae furtivae, to borrow Jerome's words, whence the Augustan road
network carried examples far and wide – to the Rhine, to Britain with the
legions and their followers.[84] In any case, the proposition of 'camp-moneyers'
must be resisted. It was not the business of the army to make coin, and
there is no mention of a *monetarius* among *immunes*, numerous as the
specialist posts were.[85] The provision of pay was the function, and the most
important function, of the procurator of every military province: *neque
quies sine armis, neque arma sine stipendiis, neque stipendia sine tributis
haberi queunt*, as Cerealis' famous words made plain to the restive Treveri

and Lingones in the year 70. 'They could not have tranquillity between peoples without armed forces, nor armed forces without pay, nor pay without tribute.'[86] The division of responsibilities between the governor and the procurator was fundamental to the Augustan scheme:[87] thus in Belgica, the governor sat in Reims and the procurator in Trier, for he was responsible for the paying of the eight Rhenish legions.[88] In Britain, the procurator was based in London,[89] and a memorandum on a tiny slip of wood found in an early well at the legionary fortress of Caerleon records a party of men sent *ad opinionem petendam*, 'to seek the "estimate" ' – that being the word for the amount calculated as needed to meet the pay. This armed convoy would presumably have gone to the procurator's office in London, whither the *ratio*, or account of what was actually disbursed, would subsequently also have been sent.[90] Figure 8 shows a countermark referable to the *fiscus*, on a Lyons As found at Abergavenny.[91] It can be seen, therefore, that the classification of material by its standard of fidelity to the originals, or in point of size or weight, necessary though some such mechanical sorting is, tends to defeat understanding: it is all too easily forgotten that those categories are an invention of the scholar, and lack ancient validity; and that all 'grades' circulated uniformly, as far as we can judge. Those which crossed the Channel from northern Gaul, for example, are far from being always, or preponderantly, of the better grades.

FIG. 8   Augustus, 'first altar series' As of Lyons, with countermark F(*isci*) T(*iberii*) AV(*gusti*)? Found at Abergavenny (Abergavenny Museum). Actual size.

Modern parallels

To close this brief conspectus, reference to later experience may be helpful. It shows that however widely scattered and multitudinous copies may be, *they are false*. At the time of great recoinage of 1696–97 in England, it was estimated that one million of the £11,000,000 in broad silver struck before 1662 and still in circulation was counterfeit; and this figure excluded the utterly base and the plated.[92] Such is the sum-total of a prolonged period of endemic counterfeiting of a principal circulating medium, such as occurred in the late Roman Republic, or the first half of the third century AD. When we turn to copper, it is astonishing to find that in 1787 only 8 per cent of a sample bore even a tolerable resemblance to the King's coin.[93] The reason for this flood is that except for the years 1770–75 there had been no mint-striking since 1754, and even at that date it had been reckoned that half the coppers in circulation were false. In 1789, after manufacturers had turned to producing their own tokens of good weight and handsome appearance, Boulton could still declare that on an average he received two-thirds counterfeit halfpence at tollgates; he added that the greater part of the wages of the poor was paid by unscrupulous employers in the form of coppers bought at a discount from 'subterranean coiners'.[94] This, then, is what 'tolerance' amounted to. Indeed the picture is not very different from that recently painted for later medieval France.[95] In Roman times a similar 'tolerance' applied to coin which was false, in that it was produced for private profit without authority, and suffered to continue until, eventually, good new coin was provided.

Claudian copies:* the background

40,000 men, half of them legionaries, the rest auxiliaries, descended on these shores in the Claudian expeditionary force of 43. The legionary at this period was paid after the rate of 225 denarii a year in three instalments; the auxiliary, five-sixths (or at least three-quarters) of that figure. Of the gross amount, however, most was retained for food, arms and equipment and also for compulsory savings, to which half or more of any donative was also credited.[96] The soldier was thus left with a sum which site-finds show was paid in *aes* – pocket-money. If, on an average, four-fifths was retained, there remained for the legionary 240 asses or the equivalent at every pay, and for the auxiliary say 192 asses. The army in Britain therefore required the huge mass of 8,500,000 assess (some in the form of dupondii and sestertii) every four months. This is not to say that a whole new mass of coin was required at that interval. We saw that the area of circulation, for coins which can be checked from their countermarks, was regional (page 107); and there, in each region, that basic quantity of coin, and whatever augmentation of it could be managed, on the whole remained. Coins received in pay would be spent, and would accordingly find their way back to source in fees and dues payable to the *fiscus*, and through the medium of the official *nummularii*, who would give silver for *aes* (page 104).

Apart from logistical difficulties – 85 tonnes ot *aes* to provide in the first instance, its augmentation every four months, its distribution often to remote and pathless places wherein, however, native or foreign traders might well have played a useful part – the problem was not new; nor were the regiments newly-raised: that had been done by Caligula four years earlier, when two new legions had been enlisted. How had the sum been found before? Until 41, the mint at Lyons as well as that at Rome had been hard at work, and Spain had helped with its numerous civic coinages. All that had now been stopped except for Rome, which in Claudius' first year produced an enormous amount of *aes*, presumably with the help of the Lyons staff. Much of his new coin went to the Rhine: there was to be no mistaking the identity of Caligula's successor, avid for the glory which even then must have been

*I here gladly place on record the open-handed help I have had from Mr. Robert Kenyon in all matters concerning Claudian copies, in advance of his own publication (note 123).

in planning, and anxious to make some showing towards the donative which, first of the Caesars to purchase the loyalty of the army, he had promised upon accession. At half the rate for the Praetorian Guard which had set him on the throne, there would have been 30,000 asses for each legionary, half or more to be saved for him.[97] Thus in 42 another great quantity was struck at Rome, identical with the previous year's issue except for the addition of P(*ater*) P(*atriae*) at the end of the titulature, an honour which the Emperor had accepted from the Senate that January (**45–46**).[98] This second issue, however, was little seen north of the Alps – only eleven out of 259 coins at Vindonissa, for example, carry the letters; two out of 86 at Camulodunum (Sheepen); one out of 17 at Silchester. The Claudian copies eschew the P.P. title: wherever the end of the legend is visible, or the spacing clear, throughout Europe this is the case.[99] They were all modelled on the first issue, and in time the initial range of copies itself was taken to provide models.

The official *aes* issues had never been adequate for the needs of the army, let alone those of civilian northern Gaul. Some Gaulish coinages seem to have been pressed into early service for the auxiliary *stipendia*, and in some instances these Gaulish issues reflected the design of the Roman coinage.[100] Imitations of Roman coins, keeping more or less closely to the pre-Claudian prototypes, exist in fair number (**33–36**).[101] But it was the closure of Lyons mint and the stopping of the Rome *aes* at the end of 42 that was to be one of the two main causes of an astonishing outbreak of false-moneying – the first in the history of Rome to transcend the bounds of endemic forgery and enter the realms of epidemic. The other was the demonetisation of Caligula's *aes*, after (we note) the completion of the Claudian strikings.[102] Withdrawal was effective in Italy, where the Tiber finds are deficient in Caligulan material;[103] the provinces made mixed response. Along the Rhine, the counter-mark TI AV, for Tiberius (Claudius) Augustus, appeared on Caligulan, earlier and early Claudian counterfeit material, its purpose to validate old or doubtful coins, but perhaps also to mark them as part of his promised donative.[104]

In lightly-garrisoned Belgica, to the rear of the great Rhenish legionary stations,[105] Gauls overstruck the Caligulan and other coins of doubtful status with copies of Claudian designs, especially the Minerva As, one of the most popular coins ever produced (**47**).[106] Overstrikes do not seem to occur along the Rhine in any number, and like countermarked coins are rare in Britain: an example is the continental Claudian Antonia dupondius from Silchester, overstruck on a Lyons 'altar' dupondius of Tiberius (**43**). Whether an order to countermark Caligulan *aes* reached Britain is unknown; many soldiers must have had it in their possession, and disproportionate numbers at Hod Hill betoken a hoard buried until the matter should have been clarified – but left behind, and destined to be eventually scattered by the plough.[107] But we may reflect that countermarking or overstriking does not increase the number of coins in circulation, and merely maintains the circulating medium: the second cause of the Claudian epidemic, therefore, is less important than the first.

Claudian copies – general

Turning now to the coins themselves, **34** at 2.23 grammes is the smallest and most barbarous imitation of a Lyons 'altar' As known to the writer; it may be compared with **33**, a typical Augustan prototype, with a Tiberian countermark.[108] The descent to a quarter or less of the right weight is a characteristic of an epidemic; the same reduction in the case of the 'barbarous radiates' or the 'falling horsemen' in later centuries brought about the 'minim'. Of other pre-Claudian *aes* found imitated on British sites, the 'Agrippa' As, with its standing Neptune commemorating Actium and earlier Mylae, is the only usual component (**35**); **36**, just under 4 grammes, is a stylistically idiosyncratic copy, belonging to a group recognised by Giard and including a die-duplicate from Hachy (near Arlon, Belgian Luxembourg).[109] Like **34**, it comes from an early fort-site at Sea Mills on the Bristol Avon. Copies of Germanicus and *Divus Augustus Pater* asses seem to be rare in Britain.

A glance through Plates III–IV reveals a wide range of competence on the part of the die-sinkers of the copies; and to this the faulty striking of the orthodox models may have contributed. The late C. H. V. Sutherland's grading system remains valuable; thus Grade I is close to the orthodox, betrayed, for example, by bad lettering or other details (**49**) even though the portrait may be good; and Grade II is competent but coarse: **50–51** show a stylistic affinity, though found respectively at Verulamium and at Salmonsbury Camp near Bourton-on-the-Water. Grade III is plainly barbarous (**52–53, 55**); Grade IV covers coins with all or part of their designs reversed, e.g. **54** with head to right instead of left and with SC backwards, an extremely poor example from a newly-found fort in the Monnow Valley, Castlefield, near Kenchurch. This last and **53** also seem to show similarities; but where there is no art, it is important not to discern style. A further category which might have been included would embrace hybrids or 'mules', wherein inappropriate obverses and reverses are matched (pages 110, 128): it occurs at all periods, not excluding that of the Claudian copies. As in the case of the 'Nerva/Trajan' dupondii and the Tetricus/Probus antoniniani, the execution may be variable in quality and grade.[110]

The examples illustrating grading are all 'Minerva' asses; indeed, one would be hard put to find sufficient representative examples among the less common 'Libertas' (**44**) and 'Constantia' issues. It is true that copies of sestertii, never common except in Italy,[111] **37** (reputedly from Colchester) being at 16.7 grammes only about two-thirds of the right weight, and the two dupondii, 'Ceres' and 'Antonia' (**38–40, 41–43**), are mostly of Grades I and II and often show considerable circulation-wear. The weights, however, may often be indistinguishable from those of the better asses, so that only their yellow *orichalcum* (brass) served as a differential. A case in point is the 'Ceres' dupondius from Usk (**42**), the obverse die being employed for another found at Ham Hill (Somerset) and for asses found at Lydney (unpublished) and Lincoln – a distribution comparable with that of the 'Nerva/Trajan' series (page 110), and further augmented by a St.-Léonard

(Mayenne) As[112] which, barbarous though it is, may stand here for various other cross-Channel links.[113] The series closes with two curiosities: **48**, a Grade I copy with the Lower German countermark Q VA[114] and **55**, the *subferratus* from Richborough mentioned above (page 116).

Sutherland found that copies occurred widely on Claudio-Neronian sites, where they outnumber the orthodox products, often by a very considerable margin. Half to two-thirds of those from Camulodunum (Sheepen), for example, were imitations;[115] so were 77 per cent from Richborough;[116] and the list could be greatly extended, yielding an average to 50 to 75 per cent.[117] What has been particularly valuable has been Giard's research in France, where among superabundant material the work of at least five die-cutters has been recognised. It is not surprising that die-linked material and further examples of these five styles should be forthcoming on British soil, as here and there along the Rhine, for the Roman army drew with it numbers of traders and camp-followers. Doubtless there was local production of Claudian copies in Britain, perhaps a considerable one; but many of those occurring at early military bases such as Camulodunum seem likely to have been struck in Gaul: as is also the case along the Rhine (page 116), there is no clustering of die-linked pieces (indeed not on any British site), as would be expected if a mint had been at work locally: stylistic similarities there are, and very strong ones, but that is all. Significantly enough, Giard has recognised three coins from Camulodunum as the work of one of his five die-sinkers, Graveur E.[118] The picture is of a *disseminated* coinage.

A decline in size and weight and a rise in the incidence of crude material[119] must have accelerated with time, for Nero was long heedless of the state of the petty coinage in the western provinces. However, provided there were image-bearing discs of some kind to be given and taken in change, both the military and the nascent urban public seem to have been content. The token quality of the imitations is strongly indicated by the variability in size, weight and style (a series of die-duplicates studied by Giard ranged from 8.7 down to 5.1 grammes),[120] of those which might be hoarded together.[121]

The mere fact that a copy is small and light and barbarous does not of itself prove that it is late in a series which continued until the tardy arrival of fine new Government coin from a Lyons mint reopened in 64.[122] Other factors enter in – the normal range of weight (as just cited, for example), and the dexterity of the die-cutter. But if *many* found on a particular site are small and light and barbarous, we would expect to find confirmation in the *sigillata* of a date towards the 60s. Indeed two stages in the Claudian epidemic, early and late, can now be distinguished. Mr. Kenyon's examination of all the Camulodunum finds,[123] well over 400, includes a number from the site of the fortress itself now identified beneath the modern town. This fortress was occupied only from 43 to 49, and the coins are not numerous; but they are all counterfeit, mostly of Grade I and II, with a couple of III. All three main grades were in early existence, therefore, as we should expect from our own **43** and **47**. For the last stage of the epidemic we may go to legionary Usk, founded towards 55 and occupied down to *c.* 70.[124] There the picture is very different, though the Colchester material comes to match it in time as regards low weight and preponderance of barbarous products. Of the Usk series of 202 Claudian aes coins, 190 were copies (25 dupondii, 165 asses):

Grades	I	I–II	II	II–III	III	IV	
Dupondii Ceres, Antonia	1	5	2	1	7	—	
Asses Agrippa Constantiae Libertas Minerva	1 — — 5	1 1 1 3	3 — 3 15	— — — 6	2 — 1 70	— — — 2	Total
	7	11	24	7	80	2	131

The remainder were too corroded, encrusted or fragmentary to assess, and the acid soil has ensured that the weights cannot usefully be taken either. Four of the coins were casts from other copies. However, to put the Usk material another way with diameter in lieu of weight, and also noting the wear,[125] we find:

Dupondii	Grade I	27 mm (1)	slightly worn (1)
	I/II	24–25 mm (3)	worn (4)
	II/III	24 mm (1)	worn-much worn (3)
	III	28 mm (1)	much worn (8)
Asses	Grade I	24–27 mm, average 25 mm (6)	very slightly worn (1)
	I/II	25–26 mm, average 25 mm (4)	slightly worn (32)
	II	20–26 mm, average 24 mm (17)	slightly worn-worn (19)
	II/III	20–25 mm, average 23 mm (6)	worn (38)
	III	18–28 mm, average 22 mm (73)	worn-much worn (2); much worn (9)
	IV	22–25 mm, average 23 mm (2)	slightly worn (1); worn (1)
		Total: 117	Total: 120

The worn state of many of these coins leads one to ask whether the needs of change had not been satisfied long before the Neronian *aes* appeared; and it is worth remark that at Exeter fortress, too – established, like Usk, towards 55[126] – the Claudian coins were also worn.[127]

Sutherland suggested that Claudian copies were produced firstly in military contexts; but however popular this 'quasi-official' explanation has been, we have already found reason to question it (page 116). Fundamentally, it is based on the belief that military craftsmen would have been more skilled, more careful and more strictly supervised than civilians, and would therefore have produced copies closer in style, size and weight to the originals. Usk must destroy that theory: there is no reason to think that the legionaries of the fifties and sixties were more maladroit than those of the forties, yet the preponderance of Grade II coins is considerable, though not apparently counterfeited on the spot; there are apparently no die-linked specimens. But we also saw that the chief reason why the theory of army-manufacture of coin must be dismissed is that the fact that the army units drew their pay against an esimate of the amount, and under an obligation to account later, from the procurator's office (page 117). In any case, the 'quasi-official' explanation is absurd: if some copies were counterfeit and others made by authority, some tolerated and some rejected as false, the result would be chaotic. It is proper, therefore, to regard them as one and all false, as we have done. Even Sutherland, in his final remark on the matter, of 1984, admitted that 'imperial acceptance of a breached imperial monopoly is not easy to understand'.[128] 'Tolerated' the Claudian copies certainly were; but only in the sense that the wheels of everyday life would not properly turn without them, any more than they could turn, centuries later, without the 92 per cent of counterfeit halfpence sampled in 1787 (page 117). We should remember, finally, two things: the Roman government had been at pains to suppress even the local *aes* in the west – Gaul and Spain – and, secondly, had at no previous time countenanced the production of coin at civic mints in the west without official sanction – *Permissu Augusti, Decreto Decurionum*, as many declare.

The appearance of the beautiful Neronian *aes*, of very full weight, in the *stipendia* from 64 onwards provided a new standard against which the Claudian copies could not but be seen as rubbish. At Usk, thirty-three coins of Nero were found: five sestertii, three dupondii, twenty-four asses and a semis or half-as[129]. What would have happened to the Claudian copies? Were they thrown away, melted, or used as fractional currency? There are very few in the Flavian forts of Wales, and this circumstance points to their immediate exclusion from the *stipendia*.[130] In his excellent account of the Southwark coin-finds, however, M. J. Hammerson has maintained that on grounds of stratification Claudian copies circulated down to Trajan, and he has espoused the concept of fractional currency.[131] No doubt in civil life they may have survived longer than among the soldiery, paid by the *fiscus* in new coin now that it was available; and it is wise to keep an open mind. Even so, reliance on stratification is ingenuous: a detailed and 'time-consuming numerical analysis' of the datable material from Valkenburg did not, after all, lead to the expected 'sharper definition of the chronology but rather to a new appreciation of the amount of upward migration of small finds in consequence of the digging of foundation-trenches pits, etc'.[132] The occasional emergence of a Claudian copy from a substantially later context[133] is hardly to be taken as significant of continuing circulation; and as to the 'fraction' theory, the use of Claudian copies in that wise would seem to have been local at the best: they were of variable size, a drawback; and there is no sign of a validating countermark of Neronian or later date, such as the SE for 'semis' found stamped on worn-out asses along the Rhine. The gutter or the melting-pot seems, in short, to have been the fate of the majority within a very short lapse of time.

The third century build-up

Père Mahudel, in describing the finds of coin-moulds in the midst of the ancient city of Lyons, on the hill of Fourvière, pointed out in 1716 that the decay of the art of engraving, considerable by the time of Septimius Severus, and that emperor's debasement of the coinage, were bound to favour false moneyers.[134] Moulds and casts are our concern in this section, which describes the growth of the epidemic of counterfeits in the first half of the third century, an epidemic which was to develop vastly and pervasively under the Gallic emperors and indeed after the recovery of Gaul down to about the year 282 or 283, a period when the place of the mould was almost wholly, though not quite, taken by the false die. Undoubtedly Mahudel was right, in that inflation consequent upon the debasing of the currency offered an opportunity to coiners: under Decius about 250, for example, denarii were being officially overstruck with antoninianus-dies, illustrating the fall in the value of the double-denarius since its original introduction, at the weight of 1½ denarii, in 212.[135] Plated and other false silver coins (63) were probably being produced in much the same quantity as in the early Empire – a quarter or a third of the circulating medium.[136] A hoard from Rottenburg (on the Neckar near Stuttgart) was composed of 117 hybrid plated denarii of the narrow period Severus-Macrinus, involving cast dies prepared from only seven original denarii.[137]

Turning to moulded coins, we may begin with the *aes*. Very little Severan *aes* reached beyond the Alps: hoards closing under Postumus consist mainly of second-century material (of course very worn for the most part) and a greater or lesser proportion of his own, overstrikes (many false), and cast or struck copies, the coiners not hesitating through ignorance or design to imitate not merely his *aes* types, but also those of his antoniniani.[138] Besides such material, there also exists in *aes* a body of light-weight casts (two were noticed above, page 108). To these, attention was first drawn by Kubitschek and, having come to light in the military stations of the Danube, they were dubbed by Elmer *Limesfalsa*, 'frontier forgeries'.[139] Their equally obscure existence in Britain went for long unremarked. They are, however, ubiquitous, and are better called 'lightweights'. A long series of current originals was called upon – in Britain mostly asses, along the Danube mostly sestertii (Figure 3) – a hint as to economic differences, orthodox sestertii not being at all scarce on the Danubian *Limes*. At Caerleon and Caerwent alone, there are a dozen or more casts from the same, badly worn As of Domitian, which had probably been rubbed down to a smaller diameter and lightly impressed several times in the clay of a two-piece slab-mould. The resultant casts weigh a third or so of the original standard. The latest piece reproduced in this way is an As of Trebonianus Gallus, *c.* 251–3,[140] from Caernarvon; but most are moulded from first-century (56) and second-century (11–12, 58–59, 61–62) or Severan pieces.[140] Manufacture was probably widespread: in 1986, half a spoilt cast Britannia As of Hadrian was reported from Carmarthen.[141] But the intrinsic date is very probably misleading, and the main period of production could well have been later even than Gallus: an As of Hadrian (57) and other *aes* were represented in the mass of Gallic Empire antoninianus moulds from Whitchurch, near Bristol[142] and much the same could be said for finds in the Rhineland, notably from Pachten (Saarland).[143] A similar dating has been claimed for the Gaulish equivalents, which are not as yet well-known.[144] But along the Danube the epidemic seems to have ended somewhat earlier, probably because of the production of official coin at Viminacium and by the authority of the Province of Dacia from the time of Gordian III and Philip.[145]

We now come to the silver. Base-looking or light denarii and antoniniani, especially denarii, are common among site-finds, many proving to be hybrid and so false,[146] and with a faulty alignment of one side to the other (180° or 360° being the regular 'die-axis'). The metal – greyish, warty, fractured – may betray a coin after its centuries of burial (page 108); and some casts seem to have been designed for a white-metal, possibly even a gold-coloured, surface given the fact that gold pieces were sometimes struck from the same or similar dies to those used for denarii.[147] A table of British finds of coin-moulds, together with a few specimen Continental finds and a summary of British lightweights, is offered below. The great majority of moulds are for Severan denarii. There are some earlier coins, betrayed by their state of wear very often, and others continue to Severus Alexander and Maximinus; with Gordian III, in 238, came the return of the antoninianus, but few deposits yield moulds for these; thus a 'tail-back' is in evidence only Lingwell Gate[148] and the recent small Guernsey find:[149]Whitchurch joins, for instance, Damery (Marne) in running on to the Gallic Empire rather than back to Severan times. At that period, running down towards Gordian, the official coinage may have been blanched at the mint to improve its colour, by dipping in some mild organic acid; but it would soon have been discoloured and dirty, and in such a circulating medium the snide coins (65, cf. 64) would have found easy entrance.

A discovery in March, 1988 among a layer of filling in the ditch of the Roman defences of London (Blomfield Street) throws considerable light on the *raison d'être* of the denarius moulds, and I am grateful to Miss Jenny Hall of the Museum of London for permitting me to examine the several hundred, mostly fragmentary, examples and to refer to them here. The denarii used as models include Maximinus and, unlike Lingwell Gate, there is not a single imprint of an antoninianus – a fact which is all the more significant, in that the new find was accompanied by a fair number of moulds for asses, including those impressed by very fresh examples, so rare on British sites, of Philip, Decius and Gallus and their families, running down therefore a good dozen years or so later than the silver being counterfeited. A curious detail reinforces the belief that no separate period of *aes*-casting is in question, for one of the end moulds of a rouleau (cf. Figure 4B) had cut on it the barred X which is the sign for a denarius – unnecessary, if that had been the only denomination in play.

It is also to be remembered that it was under Decius that a practice arose at the mint of overstamping old denarii as antoniniani, as already remarked. Old denarii were therefore at a premium compared with the antoninianus, whose sins of over-tariffing had caught up with it. The epidemic of casting must mainly, though not necessarily wholly, be linked with the reintroduction of the antoninianus in 238 and the inflationary pressures then swiftly moving to crisis-point.

The next set of moulds, from the west-country sites of Whitchurch, Kenn and Keynsham take us on to the nadir of the antoninianus under Gallienus, Claudius II, and the Gallic emperors, indeed into Aurelian's pre-Reform years.[150] One may expect to see examples in site-finds (**66**); but there are no records of moulds for the Reform coins from Britain, as there are for Diocletian's reform: they were too little distinct in appearance from the mass of Central and Gallic antoniniani which formed the bulk of coins in circulation. A very few moulds are known on the continent.[151]

Barbarous radiates

Barbarous radiates are known in prodigious numbers from Gaul and Britain, and occur in Germany, Italy, Spain and Africa.[152] They range in size from the normal for antoniniani of the period *c.* 270 (**68**), 2.90 grammes, down to very tiny pieces scarcely 7 to 5 mm across, often too small for the dies (**74, 79, 83**); twenty of the smallest coins in the Worthing hoard average only 0.3 grammes.[153] To produce reasonable material at this scale called for some skill, and it is remarkable that such skill was forthcoming. **71** is an example of a portrait of Tetricus I which is not without merit: **78–79** are engaging caricatures of Victorinus, though **84** from Lydney is confused on the   left-facing obverse, and has an extraordinary pin-man on the reverse. **80** is a rare example with the portrait of an express, Salonina; and **76** reduces the obverse to the essential crown, within a dotted border.

The makers of the barbarous radiates were no respecters of nicety, even if, and it may be doubted, they were able to understand what was required, any more than the perpetrator of the 'Nerva-Trajan' dupondii discussed above (page 110). There are frequent instances of the erroneous coupling of obverse and reverse types, as in **70**, with its Tetrician obverse combined with Aurelian's CONCORDIA AVG reverse, except that the inscription has been mistakenly engraved CONSECRATI from a Claudius II commemorative coin. Sutherland provides a thorough conspectus of types imitated, mostly straightforwardly taken, as would be expected, from the commonest Gallic and Central Empire prototypes, including the *consecratio* (altar or eagle) types issued in memory of Claudius II (**71**).[154] The latest prototypes positively known are of Probus (AD 276–82), and a range of minims in his name, with an original, is shown (**87, 91–8**) from Segontium, Caerleon and the Coygan deposit mentioned at the beginning of this essay. The PROBI

KEY X denarii + antoniniani ● aes O nummi	To HADRIAN	ANTONINE	SEVERUS to ALEXANDER	MAXIMIN to VALERIAN	GALLIENUS S.R., to QUINTILLUS	POSTUMUS to TETRICUS	TETRARCHY	CONSTANTINE	
Ancaster (Lincs.)			X						CGRB
Bartlow (Cambs)			X						CCRB
Binchester (Durham)			X						CCRB
Bottesford (Lincs.)		X	X						CCRB
Bulwick (N'hants.)			X						J. S. Burden
Castor (N'hants.)		●	X						JAABr. Is. II, 180; Artis.
Chester	X								CCRB
Colchester			X						CCRB
Dorchester (Dorset)			X						CCRB
Duston (N'hants.)								O	CCRB
Edington (Som.) and dist.		X	X	X					CCRB, VCH Som. i
Guernsey			X	+					St. Peter Port, G.C.B.
Hambleton Hill (Rut?)		X	X						B.M.
Highbridge (Som.)			?						Som. Proc. IV
Housesteads (Northd.)			X						CCRB
Kenn (Som.)					+	+			R.F. Taylor
Keynsham (Som.)						+			Britannia 1986; G.C.B.
Lincoln			X						CCRB
Lingwell Gate (Yorks.)	X	X	X	X+					CCRB
London	X	X	X	X●					Lond. & Mx. Tr. XXII. 3; Independent 11 Mar. 1988, G.C.B.
Millington (Yorks.)		?							CCRB
Nocton (Lincs.)								O	CCRB
Rivenhall (Essex)							O		CCRB
Ryton (Salop)			X						CCRB
Sleaford (Lincs.)								O	Lincs. H. & A. I
Whitchurch (Som.)	●		●+	+	+	+			Arch. J. CXXII
Wroxeter (Salop)		●X							CCRB, etc.
Bordeaux		X		+		+			BSAF 1899
Daméry (Marne)		X	+	+	+	+			RN II
Pachten (Saarland)		●X	●X/+	+					Germania 1974
Britain (lightweights)	●	●	●	●					NC 1965, etc.

(Since the above was compiled, P.J. Casey sends a note of seven moulds from Ebor Brewery, York: denarii of Commodus, Severus, and Caracalla Caesar.)

of **94** echoes a *Virtus Probi Aug* obverse legend, normally with an armed bust which is not present here. It is possible that the portrait on another Coygan minim (**99**) resembles Carus sufficiently to be identifiable as immediately post-Probus: the crown is set well back, and the brow, unlike that of Probus, is receding. Tacitus, Probus' predecessor, has a similar brow, but a much shorter nose, as the coins show (**87–90**).

One post-Gallic reverse has been mentioned; to take another to illustrate the unreal world of the counterfeiter – who had increasingly to take copies, perhaps even copies of copies, as his model – the minim (**72**), 0.62 grammes, from Dinorben near Abergele in North Wales cannot be bettered (Figure 9). It purports to show a handsome fish gaffed by a diminutive figure on a stage or platform, for which there is no prototype in the imperial coinage. However, there cannot be anything truly original in a series which is by definition imitative, and therefore what appears to be so can only be a rationalisation of something not understood. Here we have a two-figure composition, and such compositions were a great feature of the reformed coinage introduced by Aurelian. Indeed, his PROVIDEN DEOR type (**73**) provides the model, doubtless at more than one remove. On the right stands Sol, his feet apart, thus accounting for the fish's tail; on the left Providentia or Fides holds two standards, the ornaments on which have given rise to the knobbly platform.[155]

FIG. 9   Radiate minim from Dinorben, North Wales, in the name of Tetricus I, with reverse distantly modelled on Aurelian's PROVIDEN DEOR type; *see* **72**. Twice actual size.

Such objects relieve the eye, and perhaps the heart; but our remaining comments are on more important matters. Firstly, as to dating, research, (most notably that of H. B. Mattingly in the country[156] and now that of J. A. Davies[157]), has established, as already stated, that there is no certain instance whatever of a barbarous radiate modelled on an orthodox coin later than Probus (276–82): only our **99** uncertainly leads on for a year or two (283–3). By that period, the tiniest of radiate minims had been produced, as the Verulamium Theatre hoard, covered by a concrete floor of *c.* 300, declares; that hoard contained a minim in the name of Tacitus (275–6), not recognised at the time of discovery or publication.[158] There are, of course, numerous barbarous coins of Carausius, but they never fall to minim size. It is true that later originals than those admitted by H. B. Mattingly and other modern scholars have been claimed, but they are fantasies: not to mention the 'fourth-century reverse types', where the eye of faith might discern the profile of Carausius, prudence dictates Postumus (84–85). Numerian and Magnia Urbica have been claimed, but these are illusions too, even though they are tied closely in time to the last of the Proban counterfeits.[159]

Next we touch on the progressive decline in size, uniform over wide regions of western Europe.[160] The beginning of the epidemic of barbarous radiates may be placed in the reign of Victorinus (268–70), for Postumus had managed to maintain a silver standard better than that of Gallienus until late in his reign, and endemic antoniniani copies are common. Under Victorinus and Tetricus, inflation in money-prices must have been acute and with it the growth of the coining of barbarous radiates. For the further development of the epidemic, the Coygan finds mentioned at the beginning of this work are particularly significant.[161] The deposit consisted not only of copies of coins of Probus and perhaps also Carus (92–4, 97, 99) averaging 11 mm diameter and 0.42 grammes, but also of larger copies averaging 14 mm and 1.25 grammes, many of them in a distorted, half-fused condition showing that they had been collected for melting, to provide metal for the Proban minims. Within a few years of the end of the Gallic Empire in early 274, therefore, minims were replacing copies which were themselves smaller than the first imitations, close to the orthodox originals in size. A parallel situation is glimpsed at the White Woman's Hole site at the eastern end of the Mendips, where coins were divided into segments rather than melted. One of the coins so treated was an antoninianus of Postumus (9) and a second was taken from the reformed coinage, of Tacitus (10), among various Gallic originals, and a few copies, treated in the same way.[162] As already pointed out (page 115), the quartering of such material does at least prove that a full-sized antoninianus of Tacitus was not regarded as having more value than an antoninianus of Tetricus, say, or a large-sized copy; and that such coins did not command a value of more than four minims. Indeed, the 'quarters' restruck with similar designs (75) must have been in all likelihood regarded as of equal value with the larger originals. Taking the White Woman's Hole 'quarters' as an example, their weight-range is wide – from 9 mm, 0.19 grammes up to 13 mm, 0.91 grammes;[163] no precision, in point of valuation, was possible. And if they seem in their present state to be utterly valueless, we may reflect that they copied not a bronze but a silver denomination, and when issued they would in all likelihood have been plated, however speciously.

Tiny coins are by no means a phenomenon of Roman times; but the authorities may well have expected the coinage of barbarous radiates to cease upon the arrival of the reformed coinage. That did not at once happen: as we have just seen, reformed antoniniani were liable to be chopped up to make flans for minims. The value-mark XX.I etc. was introduced by Aurelian on the reformed issues of some mints, but not at a reopened mint at Lyons,[164] and seems therefore to have had little impact. Coins of Lyons account for rather more than half the contents of hoards buried in northern Gaul down to Diocletian's reform of 294, though before his seizing power in 284 something over half the coins reaching that region were, on hoard evidence, the product of Rome and Pavia (Ticinum), not Lyons (44 per cent). Under Tacitus, Lyons coinage was abundant, but much was not clearly marked as to source and seems to have been produced for the accession and other festal donatives. Only under Diocletian does Lyons become predominant in Gaul (89 per cent).[165]

Force ended the nuisance of the minim; as we saw (page 102), there is some evidence of its effect at various sites in Britain. But what of the originals? In Gaul, Gallic Empire coins appear in but negligible proportion in deposits of Diocletian's time, and the minims have gone; the usurpation of Carausius in 286, however, interrupted a process which seems to have been much more gradual in Britain than in Gaul, for massive numbers of Gallic antoniniani still formed part of the currency in the earlier 290s – over 60 per cent, in hoards such as Penard and Blackmoor, where 13 to 28 per cent might be base Central issues, and only 2 or 3 per cent reformed coins, with Carausius and Allectus adding scarcely more.[166]

Barbarous radiates used to be regarded as a kind of small-change provided for a local context; it seemed absurd that they could have had currency over distance. Nothing could be further from the truth. H. B. Mattingly showed that a considerable 'mint' was feeding not only a Midland region about 70 km across in which the Lightwood (Staffordshire) and Calverton (Nottinghamshire) hoards with their die-linked coins lay, but to some extent southern and western England also. Typical products of this mint, clandestine as it was, appeared in the Worthing hoard, the Richborough hoard, and others including Mere (Wiltshire) and Whitchurch (Somerset); and the last-named deposit added its own die-linked group suggestive of a continuing concern with (rather than for) the monetary plight of the rural west even after the obsolescence of the casting-progress (page 126) practised nearby. Other coins again from the Midland mint travelled abroad, if one can admit the stylistic rather than exact link between Calverton and a Rhenish hoard in the British Museum. Nor is this impossible: P. V. Hill found a die-link between coins found at Corbridge-on-Tyne and another from a site in the Netherlands,[167] and Mlle. Lallemand and the late M. Thirion, in publishing St.-Mard I hoard from Belgian Luxembourg, have traced more die-links between Gallic and British finds – significantly enough including the temple and fair-site at Woodeaton (Oxfordshire) as well as a hoard from Mildenhall (Suffolk).[168] J.-B. Giard, too, indefatigable in this period as in the Claudio-Neronian, has presented us with a detailed and thoughtful account of barbarous radiates in Gaul, wherein other die-links across the Channel are enumerated.[169] In putting the results of these scholars' work together some years ago, I drew the first form of Figure 10,[170] and in its present form it also incorporates the work of a new generation of researchers: E. M. Besly and R. Bland in their report on the huge find at Mildenhall (Wiltshire), J. A. Davies in his recent study of the 1972 Meare Heath (Somerset)* hoard, and Ruprecht Ziegler in the case of the Brauweiler find.[171]

---

*The continental reader may care to note that Meare and Mere, and Mildenhall and Mildenhall, are quite different places, as shown by their county, given in brackets. Indeed, the Wiltshire site is pronounced 'Mynall'.

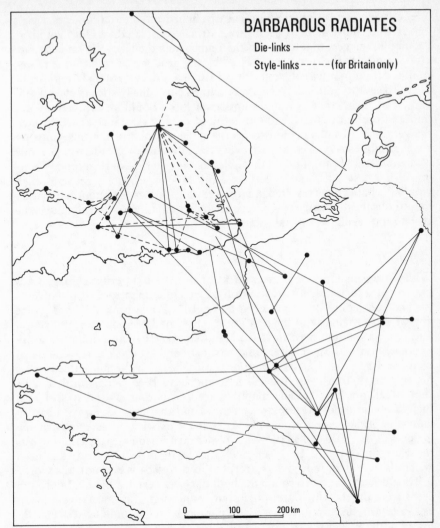

FIG. 10 Die-links between barbarous radiates in Gaul and Britain. After Giard, Huvelin and Thirion, and Ziegler, with additions from Besly and Bland, *et al.*

The elucidation of die-links between distant finds is impressive. No less impressive, in the minim hoards, is the occasional admixture of suites of die-linked material of obviously local origin. It is curious that the Caerleon minim hoard of 1955 should apparently contain no die-link with Meare Heath, Whitchurch, or Frocester (Gloucestershire), though there is a double stylistic link with Frocester and Coygan (95–97) which is worth remark.[172] There is no chronological difference to explain the lack of closer and more extensive linkage between them, more especially curious in view of the fact that they were all finds from the Bristol Channel region.

The date-crucial Verulamium Theatre hoard of some 800 pieces, all of which were illustrated, is even more strangely isolated.[173] One would be inclined to suggest that although the remarkable die-links shown in Figure 10 demonstrate the distances covered by the products of clandestine mints, so illustrating in a way the currents of trade and travel in the latter part of the third century, the local element remained exceedingly strong, even dominant. Yet, if that were so, more not fewer links would be expected in and (more importantly) between hoards found no great distance apart. In fact, the very lack of links demonstrates the dissemination of the tiny coins on a remarkable scale, even though we have to assume that the rough mode of manufacture both of dies and of blanks, (quartered coins, snipped sheeting, sliced cast rods, and pellets or droplets are vicariously recognisable), would probably have resulted in far fewer coins – dozens or hundreds rather than thousands – being struck from each combination of dies than was the case in the regulated official mints.

Carausius

With Carausius (286–93), the student of Roman counterfeit coinage finds himself in difficulties, for in addition to endemic imitations of his silver – the first such coins for a century or more (**101**) – a vast mass of crude coins appeared, particularly in the first years. There had been no mint in Britain, and as a paramount need to strike coin with his effigy and titulature arose in connexion with the military and naval stipend – for Carausius had been commander of the *Classis Britannica*, on whose loyalty and effectiveness his rule very largely depended – it would have been but natural that he should call on the erstwhile manufacturers of barbarous radiates to turn their skills into more legitimate channels, and that a good part of his coin would be struck not on new blanks, but on existing coins chiefly of the Gallic Empire (**100, 102, 104–7**). So abstract reasoning suggests. Such is the view put forward by P. H. Webb as early as 1907, and it has been generally accepted, indeed was accepted in the 1974 version of this work.

The difficulty is to determine the boundary between legitimate, but rough coins from others which are rough, but counterfeit. If overstriking is taken as a criterion, for example, there is no parallel with the counterfeit overstriking of Caligula's asses (page 119), because those coins had been decried. There is no suggestion, however, in site-finds or hoards of the last years of the third century in Britain that the Gallic Empire or reformed antoniniani had lost their legal course. Therefore overstriking may have been policy only at the start of the reign, as it had been a generation previously in the case of the obscure usurper Regalian at Carnuntum.[174]

Two further observations are worth making. The first is that Carausius' longish and perhaps rather difficult name is with few exceptions faultlessly reproduced in point of orthography, though by no means so well in point of lettering. Secondly, that rough-and-ready but accurate orthography of the name is coupled in the great majority of cases with a very few styles of bust. Indeed, throughout the reign the official style is bold and striking, very different from the products of the Continental mints. We can, if we wish, envisage the gathering of the best of the local engravers of barbarous radiates and the gradual creation, from that motley band, of a London Mint die-cutting workshop. We can almost trace the development of a particular engraver, whose work (like that of each of his several comrades) stands out in any collection of Carausian coins:[175] **105** and **107** are from the same hand, manifestly; both are overstrikes, one on a barbarous copy and with its own barbarous reverse, the other with a rather better reverse which gives the earliest recognised mintmark, the simple ML for *Moneta Londinensis*, of the new London Mint. Furthermore, if one regards the characteristics of that head, one is encouraged to think that practice made perfect, and that **108** is from the same hand.

Such is the argument. To take another, it might be suggested that London Mint from the start was able to issue coins of the confident style of **108** and that everything which did not come up to that standard is counterfeit; that the growth of skill and confidence from beginnings such as **105** and **107** is illusory, for they could merely be imitations, not early essays at a style. The trend of our previous discussions is in favour of this interpretation. But if it is correct, the obverse fidelity of even very rough coins such as **105** becomes very remarkable. Even more so, perhaps, is the total absence in the Carausian series of anything less in size than Gallic Empire antoniniani or large copies thereof, for we have seen that shortage produced a rapid decline in the size of imitations. There is perhaps a hint here as to the time-scale which governed descent to minim size generally, for the reigns of the British usurpers were brief, only ten years overall, and were followed by swift demonetization and a wholly new coinage.

The greatest service to Carausian numismatics has been that of Robert Carson, who divided the coinage into two main groups before and after 290–91, when Carausius adopted the title of *Caesar*, which had become the recognised appellation of a junior colleague in the imperial house; and the letter C for Caesar was duly incorporated before his name, e.g. on **103**,[176] product of the mint at Rouen which lay in the coastal belt of northern Gaul held by Carausius for some years.[177] In short, Carausian minims might indeed have appeared had it not been for the change in the coinage introduced *pari passu* with the *Caesar* title – the adoption of the continental XX.I standard and an increasing flow of regular material from the mints.[178] Even this might not have been enough to relieve the pressure on the currency. However, the unhindered circulation of Gallic Empire and reformed material combined with it to alleviate the needs of circulation. If, therefore, there was a 'good' Carausian coinage from the start, and Gallic and other material circulated unchecked, how may one explain the overstruck material? On the theory now under consideration it is explicable only on the assumption that the official Carausian coinage was issued at a premium, at least over Gallic material: indeed it is heavier, and overstrikes on reformed antoniniani are rare.[179]

This may indeed be the solution, for it helps in the interpretation of what is perhaps the most puzzling feature of the early coinage, the association of 'good' obverses – or at least, reasonably good – with appallingly barbarous reverses. **100** or **102** cannot be classed as anything but barbarous and counterfeit. But difficulties arise in connexion with **104**, having a 'good' obverse, reasonable (Postumian) galley on the reverse, but a totally illiterate reverse legend which might perhaps have been intended for *Laetitia* or *Felicitas Carausi*.[180] **109** is a similar case, with a decent obverse, totally reversed and barbarous on the other side. As to **110**, manifestly it was copied from a Rouen coin with the *Securit(as) Perpet(ua)* legend, though the figure is a standing Salus feeding a serpent rising from an altar. The model, however, was ill-struck and sufficiently off-centre to lose the first three letters of *SECVRIT*.[181] An inexperienced and certainly illiterate die-sinker was employed for this piece, which is rough enough in its appearance, even by the very rough standards of Rouen, to be classed as false. The mésalliance between reverse legend and type is further brought out in **111**, where a figure of Felicitas with *cornucopiae* and long *caduceus* is surrounded by the legend MART FAV, *Mart(i) Fau(tori)*, 'Mars the Favourer'. This legend is otherwise unknown. There are various novelties in the Carausian coinage, most notably the *Expectate Veni* type ('Come, O Awaited One') inspired by Virgil's *Aeneid*, and they go to show that there was a lively and interested mind with influence over the coinage. Most types, however, are the banal ones of the day, or are copies from earlier coinages, notably that of Postumus, on whom Carausius probably modelled his public image. *Minerva Fautrix* is indeed among Postumian types. That Mars could be named and the concept illustrated by a female personification, even though it was Felicitas, is too strong a juncture for any likelihood to reside in it, and banausic illiteracy is more probably the explanation.[182] So, too, with the TETVS AVG of the RSR mint representative (**112**), where the best suggestion, perhaps, is that the illiterate die-sinker copied part of a TET-RICVS name surviving as undertype on a copy of Gallienus' LIBERO P CONS AVG.[183] The same explanation may be invoked for the fourth-century 'Domino' group (page 142). It is impossible to believe that such products, despite their number, can be orthodox. It remains possible, however, that their obverses are struck from official dies which had been discarded or had been purloined from the mint.[184] Normally, it is thought, the obverse die or pile was fixed in a shock-absorbing block of wood, and the reverse die was hand-held on the heated blank placed between the two, for another workman to strike. Whether this was always so may be doubted, however, and in the case of Carausius, the Penard (Gower) hoard produced no fewer than three obverses, which with a parallel in Glasgow make four, all used with the same reverse as if that had been the fixed die.[185] Too little is known – nothing, indeed – of the day-to-day functioning of the Carausian mints, which may all have been issued with dies cut in London.[186]

It will be seen that the reader has to make up his mind as to the difficult problems outlined above. Until very much more research has been done on the *minutiae*, it will be difficult to distinguish genuine from false coins in the wide band where style, literacy, and physical form, weight and metal all seem to be indefinite. After much cogitation, it is my belief that the

Carausian mints could and did produce 'good' coins from the first, and the material which is substandard is a counterfeit reflection of it, engendered once more by shortage inspired by an artificial tariff.

The coinage of Allectus, Carausius' successor, offers little of interest to the present study. It is uniform almost to the point of dullness, like that of the continental rulers. **113**, overstruck on Carausius, bears the authentic mintmark of 293, and is scarcely to be claimed as a counterfeit: it is simply one of the first to bear the name of Carausius' murderer and successor. **114**, a well-known coin from South Shields, has shady connexions which include the use of the same obverse die, as Shiel showed, for a barbarous reverse; and its own reverse carries a London mintmark no later than *c.* 290. The lack of a legionary *cognomen*, as AVG for *Augusta*, and the appearance of a panther as the supposed emblem are grotesque, so that we may be sure the reverse is false, whatever was the status of the obverse.[187]

The Tetrarchy and Constantine

In 294, Diocletian instituted a complete reform of the coinage, restoring a gold and silver currency of good metal and weight, and below it a handsome silver-plated coin of argentiferous bronze about 4 per cent fine – the *nummus*, as it seems to have been called (often to numismatists, the *follis* – but this was really a collective noun, a 'bagful' of 12,500 denarii). It is about 25 to 27 mm in diameter and 10 grammes in weight; it was destined to become the commonest, indeed to most intents the only coin available for petty transactions. Its original subdivisions were never much seen. The plating and the silver-content placed the nummus among the silver-denominations, but all too few of the new 'sterling silver' argentei were issued to support it, and the world was not yet ready for a purely fiduciary currency such as we have today. Inflationary pressures mounted, and in 301 Diocletian issued an edict whereby the values of coins were doubled. A few months later came the celebrated edict on maximum prices which reduced the values of the coins again – at least the gold and silver – setting the equivalent of the pound weight at 72,000 and 6,000 denarii respectively. In 301 the earlier doubling of the nummus seems to have been marked (though only at Siscia and Alexandria mints) by the reappearance of the old XX.I signs, possibly now meaning twenty denarii – 'vieux francs' as it were – instead of ten. Probably five nummi went to the argenteus, and perhaps ten argentei to the gold piece.[188]

The nummus retained its weight and alloy until 307, when the standards began to slip. By 318, when Constantine reformed the coinage, the weight had fallen to only 3 grammes; in 330 to 2.5 grammes; and in 335 to 1.5 grammes, with the added silver then seldom exceeding 1.5 per cent. The plated surface, barely five microns thick, rarely survives on such coins from contexts other than Egyptian.[189]

The argenteus was rarely seen and seldom copied;[190] and indeed there seems to have been little impetus towards the illicit multiplication of the original nummus. The main series of clay moulds, for example, belongs to

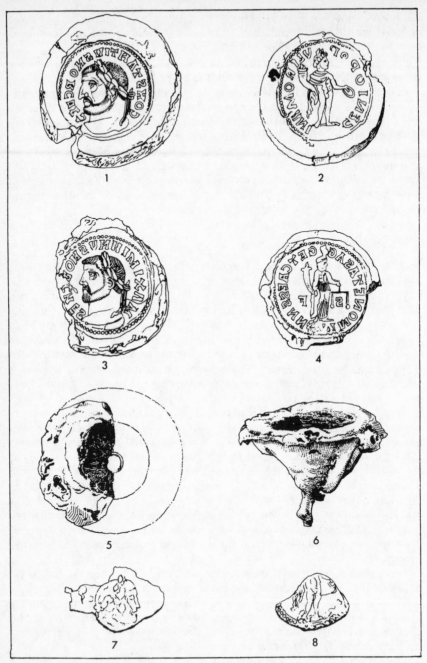

FIG. 11 Moulds (1–4) for tetrarchic nummi, from Duston (Northants.); 5–6, waste from mouths of bottle-shaped moulds; 7–8, spoilt castings. Full size. By courtesy of the Royal Numismatic Society.

the next stage. Thus the principal deposit from Duston (Northamptonshire) represents originals of Diocletian, and of Constantius I and Galerius as Caesars or junior emperors (Figure 11). Mintmarks on the impressions of the reverses of the coins moulded show that these had emanated from Trier and Pavia mints between 294 and 303–6.[191] The effect of the revaluation of 301 can therefore be distinguished, but a second reduction in 307 seems to have provoked little or no renewed outburst of casting, for we have no moulds of Constantius and Galerius as *Augusti*, or of Constantine as *Caesar* or *Augustus*. However, an isolated attempt in connexion with another reduction of the nummus in 318 furnishes us with the latest-known examples of coin-moulds from Britain – from Nocton (Lincolnshire), where they were found in the bed of the Car-dyke, the Roman land-drain, as if there had been an attempt to dispose of incriminating evidence.[192] The VICTORIAE LAETAE PRINC PERP type, which was copied at Nocton together with others, is somewhat unusual in being of a slightly better alloy than its contemporary types, and issued with a thicker or more resistant plating. This detail serves to remind us that the casts from the Nocton moulds must either have been in a white-metal or must have been treated in some way to produce a silvery surface.[193]

An attentive examination of site-finds will certainly provide instances of cast counterfeits of later date than this. But in general the counterfeiter was once more having recourse to false dies. A good Caerleon instance of a struck nummus of Galerius, not much underweight at 9.45 grammes, imitates a London Mint issue of 305–7 (115), and is perhaps a product of the inflationary doubling of the value of the nummus in 301. Counterfeiting seems to have been on a fairly small scale until the reform of 318, but that reform is something of a watershed in late Roman monetary history. Hoards tend to end or begin with it[194] and this is a fact which must point to a legislative background obscure to us: perhaps the earlier issues were demonetized, becoming *pecuniae vetitae*, to adopt the expression of a later imperial edict.[195] Certain it is that struck copies, generally of much the same module as their prototypes – a fact indicative of the heavy overtariffing of the official coinage – now appear in fair quantity (117, 118) and enter into the composition of hoards such as Llanbethery.[196]

The next watershed was the reform of 330 which introduced some of the best-known coins – the *Gloria Exercitus*, and the *Constantinopolis* and *Urbs Roma* coinages bound up with the inauguration of Constantinople as a new capital in May that year (120–22). Full-size and reduced counterfeits are common, and by no means always barbarous, though the limitations of half-tone reproduction demand that our examples (119, 123–25) are fairly obvious. Indeed, a fairly wide range of high-class copies is betrayed only by variant portraiture or an occasional letter, apart from size (123). Other mistakes are 'mules' pairing the wrong obverse and reverse (126–27) and these have sometimes entered catalogues.

The final reduction of Constantine's reign, in 335, introduced a *Gloria Exercitus* coin with only one standard between the two soldiers depicted, instead of two (128, cf. 129). There were also new types in honour of his mother Helena, and his step-mother Theodora, and these are sometimes counterfeited,[197] though the false-moneyers devoted their attention chiefly to *Gloria Exercitus* of both kinds, and the Rome and Constantinople commemorative pieces. This series was the first to be produced down to minim size for fifty years. Untypical stylistically, but interesting in themselves and in their provenance, are the examples from White Woman's Hole, the small cave at the eastern end of the Mendips which we noted above as the seat of clandestine coin-production at the end of the barbarous radiate epidemic (page 129).[198] Perhaps the third-century material had been brought in merely as scrap for the Constantinian manufacture. But it would be strange that no other equally suitable scrap occurred, and it is better to regard the deposits as separate in time, though very possibly made 'in the family'. Occupation of the cave, low-roofed as it was, ranged on the basis of coins not connected with the coining activity from Victorinus down to Arcadius.

The mode of manufacture was different at White Woman's Hole in the Constantinian period. Earlier, coins had been quartered and stamped with false dies; now the metal was cast into pencil-like rods, and slices of these formed the blanks. This method is first exemplified at third-century Draethen,[199] but was to become standard in the fourth century whenever minims were to be made. It is in evidence at Lydney[200] and, to judge by the central weakness of a fair number of Theodosian copies arising from the natural casting-process, was especially popular in late times. In most cases, the White Woman's Hole minims were smaller than the dies, as the superimposed photographs in the range (130–34) indicate. No specimen of these minims has so far been traced beyond the cave itself.

We may recall that after the collapse of the Gallic Empire some years passed before the new, reformed coinage of Aurelian made headway. A similar gap seems to have encouraged the gradual devolution of copies towards minim size in the 340s; indeed, if one takes note of the module of copies in the Appleford and Woodeaton hoards from Oxfordshire, well-illustrated in the reports,[201] one may agree that this is so. Appleford is particularly interesting inasmuch as it was the later, and included thirty copies of the substantive 'two Victories' type (136, cf. 135) which, according to J. P. C. Kent, may not have been struck until 346. Since the suspension of *Gloria Exercitus* and a few lesser issues of the same period, (our Segontium 137, cf. 138, is a rarity in Britain of *c.* 341–2),[202] there would thus have been a gap of some six years to be filled by the false-moneyer.[203] The sixty-three Appleford copies of *Gloria Exercitus* (one standard) do not descend below 12 mm, however, and likewise not the 'two Victories'. So long a cessation of minting, moreover, is a notion which is at variance with the large number of mintmarks, nine, found on the 'two Victories' type, and other scholars would prefer to date the issue from *c.* 342.[204]

What, then, of the very small copies of Constantinian coins of the 335–40 issues? The White Woman's Hole finds averaged 8 to 9 mm across, and most British numismatists would find it difficult to date them later than 346; however, in dealing with a purse of forty-three minims, (one radiate, the rest of *c.* 335–40 prototypes and many of them as low as 7 mm in diameter), found in a grave at Reims, Callu and Garnier suggested that coiners *reverted* to the imitation of these types after the fall of Magnentius in 353. The issue of the new 'falling horseman' type (151) from the Gallic mints, especially Trier, was inadequate – indeed, barbarian inroads occasioned a virtual suspension of supply from Trier, one of the most important mints. North of the Alps, too, Constantius II's final *Spes Reipublice* was available only in derisory number and, in short, scarcity again ruled circulation.[205] From the Fontaines Salées find, it could also be proved that the 'two Victories' issue was being reproduced after 353; *ex hypothesi*, therefore, so might the others – *Gloria Exercitus* (one standard), and so on. Indeed, a minim of 'falling horseman' type, with a helmeted obverse reminiscent of the Rome and Constantinople commemoratives, is recorded from a northern French hoard.[206]

It is true to say that imitations of 'falling horsemen', ubiquitous in Britain, are less common in Gaul and Germany, not to mention other regions. But one cannot say that the orthodox 'two Victories' type was other than fairly abundant in northern Gaul, where Trier struck it in vast numbers. Yet the Reims coiner was not concerned to reproduce it. Furthermore, the mere fact that barbarous 'falling horsemen' are seen as overstrikes on previous Constantinian types must tend to show that issues prior to 348 were all subsumed under the heading *pecuniae vetitae* of the edict of 356, even though the elimination of the coinage of Magnentius may have been the principal or only object of the prohibition. For these reasons I am inclined to set the Reims find before the introduction of *Fel. Temp. Reparatio* coinage in 348. There would not appear to be any reason why the production of *Gloria Exercitus*, etc. should have been inhibited before that date; indeed 129, a Lydney coin, is particularly interesting in this regard (though poorly preserved) because it displays a bust of a narrow and rather long-necked type, associated with the small *Fel. Temp. Reparatio* (phoenix) denomination, and the latest of the 'two Victories' immediately preceding it. It may be added that a recent study of the proportions of copies to orthodox coins *c.* 330–54 and 354–58 in the Rhine-Maas-Alps region throws up differences in their incidence – differences which hoard-accumulations tend to blur, so that the notion implicit in Callu and Garnier's paper of large-sized copies in time of tranquillity and of minims in time of crisis, in that case the aftermath of the Magnentian revolt and the Germanic invasions, ceases to convince.[207]

Falling horsemen and others

The most important reform of the currency since Diocletian's was undertaken in the year 348, and marked the inception of Rome's twelfth century. The FEL(*ix*) TEMP(*orum*) REPARATIO coinage was the most diverse seen for a number of years. There were several types, and three denominations. One of the commonest shows the emperor in a ship guided by Victory (144), and is frequently found counterfeited by casting, as well as by false dies; one from Usk weighs 6.74 grammes, well over the orthodox average of 5.5

grammes, and is a strong index of the substantial overvaluation applied to the series. These coins are no doubt the *majorinae* of the law-texts; another variety, showing the emperor leading a barbarian from his forest hut, is a half-unit, probably the *centenionalis*. A smaller coin again, perhaps without added silver (or rather struck from the metal of withdrawn coins) is that showing a phoenix on a globe or a pyre in obvious allusion to the 'happy renewal' indicated by the reverse legend (**156**).

The times, however, were not very happy. Of the two sons of Constantine who had initiated this set of coins, Constans was killed as a consequence of the rebellion of Magnentius in Gaul, though the other, Constantius II, was to outlive him by eleven years. Magnentius reigned from 350 to 353, and produced an interesting coinage with several new types, including the Christogram as a main reverse type on a denomination larger than the normal, majorina. This 'Salus' type (**146**) is imitated to full (**147**) as well as often to small size in common with others (**150**).[208] After the rebellion the mints began to issue a new *Fel. Temp. Reparatio* piece with a bold design of the emperor, dressed as a soldier, spearing a falling Sassanid horseman. This design had had its antecedents in the early series; but adumbrated by the last issue of the mint opened by Magnentius at Amiens, it was reduced in 354 to a weight of about 2.5 grammes (**151**), and survived until *c.* 358.

The feeble flow into Britain of subsequent official silver-bronze coinage – the authorities seem at long last to have decided to concentrate on providing a reasonable quantity of high-quality silver siliquae, and the coining of argentiferous bronze at Trier, a main mint for Britain, was virtually suspended from *c.* 353 to 364 – was no doubt the reason why copies of the falling horsemen design, down to the tiniest minims even smaller than the limit reached in the third century, came to dominate petty transactions.

Overstrikes are an initial feature of the 'falling horsemen' (**152**), occasionally occurring on *Fel. Temp. Reparatio* itself: **155** is struck on a phoenix type, though that was a lower denomination.[209] It seems certain that the originals must have commanded a high premium; and that when the overstrikes are on earlier Constantinian (or, rarely, radiate) types, they indicate demonetization, as already observed. Thus we find reference in the edict of 356 to 'moneys established for the public use' (*pecuniae in usu publico constitutae*) on the one hand, and 'prohibited moneys' (*pecuniae vetitae*) on the other.[210] **152–58** offer a range of 'falling horsemen', all but the tiniest, known from a handful of southern British sites and first from the Temple of Nodens at Lydney, where Hoard II occurred under a cement patch to a mosaic in the baths.[211]

In dealing with Lydney, it is important to realise that the fifth-century dating advanced by Mrs. Tessa Wheeler in 1932 arose from a view of the date of the building, which was understandable enough at the time but *in vacuo* and wrong, for the baths were not of later construction than the adjacent 'long building' with its floors of 367 or later.[212] Indeed, the history of the whole *temenos* is much longer than thought. Nothing later than Tetricus came from the foundations of the mosaic in question (or beneath them), though a *Gloria Exercitus* coin came from below an original floor elsewhere in the baths. As regards the minim hoard, it would have been better had attention been paid to Pearce's views on Hoard I, wherein he voiced doubts as to the dating which seemed to carry it on beyond the likely numismatic terminus. It would have been better, too, if attention had been paid to the occurrence of small *Fel. Temp. Reparatio* copies in more normal circumstances elsewhere on the same site.[213] Lastly, it is clear that the adoption of 'classes' of different *average* weight in the report on Hoard II – 0.48, 0.24, 0.12 and (the 'minimissimi') 0.06 grammes (Figure 6) – has been very misleading, for the figures are *merely* averages, and classifying them in this way predisposes the reader to think in terms of 'denominations'.

The importance of the Brean Temple excavation is that it showed a spatial difference in the distribution of minims and 'minimissimi' of Lydney type, which were confined virtually to the temple itself, and the coins found in the closely adjacent 'southern building' which had been constructed out of the materials of the temple: 183 'falling horsemen', including eight overstrikes and a full range of copies from 16 down to 2 mm, came from the temple, while the 'southern building' produced only eight. There was a Valentinianic occupation of the temple-site, probably in connexion with iron-working; but the coins found there, eighteen in number, were rather less worn than the thirty from the 'southern building', and there were only three Theodosian coins from the exterior of the temple, as against sixty-two from the 'southern building' and its immediate environs. On this basis the chronological position of the 'falling horsemen' is perfectly clear. Large or tiny, they were contemporary with the currency of their prototype, and that was generally ended by the appearance of the Valentinianic issues, which were abundant.[214] In reporting on the Brean finds in 1965, I was much impressed by the argument of B. H. St. J. O'Neil that the Valentinianic coinage did not arrive in quantity in Britain until after the *barbarica conspiratio* of 367 had been resolved; but this position is no longer tenable.[215]

Minimissimi occur not only at the sacred sites of Lydney and Brean, but also in secular contexts – baths at Canterbury, the villa at Great Staunton (Huntingdonshire), in a hoard relating to the villa at Bourton-on-Water, and a hut at Richborough.[216] Had they been known only at temples, and if more temples had produced them, they might have been dismissed as merely votive gifts. But at Pagans Hill temple (Somerset), only 25 kilometres from Brean, tiny copies were very few in a series ending after 395. Instead there were numbers of worn-out and fragmentary coins, which were the sweepings of the building. Nor does Pagans Hill stand alone.[217] We cannot therefore accept the comfortable 'votive' explanation. The tiny coins, the minimissimi, cannot be other than the legitimate and logical terminus of an epidemic episode of counterfeiting, obeying the same laws as did the Claudian copies three centuries earlier: metal has to be saved if profit is to be made. The principle is only really varied by the argentiferous bronzes current in the later third and fourth centuries, when more profit could be extracted by removing the silver. One of the best instances of cupellation of fourth-century coinage comes from Silchester, where lead phosphate (indicative of the use of bone-ash to absorb the litharge produced by melting out the silver by the addition of the lead to the pot) was observed encrusting coins from hollows in the floors of the Romano-British church near the forum.[218]

As to the usefulness of such tiny things, opinions must vary; but one must take the full range of size and weight in any given deposit: too much has been built on the 147 'minimissimi' in Lydney II, for example (whereof fifty-one 'sit quite easily on the surface of a halfpenny' an inch in diameter, cf. Figure 6), forgetting that the hoard was composed in all of 1,646 pieces, clippings, and 1,241 minims under 7.5 mm. May we be wrong in looking at individual minims? Should we be thinking in terms of packets or bags – *folles* in the literal sense – of which the Lydney hoard might have been an example? Can each and every tiny coin have been counted from hand to hand? The suggestion is highly speculative. But it is indeed true to say that for many years, since the early fourth century and before, the silvered bronze coinage had been used by the bag. The edict of 356 had as its object the suppression of speculative movements of currency from one place to another, and this it did by forbidding any merchant to carry on his own pack-animals more than 1,000 *folles* of legitimate coin (*pecuniae in usu publico constitutae*).[219] Each bag was probably equivalent to 12,500 denarii communes (perhaps in coins worth 100 denarii) and at that date must have been quite small, for instead of the 72,000 denarii of 301 the pound of gold was tariffed at an astronomical figure: A. H. M. Jones considered that the 1,000 folles of the edict, in any case allowed for travelling-expenses, would not have been worth more than one or two gold pieces (solidi).[220]

Up to the present time, there has been only one discovery to throw light upon the locality where any of the 'falling horsemen' were produced. W. A. Seaby's publication of the Ham Hill finds includes a group of nine die-linked counterfeits, sufficiently numerous to suggest that the age-old tradition of the west-country, seen hitherto in casts of Severan denarii, Gallic antoniniani and *aes* and then in struck counterfeits down to minim size, was far from extinct. Seven coins, mostly overstrikes, share one obverse, and six have the same reverse; two more have another obverse, and one the same reverse as before; there were several other imitations in the same style, again mostly overstruck, one on a tin flan. Otherwise, little success has been reported in spotting die-links in this series, a state of affairs which is quite remarkable, and must be due to the sheer mass of false coin in circulation.[221]

'Carausius II'

A special place must be allowed to the intriguing series of nineteen copies, of which a majority bear on their obverse the name of the celebrated British usurper of 286–93, though that is the only point of contact with his coinage (145, 152).[222] On nine of the coins, the name Carausius (or in two cases 'Censeris' and in two more 'Constantius' in some form) is introduced by the title DOMINO in full, so that an untendentious name for the group would be 'the Domino group' rather than as in the above subheading. The reverse types are all of *Fel. Temp. Reparatio* 'emperor in galley' (three) or 'falling horseman' (the remainder); some are overstruck and are likely to be early in the 'falling horseman' series. Specimens in the Heslington (Yorkshire) and Freckenham (Suffolk) hoards, and one from the Dinorben (North Wales) hoard (**145**), establish the period of the coins quite narrowly. As Kent has pointed out, the years 354–8 and later witnessed the undisputed sway of the central government in Britain, and it is only in Britain that 'the Domino group' is known. Consequently, the coins cannot refer to an actual individual, a rebel against the cruel imposition of Constantius II's government after the suppression of Magnentius, as was at one time thought. Possibly we may be dealing with a protest movement – Kent's suggestion that the pieces are merely evasive, like the 18th-century halfpence reading *Gulielmus Shakespeare, Pitt for Ever*, etc., instead of the king's name, is difficult to accept when there are no parallels in the Roman series, and when we remember that the historical Carausius was the great opponent of Constantius I, Constantius II's namesake and grandfather. There is a mystery here, recalling the events of sixty years before, and perhaps a mystery is not unwelcome.

Kent also suggested that the name of Constantius on the reverse of many members of the group arose in the first place from the heedless copying of an overstruck piece on which the original imperial title was still partly legible, as often is the case. The same may also apply to the word DOMINO, for some mid-Constantinian *Vota* coins carry the legend *Dominorum Nostrorum Caess* or the like. ·

PART FOUR
The last endemic stage

A considerable alteration to the coin in circulation was brought about after the ending of the 'falling horseman' issue in 357. The change consisted in the introduction of a copious supply of silver siliquae struck at a nominal 144 to the *libra* and weighing individually a rather erratic 1.9 grammes or so; a 10 per cent variation has been observed,[223] sufficient to tell us either that the coins were grossly overvalued or else that they were no longer to be allowed to pass by tale, but only by weight. At the end of the century, in 397, a further reduction to 1.3 grammes took place. From the late 350s and early 360s, considerable numbers of silver coins entered circulation for the first time for a hundred years, to be rapidly counterfeited at low weights (**142**, 1.57 grammes from Caerwent, cf. **139**, 1.79 grammes; **32**, from Silchester is in the traditional subaerate manner). Clichés do not seem to have been recorded, though the process was ideal for the multiplication of rather thin coins of high silver content – the originals were above standard[224] – as was to be shown in the medieval period (page 112). Of all the endemic counterfeits of the period, however, none is more interesting than **143**, included here at the suggestion of Stephen Minnitt of Taunton Museum. Of solid silver, 1.74 grammes, it has seen some wear, as will be noticed, but it was deemed good enough to be included in the Holway (Taunton) hoard of 1821, where its companions included many siliquae down to the end of the fourth century (Honorius), and many double siliquae or miliarensia ending with one of the usurper Eugenius (392–94). Indeed this curious little piece, a 'falling horseman' in silver, copied fairly exactly but with some defects in the legends from the ordinary argentiferous bronze type, has a die-duplicate from Burghöfe on the Danube.[225] These two pieces are testimony to the fact that the 'falling horsemen' were issued well-plated, even though the plating is only rarely preserved;[226] indeed, some may have mistaken them for silver, as in this case. Confusion must have existed in the public's mind as to the status of the various components of the currency after so many changes in the standard of the argentiferous bronze element and the reappearance of good silver.

With reasonably ample supplies of new siliquae available, the drainage of the empire's silver-resources into thoroughly base alloys ceased after a disastrous century. The silver-content of the subsidiary coinage was allowed, with only two exceptions, to drift downwards as a natural consequence of melting and remelting issues called in from time to time. Julian's large 'bull' coin of 363 was the last attempt to resuscitate a majorina of *Fel. Temp. Reparatio* style, with about 2 per cent of silver; the other exception is rather more interesting, for an edict of 371 refers to *aes dichōneutum* ('twice-melted') – presumably meaning a bronze coin formed of metal from the coinage-stock which had been cupelled for its silver, and the copper constituent recovered for this new use. The *aes dichōneutum* is shown by analysis to be the larger Valentinianic piece, with reverse type *Restitutor Reipublicae*.[227] Though the large *Fel. Temp. Reparatio* coins and the first of the Magnentian issues struck on the same basis were much counterfeited, the comparable 'bull' type was scarcely known in Britain, even though produced to some degree in the Gallic mints. Counterfeits therefore do not seem to be recorded from British sites, though known elsewhere.[228]

An abundant coinage of small *aes* was unlikely to engage the false moneyer's serious attention unless greatly overvalued, and thus counterfeits of Valentinianic nummi – the *Gloria Romanorum* (**159**) from the Wiveliscombe (Somerset) hoard is an example, with its faulty titulature, bad lettering, and globular eye – are far from common.[229] A more traditional form of endemic copying comes in again, however, with a new larger *aes* piece introduced by a reform of 381 – the *Reparatio Reipub*. This coin is scarce, but not uncommon on late sites in Britain – there are over forty from Richborough[230] – but counterfeits do not seem to have been reported, although on the Continent 16 per cent of those composing the Hemptinne (Belgium) hoard were false, and included three overstrikes. Other overstrikes of this type on Valentinianic nummi represent an unofficial upward revaluation by the false-moneyer; another, on an obsolete Constantinian nummus of 312, has been noted.[231]

It may be that even the *aes* component of the coinage was overvalued later, for it proved impossible to maintain it, in the long run, above the level of the 'fourth brass', the 12 or 13 mm nummus which formed the bulk of the subsidiary coinage introduced into Britain in the last two or three decades left to the island as a Roman province. Many of the *Victoria Auggg* and *Salus Reipublicae* coins forming the mass of this currency were badly struck, but one may frequently detect the hand of the coiner (**162–63**, cf. **161**).[232] Moreover, now that the three elements of the currency had become established – gold, silver, and *aes* – older coinage could again be brought into play. Most interesting, perhaps, are the demonetized Magnentian majorinae, cut down to 'fourth brass' size, as represented here by a Lydney piece (**148**). For the process itself we may turn to Ham Hill (Somerset), a site which had already been the haunt of false-moneyers in the 'falling horseman' period (**149**).[233]

What appears to have defeated the false-moneyer in the end, when supplies of coin ceased to reach Britain in the early fifth century, was the tendency towards the use of a very mixed small-change indeed, a point which may be illustrated with reference to hoards. A typical example at Cirencester had been concealed in a small jar 10 cm high, and consisted of only ten coins – a *Victoriae Dd Auggq Nn* 'two Victories' type of Constans; a quarter of a *Fel. Temp. Reparatio* (galley) type; a 'falling horseman'; a Valentinianic *Securitas Reipublicae*; three Theodosian (*Victoria Auggg* and two *Salus Reipublicae*); and three fourth-century illegible.[234] Larger hoards, such as that from Worlebury Camp, Weston-super-Mare, of 241 pieces, regularly go back to the 'radiate' period though ending with Honorius, and include many counterfeits – there were fifty-five diademmed minimi and another cut-down Magnentian *Salus*.[235] It would be tedious to specify many others,[236] but (as one further example) the Icklingham (Suffolk) II hoard contained seventy silver siliquae and 994 others ranging from Gallienus to Honorius and including forty-six barbarous pieces, mostly 'falling horsemen'.[237] An interesting point is that 90 per cent of those silver coins were clipped, as indeed is often the case in hoards buried, one may assume, after the reduction of the weight of the siliqua to 1.3 grammes in 397. To explain this phenomenon, numismatists have tended to seek deep and elaborate causes, even to suggest official or 'semi-official' action.[238] But it was surely as fraudulent as it was to become at times in later centuries, when the burden of circulation was carried by a silver coinage struck at so-many pieces to the pound, and so individually of somewhat varying weight.[239] We close our series of illustrations with a clipped siliqua, which is also false in itself, as its style must suggest (**141**, cf. **140**).

Thus we reach the end of the subject, for (as indicated above) there was no coinage of the 'Dark Ages' (**164**).[240] Its use is likely to have died away very rapidly once the authority which issued it no longer reached into Britain. Caerwent, for example, is noteworthy for the quantities of scattered Theodosian hoards found about the houses, as if discarded as being valueless.[241]

* * * *

> *Tace, sis, faber, qui cudere*
> *Plumbeos numos soles!*

'You leaden coin-smith, do be quiet!'

Plautus, *Mostellaria*, 892

Notes

Attention is called to two excellent new books published by Seaby in 1987, which will provide the reader with a background to much of what has been said above:
Andrew Burnett, *Coinage in the Roman World*
Richard Reece, *Coinage in Roman Britain*
It was not possible for me to take note of these works in the foregoing pages.

G.C.B.

1. *PL* XXIII, 20. The story is unique in ancient literature for such details; but there may be more in it than meets the eye. Among the apocryphal sayings of Jesus preserved in an Oxyrhyncus papyrus we find: '. . . where there is one alone, I am with him; raise the stone, and thou shalt find me' (B. P. Grenfell and A. S. Hunt, *New Sayings of Jesus* (1904), 36).

2. R. McMullen, *Soldier and Civilian in the Later Roman Empire* (1963), 51, with ref. to *CJ* IX, 24.1; cf. R. W. Davies, *AS* 1973, 199–212. Jerome's *Aegyptiorum litterae* were probably legal depositions of a kind familiar in the papyrological record, some being quoted by Davies.

3. Herodotus III, 56. He thought the tale foolish; but for the coins *cf*. R. S. Stroud, *Hesperia* XLIII (1974), 172, n. 53; K. L. Noethlichs, *Historia*, 1987, 137.

4. The 1986 Bassaleg (Gwent) hoard, to be published by my colleague, E. M. Besly, was buried *c*. 270 when the silver-content of new issues was only 2–3 per cent; among its components were counterfeit antoniniani of Philip I with 25.1 per cent and of Postumus with 11.99 to 16.28 per cent silver (analysed by J. P. Northover). On the other hand, a study of site-finds and hoards in Belgium shows that barbarous radiates may amount to 70 per cent in the former, and only 30 per cent in the latter, having been 'strained out' (J. Lallemand, *Mél. Lafaurie*, 120).

5. The first mention of aes is *CTh* xi, 21.1. The Roman law of counterfeiting is admirably treated by P. Grierson, *Essays/Mattingly*, 240–61. For a note on the punishments see e.g. J. A. Crook, *Law and Life of Rome* (1967), 272–5. Note Cassius Dio LXXVIII, 16.5 for an incident in 215 similar to that reported by Suetonius of Tiberius (*Tib.*, 58), lèse-majesté by carrying a coin into an improper place.

6. W. von Massow, *Die Grabmäler von Neumagen* (1932), no. 303; but he fails to mention the yellow paint on the coins, reported in a local newspaper soon after the discovery of the block (F. Hettner, *Rheinisches Museum*, 1881, 446–7, no. 1). A standing figure is usually described as holding a counterfeit coin for inspection, between finger and thumb; but no coin is visible there, and A. Rieche (*BJ* 1986, 183–4) shows that the figure is in reality making the standard gesture used in the finger-counting system, prevalent in antiquity, for 'hundred'. The exact number of hundreds cannot be made out.

7. E.g. Tertullian, *PL* I, 1237.

8. Actual finds of counterfeit gold coins are as rare as plated Ancient British gold is common. In *CCRB*, 42, mention is made of base gilt Severan aurei: perhaps they were the products of the denarius-moulds, and gilt or gold-coloured, the same types being often common to both aurei and denarii: the ancients could gild without gold, cf. W. A. Oddy *et al.*, *MASCA Journ.* 1981, 211–13. Note also Apuleius, *Metamorphoses* IX, 18, *novitate nimia candentes solidos aureos* 'solid gold pieces *far* too newly shining' (my translation). Plated solidi were in the old Cleeve Prior hoard (*A.* XVII (1814, 329–30). P. Bastien suggests that a well-organised workshop for producing solidi of debased metal existed in the Rhineland (*Le Monnayage de Lyon, 363–413* (1987), 151, pl. 32). Cf. also n. 134.

9. J. -M. Carrié, *DR* II, 116.

10. C. H. V. Sutherland, *The Emperor and the Coinage* (1976), 82, citing L. Breglia, in *Pompeiana* (ed. E. Maiuri, 1950), 50–63. Credit in the early Empire, as at Pompeii, see S. Mrozek, *Historia* 1985, 310–23, esp. 314.

11. T. Pekáry, *DR* II, 103–13; cf. M. Crawford, *JRS* 1970, 40–8.

12. Cicero, *Epistulae ad Atticum* IX, 9.4; see, however, *ERW*, 149.

13. Cf. the Pompeian wall-graffito recording the living-expenses of a small household over several days (*CIL* IV, 5380 – victuals and a few replacements such as a lamp; only two exceed a denarius. S. Mrozek, *Prix et rémunération dans l'Occident romain* (1975), 32 and *passim*, puts the daily cost of living in Pompeii at 8 asses on average. Much depended on the costs of transport (on which see Pekáry, *loc. cit.* n. 11), and a decorated Samian bowl by Cinnamus of Lezoux might be expensive at *Flavia Solva*, in distant Noricum: a graffito on the base-ring states, *Panna Verecundaes empta viges(sis)*, 'The pan of Verecunda, bought for 20 asses' (R. Noll. G 1972, 148–52).

14. The relationship of 16 asses to the denarius varied locally and with the passage of time; cf. S. Mrozek, *DR* I, 79–86. *Nummularii*, R. Herzog, *RE* XVII, 1415–55; cf. Crawford, *loc. cit.* n. 11, 44, n. 37. Town employee, *CIL* iii, 4035 (*Virunum*, in *Pannonia Superior*, A.D. 207). See further on banking and *nummularii*, *RE* (Suppl.) IV, 68–82; O. Schlippschuh, *Die Händler im röm. Kaiserreich in Gallien, Germanien* . . . (1974), 78–85; J. Andreau, *La vie financière dans le monde romain*, (Ec. franç de Rome, 1987).

15. Brought in a sealed bag (Apuleius, *Metamorphoses* X, 9); re-sealed, cf. Cicero, *In Verrem* II, 3.181, concerning deductions (apparently unnecessarily made) *pro spectatione et collybo, deinde pro* . . . *cerario* 'for examination and the agio, then for sealing'.

16. Herzog in *RE* has a list of the bone or ivory labels, ending in AD 88, nearly all Italian, cf. Crawford, n. 11, 44–5; Parchment, from Egypt, Herzog, *Aus der Geschichte des Bankwesens im Altertum* (1919), 33, AD 80. Presumably parchment labels entirely supplanted the bone or ivory tickets about that time. See Daremberg and Saglio, *Dictionnaire des Antiquités* fig. 495, for a banking-scene in a gold-glass, with bags of coin marked CCLV and CCCXX. This reappears in a general article on such representations by S. Karwiese, *Jahresheft des*

österreichischen archäologischen Institutes in Wien, L, Hauptblatt (1972–3), 281–95.

17. Suetonius, *Divus Augustus* 4 (*manibus collybo decoloratis . . . mensarius*). – Cloth, cf. a fragment of Suetonius (*Reliquiae*, ed. A. Reifferscheid (1860), 133, 3), but the *myrtei panni* or dark-green cloths mentioned in connexion with '*qui nummularium discunt*' can hardly have been limited to the use of apprentices. Cf. R. Bogaert, *AS* 1973, 268, 246–7 .n. 50. Clement of Alexandria, *Stromata* II, 15 uses the words *gnōrimos trapezitou*, 'banker's disciple', which gives a more correct impression of 'assistant'; the Roman army, too, used the expression *discens* to describe 'assistant' to various grades. – Portrait, Fronto, *Correspondence* I, 206 (Loeb). Counters are depicted in the accounting scenes assembled by M. Renard, *Le Pays Gaumais* 20ᵉ. Année (1959), 7–45, and also in Espérandieu, *Recueil général, passim*.

18. When Galba was Governor of Hispania Tarraconensis he had the defaulter's hands cut off and nailed to the counter (Suetonius, *Galba*, 9).

19. Cupellation or the fire-test was a matter for the mints. Archimedes' Principle is of doubtful application at this period, cf. W. A. Oddy, *Endeavour* 1986, 164–6. Lenses are a disputed subject: *pro*, R. J. Forbes, *Stud. in Ancient Technology* (1957), 186–7. Touchstone, perhaps likely in difficult cases, Oddy, *ibid.*, and below, n. 47. Magnet, useful for telling coins plated on iron cores, known (in the form of the natural stone, *magnes*), cf. F. M. Feldhaus, *Die Technik* (1914) 672–3, citing G. A. Palm, whose 52 authorities lack even a single indication that *magnes* was ever used to this end, though a party-piece (e.g. Augustine, *De Civitate Dei*, XXI, 4 *ad finem*) was to make a piece of iron move about in a silver dish in response to the movement of a piece of *magnes* underneath (I am grateful to my son Timothy Boon for identifying and locating a copy of Palm's *Maulbronn Seminar* paper of 1867).

20. Cf. Arrian, *Discourses of Epictetus* I, 20 (Loeb); Jerome, *PL* XXVI, 524; cf. R. Bogaert, *loc. cit.* n. 17, 250–1. As to smell, cf. Plautus, *Mostellaria* 267–9: 'Take the towel and wash your hands:' – 'Why, pray?' – 'As you have been holding the mirror, I fear your hands may smell of its silver. Never let Philolaches suspect you of having accepted money!' Herzog (*RE* XVII, 1418–19) says on good authority that the great antiquary, Friedländer, reckoned to tell false coins (in collections) by their odour. We forget that ancient coins have been cleansed for us by centuries' burial; in use they may have smelt abominably. No wonder *moneta nova* was desirable (cf. Martial, IV, 28.5).

21. Petronius, *Saturae*, 56.

22. D. G. Sellwood, presidential address (*NC* 1981, p. vii, pl. 38,9) illustrates a Republican denarius, the plated skin of which was not pierced by even a bold chisel-cut, a fact which he attributed to the excellent technique of soldering involved.

23. See, on the character of the coins bearing marks, especially M. Thirion, *Le trésor de Liberchies* (1972), 62–9. Premium (*aspratura*) for sharp coins, cf. *Thesaurus Linguae Latinae* II, 846. In the fourth century (*CTh*. IX, 22.1) it was laid down that all solidi had to be accepted at the same value 'although

they may differ in size' (*quamquam diversa formae mensura sit*) – a reminder, perhaps. The marking of coins died out towards the end of the first century, and is rare after Tiberius; debasement by Nero, finally by Trajan, has been suggested as an explanation; but marks occur freely on Antony's legionary denarii, certainly as base as Trajan's (five out of nine legionary denarii in the Silchester hoard of 1894, *NC* 1960, 242 have them); and gold was not debased, though it was reduced in weight (cf. C. Morrisson *et al.*, *L'Or monnayé* I (Cah. Ernest-Babelon 2, 1985), 81 and table IV. Therefore the marks should denote the best coins available on any occasion in terms of weight and fineness. It is worth remembering that the 'remedy' (or allowance of weight and fineness) in the English silver coinage was 2 dwt in the lb in respect of either – 1:120 – as late as 1817, when it was reduced to 1 dwt. Merchants and goldsmiths used to cull out the heavier coins, for they were struck so-many to the pound, not individually, and by so debilitating the currency caused great difficulty. The Roman mint cannot have worked to stricter limits than these. Bad coins were demonetized by chisel-cut, cf. G. F. Hill in J. P. Bushe-Fox, *Hengistbury Head* (1915), 71, for 'unusually suspicious' inhabitants who inflicted severe damage on coins.

24. G. C. Boon, *NC* 1978, 178–80. Cf. J.-B. Giard, *RN* 1968, pl. XI, 1648; 1970, pl. I, 4; pl. IX, 223; pl. X, 254 for A, Z, C, D; *in litt.* M. Giard, referring to coins of Claudius and Nero, said he had seen 'beaucoup imprimées de cette façon, E, I, S etc. mais jamais R.' R, however, does occur, but on a halved Nîmes As which he published in *RN* 1967, no. 64, pl. XV. RE occurs on Lyons asses (*BNC Auguste*, 223, as if for *Re(cognitus)*), but R need not have that significance. Other such marks, on a moneyer's As and a Lyons 'altar' As, see *MV*, 75 no. 924, 95 no. 2237. The B on a Claudian copy from Lincoln, mentioned but not illustrated by G. F. Hill in *NC* 1921, 314 is of the same incuse character, as Mr. Robert Kenyon confirmed.

25. Other *aes* with peck-marks J.-B. Giard, *RN* 1967, 121, pls. XIII-XIX *passim*, Nîmes and Lyons asses etc.; many others were battered. I know of no examples of Nîmes which were plated; but this is an indication that they existed. Pecking sometimes, but rarely, appears on Roman silver; I have not seen it on gold, but it may well occur. It is very similar to the widely-prevalent pecking of Anglo-Saxon pennies in Scandinavian finds.

26. W. A. Seaby, *NC*, 169. He calls the battering 'modern', but in the light of the parallels its ancient character is quite certain (cf. last note). An obverse die-duplicate (with reverse OB CIVES SERVATOS, not as here, SPES AUGUSTA), was offered in *NCirc* Oct. 1987, no. 5674, from 'Wiltshire', and was bought by Devizes Museum.

27. *Sententiae receptae a Paulo* V, 25.1; cf. Arrian, *Discourses of Epictetus* III, 3.3. (Loeb).

28. The notion that the PROB mark was British was MacDowall's (cited by Kraay, *Essays/Mattingly* 130, n. 2). I am grateful to Mr. Kenyon for information as to the PROB sestertii in Britain; see his account in *NC* 1988 forthcoming of which he obliged me with a proof; but our views differ. Tiber finds, H.-M. von Kaenel, *Bolletino di Numismatica* II/III (1984), 101–3. A consignment of Claudian *aes*, apparently straight from the mint, was found in an amphora near

Tarragona, perhaps intended for the *stipendia* of the legion at Léon (H.-M. von Kaenel, M. Campo and J. -C. Richard, *El tesoro de la Pobla de Mafumet* (1981)). There were no countermarked pieces in what is preserved of the find.

29. Cf. von Kaenel, *loc. cit.* n. 28.

30. Cf. Kraay, *Essays/Mattingly*, 131, and note the coin shown *ibid.*, pl. VI, 8. The DVP mark is there far fresher than the others, but that is not the impression gained from our piece. – Temper of soldiery, cf. Tacitus, *Annales* I, 17; 35.

31. M. Crawford remarks (*JRS* 1970, 47 n. 77) that 'the notion of Roman Imperial countermarks systematically validating the coins to which they were applied seems misplaced', but does not explain why; probably because only a proportion of the coins was so marked. C. H. V. Sutherland, in *RHC*, 44, suggests that Tiberian countermarks on worn *aes* did validate it for use 'until fresh supplies could be struck', but that they might equally reflect Tiberius' desire to emphasize his position and authority as the new *Imperator*. He draws attention to the 'intensity' of countermarking at that period, 'never seen before or afterwards'.

32. Cassius Dio, LXIV, 6.

33. It is uncommon in the Flavian forts of Wales: e.g. at Caerleon fortress, down to 1980, there are recorded five pre-Claudian, thirteen Claudian, eight Neronian, three Galban/Vitellian, and 115 of Vespasian, all *aes*; at Brecon Gaer, one of Caligula, one of Claudius, none of Nero, four of Vespasian, all *aes*; Caernarvon, one of Nero, twenty of Vespasian; at Holt, one of Claudius, none of Nero, seven of Vespasian. In the civil districts the coinage of Nero appears to have circulated more freely, e.g. at Silchester there were on record (to 1986) twenty-five *aes* to 112 Claudian, of which latter seventeen were orthodox. The coinage in general, especially the *aes*, was introduced *via* the military pay; it is the military picture, therefore, that is important. The various alterations to coins described are in themselves an indication of demonetization. Cf. Arrian, *Discourses of Epictetus* IV, 5.17, for a *tetrassaron* (sestertius) of Nero described as obsolete (literally, 'rotten' – *sapron*), unlike one of Trajan. See also n. 102 below.

34. Probably from 69 to 71, before Vespasian's own coinage began to pour from the mints; cf. J.-B. Giard, in *Actes du 8ᵉ Congrès internat. de Numismatique 1973* (1976), 284. In Gaul it appears that no hindrance was imposed on the circulation of Neronian aes, either orthodox or (cf. his pl. 32, 28), imitative; indeed, imitative Neronian *aes* seem virtually confined in production to the border region of the Suessiones and Remi, and is not much found elsewhere: isolated British examples are mentioned by Sutherland (*CCRB*, 13), but I have not found the Silchester specimen to which he alludes; there is one from Prof. Fulford's new excavations. One is shown by C. E. King in *CHRB* in (1986), 20, no. 9 (6.6 g), in what cannot have been a single hoard, from the Thames at Kempsford (Glos.). Some silver was also countermarked IMPVES (*BMCRE*, II, p. XVII), very worn, some Republican: so a case of validation.

35. *NCirc.* 1974, 11. Cf. V. Zedelius, 'Nero Calvus?' ('Bald Nero?'), *Berichte aus der Arbeit* (Rhein. Landesmus. Bonn) 1979, 2, 20–2. Zedelius mentions a paral-

lel to the crown cut on **6**, from a site in the Netherlands; the crown came to be the mark of the dupondius in Flavian times, so the motive is plain, namely to double, hopefully, the value of the coin; R. A. G. Carson (*NC 1955*, 230–1) refers to an 'antoninianus' of Alexander – who issued no such coin – from the Mattishall hoard (and therefore an ancient forgery, not a modern one, and such are known), made by carefully cutting a crown on a good broad denarius. Another at Cardiff is very well done, but without provenance.

36. *CA*, 16 no. 37. Another was found at Wroxeter (*Wroxeter 1913*, 57 no. 10) and a third at Fishbourne (R. Reece in B. W. Cunliffe, *Fishbourne Report* (1971) II, 93, under 2a). The similar mark PR occurred at Richborough (*Richborough Report* IV (1949), 284, no. 22520).

37. This is one of the most important results of Kraay's study on 'the behaviour of early imperial countermarks' in *Essays/Mattingly*, 113–36; note his figs. 5–6. Note, too, D. W. MacDowall on the Pannonian mark (*NC 1960*, 103–12): GALBA across the head of Nero (in Greek letters); VTE for Vitellius is recorded in *BMCRE* I, p. XXXVII.

38. C. J. Howgego, *Greek Imperial Countermarks* (1985), 17–20. Though the Rhenish legions did not apply countermarks, *Legio VI Victrix* did so in Spain and *Legio X Gemina* both in Spain and Pannonia (*ibid.*), though one suspects only because of the commotions of 68–9. *Bucranium* countermarks on Trajanic asses are known from Richborough, Bath, Coventina's Well, and the bed of the Mayenne in Gaul (*ibid.*, 294 no. 160), brought back by returning soldiers from Trajan's last campaign. The Richborough piece is listed wrongly by R. Reece in *BIAL* XVII (1981), 57.

39. The Caerleon piece is *NC 1965*, pl. 16, 17. The Lydney piece is the 7th down, in W. H. Bathurst and C. W. King, *Roman Remains at Lydney Park, Glos.* (1879), 80.

40. *NC 1965*, 163: Cu 67.1, Sn 11.1, Zn 0.1, Pb 19.1 per cent.

41. These analyses were carried out in 1987 by Dr. J. P. Northover for the purposes of this paper. The alloy might be described as 'speculum metal'. At Edington (Somerset) a lump of metal 'principally tin' is reported, and the same stated to be the alloy of a coin still lodged in the mould (J. Poole, *A.* XIV (1803), 102). Base metal was also employed at Lyons (*ibid.*), and at Carnuntum the alloy was said to be 'silver-like' (G. Elmer, *NZ* 1933, 58). A small forger's hoard from the Isle of Wight (R. Bland and M. Cowell, *CHRB* VI (1986), 31–4) was composed, apart from an as of Domitian, of fifteen casts of denarii running down to the 170s, made of a tin-lead alloy, with a golden coating on one which recalls the false gilding, above n. 8. Another find is that of pure tin denarii, with two original coins, from the well at Bar Hill fort on the Antonine Wall (G. Macdonald, *NC* 1905, 10–17). Another base hoard from London is published by J. Hall (*CHRB* VI, 57–8). The Whitchurch moulds, on the contrary, seem to have been contaminated with silver; but a mould for an As of Hadrian (57) also gave that result, which is therefore anomalous; perhaps it is derived from contact with the dross arising from cupellation of silver in orthodox coins (*AJ* 1966, 44–6).

42. Note in particular the careful and interesting distinction drawn between various categories of cast counterfeit in the *Cunetio* hoard (*CT*, 165–7, pl. 40): 'with traces of silver coating . . . thick silver or tin coating . . . base white-metal coating . . . no apparent coating.' Contrast pls. 32–39, struck counterfeits.

43. The figure is from G. Behrens, *Mainzer Zeitschrift* XV-XVI (1920–1), 25–31, Abb. 1–3, modified. Note the Damery feeder with 12 stubs corresponding to the 12 coins in each rouleau. In August 1976, Dr. G. J. Dawson (*in litt.*) pointed out that the Whitchurch moulds (*AJ* 1966, 13–51) may also have been cast in rouleaux of a dozen: 'in any rouleau there will be two single-faced moulds at the ends and *x* double-faced between them. If therefore one divided half the number of single-faced moulds into the number of double-faced, and added one, that would be the number of coins in a rouleau, assuming that the sample of moulds is representative and the rouleaux standard: there are 17 singles and 93 doubles tabulated; dividing 93 by 8.5 gives 10.94, say 11, and adding one gives 12.' On the same basis, the 302 singles and 1,134 doubles of the Pachten, Saarland, find (M. R. -Alföldi, *G* 1974, 440, table) yield 7.5+1, say eight or nine per rouleau.

44. Gilding without gold, n. 8. Quotation, M. Crawford in dealing with a Dacian hoard, *SCN* VII (1983), 57.

45. P.-H. Mitard, *RN* 1963, 116–18, pl. XIIa–e.

46. R. E. M. and T. V. Wheeler, *Verulamium Report* (1936), 222, fig. 49, but not there identified as false; and from 'South Humberside', Bonham's sale 14–15 Sept. 1981, lot 391 (a ref. from E.M. Besly).

47. Mr. E. M. Besly pointed out this pair of coins in the Bassaleg hoard (n. 4 above); analysis by J. P. Northover. It was in the third century that men became especially sensitive to the silver content, betraying thus a capacity to distinguish on the basis of streak or other tests, even when the surface was blanched by the use of tartaric acid (as in the Royal Mint with sterling silver): note the greater proportion of the slightly richer Cologne coins of the Joint Reign of Valerian and Gallienus in hoards, as opposed to site finds, compared with issues of Rome mint (J. Lallemand, *Mél. Lafaurie*, 118, cf. 119). Overvaluation, cf. D. R. Walker, *Metrology of the Roman Silver Coinage* III (BAR Suppl. Ser. 40, 1978), 139.

48. G. C. Boon, *Monmouthshire Antiquary* II (1965–8), 52–3, 119; Wroxeter, coin kindly notified by Mr. Robert Kenyon, whose colleague Mr. K. Butcher saw it in the collections of Rowley's House Museum, Shrewsbury; Chichester, kindly notified by Dr. J. P. Goddard who published it in *NCirc.* 1984, 76. Camarthen, Dyfed Arch. Trust excavations, shown N.M.W. 1988; duplicate of our Pl. II, 25.

49. *CA*, 125, pl. IV, 77–78. It was P. J. Seaby who noticed the obverse link between the aureus in Paris, from the RSR mint, and another Little Orme coin (*CA*, 125, pl. IV, 72–73) with *Moneta* reverse; unfortunately the findspot of the gold coin is unrecorded (cf. Shiel, *Carausius*, 146, no. 5).

50. L. H. Cope, *Metallurgia* 1967, 15–20. Max von Bahrfeldt estimated that the plating usually accounted for a ninth part of the weight of a coin (cited by M. Crawford, *RRC* I, 560).

51. *Ibid.*, 581. According to Tacitus, however, the ancient Germans preferred old coins, '*serrati, bigati*' (*Germania*, 5). L. A. Lawrence, *NC* 1940, 190–1, reports a Royal Mint experiment in plating serrated blanks with silver granules.

52. Lawrence, *ibid.*, 192. Another list of 240 down to 48 BC, P. P. Serafin, *AIIN* 1968, 9–30; *ibid.* 11 for the suggested total of plated pieces. Her dating, however, needs bringing into line with Crawford's. For the total of denarii in circulation, cf. K. Hopkins, *JRS* 1980, 109, fig. 2 for a histogram to compare with Serafin's. The nuisance of plated denarii continued under Augustus and Tiberius, when some 30 per cent of those in circulation may have been false, in the estimation of C. Rodewalt, *Money in the Age of Tiberius* (1976), 80. Part of a large Vespasianic hoard of plated coins, perhaps made under Trajan, is published by I. Carradice, *NCirc.* 1980, 306–7; M. Curry had listed others *ibid.* 1973, 335.

53. M. Crawford, initially in *NC* 1968, 55–9, revised in *RRC* 560–5 with better photographs.

54. J.-B. Giard has claimed that in some cases the dies used for orthodox and plated material were 'rigoureusement les mêmes' (*BNCAuguste*, 22). Theft from the mint is the best explanation of that fact. Misuse of dies is envisaged for a somewhat later date by Ulpian, cited in *Digest* XLVIII, 13.8. Since the *nummularii* had the official task of 'spotting the copper through the silver' (n. 21), it would have been absurd to have introduced plated coins officially. Mommsen (*RM*, 386–7) accepted plated coins as a fiduciary element in the currency, perhaps under the influence of his everyday experience with the fiduciary coinage of German states, the *Scheidemünzen* (literally 'sheathed', i.e. plated): though by his time the issues were of copper without plating, a coat had earlier been applied, and survives on 18th-19th century pieces.

55. L. A. Lawrence, *NC* 1940, 185–9. Bronze or copper and also iron cores, plainly, upon inspection. Crawford in *RRC* and also *Coinage and Money under the Roman Republic* (1985), 189–90, cannot believe that coins could be made with an iron core: 'iron and silver are virtually immiscible' (the reference is to Pliny's remark that Antony *miscuit denario ferrum, Nat. Hist.* XXXIII, 132). But the plating was accomplished, as it must have been with bronze counterfeits with iron cores, by filing bright the cores and hot-dipping. It seems likely that Pliny had seen an example of Antony's denarii falsified in this way, and drew a general conclusion; cf. J. Pinkerton, *Essay on Medals* (1784) I, 43, 'I have seen, and tried, a denarius of Antony LEG.VI which flies to the magnet like iron'.
     Another hoard, with poor silver or subaerate Republican (14) and one Vespasianic denarii, to prove late imitation of the former, M. Chiṭescu, *SCN* IV (1968), 127–37, Bozieni, Moldova.

56. I am grateful to Dr. A. Burnett for the photographs.

57. R. A. Brown, *NC* 1981, 145–6. I am obliged to Mr. Brown for lending me his negative. Other techniques, cf. W. A. Campbell, *Greek and Roman Plated Coins* (*NNM* 57, 1933). The very thin plating of late Roman times is mentioned below, n. 60.

58. Cf. n. 23 *ad finem*.

59. The technique is explained (with particular reference to medieval examples) by W. A. Oddy and M. M. Archibald in *Sci. Stud. in Num.* (BM Occas. Ppr. 18, 1980), 81–90. The Silchester specimen, published here by kind permission of Prof. Michael Fulford, occurred with much evidence of contemporary metal-working in the Basilica. Another example, from Kenchester, bears the impression of a denarius of Titus, but has no channel for the molten metal. Another, from Lydney, is badly damaged but seem to have been for antoniniani of Postumus rather than the fourth-century coin suggested by Collingwood (in *Lydney Report* (1932), 101 no. 5, cf. fig. 28). A channel is evident. The strip of lead had earlier been used to carry a magical alphabet. Not all imprints of coins on lead, however, are connected with counterfeiting. A lead backing was necessary to make re-poussé ornaments in bronze from coins (*inter alia*); and an unpublished scrap of bronze at Lydney carries an obverse impression of a majorina of Constans, within a hand-raised dotted border. Impressions of coins of Numerian, Constantine I and Crispus are reported from Woodeaton temple-site (J. R. Kirk, *Oxoniensia* XIV (1951), 44). These imprints were used to decorate caskets, and in regalia, etc.

60. Plating of late coins, cf. E. S. Hedges and D. A. Robins, *NC* 1963, 237–40; L. H. Cope, *NC* 1968, 144. *Idem*, in *Methods of Scientific Examination of Ancient Coinage* (1972), 261–78, suggests that molten silver chloride might have been used; C. E. King and R. E. M. Hedges, *Archaeometry* XVI (1974), 195–8. Cf. also P. le Gentilhomme, *RN* 1942, 165–6 and P. Bastien, *Le Monnayage de Magnence* (1983), 75–7, for tin coatings.

61. *Gallia* 1972, 428–9, fig. 17.

62. H. Cüppers, *Trierer Zeitschrift* 1968, 217–18, Abb. 5.

63. Antoninus Pius (*NC* 1965, 173, Caerleon; *BSFN* 1981, 158–9, Bapaume); Faustina I (*NC* 1985, 233, Colchester); Alexander (*NC* 1971, 183–4, Gare hoard, Cornwall); cf. M. Thirion, *BCEN* 1975, 41–4, 64–5. Postumus, a lead mould (*BSFN* 1981, 105). First-century examples seem lacking.

64. Augustus (*BNCAuguste*, 23); Claudius and Nero (*RN* 1968, 116, 126–7, *JS* 1975, the latter, same obv. as two overstruck on asses of Caligula): Claudius again, sharing an obv. die with a coin of solid copper from Richborough (55) and Colchester – I thank Mr. Robert Kenyon, who supplied the negative; then Antonine and third-century Lucilla (*BSFN* 1970, 509, our **16**, with thanks to M. P.-H. Mitard for the photograph); Commodus and Severus (*NZ* 1933, 67, *Carnuntum*); Commodus (*DR* I, facing 106, no. 3, Britain); Gordian III (*NC* 1965, 173 = 1951, 32, Silchester); and Postumus (*BCEN* 1976, 30–2, but the same die was *not* used, as suggested, to strike coins in solid metal: the slightly reduced dimensions indicate a cast die, cf. p. 108 and n. 45.

65. S. Bolin, *State and Currency in the Roman Empire to* AD 300 (1958), 303, n. 6. It has been suggested (E. Lo Cascio, *JRS* 1981, 79) that the debasement of the silver coinage in the first and second centuries may have arisen from the appearance of vast quantities of gold coins struck from captured metal (e.g. the gold of Dacia under Trajan): gold becoming commoner, silver rose in relative value, and the denarius needed to be issued less fine to keep the bimetallism in

balance. This operation would have had its effect on the *aes*-silver coin relationship and therefore on the activities of counterfeiters.

66. 'Trays' of offcuts, turnings and droplets, S. S. Frere, *Verulamium Excav.* I (1972), 18; likewise at Silchester, 1961, unpublished. Statue-fragments were also carefully collected and stored, whether from *damnatio memoriae* ceremonies or other sources, and stored at legionary (also auxiliary) headquarters (T. Sarnowski, *G* 1985, 521–40; cf. my *Legionary Fortress of Caerleon-Isca, a Brief Guide* (1987), 43.

67. *RIB* no. 274. The statuette was kindly weighed by Miss C. M. Johns of the British Museum and turns the scale at 1642.6 grammes or 5 *librae*, including the base, which seems to be of the same metal though separately cast. It is curious that the given bronze should have been priced in denarii and the finished object in sestertii. I used to think that this variety of reference might mean that goods priced in one unit had to be paid for in that unit, but that does not seem to be the case, cf. n. 13.

68. J.-B. Giard, *JS* 1969, pl. II, 22 (Le Petit-Couronne hoard); similar but coarser, P. Le Gentilhomme, *RN* 1942, pl. VIII, 29–30 (La Vineuse hoard); quartered, Boon *PUBSS* XIII.1 (1972), 70–80, *DR* I, 104–5.

69. T. V. Wheeler in R. E. M. and T. V. Wheeler, *Lydney Report* (1932), 116–31. Our fig. 6 is based on a card exhibited at Lydney Park; the central circle shows a modern 2p piece instead of the one-inch halfpenny used originally for comparison. The circles containing the Class E and F minims represent the 18 mm module of the 'falling horseman' of *c.* 354.

70. G. C. Boon, in G. J. Wainwright, *Coygan Camp* (Cambrian Arch. Assn., 1967). 119–20, 124, Group E.

71. D. Nash, *Essays/Sutherland*, 24–7, J. -B. Giard draws attention to a late coinage of the Bellovaci imitating the Lyon 'altar' coinage at reduced module, the crude obverse die known for another reverse showing a bird (*QT* 1985, 238, tav. 1, 1); cf. also S. Scheers, *Traité de Numismatique celtique* II (1977), 806–8, nos. 722–36. The *locus classicus* is E. Ritterling, *Hofheim* (1913), 98–117, table at 112; cf. H. Chantraine, *Novaesium* III (1968). On the production and use of certain Gaulish coins for the *stipendia* of auxiliary troops, cf. A. Furger-Gunti, *AK* 1981, 231–46. M. Crawford has commented on the scarcity of the smallest denominations in the west, cf. *JRS* 1970, 44–5; and this is how it was made good.

72. For these see *MV* 24–5: in general, T. V. Buttrey, *American Journ. of Archaeology* 1972, 31–48. Only very occasional quartered or thirded early *aes* coins appear in Britain: one at Usk, two at Silchester. It is believed that the cutting of Republican, Nîmes and Lyons asses may have arisen from a retariffing as dupondii: cf. now H. M. Crawford, *Coinage and Money under the Roman Republic* (1985), 261.

73. 8.7 down to 5.1 grammes in a case noted by Giard (*RN* 1968, 115, nos. 1669–70); in the Puy-de-Dôme hoard, imitations of Lyons asses ranged, over five examples, from 6.43 down to 3.62 grammes, and of Nero's Victory asses

from 8.0 down to 4.66 grammes (*RN* 1964, 151–7). The Worcester hoard of Claudian copies consisted of ten coins, 9.46 down to 4.7 grammes. (Sutherland, *NC* 1963, 57–9); Hoard B at Usk was composed of five dupondii 11.98 down to 9.85 grammes, and two asses, 7.96 and 4.29 grammes (Boon, *Usk*, 16).

74. Cf. n. 33.

75. Carinus appears to have been engaged in successful operations *sub Arcto felici* – 'neath blessed northern skies' – according to Nemesian, *Cynegeticon* 69–70, but this seems an unduly exaggerated reference to the suppression of counterfeiting activity, if reference it is; however, extirpating false-moneyers may have been part of wider activities which in some measure presumably justified the title of *Britannicus Maximus* which he enjoyed, and shared with his brother, Numerian (*CIL* XIV, 126).

76. It would be tedious to trace the development of this myth in any detail, even though it became almost an article of faith. As early as 1872, Thomas Wright (*Uriconium*, 337–8, with woodcuts, our fig. 7) was assuming that radiate minims with barbarous reverses which he identified as copied from fourth-century types, *Gloria Exercitus* and *Gloria Romanorum*, belonged to the period after the Roman occupation and before the coming of the Saxons. The identifications are fanciful, needless to add; scarcely less so are coins such as *CCRB* pl. XIV, 13–14, or our **164** *Gloria Romanorum* (of Valentinianic date) with radiate obverses. When eventually we arrive at 'sceatta-like imitations' the final contact with archaeological reality has been lost (e.g. *ibid.* 107 and n. 1). For the theory of a sub-Roman coinage persisting until the 6th century, see P. V. Hill, *Barbarous Radiates* (NNM 40, 1949), and *idem*, *NC* 1951, 91–108. As late as 1973 C. H. V. Sutherland was fighting a rearguard action, in maintaining that 'ageing copper supplemented by poor, small copies of former Roman issues' circulated down to 450 (*English Coinage*, 2). See further, p. 140, regarding the 'fifth-century' Lydney dating, and n. 241. Where a base-metal currency could survive, it did, as in N. Africa: cf. the Ain Kelba hoard, Algeria, C. Morrisson, *Mél. Lafaurie*, 239–48: of some 1,200 pieces in a pot ending in the 520s, but going back to a few late third and fourth-century material, as well as a few Punic.

77. See note 158.

78. G. C. Boon, *NC* 1961, 191–7.

79. B. H. St. J. O'Neil, *AJ* 1945, 50: 'numismatists must be prepared in future to find that minimissimi were also current by 367 and are by no means proof of a fifth-century date' (this was in connexion with finds at the Park Street villa near St. Albans). Cf. J. P. C. Kent, 'Barbarous copies of Roman coins,' in *Limes-Studien* (Vorträge des 3. internationalen Limes-Kongresses 1957 (1959)), 61–8. Brean Down, G. C. Boon, *NC* 1961, 191–7; *idem*, *PUBSS* X. 3 (1965), 232–48.

80. It is interesting to record that O'Neil, a practised excavator, good archaeologist and competent numismatist was, despite his pronouncement quoted in n. 79, compelled by the force of the myth to posit, in the case of finds at Canterbury, a wooden floor in the bath-house concerned, which allowed small Constantinian coins and minimissimi (down to 1½ mm) to fall through cracks, also a single

Theodosian coin, but not the 'relatively large' Valentinianic pieces (*NC* 1948, 226–9). He nevertheless observed that it was 'futile to search for evidence of currency among dwellers in a Dark Age, who had no use for it', though admitting at the same time that minimissimi may have been current *c.* 410–40. Cf. C. H. V. Sutherland's observations on the Canterbury find (*NC* 1949, 242–4). The fancies of numismatists conjured up a 'metal shortage' which was devoutly believed by archaeologists as well; the argument was a perfectly circular one (cf. H. Mattingly and W. P. Stebbing, *NC* 1939, 119, 'the suggestion of an age of extreme poverty, in which the barest scraps and strays of metal were jealously treasured') though every Roman site is prolific of scrap bronze even today. The Romans did indeed save offcuts and scraps were indeed saved, cf. n. 66; but throughout the period of the occupation, and as a matter of course. The 'fancies' are very different from the matter-of-fact approach of later years, e.g. R. Reece in the *Richborough Report* V (1968), 191, where he remarks of the celebrated 'radiate hoard' (*NNM* 80 (1938)) that 'the late dating has . . . been mainly on stylistic grounds and cannot now be held to have any secure external confirmation', and of the equally celebrated 'diademmed hoard', 'to put the hoard in the fifth century makes the hoarder a highly discriminating eccentric who had taken a dislike to the prolific issues of the houses of Valentinian and Theodosius'.

81. *JS* 1975, 85 (obv. die used for two Minerva overstrikes on Caligulan asses and for the plated 'Constantia' piece from Condé-sur-Aisne).

82. *RBI*, 23–4; cf. *CCRB*, 13. On 'semi-official' copies, cf. C. E. King, who classifying the 'unmarked' coins of Carausius observed (*BNJ* 1984, 2) that 'in theory this is a category which should not exist, since in effect its creation is an admission that the criteria by which genuine pieces are distinguished from ancient copies are not sufficiently rigorous' (*ibid.*, 2).

83. For these finds cf. J.-B. Giard, *RN* 1968, 76–7; *idem*, on the Montereau discoveries, *Bull. du Groupement archéol. de Seine-et-Marne* 18/19 (1977–8), 68–9. For river-finds in Britain cf. e.g. my own note on those from the Thames in Reading Museum, *Oxoniensia* XIX (1954), 38–9 – *aes* collections (1) Claudian copies down to Aurelius, Whitchurch Weir pool; (2) . . . Flavian, with two brooches . . . Goring; (3) Claudian copy down to Hadrian, Mapledurham; and (4) Tiberius down to Hadrian, sestertii, Caversham bridge. Another deposit (Claudius-Victorinus) from a tributary of the Thames, the Bulbourne, at Bourne End, A. Burnett. *Coin Hoards* III (1977), 77–8; another, Thames at Kempsford, is cited n. 34 above. This list is random.

84. J.-B. Giard, *RN* 1970, 51–6; *JS* 1975, 94 for die-links; below, p. 121. The Civil War coinages 'in mints moving with' the principal contestants are exceptions to prove the rule.

85. *Immunes*, cf. Tarruntenus Paternus' extensive list in *D* 1, 6.7 (conveniently, G. R. Watson, *The Roman Soldier* (1969), 181, n. 178): '*hi omnes inter immunes habentur*' seems to exclude a complete total. An attempt to show from Livy XXIII, 48 that the army in Spain was ready to strike its own coin in 215 BC does violence to the historian's meaning (cf. *NC* 1986, 83); and the instrument ('hub') on which the note is based is false in any case (Prof. Crawford, *in litt.* 5 Nov. 1987).

158   Coins and the archaeologist

86. Tacitus, *Historiae* IV, 74.

87. J. Marquardt, *Römische Staatsverwaltung* (1876) II, 303. Coins countermarked by the fisc, cf. M. Grant, *From Imperium to Auctoritas* (1946), 95.

88. E. Wightman, *Gallia Belgica* (1985), 61–3.

89. By A. D. 60, on the basis of *RIB*, 12; cf., neatly, R. P. Wright, *B*, 1984, 257–8.

90. R. S. O. Tomlin, *B* 1986, 450–2. Cf. R. W. Davies, *Historia* XVI (1967), 115–18, for *opinio* and *ratio*. Cf. for further detail, *ERW*, 151 n. 65.

91. FTAV, *Fisci Tiberii Augusti* (?), three others known, including one from Vindonissa, see my note in *MA* ii, 4 (1968–9), 176–7, and J.-B. Giard, *BNCAuguste*, 38.

92. Sir J. Craig, *The Mint* (1953), 193.

93. *Ibid.*, 253.

94. H. W. Dickinson, *Matthew Boulton* (1936), 138–9. A few examples are illustrated, *NC* 1986, pl. 23. It is worth remark that many of these counterfeits are utterly barbarous (though some are of excellent style – as in the Roman series). That they became lightweight but never sank to a very small size is due to the existence of a lower denomination, the farthing; though that was less imitated.

95. L. Feller, *Faux-monnayeurs et fausses monnaies en France à la fin du moyen age* (1986), ch. XI esp. p. 177: '. . . une marchandise dont la circulation et la diffusion ont suivi les mêmes routes, atteint les mêmes régions qu' irriguait le commerce international . . . *une donnée structurelle de l'économie, malgré les efforts de répression* . . . On avait trop besoin d'espèces pour examiner de près leur exacte provenance . . . même si la circulation . . . n'a pu que demeurer finalement marginale' (my italics).

96. H. Zehnacker, *RIN* 1983, 115–15, shows that the army ceased to be paid in silver from 29/28 BC when the great emissions of *aes* began for the first time since Sulla. Thus, a quarter of known Vesta asses of Caligula come from Vindonissa alone (R. Martini, *RIN* 1980, 64). Cf. also M. Crawford, *ANRW* II.2 (1975), 654; Howgego, *op. cit.* n. 38, 20–1. The issue of a sestertius to commemorate Domitian's award of a fourth *stipendium* in 84 (C. M. Kraay, *MN* IX (1960), 114–16) – only one example survives, though curiously enough the imprint of the obverse of another, on a fragment of glass, is also known (*BSFN* 1986, 33–5; both in Paris) tends to show pay at the date was in *aes*. But it is necessary here to think specifically in terms of the *free or nett pay*: the gross sum would surely, for ease of transport, have been consigned in aurei or denarii or both. Suetonius, indeed, refers (*Domit.*, 7) to the *quartum stipendium* as *aurei terni*, three gold pieces a man. That gold did circulate among legionaries is shown, e.g. by the Caerleon (Myrtle Cottage) hoard of five aurei down to AD 74 (my *Brief Guide* (1987), 27, including the present 1; *AC* 1940, 106, 123–4), and other finds such as the famous Thorngrafton Quarry arm-purse with its three aurei and sixty denarii down to Hadrian (J. C. Bruce, *The Roman Wall*

(1867 ed.), 417–26). The *viaticum* on joining the army was expressed as three aurei (G. R. Watson, *The Roman Soldier* (1969), 44). As to the silver, Caligula gave (as promised) 100 denarii a man to the vast force assembled for the invasion of Britain (Suetonius, *Caligula*, 46). Sutherland (*RHC* 70) has some interesting speculations as to how the legacy of Tiberius might have been paid, 1,000 sestertii per man, weighing 60 lb., being unlikely. He suggests perhaps 9½ aurei, 12 denarii and two of the commemorative sestertii only. This mixed coin would weigh only 1½ lb. The extreme rarity of the Domitianic sestertius cited above suggests that the extra *stipendium* may have been consigned in mixed coin also. The annual cost of the Roman army is put by J. Hopkins (*JRS* 1980, 124–5) at 445,000,000±50,000,000 sestertii; J. B. Campbell (*The Emperor and the Roman Army* (1984), 162–3) thinks this figure is altogether too high, and suggests 350 to 380,000,000. C. Nicolet (*DR* I, 225) points out that the Romans originally regarded army pay, for a citizen militia, as 'maintenance' – *opsōnion* (Dionysius of Halicarnassus IV, 19.3): hence the heavy deductions, by imperial times traditional, leaving only (as stated) 'pocket-money'.

97. Suetonius, *Divus Claudius*, 10; Watson, *op. cit.* n. 96, 108–10, for donatives, though the proportion of the Praetorian figure is disputed. The amounts – the *deposita* – placed in the legions' savings-bank were very considerable. Domitian set a limit of 1,000 sestertii (taking this as a unit of account, not necessarily therefore in aes coins) per man, because in the revolt of 89 Saturninus had found the combined savings of the two legions then in garrison at Mainz sufficient to float his attempt (Suetonius, *Domitian*, 7). There would also have been substantial funds for the day-to-day requirements of the legions.

98. D. W. MacDowall (*Essays/Sutherland*, 38) for the first time noted that in Italy coins with and without P.P. were equally represented in finds. In *RIC* I², Sutherland still maintained the older (Kraay) notion of *aes* being struck from 41 to 50 without, and from 50–54, with, P.P. Even for MacDowall, the dating remained as in *MV*, 36–7. Now, however, we have H.-M. von Kaenel's new appraisal, cf. his *Münzprägung und Münzbildnis des Claudius* (1986), esp. 226–8, building on his other work, cited n. 28. No interval can have lain between the two issues, given their very strong stylistic affinity; sestertii bulk large, the accession-donative being perhaps the cause.

99. Cf. Giard, *RN* 1968, 30; 1970, 34 and n. 2. The Southants. hoard example (*NC* 1911 pl. 3, 4) does not have the letters P.P.; there was a mistaken Cohen reference in the text. Others from Lincoln (*NC* 1931, 314) and Ham Hill, Som. (*NC* 1949, 169) are likewise mistaken. In the first case, the mistake was my own (a misreading); but I have looked at the material in Taunton and have failed to find a P.P. copy among it: for *NC* 1949, 169 no. 16, therefore, read not 'with' but 'without' P.P.

100. Cf. Giard, *JS* 1975, 81–102 and *RN* 1967, 131.

101. Cf. Giard, *RN* 1967, 131; 1968, 105–13 *passim*; *CCRB*, 10–11.

102. Cassius Dio LX, 22. Sutherland, *RHC* 79–80, says it is 'beyond belief' that the Senate 'could even contemplate, let alone achieve, the melting down of *all* the portrait-bearing *aes* coinage of Gaius' and suggests that merely a token

destruction took place. He adds that 'a previous coinage was withdrawn (or more probably sifted out over a period by the *mensarii* or at the *aerarium* itself) only when it had become worn to virtual illegibility . . . or when currency reform, in reducing the weight-standard, left earlier coinage circulating at a too obviously heavy standard.' But the site-evidence, as mentioned in these pages, is not in favour of that view. The overstriking of the 'portrait' (*Vesta*) asses and for good measure of other earlier coins including some of Germanicus issued under Caligula (47) and of Lyons 'altar' type (43), and the apposition of countermarks on coins far from worn to that degree (33) show that these various pre-Claudian coins were otherwise valueless ('rotten', cf. Epictetus, cited n. 33). Naturally, demonetization, being a decision taken without the means of universal enforcement, was unable to command universal implementation; negative evidence of occurrence apart (n. 33), sufficient coins countermarked, overstruck or hoarded (n. 106) exist, however, to prove the wide promulgation of the senatorial decree regarding Caligula's *aes* and show that itwas by no means ineffectual. We might note the derogatory reference in Statius, *Silvae* IV, 9.23 to would-be literary work bought '*plus minus asse Gaiano*', when reference to an As by itself (as in Catullus, 5,3) would surely have been opprobrious enough. This passage is in some editions connected with a supposed reduction of the weight of the As under Caligula, but this was not the case (cf. *RIC* I², 102, 118). A general study of the countermarks (and other markings) on asses of Caligula, R. Martini, *RIN* 1980, 53–83; he stresses the 'political' interpretation of the Claudian countermarks on the coins found in the Rhenish fortresses; applied to the reverse of the Vesta asses in the main, they cause the obverse to be flattened at a point which preserved the GERMANICUS element of the titulature, so that Claudius might equally profit by continuing reference to the hero, after all his brother. This point is worth making; but at Vindonissa only two out of 275 such asses are so countermarked (cf. Kraay, *Essays/Mattingly*, 127).

103. Von Kaenel, *op. cit.* n. 98, 231.

104. Kraay, *MV* 48–9 and *Essays/Mattingly*, passim; M. de Weerd, in *Ex Horreo* (*Cingula* IV, 1977), 268–9. Note the Glasgow coin on which Kraay commented (*JRS* 1963, 178) with TI AV over PROB, itself known only on the issue of 41; note too a pair of Caligulan asses overstruck with Claudian types after being countermarked TI.C.A. (*RN* 1970, 49, no. 74, 50 no. 96). In *RBI* pl. I, 2, Sutherland shows an imitative sestertius of Claudius with the mark TI AV; it may be that all Claudian coins with this countermark are counterfeits of an acceptable standard, like those marked PROB or IMP PRO (p. 106): some certainly are, cf. *JRS* 1975, 90. M. Crawford (n. 31) suggests that the notion of systematic validation by countermarks 'seems misplaced', but it is manifest that countermarks validate or affect the acceptability or circulation-area of coins, for otherwise there would be no reason to apply them, except a political one which the character of the marks does perhaps sometimes support.

105. A mobile policing unit – the *Ala Vocontiorum*, a cavalry regiment of 500 strong – was based at Arlaines, 11 km west of Soissons from Augustan times, and its fort was rebuilt in stone under the Flavians: M. Reddé, *Cah. du Groupe de recherches sur l'Armée romaine et les provinces* I (1977), 35–69. Its presence might account for the plenitude of early *aes* at the ford of Condé-sur-Aisne;

in that case a garrison near other fords might be sought, near also, thus, to new cantonal capitals.

106. Cf. Giard, *RN* 1970, 48–51; *JS* 1975, 86–7; E. C. Vidal, *Ampurias* XXXI-II (1969–70), 256–7, mentions a *Caesaraugusta* coin overstruck with a Claudian (*Libertas*) type. The Mafumet amphora of *aes* (n. 28) may have been sent as a result of the suppression of the Spanish local coinages and a consequent shortage. Claudian copies are frequent in Spain (C. H. V. Sutherland, *The Romans in Spain* (1939, repr. 1971), 175–6). We may also note as a matter of interest *RBI* pl. VIII, 3 which appears on the reverse to reproduce lettering foreign to the Minerva type: it may have persisted from an original coin which, overstruck, was taken as the proximal model for this piece. We shall find other instances of such blind imitation (pp. 126, 134).

107. I. A. Richmond, *Hod Hill* II (1968), 92–103, thirty-four to fifteen Claudian, including with the latter five copies. At neighbouring Waddon Hill fort (G. Webster, *Proc. Dorset N. H. & Arch. Soc.* CI (1981, 58) there were two to twenty-one Claudian, only two copies apparently; Richborough, 33 to 345 (R. Reece, *BIAL* 1981, 57); at Sheepen, Colchester, 56 to 138, including 68 copies (Sutherland in *Camulodunum* (1947), 145–56); at Silchester down to 1986, 5 to 117 including 95 copies (my own figures).

108. For the countermark TIB in nicked circle, cf. Kraay, *Essays/Mattingly* 122–5, emanating from Strasbourg, then seat of *Legio II Augusta*.

109. J. Noël, *BCEN* 1967, 61, 7.14 grammes, from a grave of the later 1st century; Giard, *JS* 1975, 94, 98, pl. III nos. 28 (ours) and 29 (Copenhagen).

110. *CA* pl. I, 25 is a Silchester example (Claudius/Antonia); cf. Giard, *RN* 1970, 35–6, 37–8, pl. III, 37, similar; 39, 43; *JS* 1975, 84 86–9, pls. IX-X *passim*.

111. Cf. von Kaenel, *loc. cit.* n. 28, 107–8, 34 out of 68 Spes sestertii false, but of good style; only 4 out of 90 Minerva asses and 2 out of 80 Constantia asses were false; all copies without P.P. Giard shows a very barbarous sestertius from Ostia (Gallic or British?) in *QT* 1985, 236, pl. I, 7. – 'An emphatically metropolitan denomination' – Sutherland, *RHC*, 49.

112. Boon, *Usk*, 16, B/I; W. A. Seaby, *NC* 1949, 169, no. 14; *RBI* pl. V, 5 (*CCRB* pl. II, 2); *RN* 1970, pl. I, 4, again Minerva type, with countermark Z (p. 106); cf. Giard, *ibid.* 35, 13–15, 254–5, pls. II, X. For die-linked sestertii from Ham Hill and a Wiltshire site, see n. 26 above. For a British find, 13.52 grammes, similar to 37, see Schweiz. Kreditanstalt Sale, 27–28 Oct. 1987, lot 1107.

113. Giard, *JS* 1975, 94–5, pl. IX, 96. His list of die-links *ibid.* is fullest. Cf. *RN* 1968, 115 no. 1672, pl. XI (Condé-sur-Aisne); *RBI* pl. VIII, 1–2, British and Maidstone Museums; *CA* pl. III, 32 (Silchester), and *CCRB* pl. III, 32 (Silchester), and *CCRB* pl. III, 4. Another, *RN* 1968, pl. XI, 1582 (Condé) and *CCRB* pl. III, 4 (Pangbourne-on-Thames), these last two weighing only 3.00 and 2.10 grammes respectively.

114. *RN* 1968, 94 refers to examples from Condé-sur-Aisne, St.-Léonard, Neuss,

Neuss-Sels, and Nijmegen; add Vechten (J. H. Jongkees, *JMP* XLVIII (1961), 86–7), besides Silchester. In *JS* 1975, 90, Giard points out that these could well have been counterfeit countermarks: Q.Va(*lerius*) might have been a *nummularius* (*ibid.*, 93, 96) who stamped only much worn imitations – eight examples range from 8.21 grammes (the Silchester specimen) down to 4.11 grammes: but J. H. Jongkees (*loc. cit.*) has suggested a connexion with the consul of 46. He seems to have done nothing in the region, however, unlike L. Apronius (*cos* AD 8) who in 15 was left in the rear by Germanicus during the Cattian campaign to build roads and embank rivers against the possibility of flooding (Tacitus, *Annales* I, 56). The stamp L. APRON must be his, just as VAR must refer to the ill-fated Quinctilius Varus. These were early days, and such personal guarantees would not have been allowed later on, when greatness was tolerated only up to a certain point (as in the case of Julius Frontinus, cf. Tacitus, *Agricola*, 17.2). I judge, therefore, that Q.VA has reference to an individual far inferior to a consular. False countermarks M and PRO on a hybrid 'Antonia' dupondius (Grade III) with Claudius obverse, 8.47 grammes, now in the National Museum of Wales, Münzzentrum Köln Auktion 62, 1987, lot 38.

115. C. H. V. Sutherland in C. F. C. Hawkes and M. R. Hull, *Camulodunum* (1947), 145–56.

116. R. Reece, *BIAL* 1981, 57.

117. M. J. Hammerson in Southwark Excav. *1972–74* n.d. II, 588–9, lists some percentages; Silchester down to 1986, 95 copies in 117. Cf. also R. Kenyon in H. R. Hurst, *Kingsholm* (1985), 23–5, table at 25; L. F. Pitts, *ibid.*, 27, table showing a minimal 20 orthodox to 56 copies, but cf. Hurst, at 124, for 38: 109 including Nero. Kingsholm was occupied from *c.* 49 to 66/7.

118. J.-B. Giard, *RN* 1970, 51–6, pls. V-XI, 261 is from Camulodunum.

119. Giard (*QT* XIV (1985), 235) comments on the absence of any leavening of Celtic art in the design of the Claudian copies. The 'Celtic' *élan* could scarcely flourish in the workaday commercial world of the false-moneyer: to suggest that an Antonia dupondius and a *Spes* sestertius copy had 'keltische Stil' (Schweiz. Kreditanstalt sale, 27–28 October 1987, lots 1101 and 1107) is forlorn. The last Bellovacian issue is a depressingly inartistic thing (n. 71).

120. *RN* 1968, 115, see under nos. 1669–70.

121. Cf. n. 73.

122. It may be of interest to sketch briefly what happened to this new coinage. On the figures of M. Grant (*NC* 1955, 21–37, esp. 32; 1957, 229–30), the bulk of Rome production went to Italy, and that of Lyons, apart from what went to pay the army on the Rhine and in Britain, remained in Lugdunensis and Aquitania, thus encouraging a burst of counterfeiting in Belgica (Giard, *loc. cit.* n. 34, 279–96) and scarcely at all elsewhere. This rose to about 11½ per cent of the orthodox material. As already remarked (p. 115; n. 33), Nero's coinage seems to have been rapidly withdrawn by Vespasian where that action was practicable – in making up the stipend.

123. R. Kenyon, in N. Crummy (ed.), *Colchester Archaeological Reports*, No. 4: *The Coins from Excav. in Colchester 1971–9* (1987), 24–42; and a second report in that series, in preparation.

124. Boon, *Usk*, 1–42. The series includes a cast Minerva As (from a Grade I original) which much resembles a cast 'eagle' As of Vespasian (list nos. 60, 263, – 6.75, 6.95 grammes) as if suggestive of contemporary manufacture; but this would be an illusion, probably arising from a similarity of the alloy used. However, J. -P. Bost and I. Pereira, *Numisma* XXIII-IV (1973–4), 172–3, record a Claudian obverse with a Vespasianic *Aequitas* reverse, clear but barbarous to an extreme: perhaps another exception to prove the rule that copies are contemporary with the currency of their prototype. On the piece cf. Giard's comment, *JS* 1975, 90, n. 30, 'un cas isolé' – as the two authors of the note had likewise observed. Giard suspects that the piece was inspired by the 'restored' coinage issued under Titus.

125. 'Worn' means that the very highest detail, a laurel-wreath or a lock of hair, has been obliterated by circulation-wear and has merged with the next lowest.

126. Exeter, *c.* 50–52 'or very shortly afterwards' (M. Todd, *The South-West to AD 1000* (1987), 196) – perhaps rather too early a date; Usk, *c.* 55 on pottery, Boon, *Usk*, 3 citing Manning. These two fortresses, with Wroxeter making a third, were founded as part of the same programme of frontier stabilisation, in Manning's view.

127. N. Shiel and R. Reece in P. T. Bidwell, *The Legionary Bath-house . . . at Exeter* (1979), 162–7.

128. *RIC* I² (1984), 115; cf. C. E. King, quoted n. 82 above.

129. Boon, *Usk*, 4–5, 32–4.

130. *Aes*: at the Brecon Gaer were one of Caligula (a rare find!), one of Claudius, none of Nero, four of Vespasian; at Caernarvon, one of Nero, twenty of Vespasian; at Holt, one of Claudius, none of Nero, seven of Vespasian. At Caerleon down to 1980 there were five pre-Claudian, thirteen Claudian, eight Neronian, three Galban and Vitellian, and no fewer than 115 of Vespasian. Cf. n. 33.

·131. Hammerson, *l.c.* n. 117, 590–1; of Nero he listed only five, *ibid.* 155, 285, 390.

132. W. Glasbergen, *De romeinse Castella te Valkenburg* (*Cingula* I, 1972), 151. For a reappraisal of the stratification of the pre-Flavian coins, see de Weerd in *Ex Horreo* (*Cingula* IV, 1977), 266–7. – 'Moving up' through divers causes will perhaps explain the classical difficulties of Hawkes and Hull in interpreting stratified Sheepen deposits (*Cam. Report*, 174–9).

133. Icklingham is the latest hoard, I think, *c.* 395 (*NC* 1929, 319); Hammerson, *l.c.* n. 117, 590 for others. A hoard discovered and put to use in Constantinian times at Brean Down (Weston-super-Mare) is published by me in *PUBSS* X. 3 (1965), 236: one Minerva copy and a few sestertii, Trajan, Pius, Faustina II, Commodus (2) and another illegible.

134. N. Mahudel, *Hist. de l'Acad. roy. des Inscriptions et Belles-Lettres* III (1723), 218–24; translated by J. Akerman, *CCRB*, 74–6. Counterfeits were so common by the time of Caracalla that the contemporary historian, Cassius Dio (LXXVIII, 14.4) refers to silver-plated lead and gilt copper as official issues.

135. One from the Sully hoard, which had two, is illustrated as *CA* (5). The same practice began a little earlier among the coiners: S. Michon, *BSFN* 1986, 177–8, illustrates a Severan denarius overstruck as an antoninianus of Otacilia, Philip I's empress, died 249. Cf. the factitious antoninianus, above n. 35.

136. Above, n. 52.

137. *FMRD* II/3 (1964), no. 3322.

138. A British hoard is Leysdown (R. A. G. Carson, *NC* 1971, esp. 182). One of the worst casts known is of a Postumian sestertius, from Chateaubleau (S.-et-M.), a site which earlier produced moulds running from Julia Domna to Tetricus II (P.-H. Mitard, *RN* 1963, 115, pl. XII, I, 119, ref.). Another Postumian mould is noted by P. Bastien (*BSFN* 1976, 823) and further casts by H. Huvelin and D. Nony, in the Néry hoard (*RN* 1978, 89–109), 58 out of 65 being false. Cf. P. Bastien, *Le Monnayage de Bronze de Postume* (1967), ch. V; cf. *PM*, 116–30. Moulds for Antonine sestertii are known from Central Gaul (A. Morlet, *Vichy gallo-romaine* (1957), 172–3, fig. 110).

139. *NZ* 1921, 153–70. Cf. E. Lacom, *Mitt. Num. Gesellschaft Wien* 1929, 6; G. Elmer, *NZ* 1933, 56–67, tables.

140. Boon, *NC* 1965, 161–74; Gallus, *AC* 1976, 54 no. 117, illus. No. 56, from same original as four from Bath, Sacred Spring (D.R. Walker, in B. Cunliffe (ed.), *The Temple of Sulis Minerva* ii (Oxford 1988), 291, Pl. XXXII, with 36 others of similar appearance beyond much doubt locating manufacture at Bath, perhaps for the visitor-trade. Dr. Walker would date production *c.* 122–24.

141. From excavations of the Dyfed Archaeological Trust; kindly shown by Mrs. H. James.

142. G. C. Boon and P. A. Rahtz, *AJ* 1966, 13–51; cf. above, n. 35. Similarly, a lightweight (6.35 g) cast As of Maximus Caesar, son of Maximin I, was in the Cunetio hoard (*CT* no. 3053).

143. M. R.-Alföldi, *G* 1974, 426–47.

144. *PM* 125, n. 1. Mr. G. B. Rogers kindly sent me a lightweight As of Hadrian (4.15 grammes) which he had himself found at Fréjus. But such things appear to be scarce away from the frontier provinces.

145. The following table is drawn up from Elmer's data (n. 139 above) and from Reece, *Richborough Report*, V, 204–5.

ORTHODOX AES AT CARNUNTUM (I) AND RICHBOROUGH (II)

Emperor, etc.	Sestertius		Dupondius		As		Viminacium, Dacia – I	Greek
	I	II	I	II	I	II		I
Antonius Pius	91	28	76	18	145	37		7
M. Aurelius	134	12	103	16	125	2		10
Commodus	57	9	40	—	34	2		1
Severus	17*	1	1	—	5	—		4
Caracalla	8	—	4	—	8	—		14
Elagabalus	3	—	—	—	7**	—		2
Alexander	60	—	1	—	10	—		3
Maximin I	18	—	2	—	3	—		1
Gordian III	32	—	2	—	10	—	86	4
Philip	20	—	1	—	—	—	109	1
Decius	4***	—	3	—	2	—	86	—
Aemilian-Gallienus (J.R.)	—	—					17	1

  * with sestertius of Didius Julianus
 ** with two asses of Macrinus
*** includes a double sestertius
(No Greek *aes* are noted at Richborough in the list quoted, but they do occur sparingly on most sites with a long coin-series, and across the country; it would be interesting to see a list assembled.)

146. But some hybrids, as between the coins of joint emperors struck at the same period, are not false but arise from accidental confusion of dies.

147. See n. 41, and for the surface, nn. 8, 42 and 60.

.148. *CCRB* 44 and n. 9, the Liverpool pieces.

149. Two moulds were submitted for examination by R. B. Burns, Guernsey Museum, from St. Peter Port. Both were double-sided: (*1a*), denarius of Alexander; (*1b*), rev. of denarius of Elagabalus, Sol standing, PM TR P II COS II P P; (*2a*), antoninianus of Gordian III; (*2b*), rev. of denarius of Alexander, *Annona* type, rubbed.

150. *AJ* 1966, 20, no. 2, for the Aurelian, of Siscia, *RIC* 193 (*CA* (**49**)). Moulds from Kenn consist of three fragments for Gallienus and Tetricus I (Lilly and Usher, *PUBSS* XIII.1 (1972), 39, no. 5, and my own inspection at Taunton). One of the two legible moulds from Keynsham is for a sole reign antoninianus of Gallienus. R. Schindler refers to a mould for Tetricus from a burial at Saarlouis (*Beitr. saarl. Arch. u. Kunstges.* 1964, 21). Cf. the Chateaubleau

finds, n. 138 above. For a cast antoninianus of Claudius II having a Milan obv. and Rome rev., cf. P. Bastien, *BSFN* 1975, 823–4 – Fresnoy-lès-Roye (Somme) hoard. Note also the Silchester cliché mould, p. 112 above.

151. Mould(s) for Probus in a curious mass ranging apparently from Pius to Constantius I ('mais on ne sait pas exactement si tous ces objets ont été déterrés ensemble'), *PM* 456, n. 1. Probus moulds, for antoniniani not tetradrachms, in Egypt, *ibid.* 308, n. 3. Bibliography of moulds, M. Jungfleisch and J. Schwartz, *Suppl. aux Annales du Service des Antiquités de l'Egypte* (1952); and Schwartz, Supplement, *Schweiz. Münzblätter*, 1963, 12–14.

152. Excluding the *consecratio*-issues of Claudius II, many of which are counterfeit, numbers in Italy seem to be small. Spain has them in uncertain proportion. Africa, *PM* 303, n. 3; cf. Giard, *JS* 1969, 26, note. For Britain, see *CCRB* 57–61 and the works cited *nn.seqq.*; Gaul, J.-B. Giard, *JS* 1969, 5–34, and École pratique des Htes. Études, *Annuaire* 1965/6, IVᵉ Section, 461–8 and R. Weiller, *Helinium* VIII (1968), 131–48, and *NC* 1969, 163–75 (Luxembourg): cf. also J. Lafaurie in *ANRW* II.2 (1975), 895–8.

153. Analysis of barbarous radiates (P. Le Gentilhomme, *RN* 1962, 165) showed *nil* silver; but cast rod and blanks from the Sprotborough find (W. J. C. Price, *NC* 1982, 31) showed about 1½ per cent, corresponding to that in the official coinage of the time and so indicating the source. Cf. Le Gentilhomme, *ibid.*, 164–5 for analyses of the official coinage. Worthing, G. D. Lewis and H. B. Mattingly, *NC* 1964, 189–99 (the weights supplied by Worthing museum).

154. *CCRB passim*; note also the valuable series published elsewhere, notably in *CT* pls. 32–39 for struck forgeries, with plenty of comparative material on the preceding plates; for *Divo Claudio* cf. J. Lallemand in *Mél. Lafaurie*, 119 – a prolonged period of striking after the prototypes had ceased to be coined.

155. Boon in W. Gardner and H. N. Savory, *Dinorben* (1964), 119; no. 158. Cf. J. C. Bruce, *Lapid. Septent.* (1875), 209 no. 421 (*Corpus Signorum Imperii Romani, Gt. Britain* I, 6 (1988), no. 162), for a deity with shield bearing a vertical fish; could there be a connexion? Such transformations are, not surprisingly, rare: another published by P. V. Hill (*NC* 1948, 93–4, fig. 1 = *BNJ* 1949–51, 20 no. 33, pl. I), die-linked to a coin in Paris, shows a large central figure with arms around a smaller personage on either side. *Not* 'late, un-Roman' (Hill); *possibly* 'a mother-goddess' (Giard, *JS* 1969, 8); but in any case derived from a *Fides Militum* two-standard type. The 'long cross and pellets' of a Richborough radiate-hoard specimen (Hill, *BNJ* no. 24) is more readily derived from the *consecratio* 'altar' type for Claudius II.

156. See his papers on the Worthing hoard (with G. D. Lewis, *NC* 1964, 189–99) and others – Lightwood and Calverton (*N. Staffs. Journ. Field Stud.* III (1961), 19–36), Goring-on-Sea (*Sussex Arch. Colls.* CV (1967), 56–61), London, Paternoster Row (*NC* 1967, 61–9), Verulamium 1960 (*B* 1971, 196–9); Frocester (*TBGAS.* LXXXI (1970), 83–6, no illus.), and Sprotborough (with M. J. Dolby, *NC* 1982, 21–33). We might remember that the late C. H. V. Sutherland was the first to identify the name of Probus on barbarous radiates from Richborough (*NC* 1935, 228–9).

157. See his papers on Richborough radiates, *BNJ* 1982, 17–28, the Meare hoard, *NC* 1986, 107–118, and the Colchester finds, *loc. cit.* n. 123. A doctoral thesis is also in preparation.

158. T. V. Wheeler (ed. B. H. St. J. O'Neil), *NC* 1937, 221–28; pl. XXVII, no. 645 for the Tacitus. Sutherland's remarks on the significance of this hoard (*Trans. Internat. Num. Congr. 1936* (1938), 252–61) are in hindsight interesting in their use of very poor comparanda. Similarly there is neither evidence nor likelihood for the *c.* 500–550 date suggested by R. Turcan for an Algerian hoard (*Latomus* XXXI (1972), 130–45, esp. 144).

159. P. V. Hill, *Barbarous Radiates* (NNM 60, 1949), 8. The 'Magnia' was in point of fact a Constantinian minim of a somewhat unusual kind, in the name of Fl. Maxima Theodora, as Hill's illustration shows. The 'Numerian', I imagine, was 'Aurelian' misread. Even in the true barbarous radiate series, empresses are very rare. Salonina is the only likely candidate and she appears on a *Segontium* minim (*AC* 1976, 58, no. 254, illus.) (80), p. 126 above.

160. Cf. H. B. Mattingly on the Verulamium II hoard (*B* 1971, 196–9), noting this chronological decline and using it to explain why the later Theatre hoard offered no die-links despite coming from the same site (*ibid.*, 197).

161. G. C. Boon in G. J. Wainwright, *Coygan Camp* (1967), 116–26.

162. *Idem, PUBSS* XIII.1 (1972). I showed a Coygan and quartered White Woman's Hole material in *DR* I, facing 106.

163. *PUBSS* XIII.1, 72 for a schedule.

164. The meaning of the mark XX.I and its variants has been much discussed. The notion championed by L. H. Cope (*NC* 1968, 118, with reference to other ideas) was that it signified an alloy of 20 *oboli* of silver to 1 *libra* of bronze. This conclusion has been denied, however, by M. H. Crawford on the basis of Cope's own figures (*ANRW* II.2, 581 n. 82). He inclines to make it a 5-*denarius* piece, i.e. 20 sestertii to 1, as proposed by Sutherland (*JRS* 1961, 94).

165. Cf. P. Bastien, *Rev. du Nord* IX, no. 239 (1978), 801–2; *idem, Le Monnayage de l'atelier de Lyon,* 274–85 (1976), 40–1, cf. his fuller treatment in *Festoen: opgedragen aan A. N. Zadoks-Josephus Jitta (Scripta Arch. Groningana* VI, 1976), 75–81. Cf. J. Lallemand in *Mél. Lafaurie,* 121–2, for an important study of the pattern of Reform antoniniani in Belgium: hoards are *poorer* in such finds, because they are *late*, mostly buried under Diocletian.

166. Penard, G. C. Boon, *BBCS* XXII (1967), 291–7; Blackmoor, R. Bland, *CHRB,* III (1982), with Christie's sale catalogue, Dec. 9th 1975. But central reformed pieces might be recognized gradually as 'different' from Gallic material, as stratification in the Penard and Tattershall hoards suggests (Boon, *ibid.*, 294; Besly and Bland, *CHRB* IV (1984), 106); cf. Bland and Carradice on the Oliver's Orchard (Colchester) multiple hoard, where the fine coins had been added last (*CHRB* VI (1986), 65). The Gloucester Bon Marché hoard of 1960

held some 15,000 coins, all reformed except two of Allectus and one of Victorinus (cf. *NC* 1962, 63, and information from R. A. G. Carson). The persistence of radiate minims in British circulation, down to the earliest years of Carausius, is suggested by finds such as the Segontium hoard (Boon, *AC* 1976, 43–5) – 35 coins, Gallienus – Tetricus II, 5 large, 15 small (12–8 mm) copies, 0.99–0.24 g., and one early Carausius.

167. H. Mattingly and W. P. Stebbing, *The Richborough Hoard of 'Radiates'*, 1931, (*NNM* 80, 1938); Whitchurch (Som.), C. H. V. Sutherland, *NC* 1934, 300. The others, with Calverton subsumed under Lightwood, see above n. 118. The Rhenish findspot is unknown. The other link is cited by Mattingly in his Calverton paper, *loc. cit.* n. 156, 24.

168. Lallemand and Thirion, *Le trésor de Saint-Mard I* (1970), 67–72.

169. Giard, *JS* 1969, 13, mentions four die-links with specimens in British collections. Woodeaton is interesting, cf. J. G. Milne, *JRS* 1931, 101–9, esp. 101–2, with Goodchild and Kirk, *Oxoniensia* XIX (1954), 15–37, cf. 27. Mildenhall (Suffolk), A. S. Robertson, *NC* 1954, pl. 5, 3 (17 examples, obv. shared with pl. 5,2 and rev. with pl. 5,24). The barbarous rev. of no. 3 is presumably a replacement for a worn rev., no. 2, the already cracked obv. die then itself being replaced. It is unusual to find this kind of evidence in the barbarous radiate series; cracked dies scarcely appear. A slightly earlier link (towards 260) is noted by Lallemand, *Mél. Lafaurie*, 117–18 (Oombergen/Alost - Dorchester, Dorset).

170. *Sci. American* Dec. 1974, 120–30, at p. 29.

171. *CT*, 67–70, esp. 68; Davies, *loc. cit.* n. 157; R. Ziegler, *Der Schatzfund von Brauweiler* (Beihefte, *BJ*, Bd. 42, 1983), 74–81.

172. The Caerleon hoard consisted of a large Tetricus I imitation, 18 mm 2.9 grammes, one 16 and two 15 mm copies a gramme lighter, and 91 minims 13 mm 2.9 grammes down to 6 mm and 0.1 grammes. Frocester, above n. 172.

173. *Loc. cit.* n. 158. Mattingly in *NC* 1964, 194, refers to a stylistic link between Verulamium (no. 655) and the products of the Midlands mint. This is not much in so large a hoard. As noted above, there is a Tacitus copy (no. 645) in the Verulamium hoard, making it formally contemporary with Lightwood rather than later, as Mattingly suggested; going solely by size, narrowly, is perilous. Mattingly suggested that the Verulamium hoard was probably somewhat earlier than the date of *c.* 300 placed on the concrete floor above. There is no problem, archaeologically.

174. *Cf. RIC*, V. 2, 586–8, pl. 20, Regalian. In *CA* 147, n. 124, I mentioned a *regular* overstruck coin of Carausius from a N. Wales hoard, with LEG II AVG/ML reverse of *c.* 286. On re-examination I find it is merely doubly-struck on the obverse, not overstruck at all.

175. See a study of C. E. King, *BNJ* 1984, 2–9, where particular attention is given to the portraiture on the 'unmarked' series (viz. lacking mint-marks).

176. R. A. G. Carson, *Journ. Brit. Arch. Assn.* 1959, 33–40; in *Mints Dies and Currency* (1971), 57–65. Shiel's modification, starting the C or G mint in 289/90, is acceptable (*Carausius*, 184–5).

177. Rouen, see B. Beauhard and H. Huvelin, 'Le trésor de Rouen . . .', *Histoire et numismatique en Haute-Normandie* (ed. N. Gautier, *Cah. des Annales de Normandie*, no. 12A, 1980), 63–91. See also A. Burnett and J. Casey, *BNJ* 1984, 10–20.

178. But for the obvious Postumian prototype, and the absence of a suggestive legend, coins such as **84–85** might not unreasonably be attributed to Carausian originals, were it not for the gap in named minims after Probus.

179. *CCRB*, 63, mentions Carinus, Maximian and Diocletian; the second is, I think, acceptable, and is a component of a Silchester hoard somewhat inaccurately described in the ref. cited by Sutherland; there were only four overstrikes in forty coins, by no means an uncommon proportion (Boon, *NC* 1960, 246–7, Hoard III). The original MS list by the excavator, J. G. Joyce, who was a good numismatist, may be relied upon though the coin, with others, was mounted between glass plates at Stratfield Saye (*CA*, 147, no. 123), which I was understandably not allowed to remove.

180. No such reverses, however, are recorded. The number of strokes following those reasonably taken to represent LAETITIA or FELICITAS – normal legends for the galley-type – requires something longer than AVG, and C appears to begin the second word.

181. This coin is actually *RIC* 704. It is not in quite the same case as Stukeley's ORIVNA AVG coin from Silchester, where the F of *Fortuna* is lost in a split, and the T is very narrow; but 'I never saw the real coin' says Stukeley (see my note, *NCirc* 1974), 428).

182. Cf. my note in H. N. Savory, *Excav. at Dinorben 1965–9* (1971), 33–4, no. 204; H. A. Seaby on the Little Orme's Head hoard, *NC* 1956, 219, no. 148, both in Cardiff; as the present text shows, I have changed my view of this piece.

183. Penard hoard; cf. Boon, *BBCS* XXII.3 (1967), 291–7, pl. V, 12. Shiel, (*Carausius*, 168) suggests that the legend might have been intended for LE[G . . .], but this is not acceptable. On a similar line of argument, it appears that Stukeley's celebrated but unconfirmed mintmark CLA (*Medallic History of Carausius* (1757–9) II, pl. 29, 2) on a barbarous reverse was really no more than part of the name CLAVDIVS surviving as undertype. However, the mysterious mintmark BRI on a small group of Carausian pieces (Shiel, *ibid.*, 177–80) is not explainable in this manner. It is scratched rather roughly into the dies, apparently as an afterthought, 'signing' an unmarked (and so silverless, L.H. Cope, cited by R. Bland, *BNJ* 1984, 41) issue of early date, without the C(*aesar*). One is shown in *CA*, pl. IV, no. 71.

184. The base denarius [101] would appear to be a good case in point, the reverse having been struck from an antoninianus-die of rather a rough kind, as noted by Shiel, *NCirc.* 1973, 332, no. 10.

185. This LITI AV reverse is shown in *BBCS* XXII.3 (1967), nos. 9 (two out of three from Penard) and in *Hunter Cabinet* (ed. A. S. Robertson) IV (1975), pl. 58, 66.

186. The L and C (or G) mints certainly shared the services of one die-cutting shop from time to time and perhaps generally, as any comparison of the obverses will show; likewise the 'base' or unmarked mint/issues (cf. L. H. Cope's analytical results cited above, n. 183) and the RSR or 'treasury' mint; for BRI see n. 183. It will be noted that I cannot now agree, as I previously did, with E. Fantecchi, RIN 1960, 134–45, on the source of the RSR coinage.

187. Shiel, *B* 1973, 224–6. Mr. Shiel kindly lent his negative through the British Museum. Cf. C. Oman, *NC* 1918, 80–96 and 1924, 53–68, for legionary coins.

188. Some of this matter is still highly contentious. Crawford's account in *ANRW* II.2 (1975), 579–80, and the introductory matter in *RIC* VI, VII, VIII and IX demand caution. Cf. J. Lafaurie, *RN* 1975, 73–138 for the most important study (p. 109 for gold and silver prices in the maximal edict, following M. Giacchero's edition (*Edictum Diocletiani et Collegarum de Pretiis Rerum Venalium* (Genoa, 1974), 115, 206–7), with the Aezani (Phrygia) fragments settling these for the first time.

189. See n. 60.

190. J. Gricourt noted two, *BCEN* 1972, 49–50, one a mere hybrid, the other barbarous, only 1.7 grammes against 3 grammes or so. Cf. P. Bastien, *BCEN* 1981, 32–9, no. 1 in an interesting series of imitations, down to Julian's 'bull' type.

191. S. Sharp, *NC* 1871, 28–41. The only variation from this account concerns 14 fragments said to read GAL VAL MAXIMIANVS AVG which on inspection conflate GAL VAL MAXIMIANVS N C and IMP DIOCLETIANVS P AVG. The very common Egyptian finds complement the dating: the Behnesa deposits are of 308–10 and 316–17 and later (*NC* 1905, 342–53; A. el-M. el-Kachab, *Serv. Ant. de l'Égypte* LI (1951), 29–51. Cf. also J. Schwartz's comment on my Rome paper, *DR* I, 106. I do not see how an unofficial reproduction of coin by casting can be anything other than the work of false-moneyers since the products are not authentic; they may havȩ been *accepted* as a 'money of necessity' but were uttered for *profit*.

192. *AJ* 1934, 119, 176, cf. *BM Guide to Antiq. of Roman Britain* (1922), 72, 'Constantine and Helena' – but there are no moulds for coins of Helena in the British Museum (where I studied the material in 1973). Another mystery attending the Nocton series is the presence with the fourth-century moulds of a numerous group of others for denarii and at least one antoninianus, closely similar in appearance and condition, and different from other sets of moulds in the British Museum. There appears to be no record of the origin of this wholly earlier material.

193. Kent, *RIC* VIII (1981), 78–9 for the most recent statement on this issue; and

cf. the radiate imitations in the Cunetio hoard (n. 42) as to what could be achieved in the way of plating.

194. P. Bruun, *RIC* VII (1966), 13.

195. *CTh* IX, 23.1.

196. Boon, *NC* 1960, 253–65; cf. Kent, *RIC* VIII, 90.

197. Examples in *CA* [**106, 107**], latter from Richborough.

198. Boon, *PUBSS* XIII.1 (1976), 70–82.

199. *Ibid.*, 79–82.

200. D. A. Casey in *Lydney Report* (1932), 129–131.

201. C. E. King, *RBN* 1977, 41–100; *NC* 1978, 38–65, analyses in *PACT* I (1977), 86–100, esp. 96–7 for copies: the absence of silver might point to cupellation, cf. n. 172; cf. also *eadem, Coin Hoards* VI (1981), 40–9, on comparable material from Bancroft villa, Milton Keynes.

202. We may note this very rare copy of the Siscia VICTORIA AVGG single Victory type (*AC* 1976, 73 no. 697, pl. V). Originals scarcely appear in Britain; there is one from Kenchester [**138**].

203. In an important study of imitations 318–63, P. Bastien, *MN* 30 (1985), 143–77, esp. 173; J. P. Callu and J. P. Garnier, *QT* VI (1977), 286. The problem is Gaulish and British, copies from beyond the Alps being rather few (*ibid.* and n. 26) for 330–48 as for 348–63. In all there were twenty-five fourth-century copies in the Matreille A wreck of *c*. 400–25; they included three *Spes Reipublice* in twenty-nine of that type (G. Depeyrot, *Archaeonautica* III (1981), 213, table). This type is quite rare in Britain.

204. R. Delmaire, *BSFN* 1983, 342; G. Fabre and M. Mainjonet, *Gallia* 1965, pl. IV, 86–9 for the 'Magnentian' copies, cf. also Callu and Garnier, *loc. cit.* n. 203, 288 and *ibid.* n. 33. Bastien's parallel (*loc. cit.* note 203, 170) is not very significant, cf. the Tetricus/Probus copies noted above, p. 114.

205. D. Wigg, *AK* 1987, 111–20. Note his Abb. 4 for the heavy incidence of 'falling horsemen' in Britain and the Lower Rhine region, with very little south-east of the Mosel and the Nahe. In general see *RIC* VIII, 90–1; further afield, note Carson and Kent, *JNG* XXI (1971), 138, only thirteen copies in one, 186 coins of a large hoard from Izmir; only two in three Romanian hoards together totalling 2,922 coins, all but 35 of them orthodox 'falling horsemen': E. Chirilă *et al., Drei Münzhorte aus dem Banat* (1974). For *Spes Reipublice* note e.g. the contrast in south-east Spain, cf. M. L. Galindo, *Antigüedad y Cristianismo*, II (Univ. Murcia, 1986), 195–213: no counterfeits, it seems, for the period *c*. 348–63.

206. Fabre and Mainjonet, *loc. cit.* n. 204; 'falling horsemen' making the hoard

later than supposed, nos. 23–6, 73, 167–9, 171–4. The authors' comment, 'un reflet de la confusion qui régnait dans le monnayage' is just.

207. *Loc. cit.* n. 203. Note, too, M. R.-Alföldi's report on a well at Cologne (*Kölner Jahrbuch für Vor- und Frühgeschichte* V (1960–1), 80–4. The coins go down to 'falling horsemen' – one of only 9 mm – from *c.* 330; the filling is dated to the aftermath of the barbarian invasion of 355.

208. A 9 mm example, in the Redenhall (Norfolk) hoard, *NC* 1946, 157, bizarrely misdescribed as a fifth-century imitation (for which no prototype exists in bronze) by P. V. Hill, *BNJ* 1949–51, 19, pl. I, 18. It is a particularly neat *Salus* copy, with clear Chi-Rho, and part of an Arles mintmark legible.

209. Cf. J. W. E. Pearce, *NC* 1939, 266–80; pl. XV, 14–15, are eastern copies overstruck on the same type, through carelessness; cf. Kent, *NC* 1957, pl. VIII, 22 – another such. Note, the apparently numerous overstrikes on the same type in the Heslington hoard result from a slip in description (*NC* 1971, 224). Examination shows only one possible. Fourteen are on 'phoenix', five being doubtful; seven are on uncertain undertype: total, twenty-two. There were no fewer than 297 overstrikes in the hoard, two being of Magnentian type, one 'galley' on 'phoenix', rest 'falling horsemen' on various earlier coins.

210. *CTh* IX, 23.1.

211. R. E. M. and T. V. Wheeler, *Lydney Report* (1932), 116–31.

212. *Ibid.*, 156–7; relation of long building to bath-house, *B* 1980, 357. The long building had floors sealing Valentinianic material. But the site had a longer structural history in general than the Wheelers supposed.

213. Pearce, *ibid.*, 114; other finds, 47, 50, 59–60, in contexts which held nothing later than Valentinianic.

214. Boon, *NC* 1961, 191–7; *PUBSS* X.3 (1965), 232–48. There is (as there was with the radiate minims, cf. n. 166) slender evidence to show a persistence into the next – here the Valentinianic – period, see n. 216 below, and note the few from the temple itself.

215. O'Neil in *AJ* 1945, 59. But it has been abundantly shown by R. J. Brickstock (whose M. Phil. thesis was most kindly made available to me by Mr. John Casey in August, 1987) that the first issue, 364–7, of Valentinian and Valens certainly did arrive in Britain in quantity before the *'barbarica conspiratio'* took effect. I am grateful to Mr. Brickstock for his kind permission to refer to this finding here.

216. B. H. St. J. O'Neil, *NC* 1948, 226–9 for Canterbury; Great Staughton, *JRS* 1959, 118; Richborough, H. Mattingly and W. P. Stebbing, *NC* 1939, 112–19, pls. VI–VII; Bourton-on-the-Water, O'Neil, *NC* 1935, 284–6, and more particularly in TBGAS 1934, 133–9: in a pot, with a coin of Decentius and a silver Valens. This latter, if reliably associated – and the record is old – point to a period after *c.* 363 for the continuing usefulness of these tiny pieces. In

Brittany, too, use of 'falling horsemen' – though not, I think, 'minimissimi' which are a British phenomenon only – down to the 380s is claimed by P. Galliou in *Océan atlantique et péninsule armoricaine* (107ᵉ Congrès des soc. sav., Brest 1982 (1985)), 115. In that region, supplies of official coinage are said to end in the 360s.

217. Boon in *Proc. Som. Arch.* and *N. H. Soc.* XCVI (1951), 128. Note, too, the similar finds (including a 'minimissimus') from Frilford Temple (Berks.), C. H. V. Sutherland, *Oxoniensia* IV (1939), 49–53.

218. S. S. Frere, *A CV* (1976), 287–8; Werner and Bimson, *ibid.* 297–8; cf. also Boon, *Silchester, The Roman Town of Calleva* (1974), 275–7, 312, n. 24; *idem, BBCS* XXXII (1985), 382, coins strongly heated with lead; *idem,* in J. D. Zienkiewicz, *The Legionary Fortress Baths at Caerleon* (1986) II, 38, no. 232. Cf. *CTh* IX, 21.6, of 349 regarding the 'purging' of silver from copper.

219. *Loc. cit.* 195; cf. A. H. M. Jones, *JRS* 1959, 34–8. *Folles* as bags of coin, e.g. in T. C. Skeat (ed.), *Papyri from Panopolis* (1964), Pap. 2, 104–7, for *Legio III Diocletiana*, 50 lb of silver and four *folles* of money, etc., and cart with four mules and driver to convey it.

220. Jones, *ibid.*, cf. *CTh* VII, 20.3; value, see n. 188.

221. W. A. Seaby, *NC* 1949, 175–6, pl. II, 12–18 (no. 17 being of tin). On the *absence* of die-links in another hoard (Poundbury, Dorchester, Dorset) cf. A. S. Robertson, *NC* 1952, 91–2.

222. The earlier material is assembled by C. H. V. Sutherland, *NC* 1945, 125–33. See also P. V. Hill, *NC* 1948, 91–3; H. Mattingly, *NC* 1953, 72; Boon, *NC* 1955, 235–7; Kent, *NC* 1957, 78–83, and with Carson, 1971, 225; C. E. King, *NC* 1976, 227. The Dinorben specimen and brief discussion, Boon, *BBCS* XXXII (1985), 379–82.

223. Kent, *RIC* VIII, 57–8.

224. M. Amandry *et al., QT* XI (1982), 283–4. Mintmarks soon carry the letters PS for *pusulatum,* 'refined'.

225. F. Haverfield, *Victoria History of Somerset,* I (1906), 356; cf. S. Archer in P. J. Casey (ed.), *The End of Roman Britain* (BAR 71, 1979), 44, no. 26; Lawrence Fine Art of Crewkerne, Sale cat. 2 October 1986, Lot 7; now at Taunton, 1.74 g Burghöfe, B. Overbeck in *Mélanges de numismatique offerts à P. Bastien* (ed. H. Huvelin *et al.,* 1987), 251–3, pl. 18; 2.03 g but chipped. Cf. Kent in *RIC* VIII, 167.

226. *Ibid.,* 60. A Heslington overstrike (n. 209) retains silvering (?) of the original.

227. *Dichōneutum, CTh* XI, 21.1. Analyses at first seemed to give the Valentinianic '3 Æ' a silver-free alloy (A. Ravetz, *Archaeometry* 1963, 46–55, cf. *eadem, NC* 1964, 216–17) but later and more numerous ones have redressed the picture and pointed up the contrast between Julian's 'bull' type and the Valen-

tinianic *Restitutor Reipublicae*, clearly a matter of policy (Amandry *et al.*, *l.c.* n. 224, 284–9).

228. Kent, *RIC* VIII, 65–6, 90. Cf. P. Bastien, *MN* 30, 156–7, cf. his fig. 51; Hill, *NC* 1955, pl. I, 18, no provenance given.

229. Hill, NC 1946, 163, shown *idem, NC* 1950, pl. 15, 14; 2.43 grammes. It is not 'overstruck' as he says. It has been badly defaced in ancient times, probably because it was recognised as false. Other Valentinianic copies, Hill, *BNJ* 1949–51, pl. I, 5; M. J. Hammerson, *Trans. London & Middx. Arch. Soc.* XXIII.1 (1971), pl. E, 125.

230. Reece, *BIAL* XVIII, 65–6.

231. Hemptinne hoard, as mentioned by G. Depeyrot and D. Rouquette, *BSFN* 1981, 14; slightly different figures are given by M. Amandry, *ibid.* 13, but do not affect the general picture. Amandry publishes two overstrikes, *ibid.* 12–13, one on *Soli Invicto Comiti*; the other is of Gratian's CONCORDIA AVGG type on *Securitas Reipublicae* of Valens. Depeyrot and Rouquette publish *ibid.* 13–14 a *Reparatio Reipub.* struck over a *Securitas Reipublicae* of Gratian himself. On Lyons *Reiparatio Reipub.* of Maximus, counterfeited, cf. *BSFN* 1988, 314–15, illus.

232. Hill, *BNJ* 1949–51, 18, pl. 1, 3 and 4 shows respectively a fine example of a Theodosius, *Victoria Auggg*, struck copy (misidentified) and a cast copy of *Salus Reipublice* type; another, from the Bermondsey hoard, *idem, NC* 1950, pl. 15, 18; cf. *NC* 1946, 167–9. The most notorious of these Theodosian counterfeits is the surprisingly neat Richborough piece (*Report* II, no. 19, 315, pl. 36, 2) with obverse titulature somewhat less so, reading 'Pavunius' or 'Pruumus' (F. Salisbury, *NC* 1934, 135–6, 309–10; cf. *CCRB* 100, pl. 14, 16).

233. Above, n. 221; an unusual example of trimming is offered by no. 405 in the Brean Down list (*PUBSS* 1965, 247), being a Valentinianic *Securitas Reipublicae* cut down to 13 mm.

234. *Antiq. Journ.* 1949, 83–4.

235. Hill, *NC* 1946, 153–6.

236. Hill *ibid.* publishes hoards from Redenhall (Norfolk), 157–9; and Wiveliscombe (Som.), 163–5. Cf. also Bermondsey, H. Mattingly, *ibid.*, 167–9.

237. Mattingly, *NC* 1929, 319–27; 1938, 59–61.

238. C. E. King, *BNJ* 1981, 5–31, has a good study of these hoards and the 'problem' of clipped siliquae, but makes too much of them; I cannot believe in 'weight-standards'.

239. It is worth recalling that it was a grave offence to clip solidi within the outer ring, for they had to be regarded as all having the same value (*CTh* IX, 22.1). No such regulation is recorded for silver, but as gold and silver had always

been classed together under the law relating to forgery (above, p. 103 and n. 5) one may presume that clipping of siliquae would have been equally punished. Curiously enough, the large silver *miliarensis* was not clipped, perhaps because it was little seen in circulation – 'une monnaie de thésaurisation'.

240. 'An illusion . . . the resemblance was persuasive, but . . . this irregular coinage *does* play strange tricks on us' (H. B. Mattingly, *NC* 1964, 192).

241. Cf. *BBCS* XXII.3 (1967), 310. In conclusion, 'we see how Roman Britain formally ended, with the repudiation of a usurped imperial authority and the refusal of the legitimate emperor to resume responsibility. This will have meant: no fresh appointment of officials, no despatch of gold for pay, no small change to redeem that pay. It is surely no longer necessary to point out that coins in the Roman world 'drifted' but little, but were moved swiftly and deliberately, then remained close to their place of issue until deposition or loss. So Britain began a rapid reversion to a coinless economy. . . . There is no evidence that coinage was struck in Britain by any sub-Roman government. It is not unthinkable that coinage in gold or silver in the name of Honorius or even of Valentinian III should have been produced, but there is no indication that this actually happened; it is probable that the need for coined money disappeared with the Roman fiscal system. With so fragile a basis, the economy will not have required small change. . . .' J. P. C. Kent, *The End of Roman Britain* (ed. J. Casey, *BAR* 71, 1979), 18, 22.

Abbreviations

A	*Archaeologia or Miscellaneous Tracts*, Society of Antiquaries of London.
AC	*Archaeologia Cambrensis*, Cambrian Archaeological Association.
AIIN	*Annali*, Instituto italiana di Numismatica.
AJ	*Archaeological Journal*, Royal Archaeological Institute.
AK	*Archäologisches Korrespondenzblatt*.
ANRW	*Aufstieg und Niedergang der römischen Welt*.
AS	*Ancient Society*.
B	*Britannia*.
BBCS	*Bulletin*, Board of Celtic Studies, University of Wales.
BCEN	*Bulletin*, Cercle d'études numismatiques.
BIAL	*Bulletin*, Institute of Archaeology, University of London.
BICSL	*Bulletin*, Institute of Classical Studies, University of London.
BJ	*Bonner Jahrbücher*.
BMCRE	British Museum Catalogue, *Coins of the Roman Empire*.
BNC *Auguste*	Bibliothèque Nationale, *Catalogue des monnaies de l'Empire romain*, I: *Auguste*, by J.-B. Giard. Paris, 1976.
BNJ	*British Numismatic Journal*.
Boon, *Usk*	*Report on the Excavations at Usk 1965–1976. The Coins Inscriptions and Graffiti*, by George C. Boon and Mark Hassall. Cardiff, 1982.

BSFN	*Bulletin*, Société française de numismatique.
CA	*Coins and the Archaeologist*, edited by John Casey and Richard Reece. British Archaeological Reports, 4, 1974.
CCRB	*Coinage and Currency in Roman Britain*, by C. H. V. Sutherland. Oxford, 1937.
CHRB	*Coin Hoards from Roman Britain*. British Museum Occasional Papers.
CJ	*Codex Justinianus*.
CRRB	*Coins of the Romans relating to Britain*, by J. K. Akerman. London, 1844.
CT	British Museum, *The Cunetio Treasure*, by E. Besly and R. Bland, London, 1983.
CTh	*Codex Theodosianus*.
Dri-ii	École française de Rome. *Les 'Dévaluations' à Rome*, I (1978) – II (1980).
ERW	*The Emperor in the Roman World*, by Fergus Millar, London, 1977.
Essays/Mattingly	*Essays in Roman Coinage presented to Harold Mattingly*, edited by R. A. G. Carson and C. H. V. Sutherland. Oxford, 1956.
Essays/ Sutherland	*Scripta Nummaria Romana*, Essays presented to Humphrey Sutherland, edited by R. A. G. Carson and C. M. Kraay. London, 1978.
FMRD	*Die Fundmünzen des römischen Deutschlands*.
G	*Germania*.
JMP	*Jaarboek voor Munt- en Penningkunde*.
JNG	*Jahrbuch für Numismatik und Geldgeschichte*.
JRS	*Journal of Roman Studies*.
JS	*Journal des Savants*
Mél. Lafaurie	*Mélanges de numismatique, d'archéologie et d'histoire offerts à Jean Lafaurie*, ed. P. Bastien *et al.*, Paris, 1980.
MN	American Numismatic Society, *Museum Notes*.
MV	C. M. Kraay, *Die Münzfunde von Vindonissa (bis Trajan)*. Veröffentlichungen der Gesellschaft Pro Vindonissa, V, 1962.
NC	*Numismatic Chronicle*.
NCirc.	Spink's *Numismatic Circular*.
NNM	American Numismatic Society, *Numismatic Notes and Monographs*.
NZ	*Numismatische Zeitschrift*.
PL	J. P. Migne, *Patrologia Latina, Cursus Completus*.
PM	J. P. Callu, *Politique monétaire des empereurs romains de 238 à 311*. Paris, 1969.
PUBSS	*Proceedings*, University of Bristol Spelaeological Society.
RBN	*Revue belge de numismatique*.
RE	Pauly's *Reallexicon der klassichen Altertumswissenschaft*, ed. G. Wissowa *et al*.
RBI	C. H. V. Sutherland, *Romano-British Imitations of Bronze coins of Claudius I* (NNM no. 65, 1935).
RHC	*Roman History and Coinage 44 BC–AD 69*, by C. H. V. Sutherland, Oxford, 1987.
RIB	*The Roman Inscriptions of Britain*, ed. R. G. Collingwood and R. P. Wright, vol. i. Oxford, 1965.
RIC	*The Roman Imperial Coinage*.

RIN	*Rivista italiana di Numismatica.*
RM	*Geschichte des römischen Münzwesens*, by Theodor Mommsen. Berlin, 1860, repr. Graz, 1956.
RN	*Revue numismatique.*
RRC	*Roman Republican Coinage*, by M. H. Crawford. Cambridge, 1976.
SCN	*Studii şi Cercetări de Numismatica.*
Shiel, *Carausius*	*The Episode of Carausius and Allectus*, by Normal Shiel (BAR 40, 1977).
TBGAS	*Transactions*, Bristol and Gloucestershire Archaeological Society.

List of illustrations

All coins, etc., shown full size; asterisks distinguish orthodox pieces. NMW – National Museum of Wales.

Pl. I

*1. Titus, aureus, Rome, 74. 7.30 grammes. Obverse with *nummularius'* mark (M engraved). Caerleon; Myrtle Cottage hoard, NMW. P. 104.

*2. Nero, As, Lyons, 66. 9.25 grammes. Obverse with radiate crown engraved on the head, for 'dupondius'; reverse with peckmarks to test for plating, and (arrowed) incuse R. Exeter, excavations. Royal Albert Memorial Museum. P. 106.

3. Claudius, Grade I sestertius, 24.46 grammes, with portrait battered to test for plating. Ham Hill, Som. Taunton, Somerset County Museum. P. 106.

4. Similar, 27.57 grammes, with battered portrait and countermark [P]ROB. Silchester; Reading Museum. P. 106.

5. Similar, much worn, 22.04 grammes. Obverse countermarks IMP and PRO, and on the reverse an edge-cut to test for plating and countermark DVP reducing the value. Germania Inferior; NMW. P. 106.

*6. Nero, As, Lyons, 66. 8.06 grammes. Obverse showing test-cut across the neck, with possible political significance. Silchester; Reading Museum. P. 107.

*7. Similar, 11.20 grammes. With countermark of validation, VESPAS. NMW. p. 107.

*8. Augustus, As, Nîmes, *c.* 10–14, 13.00 grammes. Filed between the heads of Augustus and Agrippa to be divided into two. NMW. P. 115.

*9. Postumus, antoninianus, Milan, 268, 2.13 grammes. Marked to be divided into quarters for restriking as minims, and one segment detached. White Woman's Hole, Mendip. Bristol City Museum. P. 129

*10. Tacitus, 275–6. Quarter of an antoninianus, Lyons, 0.53 gramme. Intended for restriking as a minim, cf. Pl. V, 75. White Woman's Hole; Bristol City Museum. P. 129.

11. Antoninus Pius, 138–61. Lightweight cast As, 5.57 grammes, Lydney; Collection of Lord Bledisloe. P. 108.

12. Similar (part missing), originally *c.* 3.5 grammes. Cast from an original from the same mould as 11. Caerleon; NMW. P. 108.

13. Marcus Aurelius, 161–80. Cast As, 8.7 grammes. Caerleon; NMW. P. 108.

*14. Philip I, 244–9, antoninianus, Rome, 2.80 grammes. Bassaleg hoard, Gwent; NMW. P. 110.

15. Struck copy of the preceding type, 4.20 grammes. Bassaleg hoard; NMW. P. 110.

16. Lucilla, *c.* 164–9. Dupondius, bronze plated on iron core. Vendeuvre-du-Poitou; by courtesy of M. P.-H. Mitard. P. 112.

Pl. II

17. Keyed clay mould for an antoninianus of Postumus, Lyons; by courtesy of Rouen Museum, photo Ellebé. P. 102.

18. Unkeyed clay mould for an antoninianus of Tetricus I, 271–74. The obverse mould retains part of the outer casing, being the lowest mould in a pile. Whitchurch, Som. Bristol City Museum. P. 108.

19. Unkeyed clay mould for the INVICTUS reverse of an antoninianus of Victorinus, 269–71. Whitchurch; Bristol City Museum. P. 108.

20. Bronze die for a false denarius of Hadrian, 117–38 (iron sleeve missing). Verulamium – St. Albans, in excavations. Verulamium Museum. P. 110.

21. Keyed lead cliché mould for a false antoninianus of Tetricus II, 273–4, and modern plaster cast. Silchester excavations; by courtesy of M. G. Fulford. P. 112.

*22. Nerva, dupondius, Rome, 96–8. 15.29 grammes. NMW.

*23. Trajan, dupondius, Rome 98–9. 14.37 grammes. NMW.

*24. Trajan, dupondius, Rome 103–11. 14.24 grammes. NMW.

25. 'Nerva-Trajan' dupondius, *c.* 104 (?), SPQR OPTIMO PRINCIPI reverse, 11.30 grammes. Caerleon; NMW. P. 110.

26. 'Nerva-Trajan' dupondius, obverse, 13.40 grammes, Ffrith, Flints., NMW. P. 110.

27. Same die, Wroxeter, Salop. Kindly notified by R. Kenyon. Shrewsbury, Rowley's House Museum. P. 110.

28. L. Scipio Asiagenus, 106 BC. Plated copper denarius, 2.73 grammes, serrate. NMW. P. 111.

29. Nero, plated denarius with central leaf of silver thickening at the edge. Woodcock Hall, Saham Toney, Norfolk. By courtesy of R. A. Brown. Norwich Museum. P. 111.

30–31. Octavian and Antony, denarius. 39 BC. Silver-plated on iron cores. Two examples from the same false die: note *nummularius'* mark on the neck. St. Swithin's lane, London. British Museum. P. 111.

32. Valentinian I, 364–75. Siliqua, silver-plated copper, halved. Silchester; Reading Museum. P. 143.

Pl. III

*33. Augustus, As, Lyons (1st series), *c.* 10–2 BC. 10.00 grammes. With countermark TIB. NMW. P. 120.

34. Grade III copy of the preceding, 2.23 grammes. Sea Mills, Avon. Bristol City Museum. P. 120.

*35. Agrippa, As (under Tiberius, 14–37), 11.38 grammes. NMW. P. 120.

36. Grade II–III copy of the preceding, 3.96 grammes. Sea Mills. Bristol City Museum. P. 120.

37. Claudius, sestertius, Grade II–III copy, 16.68 grammes. 'Near Colchester'. NMW. P. 120.

*38. Claudius, dupondius, CERES AUGUSTA, 41. 14.01 grammes. NMW. P. 120.

39. Grade I–II copy of the preceding, obverse, 11.98 grammes. Usk, excavation; NMW. P. 120.

40. Similar; reverse, 11.59 grammes. Sea Mills; Bristol City Museum. P. 120.

*41. Claudius, dupondius for Antonia, 41. 15.50 grammes. NMW. P. 120.

42. Grade I–II copy of the preceding, 9.85 grammes, Usk. NMW. P. 120.

43. Grade III copy of **41**, overstruck on Lyons dupondius of Tiberius, 13.02 grammes. Silchester, by courtesy of M. G. Fulford. P. 119.

44. Claudius, As, LIBERTAS AUGUSTA type. Grade I. 7.37 grammes, Silchester; Reading Museum. P. 120.

Pl. IV

*45. Claudius, As, Minerva type, 41. 11.60 grammes. Rodd Nash Farm, Rads. NMW. P. 119.

*46. Claudius, dupondius, 42. With obv. legend ending in PP for *Pater Patriae*. 16.8 grammes, British Museum. P. 119.

47. Grade III copy, Minerva type, overstruck on an As of Germanicus (time of Caligula): part of the legends survives, especially on the reverse. 10.33 grammes. Northern Gaul. NMW. P. 119.

48. Grade I copy, Minerva type, much-worn, 8.21 grammes, with countermark Q.VA; Germania Inferior, found at Silchester. Reading Museum. P. 121.

49. Grade I copy, Minerva type, 10.40 grammes. Silchester, by courtesy of M. G. Fulford. P. 120.

50. Grade II copy, Minerva type, 6.74 grammes. Silchester, by courtesy of M. G. Fulford. P. 120.

51. Similar style, 6.90 grammes, Salmonsbury Camp, Bourton-on-the Water, Glos. Cheltenham Museum. P. 120.

52. Grade III copy, Minerva type, 6.78 grammes, Silchester. Reading Museum. P. 120.

53. Grade III copy, Minerva type, 9.5 grammes, Verulamium excav., by courtesy of S. S. Frere. P. 120.

54. Grade IV copy, Minerva type (head R. and SC reversed), 3.74 grammes. Castlefield, Kenchurch, Herefordshire; By courtesy of S. Clarke. P. 120.

55. Grade III copy, Minerva type, copper plated on iron. Richborough. By courtesy of R. Kenyon. Site Museum. P. 120.

Pl. V

56. Domitian, lightweight cast As, 4.92 grammes. Usk. NMW. P. 125. See P. 164, note 140.

57. Clay mould for a worn As of Hadrian, and modern cast. Whitchurch, Som. Bristol City Museum. P. 125.

58. Faustina II, lightweight cast As, 3.22 grammes. Caerleon; NMW. P. 125.

59. Similar, 2.97 grammes. Probably cast at the same time as the preceding: note the 'crack' or inhomogeneity near the casting-jet in both, due to the cooling of the metal. Caerleon; NMW. P. 125.

*60. Commodus, As, Rome, 189–90, showing the Emperor plough-
ing the bounds of a new colony, 11.55 grammes, British Museum. For comparison with nos. 61–2.

61. Commodus, lightweight cast with reverse similar to the preceding, 3.40 grammes. Caerleon. NMW. P. 125.

62. Similar, 3.08 grammes. Caerleon, NMW. P. 125.

63. Severus Alexander, 222–235, denarius, silver-plated on copper,
1.70 grammes. Caerleon; NMW. P.124.

*64. Gordian III, 238–44, denarius, 2.8 grammes. NMW. P. 125.

65. Gordian III, base cast denarius, 2.69 grammes. Caerleon; NMW.
P.125

66. Tetricus II, 272–4, antoninianus, cast, 2.28 grammes. Caerleon;
NMW. P. 126.

*67. Tetricus I, 270–4, antoninianus, 2.32 grammes. NMW.
For comparison with nos. 68ff.

68. Tetricus I, 'barbarous radiate', 2.90 grammes. Caerleon minim
hoard; NMW. P. 126.

69. Similar, heavily silver-plated, 2.00 grammes. By courtesy of
P. J. Casey. P. 112.

70. Similar, but with reverse CONSECRATI and type from Aurelian's coinage, 2.21 grammes. South Wales; NMW. P. 126.

71. Radiate minim with Tetricus' name and portrait, and 'altar'
reverse, 0.62 gramme. Caerleon minim hoard. NMW. P. 126.

72. Similar, but with reverse drawn from Aurelian's PROVIDEN
DEOR type; 0.62 gramme. Dinorben, Abergele, Denbs. NMW.
P. 128.

*73. Aurelian, reformed antoninianus, with the type mentioned
under the preceding. Bon Marché hoard, Gloucester. British
Museum. P. 128.

74. Radiate minim with obv. portrait of Tetricus II, 0.31 gramme.
Caerleon minim hoard, NMW. P. 128.

75. Barbarous radiate struck on a quarter of an antoninianus, 0.58
gramme. White Woman's Hole, Mendip. Bristol City Museum.
P. 129.

76. Radiate minim, 0.48 gramme. Caerleon minim hoard; NMW.
P. 126.

PLATE I

PLATE II

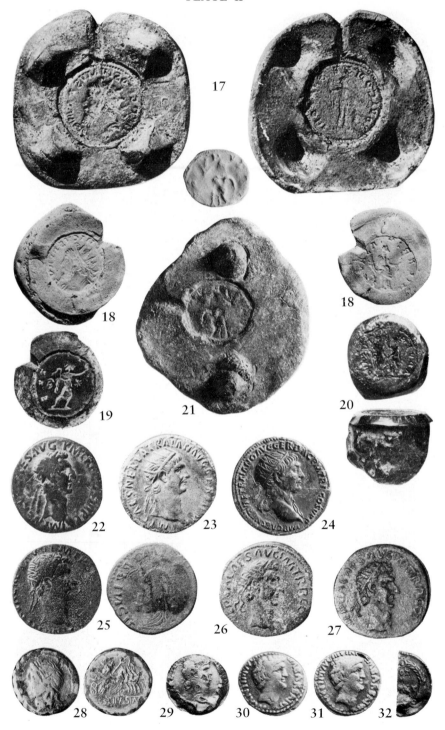

17

18

18

21

18

19

20

22

23

24

25

26

27

28

29

30

31

32

PLATE III

33

34

35

36

37

38

39

40

41

42

43

44

PLATE IV

PLATE V

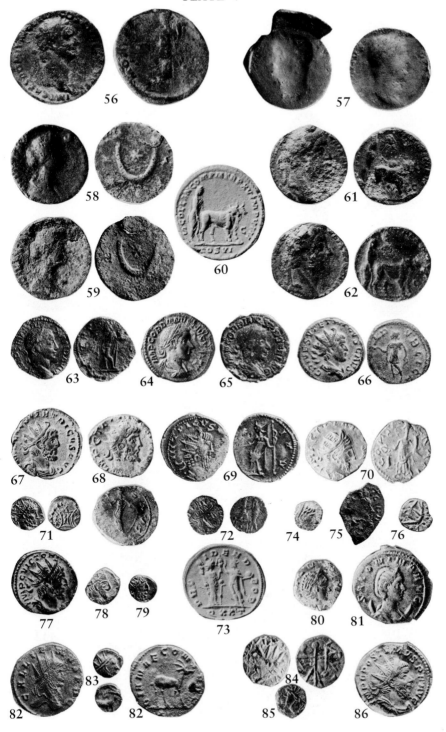

PLATE VI

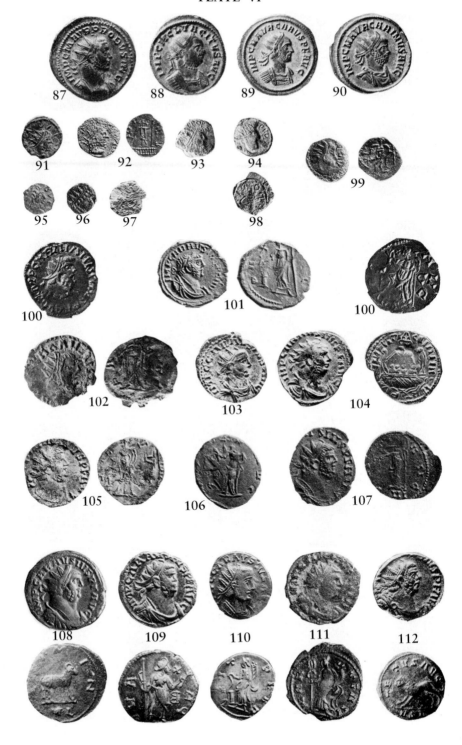

PLATE VII

PLATE VIII

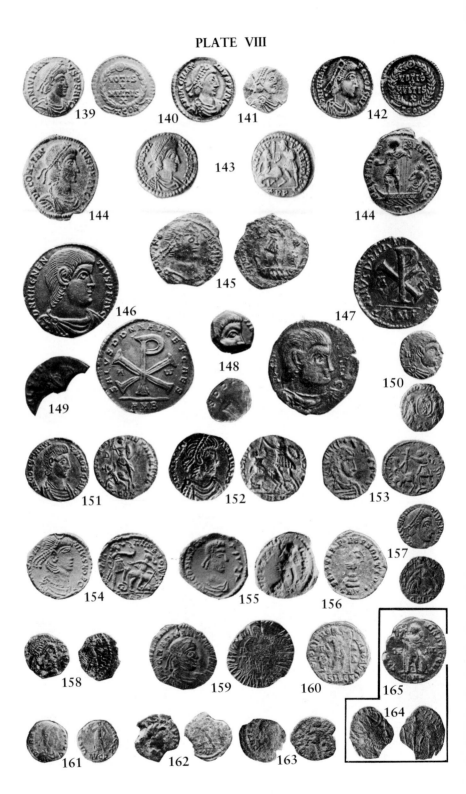

139

140

141

142

143

144

144

145

146

147

148

149

150

151

152

153

154

155

156

157

158

159

160

161

162

163

164

165

*77. Victorinus, antoninianus, 3.23 grammes. NMW.
For comparison with nos. 78–9.

78. Radiate minim Victorinus portrait. 0.52 gramme. Caerleon
minim hoard; NMW. P. 126.

79. Another, 0.22 gramme, same source. P. 126.

80. Barbarous radiate with portrait of Salonina, 0.64 gramme.
Segontium; NMW. P. 126.

*81. Salonina 253–60–68, antoninianus, Rome, 3.00 grammes.
Bassaleg hoard; NMW. For comparison with no. 80.

*82. Gallienus, 260–8, antoninianus, Rome, with antelope on re-
verse, 4.31 gramme. Llanedeyrn hoard, Cardiff; NMW. See
no. 83.

83. Radiate minim based on the preceding type, 0.25 gramme.
Lydney; Collection of Lord Bledisloe. P. 126.

84. Radiate minim with left-facing Postumus bust and pin-figure
reverse, 0.79 gramme. Lydney; Collection of Lord Bledisloe.
P. 129.

85. Radiate minim with similar bust, 0.37 gramme. Caerleon minim
hoard; NMW. P. 129.

*86. Postumus, 259–68, antoninianus, Gaul. 3.28 gramme. Bassaleg
hoard; NMW. For comparison with nos. 84–5.

Pl. VI   *87. Probus, 276–82, antoninianus, Lyons, 4.32 gramme. Penard
hoard; NMW. P. 128.

*88. Tacitus, 275–6, antoninianus, Ticinum, Penard hoard; 3.60
gramme. NMW. P. 128.

*89. Carus, 282–3, antoninianus, Rome. 4.16 gramme. NMW.
P. 128.

*90. Carinus, 283–5, antoninianus, Rome. 3.89 gramme. NMW.
P. 128.

91. Radiate minim in Probus' name, 0.98 gramme. Segontium;
NMW. P. 126.

92. Similar, 0.48 gramme, Coygan, Carms. counterfeiter's deposit;
NMW. P. 129.

93. Same obv. as preceding, 0.42 gramme. Coygan; NMW. P. 129.

94. Similar, 0.70 gramme. Caerleon minim hoard; NMW. P. 129.

95. Similar, Frocester Court Villa, hoard, Gloucester Museum. P. 131.

96. Similar obverse style to the preceding, 0.24 gramme. Caerleon minim hoard; NMW. P. 131.

97. Similar obverse style to the two preceding. 0.24 gramme. Coygan counterfeiters' deposit; NMW. P. 131.

98. Radiate minim, with reverse PROBI (reversed). 0.50 grammes. Coygan, counterfeiters' deposit; NMW. P. 126.

99. Radiate minim with portrait reminiscent of Carus, 0.54 gramme. Coygan, counterfeiters' deposit; NMW. P. 128.

100. Carausius, 286–83, antoninianus. Barbarous overstrike on Tetricus I. 2.67 grammes. Little Orme's Head hoard, no. 97. NMW. P. 132.

101. Carausius, base denarius, with reverse from an antoninianus-die. Silchester. Weight unknown. P. 132.

102. Barbarous Carausius, overstruck on Tetricus I, 2.72 grammes. Silchester; Reading Museum. P. 132.

*103. Carausius, antoninianus, Rouen, 3.61 grammes. Little Orme's Head hoard, no. 98; NMW. P. 133.

104. Carausius, antoninianus with barbarous reverse, overstruck on Tetricus I. 2.64 grammes. Little Orme's Head hoard, no. 112; NMW. P. 132.

105. Carausius, barbarous antoninianus overstruck on a barbarous radiate; silvered surface, 1.80 grammes. Penard (Gower) hoard; NMW. P. 132.

106. Same obverse die (not shown) and similar reverse, less barbarous, also overstruck, 2.64 grammes. Penard hoard; NMW. P. 132.

107. Similar obverse, semi-barbarous reverse. *Pax* type, with early mintmarks of London ML, 1.89 grammes. Penard hoard; NMW. P. 132.

*108. Carausius, antoninianus, London, 287, in honour of *Legio I Minervia*, 4.09 grammes. Little Orme's Head hoard, no. 56; NMW. P. 134.

109. Carausius, antoninianus, 4.82 grammes with barbarous reverse (turned L. for R.) copying the BE/MLXXI mark of 290–1. Little Orme's Head hoard, no. 109; NMW. P. 134.

110. Barbarous copy of Rouen *Securit. Perpet.* type, given a *Salus* figure; 3.10 grammes. Little Orme's Head hoard, no. 100; NMW. P. 134.

111. Carausius, antoninianus, with barbarous reverse MART FAV, and figure of *Felicitas*. Die-duplicate from Dinorben, Abergele, 4.47 grammes, and Little Orme's Head hoard, no. 148, 4.00 grammes, both reverses used to make up the photograph here; both NMW. P. 134.

112. Carausius, antoninianus with barbarous reverse of the RSR mint, 3.67 grammes. TE TVS AVG may present part of the name of TETRICUS showing through, as undertype, on the prototype. The lion or panther betokens an ultimate original in Gallienus' 'animal' series; NMW. P. 134.

Pl. VII *113. Allectus, 293–6, antoninianus overstruck on Carausius, with the SF|C mark of 293 at the C mint. Silchester; Reading Museum. P. 135.

114. Allectus, false 'legionary' antoninianus showing a panther L. and early Carausian mintmark of London. 6.31 grammes. South Shields; site museum. By courtesy of N. Shiel. P. 136.

115. Galerius Caesar, 293–305, nummus, London, struck copy, 9.45 grammes, *c.* 300–5. Caerleon; NMW. P. 137.

*116. Galerius, nummus, London, 9.47 grammes, *c.* 300–5. Lydney: Collection of Lord Bledisloe. For comparison with no. 115.

117. Constantine I, 306–7. Copy of VICTORIAE LAETAE PRINC PERP type of Trier, *c.* 318–19, 2.04 grammes. Silchester; Reading Museum. P. 137.

118. Constantine I, copy of VOTA type for the Caesars: CESRVM NOSTRORVM and Trier mintmark of *c.* 323–4, 2.00 grammes. Llanbethery (Barry) hoard; NMW. P. 137.

119. Constantine II Caesar, copy of PROVIDENTIAE type of *c.* 326–30 with camp-gate, but GL[ORIA EX]ERCITUS legend and Arles mintmark; 1.67 grammes. Caerwent; NMW. P. 137.

*120. Constantine I, nummus, Trier, 332, 2.47 grammes, GLORIA EXERCITUS (two standard) type; Llanberthery hoard; NMW. P. 137.

*121. *Constantinopolis*, Trier, 332, 2.42 grammes. Llanbethery hoard; NMW. P. 137.

*122. *Urbs Roma*, Lyons, 332, 2.46 grammes. Llanbethery hoard; NMW. P. 137.

123. Reduced copy of the type of no. 120, 1.40 grammes. Llanbethery hoard; NMW. P. 137.

124. *Constantinopolis* copy, types reversed, 2.41 grammes. Llanbethery hoard; NMW. P. 137.

125. *Urbs Roma* copy with Trier reverse (? orthodox) of 331. Llanbethery hoard; NMW. P. 137.

126. *Constantinopolis/Gloria Exercitus* (two standards) mule, 1.06 grammes. Caerleon; NMW. P. 137.

127. *Urbs Roma/Constantinopolis* mule, 1.92 grammes. Llanbethery hoard; NMW. P. 137.

*128. Constanţine I, nummus of Arles, 335–6, 1.54 grammes. GLORIA EXERCITUS (one standard) type; Llanbethery hoard; NMW. P. 137.

129. Constans Augustus, 337–40. *Gloria Exercitus* (one standard) type, with narrow long-necked bust typical of the period *c.* 348, 1.26 grammes. Lydney; Collection of Lord Bledisloe. (cf. **156**, for reverse and details, Pl. VIII. P. 139.)

130–131. *Constantinopolis* and –

132–134. *Constantinopolis/Gloria Exercitus* (one standard) minims in a die-linked series weighing between 0.42 and 0.67 gramme. Several have been superimposed to indicate the designs as fully as possible, the flans in general being too small. White Woman's Hole, Som. Bristol City Museum. P. 138.

*135. Constantius II Augustus, 342–8(?). VICTORIAE DD AVGGQ NN 'two Victories' type. Trier, 1.10 grammes. Caerleon; NMW. P. 138.

136. Copy of the preceding type, 0.71 grammes, Silchester. Reading Museum. P. 138.

137. Constans, VICTORIA AVGG type, Siscia, 0.77 grammes. Segontium; NMW. P. 138.

*138. Constans, orthodox specimen of the preceding type, cf. *c.* 341–2, 1.53 grammes. Kenchester; Hereford Museum. P. 138.

Pl. VIII　　*139. Julian Caesar, 360–63. Siliqua, Arles, 1.79 grammes. Cleeve Prior hoard. Lydney; Collection of Lord Bledisloe. P. 143.

*140. Magnus Maximus, 383–8. Siliqua, Trier, 1.94 grammes. Cleeve Prior hoard. NMW. P. 145.

141. Counterfeit siliqua, possibly of Maximus; clipped, 0.70 gramme. Holyhead Mountain signal-station. By courtesy of P. Crew. P. 145.

142. Struck copy of a siliqua of Julian II (named as *Caesar*, 355–50), 'Arles' mintmark given as TCOR; 1.57 grammes. Caerwent; NMW. P. 143.

143. 'Falling horseman' with 'Trier' mark, 1.74 in *silver*; Holway hoard, Taunton. Somerset County Museum, Taunton; P. 143.

*144. Constantius II, majorina, Rome, 5.20 grammes. retaining silvered surface; FEL. TEMP. REPARATIO (Emperor in galley) type, 348–50. Dinorben hoard; NMW. P. 139.

145. 'Domino Group' imitation, overstruck on *Gloria Exercitus* (two standards), 2.15 grammes. Dinorben hoard; NMW. P. 142.

*146. Magnentius, 350–3. Large *Salus Chi-Rho* type, Amiens, 8.2 grammes. NMW. P. 140.

147. Copy of the preceding. Wookey Hole Cave; Wells Museum. P. 140.

148. Magnentian *Salus* type, cut-down to the size of Theodosian small aes. Lydney; Collection of Lord Bledisloe. P. 145.

149. Specimen offcut from cutting down Magnentian Salus majorinae, Ham Hill; Somerset County Museum, Taunton. P. 145.

150. Minim, Magnentian 'two Victories' type. 1.13 grammes as against a normal 4.5–5.0 grammes. Lydney; Collection of Lord Bledisloe. P. 140.

*151. Constantius Gallus, 351–5, *centenionalis*, Arles, FEL TEMP REPARATIO (falling horseman) type, 2.50 grammes. Caerwent; NMW. P. 139.

152. 'Domino Group' ('Carausius II') falling horseman type, overstruck on *Gloria Exercitus* (two standards), 2.51 grammes. Silchester; Reading Museum. P. 142.

153. Barbarous 'falling horseman', overstruck; Silchester; Reading Museum. P. 140.

154. Similar, in name of Constantius Gallus, reversed rev., Heslington hoard, York. Yorkshire Museum. P. 140.

155. Similar overstruck on FEL. TEMP. REPARATIO (phoenix on pyre) type, Gloucester; Gloucester City Museum. P. 140.

*156. Constans (obverse on Pl. VII). FEL TEMP REPARATIO (phoenix on pyre) type, 2.29 grammes. Lydney, Collection of Lord Bledisloe. P. 140.

157. Small 'falling horseman' with 'Lyons' mint-mark, 0.79 gramme, Silchester; Reading Museum. P. 140.

158. Barbarous 'falling horseman', 0.89 gramme, White Woman's Hole; Bristol City Museum. P. 140.

159. Gratian, 367–83. Barbarous and defaced GLORIA ROMANORUM of Siscia, 2.43 grammes, DNGNATIANVS ... Wiveliscombe hoard; Somerset County Museum, Taunton. P. 144.

*160. Reverse for comparison, 2.05 grammes, Lydney, Collection of Lord Bledisloe.

*161. Arcadius, 383–408. VICTORIA AVGGG nummus, Lyons, 0.77 gramme. Llys Awel votive cache, Abergele; NMW. P. 145.

162. Copy of the preceding type, 'Arles' mintmark, 1.23 grammes, Caerwent; NMW. P. 145.

163. Copy of Theodosius I, 379–95, SALUS REIPUBLICE type, 0.72 gramme, DNTEOD. Silchester Reading Museum. P. 145.

164. Barbarous radiate, with reverse showing a standing figure bearing a vague resemblance to the Valentinianic *Gloria Romanorum* [160] or *Gloria Novi Saeculi* [165] types. 0.75 gramme. Silchester; Reading Museum. P. 116.

*165. Gratian, 367–83. GLORIA NOVI SAECULI type (reverse). For comparison with no. 164.

8
Data for dating
John Collis

Summary

In its progress from the moneyer's die to the excavator's finds tray, a coin has undergone a series of varied selection processes. Correct evaluation of a coin's significance depends on a careful consideration of these processes, and a failure to do so has in the past led to some glaring misinterpretations. On the specific problem of using Roman coins for dating evidence, we have still failed to evaluate the length of circulation of individual coin types. Seriation seems to offer the best potential approach to this question.

Introduction

One of the more pleasant and stimulating aspects of the conference was the contrast of views expressed, often leading to a lively discussion at the end of various papers which could only be stifled by that most potent of threats, no tea break. As representing one of the extremes of thought at the conference, and also one of the more vocal elements in the audience, I thought it might be worthwhile to expand some of my views and ideas, and to suggest at least one method, seriation, which may allow us to make more objective and meaningful use of coins for dating.

Several speakers professed a feeling of despondency if not downright despair about the use of coins to archaeologists, especially their value as dating evidence. This despair came mainly from the archaeologists, but one suspects this is largely due to the expectation in the past of too much information from single coin finds, and only now are we beginning to grapple with the complex factors which affected coin use, distribution and, eventually, loss. For too long we have accepted coins at their face value, and that a highly inflated value. The pound in our pocket is not what it used to be, and neither is the follis in the feature nor the penny in the pit.

Personally, I am not so pessimistic. Certainly in the past too many assumptions have been made, and much written, especially by archaeologists, will have to be totally reviewed. In the meantime we must start questioning many of our previous assumptions, trying to establish as precisely as possible the different factors which may affect our interpretation. This is what I want to do in this paper, even if it sometimes involves stating the obvious. I hope out of it we will be able to evolve standard procedures, and standard evaluations of site evidence which everyone will be able to understand.

One thing was clear from the conference, that the revolution of quantification is only just beginning to hit numismatists. However, none of us progressed much beyond the stage of using simple graphs and bar-charts to illustrate our quantified material, and there was little reference in the lectures to the statistical techniques which are so developed in other fields, including that of archaeology. Coins are of course artefacts, and can be expected to follow the same rules as any other artefact type that an archaeologist has to deal with, so the same techniques can be applied. One major problem, however, that the archaeologist has had to contend with is the often indifferent quality of his data, but with coinage we have a body of information probably of higher quality than any other archaeological data.

Bias in the sample

Two or three speakers used the word 'sample' to describe the group of coins they were discussing. The simple use of the word implies a marked change of attitude, for no longer is the individual coin seen in isolation, but it is seen in its total background as a representative of the coins which were circulating at one time. But in addition the idea of a sample suggests to us the application of that body of statistical theory, which is sitting unopened on many of our bookshelves (e.g. Moroney 1951, Reichmann 1961). It introduces to us all the concepts of means, averages, sampling errors, Chi-square tests and the like, and teaches us to be more exact and more thoughtful in what we say, and also, we hope, to make our interpretations more meaningful.

The first thing we must realise is that the coins we are dealing with represent only the minutest fraction of the coins struck, and before they reach the vaults of our museums they have gone through a series of selection processes of very different kinds. We can perhaps talk of different 'levels' at which selection has taken place. We must consider these levels of selection and the actual processes involved, noting the distinction between what we can actually observe and what only infer. All these levels and processes I have tabulated (Table 1), thinking very much in terms of Roman coinage in Britain.

I will now expand on these different factors, and give examples:

(Level 1) All coins minted. At the first level, it is obviously significant that coin production varies from period to period, both in quantity and quality. Factors like the usurper's need for prestige were mentioned in the conference, or the central government's inability or disinterest in producing the required coinage, which could lead on to the production of the semi-official or unofficial coinage as described in Mr. Boon's paper.

(Level 2) Coins circulating in a province. At this level imperial policy also had its effect, for instance in the movement and payment of troops. Divisions in the empire are also likely to cause a blockage in coin circulation and trade, as for instance the formation of the Gallic empire limiting the circulation of Italian coins in Britain. To take extreme examples the decision of Claudius to invade, and the inability of Honorius to help both profoundly affected coin circulation in Britain. Also perhaps self-evidently the siting of

191

LEVEL	SAMPLE	SELECTION PROCESSES
1	All coins minted	(1) Imperial policy (2) Availability of raw materials (3) Economic pressures (inflation etc.)
2	Coins circulating in a Province e.g. Britain	(1) Imperial policy (2) siting of mints (3) trade
3	Coins circulating on an individual site	(1) Character of site (fort, market etc.) (2) date of site
4	Total coins lost or discarded (single losses, hoards, votive deposits)	(1) Activity on site (e.g. retail, wealth storage etc.) (2) value of coin
5	Total coins discovered on individual site	(1) Intensity of excavation and collection (2) Chance
6	Total coins from an excavation or part of site	(1) Nature of activity in area (e.g. market, rubbish dump, private house etc.) (2) Date of occupation
7	Total coins from a feature	(1) Date of feature (2) Function of feature

UNOBSERVABLE DATA / OBSERVABLE DATA

TABLE 1

mints is important, so coins of Antioch, Siscia and the like are bound to be much rarer in Britain than those of Lyons, Trier, and other Gaulish mints.

(Level 3) Coins circulating on a site. The actual coinage circulating on an individual site will be influenced by factors like the official consignment of pay to a fort, or the importance of small change on a market or fair site. Obviously the date of occupation will also affect the coins circulating on a site – Claudian troops were not using Constantinian coins.

(Level 4) Total coins lost. This level of interpretation is the most difficult, representing the break between data which we can observe directly, and that which can only be inferred. Obviously the gold and silver 'in circulation' will generally be hoarded away, and only change hands rarely for major transactions, whereas small value coins will be changing hands frequently and a higher percentage will be lost. Coins can be lost singly, or in groups (e.g. the lost purse); or coins can be deliberately discarded, singly (e.g. Coventina's Well), or in hoards. All of these types of coin loss are samples of the total coinage in circulation, and the selection factors can be very difficult to judge, especially with hoards. Hoard evidence must obviously be taken into account when attempting to reconstruct the coinage in circulation, but here we shall only be considering the evidence of the single coins accidentally lost. Even so, with single losses there is a bias in the loss. For instance, a poor man will hunt more diligently for a lost coin than a rich man. Different types of sites may have different patterns of coin loss, a contrast between the market where small change is changing hands, or the farm where the farmer keeps his gold and silver in his sock.

(Level 5) Total coins from a site. Factors of discovery, such as the nature of prospecting and the size and value of the coin, are of major importance, and before we can assume that the pattern of coin discovery reflects the pattern of coin loss, we must investigate possible biases, such as the loss of late deposits or the failure to expose earlier ones, the accidental inclusion of hoards and so on. The major factor however is sample size. How many coin finds are necessary before chance biases in the samples have been eliminated? Only experimentation can tell us this, and there the work of John Casey and Richard Reece is most important, for their histograms of site finds sometimes covering several thousand coins. The important point is reached when new discoveries do not substantially alter the pattern already established. The vital threshold for a Roman site seems to be about 1,500 finds. So two samples of 1,500 coins from the same site should give almost exactly the same pattern. One query raised by Brian Hobley at the conference, specifically thinking of his excavation at the Lunt, was: 'Can one say anything meaningful about a completely excavated site where the number of coins is substantially below the threshold number?' If date of abandonment is required, one approach would be to compare the sample with that obtained for the surrounding area or from a site with a sufficient number of finds, e.g. Wroxeter, and using statistical methods try to say that coins after a certain date are significantly absent. But a more promising approach I shall discuss below.

We should perhaps also emphasise the problem of the quality of excavation. Obviously there is going to be a considerable contrast in the rates of recovery on an excavation, between discoveries made during mechanical excavation, picking, shovelling and trowelling, with an obvious bias towards the larger coins in the more coarse excavation. In making comparison between different sites this is perhaps not of major importance, but if we are to construct 'coins lost' from 'coins found' (level 4 from level 5) we must try to work out how much we are likely to be missing. I would recommend that when coins are published the method of excavation under which they were found should be mentioned, so that higher quality data can be separated from poor quality. Also, as we all know, some volunteers have a better eye than others, and when volunteers are trained to look for the black stains in the soil rather than the coins themselves, the number of minims rapidly increases. So the names of the discoverers should also be recorded, to distinguish between high and low quality workers. However, perhaps it is time that Roman archaeologists admitted that their present excavation techniques are not adequate to tackle this sort of question, and when sample sieving is introduced we shall have as unpleasant a shock as prehistorians have recently suffered (Payne 1972).

(Level 6) Total coins from part of a site. Coins from an individual area can under normal circumstances be expected to reflect the total coin pattern from the whole settlement. Where it does seem to be aberrant, two possibilities are available:

  (a) The sample is too small, and chance sampling errors are distorting the picture. There are statistical tests such as the Chi-square test for eliminating this as a possibility.
  (b) The difference is significant, and speculating can start on the reasons why. One possibility maybe a shift in the focus of the settlement, or the example given by Peter Curnow, where the construction of the city wall at Verulamium caused the abandonment of a suburb, which therefore produced almost no later coins.

(Level 7) Total coins from a feature. Finds from individual features are more difficult to deal with as they are usually very small samples of a few coins at most. Yet even where two coins are found together, they do tell us something about the coinage in circulation at a given point in time. But often more relevant to the excavator is to establish the date at which his feature was filled in. The date-after-which is of course established by the latest coin in the group, but what about establishing a date-before-which? At present the only way we can get any clue to the significance of the absence of later coins is by studying the master chart for the whole site or area. Thus, a pit ending with coins of the Tetrici *c.* 272 could date to 285 simply because coins of the intervening emperors are so rare in this country. But to this problem I shall return later.

Much of what is written above may be deemed as self-evident, but it is clear from the literature and from comments made at the conference that there is some confusion about what statements can legitimately be made

Coins and the archaeologist

from what evidence. John Casey made mention of one example where the abundance of coins of one period on a settlement was taken by the excavator as denoting a change in character if not ownership, yet that abundance merely reflected the national pattern. In other words, my level 6 was assumed to directly reflect level 3. Another example is a statement that the lack of first and second-century coins on a class of rural settlements showed that those settlements played no part in the money market economy, but again this lack of coins reflects the national situation. It is self-evident that one cannot state what coins were being struck in the Roman empire from the evidence of a single pit somewhere in Britain, and so we must be extremely careful before we make any attempt to postulate from observed data at levels 5, 6 or 7 what the situation may have been at levels 4, 3, 2, or 1. Even writing this article I have found myself slipping into the same sort of error, referring to coin losses when I mean coin finds, two categories which can be very different.

The scheme laid out on Table 1 does also give a framework within which archaeologists and numismatists can work, and see their relationship to the whole field of study. John Casey and Richard Reece presented papers at level 5, whereas that self-styled 'numismatic hack' Peter Curnow was on level 6, but his paper demonstrates most clearly that this is no caste system and exciting and stimulating work can be done at any level and requires skill and imagination. Historians tend to be interested in level 1, archaeologists in level 7, but as an archaeologist I would certainly not consider myself inferior to an historian. Quite the opposite.

Coins circulating and coins lost

The coins in circulation at a given point of time will naturally be biased towards those recently issued, whereas earlier coins, though still circulating, will be rarer due to coins being lost or withdrawn. On the other hand, coins most recently minted will also be rare, as they are not yet in full circulation. If, for the sake of argument, we take the old penny and assume uniform production and withdrawal rates in the period between 1860 and 1960 we can make a number of hypothetical statements about the pattern of circulation over those 100 years.

Firstly, let us consider the pennies in circulation in 1940. It would include only a few of 1940, but a lot from the late 1930s. On the other hand, pennies of the 1860s and 1870s will be quite rare. If we plot this distribution as a graph of the number of pennies against the date of issue the pattern ought to follow that in Figure 1.

This distribution is the classic skew-curve. The pennies *lost* in 1940 will also follow this pattern, and so if a pit of 1940 were excavated, it is very unlikely it would actually contain a coin of that date. Any date between 1860 and 1940 would be possible but the late 1930s would be the most likely. In other words, for 'pennies circulating in 1940' in Figure 1 we can read 'pennies lost in 1940'.

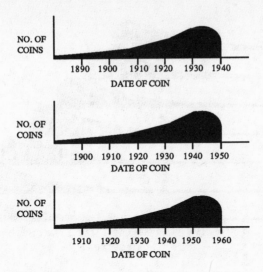

NO. OF COINS

1890 1900 1910 1920 1930 1940
DATE OF COIN

NO. OF COINS

1900 1910 1920 1930 1940 1950
DATE OF COIN

NO. OF COINS

1910 1920 1930 1940 1950 1960
DATE OF COIN

FIG. 1 – 3

If we now consider the situation ten years later in 1950, the pattern will be exactly the same, except pennies of the late 1940s will be in preponderance, and pennies of the 1860s and 1870s will have all but gone out of circulation. Likewise in 1960, except the skew-curve will have crawled a bit further along the axis. If we take the curves for all the years from 1900 onwards and tabulate them one above the other, we obtain the pattern on Figure 4.

Now, instead of looking at this chart horizontally, let us look at it vertically. Coins of the 1860s will be at their maximum circulation and loss around 1900, but by 1910 the numbers will have started dropping, and they will become excessively rarer through 1920, 1930, 1940, etc. So if we express Figure 4 in a different way to show the rate of loss of the coins of different years, we will end up with a pattern in Figure 5. In other words we again encounter the classic skew-curve.

This pattern is one familiar to archaeologists, and reflects the life cycle of birth, maturity and death which many archaeological phenomena pass through, be they attributes, artefact types or cultures (Clarke 1968). It has been most admirably demonstrated in the study of the styles of tomb-types in the eighteenth and nineteenth centuries in towns in New England (Dethlefsen and Deetz 1966), and has been used as a model, for instance, to test the chronology of British Beakers (Clarke 1970). Where the pattern is unknown, it can be established by studying the associations of one type with another. This technique of 'seriation' is no new phenomenon, and was used by Flinders Petrie to work out a sequence of tombs, but its application has been greatly extended with the development of the computer.

Returning to our hypothetical pennies, it should be possible, using the data on Figure 5, to talk about the rate of loss of coins in numerical terms.

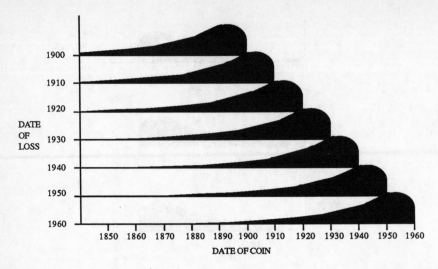

FIG. 4

So, in theory, we should be able to make statements like 30 per cent of the coins of 1900 which will ever be lost will have been lost by 1910, another 20 per cent by 1920, and another 12 per cent by 1930 and so on, though in theory we can never reach 100 per cent, as long as any coins exist to be lost. By adding these figures together we can construct a hypothetical cumulative percentage curve of coin losses.

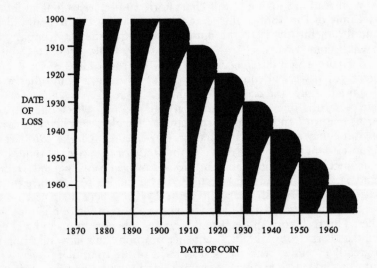

FIG. 5

Reading off this diagram (*see* Figure 6) one can say that 50 per cent of the pennies of 1900 will have been lost by 1920, 75 per cent by 1940 etc. In other words, if an archaeologist finds a coin of 1900 in a pit there is a 1:1 chance the pit was filled by 1920 and a 3:1 chance by 1940, and so on. The rate of loss will of course be the same for all pennies irrespective of how many were minted, as long as they went into normal circulation.

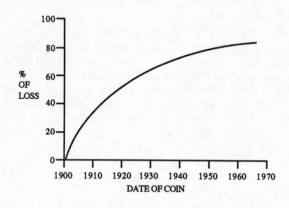

FIG. 6

Circulation observed

So far I have continually made modifying statements like 'assuming uniform production withdrawal rates'. Of course in reality the situation is much more complicated, with factors like inflation, debasement of the coinage, changing rates of withdrawal of old currency, demonitisation, and so on. To my knowledge, information about what pennies were in circulation simply does not exist, and it most certainly does not exist for Roman coinage. ·We know little about the length of circulation of individual coin types, and one wonders, for instance, if there was a monetary reform, how much old coins continued in circulation, especially in a province like Britain.

How can we reconstruct the curves, how can we establish what coinage was circulating at any one point in time, or work out the range of circulation life of individual coin types? The only way is to use the evidence of associations. Hoard evidence is one body of information, but as the selection factors are so varied and unpredictable, it can only be used to supplement other data. The other sources of information come from pit groups and other associated finds which were lost over a short period of time. Every time two or more coins are found together in a pit or feature we have an association. There must be hundreds of such associations published and dozens more found each year, but no one has yet started to gather this body of data together.

Using this sort of data it should eventually be possible to make statements like: 50 per cent of the coins of Tetrici are found with no later coins, 30 per cent are found with coins of the British usurpers, 10 per cent with coins of Diocletian and early Constantine. Or from another point of view: when coins from 330–340 are the latest in the group, 10 per cent of the associated coins will be radiates, 10 per cent Diocletian and early Constantine, 60 per cent contemporary coins, thus giving us a picture of the coin losses in the 330s. This has been done for other classes of archaeological data, and should be possible for coins.

With all these wonders of statistics, human judgement will still have to play a major role. When can one accept a deposit as being of short duration? Is there evidence of deliberate infill using earlier deposits which may already contain earlier coins? When is a group of associated coins a group and when is it a hoard? The human archaeologist is not redundant yet. The result we hope will be the possibility of stating exactly what the significance of a single coin, or a group of coins is, that they are likely to have been deposited by such-and-such a date, and unlikely to be later than a somewhat later date. This is what the archaeologist most desperately needs.

A plea for data

To build up a trustworthy seriation, hundreds if not thousands of observations are needed of coins found in close association and obviously lost at the same time. The more observations, the less important become statistical errors, or those rogue associations caused by Roman George Boons carrying coin collections around in their toga pockets.

Before inclusion, the following factors must be taken into consideration:
(1) The coins should represent chance losses, and not hoards.
(2) They should come from a deposit which in the excavator's opinion represent only a brief period of build-up, e.g. the infill or pit or a post-hole, and not from long duration deposits, such as occupation levels.
(3) There should be no evidence of a substantial amount of earlier material, such as deliberate infill of a pit using material derived from earlier deposits. However, if the two coins come from the bottom of a pit which has later been deliberately filled up, these can be accepted as associated, whereas if one coin comes from the bottom fill, and the other from the deliberate infill, these would not count.
(4) Both coins must be identifiable at least to an emperor or coin series (e.g. Fel Temp etc.). 'Unlikely' associations such as a coin of Claudius with one of Honorius *must* be included, as should all minims and barbarous coins, even if not assignable to an emperor.

In addition to the obvious data, excavators should also record information on prospecting methods and coin size in the hope of learning more about what we are *missing*, and so of getting nearer a reconstruction of actual coin losses.

Bibliography

Clarke D. L. (1968) *Analytical Archaeology.*

Clarke, D. L. (1970) *Beaker Pottery of Great Britain and Ireland.*

Dethlefsen, E. and Deetz, J. (1966) 'Death's Heads, Cherubs, and Willow Trees: Experimental Archaeology in Colonial Cemeteries'. *American Archaeology*, 31, no. 4, 502–10.

Moroney, M. J. (1951) *Facts from Figures.*

Payne, S. (1972) 'Partial Recovery and Sample Bias: the Results of some Sieving Experiments'. In E. S. Higgs ed. *Papers in Economic Prehistory.*

Reichmann, W. J. (1961) *Use and Abuse of Statistics.*

Data for dating

This was one of those pieces of research which never got off the ground. However, it would still be eminently worthwhile doing. The approach has however only so far been applied to pre-Roman coinage (Haselgrove 1986), an application which I had not envisaged when I wrote in 1974. However, Haselgrove has adequately demonstrated the nature of the time-lag, which will cause us all to rethink the interpretations we have placed on pre-Roman coinage. Something similar could happen for Roman coinage, especially for the end of the fourth and beginning of the fifth centuries. Our over-ambitious hope of computer storage of coin data (Haselgrove and Collis 1981) has now become a reality with the appearance of computers with greater storage capacity and more sophisticated relational databases, such as dBase III plus and Prime Information. This year will see the first entries, and we are also thinking about sceattas. What about Roman and medieval coinage? These problems have also persuaded me to improve my recording methods. All printed site labels have spaces to note the name of the finder and the method of excavation – sieving, trowel, pick and shovel, fieldwalking. I urge all excavators to do likewise.

Department of Archaeology and Prehistory
University of Sheffield

Bibliography

Haselgrove, C. (1986) *Iron Age Coinage in South-East Britain: the archaeological context*. Unpublished Ph.D. dissertation, Cambridge.

Haselgrove, C. and Collis, J. (1981) 'A computer-based information storage and retrieval scheme for Iron Age coin finds in Britain'. In B. W. Cunliffe, 'Coinage and Society in Britain and Gaul: some current problems', pp. 57–60. *Council for British Archaeology*, Research Report No. 38, London.

9
Interpreting coin-finds
J. P. C. Kent

'They did discourse very finely to us of the probability that there is a vast deal of money hid in the land'. Pepys' *Diary*, 19 May 1663.

If numismatists had effectively persuaded their archaeological, economic and historical colleagues of the essential validity of their techniques and conclusions, it would not have been necessary to hold this conference at all. It is the measure of our corporate failure that our most confident and carefully thought-out pronouncements and statements of method seem to command attention mainly when they happen to reinforce a fashionable or deeply held opinion deduced quite independently from the coins; if our coin evidence fits, we may achieve acclaim, if it does not, it may be safely disregarded.

Numismatists do not, any more than their colleagues, speak with a united voice; it would be surprising if they did – though I have heard archaeologists more than once demand a 'consensus' before committing themselves to a particular numismatic proposition. The nemesis of the mystique that an ancient science – or is it not rather an art? – has cast over itself is that colleagues deeply learned in many branches of their subject tend to retreat baffled and suspicious in the face of the evidence we offer.

Certain university appointments of recent years seem to reflect a cautious desire of departments of history and archaeology to emancipate themselves from the tyranny of the classically trained numismatist. In very truth this bogey, though still from time to time invoked,[1] is something of a myth. The 'professional numismatist' – to use the phrase in its true, rather than in its euphemistic sense – is, increasingly, a person with historical and/or archaeological training and experience, who has chanced to specialise in the study of coins and who might equally well have turned to university teaching, general museum work, or even industry. His classically trained colleagues, whose detachment from the pressures of archaeological controversy is itself valuable, cannot and do not wish to, escape from the realities of the wider body of evidence, and the world of learning of which we are all a part. In this context, diversity of numismatic opinion is a precious sign of intellectual vigour and integrity in the ivory towers and a guarantee that the discipline remains outward-looking and dynamic.

Coinage has long been recognised to have characteristics which distinguish it from most other artefacts – those, at least, which are regularly found in archaeological contexts. Most significant of these distinctions are, firstly, its official nature (or, in the case of forgeries, its direct relationship to official

201

objects), and secondly, its documentary character. From it, in consequence, is sought evidence of an especially specific kind in respect both of date and of interpretation. The numismatist's responsibility is correspondingly oner-ous, and this essay seeks to discuss, if not to determine, the degree to which we succeed in tackling our major classes of evidence.

The basic, 'simplistic' level of interpretation, which, like all such, contains just enough truth to be plausible, divides hoards into two basic groups, defined respectively as 'currency' and 'savings'. The first group, it is held, discloses a cross-section of the available currency in the desired denomina-tions at the date of deposition. Such hoards will reveal a gradation of wear from the earliest to the most recent coin. The second results from careful men putting aside coins from time to time over a lengthy period; such hoards contain random peaks of material, corresponding to fluctuations in their collectors' prosperity, and do not show gradation of wear to the same extent. Hoards of unusual magnitude may be deemed to have been 'military chests', or to have had some other official character. A corollary to these premises continues as follows: hoards are deposited close to the date of the latest coin. Plotted on maps, they can show movements of armies and peoples, areas of unrest, regions of wealth etc.[2]

This comfortingly coherent set of yard-sticks is seemingly valuable when applied to periods when literary evidence is negligible or scanty. Its principles are, however, merely deduced *a priori*; they must be proved valid in an unambiguously documented context if we are to accept them as axiomatic. The truth is, as usual, much more complex.

All hoards tell us something about the currency of their time, inasmuch as they contain coins worth putting on one side, and available to be hoarded. Each find has, therefore, a psychological aspect individual to the depositor, i.e. the determination of his quest for the most desirable coins, usually those of the finest metal, highest weight and best condition. Against this must be set the historical circumstances of selection and deposit, i.e. the availability of and accessibility to the desired coins in the depositor's economic *milieu*, and the speed with which concealment had to be undertaken. It is, of course, well known that, in general, hoards contain a lower proportion of false pieces than do site-finds of the same period; hoards are systematically weigh-ted in favour of what was best in the currency, site-finds with what, like broken crockery, was best discarded. Hoards tend to contain a larger prop-ortion of the higher denominations than do site-finds; we might have deduced *a priori* what the Central Statistical Office has demonstrated graphically, that small coins are more readily lost than large ones, and that low denomi-nations survive less readily (and, we might add, in worse condition) than pieces of high value. Even in 1967 it appeared that the currency of Great Britain was not uniform, there being a marked increase in the proportion of older coins in circulation outside London. *A fortiori*, uniformity of cur-rency in remoter times is not readily to be accepted, nor used as the basis of further hypotheses.[3]

Since hoards are individual to the person, time, place and circumstance of their acquisition, we need not be surprised at the diversity which they show, however we choose to categorize them. Some examples, not in themselves 'untypical', are representative of the infinite variety of hoard structure:

False coin
London, St. Swithin's Lane (Roman)   *NC* 1940.185
Scarborough Castle, Yorks (Charles I)   *Num. Circ.* 1907.9940
Great Barr, Birmingham (Charles II)   *Daily Telegraph* 5 Oct. 1956

Coins of predominantly low denomination and poor condition, often including false pieces
London, Paternoster Row (Roman)   *NC* 1967.61
'St. Leonard's-on-Sea, Sussex' (Roman)   *NC* 1951.91
There are many similar finds in third-century Britain.
Buttington, Montgomery (Elizabeth I)   *BNJ* 1964.152
Upton, Berks (Charles I)   *BNJ* 1968.139

Selective exclusion of lowest denominations
Sheerness, Isle of Sheppey, Kent (Charles I) *BNJ* 1969.163
Acton, Suffolk (Charles II)   unpublished
These hoards exclude the abundant sixteenth-century sixpences regularly found in such minor hoards.

Containing coins predominantly of a single issue only
Karanis, Egypt (Roman)   *Coins of Karanis,* 14

This characteristic is also found in periods when the coinage is immobilised, or subject to systematic type changes.

Ending exceptionally strongly
Colchester, Essex (Henry III)   *BNJ* forthcoming
Fishpool, Notts (Edward IV)   *NC* 1967.133

Ending exceptionally weakly
Llangarren, Herefordshire (Roman)   *NC* 1956.83

Having a false end
Reka-Devnia, Bulgaria (Roman)[4]
This hoard 'terminates' in the middle of the reign of Gordian III. It omits coins of the Philips, but includes the sons of Decius.

Contents politically motivated
Gloucester (Roman)   unpublished
East Harnham, Wilts (Roman)   *NC* 1949.248
Cheddar, Somerset (Roman)   *JBAA* 1847.270

An interesting group of finds which appears to discriminate against the coinage of Carausius in his own name, while admitting the issues struck by him in the names of Diocletian and Maximian. From the time of Aurelian's recovery of Gaul, hoards suggest a consistent discrimination against the coinage of the Gallic Empire; other examples might be cited, and more may be suspected.

Enclosed in more than one container

At least eleven per cent of the hoards listed by Thirion for the Celtic and Roman periods in Belgium were contained in more than one vessel.[5] Other hoards have been discovered divided into two portions and buried some distance apart:

Vidy, Lausanne, Switzerland (Roman)   *SNR* 1967.312

Such divided finds are not necessarily recovered intact:

Alderwasley, Derbyshire (17th Century)   *BNJ* 1906.337
                                          and unpublished

The first pot-full of this hoard of coin-clippings was found in 1846, a second was recovered in 1971 adjacent to the find-spot of the first. Multiple-container hoards are not easy to distinguish from successive concealments in the same area:

Colchester, Essex (Henry III)   *NC* 1903.111 and
                                          BNJ forthcoming

In 1969 a large find consisting overwhelmingly of Long-Cross pence was discovered close to the place where in 1902 a substantial hoard of short-cross pence had appeared. It is improbable that these two classes of coin were ever concurrent to such an extent that a single deposit could have consisted of large numbers of each type segregated into separate containers. It is, however, less easy to establish the relationship between the numerous hoards deposited in close proximity to one another at:

Beachy Head, Sussex (Roman)

Icklingham, Suffolk (Roman)

In some cases, the circumstances of discovery make it virtually certain that no further part of the deposit remains to be found. More frequently, we have no means of judging the completeness of a find. We have seen that portions of the same hoard can turn up more than a century apart: hoard records seldom antedate the eighteenth century, whereas hoards themselves, or parts of them, may be disinterred any time after their burial.

Bromley, Kent (George VI)   *BNJ* 1968.145

The latest coins of this hoard, found in 1966, bore the date 1941. The Anglo-Saxon Chronicle implies the unearthing of Roman coin-hoards. The immemorial law of Treasure Trove is not readily to be explained unless the periodic discovery of gold and silver was sufficiently important to be of perceptible benefit to primitive treasuries.[6] It is possible that hoards with unusually 'weak' endings are to be explained, in some cases at least, as one portion of a multiple-container deposit; other parts may await discovery, or may have been found long ago.

Dispersed hoards

This class of find is occasioned by the disturbance of the find-spot in former times, without recovery of the hoard. This may arise owing to the destruction of the superstructure of a building, in which the hoard has been secreted:

Lydney, Glos. (Roman)[7]

The coins recovered from the floor of the temple site have the appearance of a hoard dispersed thus rather than of a random (and quite inexplicable) scatter of casual losses on a hard floor in constant use.

Chadwell St. Mary, Essex (Roman)   NC 1956.238

The excavation of this hoard in 1956 furnishes a classic instance of the recovery of a deposit scattered by cultivation. Commencing at the top-soil, the dispersed coins constituted an inverted cone, at the apex of which lay the remains of the neck of the pottery container, set upside down into the natural soil. Dispersed hoards are relatively abundant at all periods, and on large excavated sites such as Corbridge, where they may be gradually recovered over a half century or longer, they are readily confused with pieces lost in the normal way. All general site-lists require scrutiny with this possibility in mind.

Though it is a common practice, particularly in periods when hoards are scanty and literary evidence slight, to try to link such hoards as we know with such events or even personages as are recorded,[8] the validity of such assumptions is in general doubtful. One of the few comprehensive accounts of the collection, concealment and recovery of a hoard is related in Pepys' *Diary*. The tale is worth recounting. At the Restoration of 1660, Samuel Pepys declared himself to be earning £50 a year, and to have £40 cash in hand. By the end of 1666, his average annual income exceeded £3,000, and he was 'worth in money, all good', above £6,200, beside two-and-a-half dozen silver vessels. Like many of his thrifty contemporaries, he kept his surplus cash under lock and key in his own house; the unfortunate Mr. Tryan, of Lime Street, who kept the key of his cash-chest in his desk, was robbed of £1,050 in money and of £4,000 in jewels held as securities for loans.[9] In June 1667, deeply worried by the penetration of the Dutch fleet into the Thames estuary, Pepys resolved to conceal his money. He was at first undecided whether to conceal it elsewhere in London or to despatch it to the family estate in Brampton, Northamptonshire. The latter counsel prevailed and his father and wife took coach, with a bag containing some £1,300.[10] Finding himself unable to convert his silver in hand for gold – he had been forestalled by others – Pepys sent on another 1,000 gold pieces by special messenger, and carried on his own person another £300 worth, together with 'directions where to find £500 and more in gold and silver'. Recovery of the treasure in October of the same year proved a gruelling experience. His wife gave him 'so bad an account of her and my father's method in the burying of our gold, that made me mad; and she herself is not pleased with it, she believing that my sister knows of it. My father and she did it on Sunday, when they were gone to church, in open daylight, in the midst of the garden, where for aught they knew, many eyes might see them; which put me into trouble, and I presently cast about, how to have it back again to secure it here, the times being a little better now'. Recovery began at night, with a dark lantern, but 'they could not justly tell where it was', and Pepys began to fear the worst; but 'by poking with a spit', it was at length located, 'not half a foot under ground'. Frantic digging merely succeeded in scattering the coins in the grass and loose earth. Finally, coins, dirt and all, were raised and washed. To Pepys' chagrin, he found himself about one hundred pieces short, and fearing that the neighbours might have observed him, and come searching on their own account, he and his servant sieved through the earth until they had recovered a further seventy-nine. Pepys considered it quite acceptable that his special messenger should have lost some twenty to thirty pieces *en route*, and regarded himself as well content with the matter when all was finally safe back in London, 'under a bed in our chamber'.

This true story prompts several reflections. Pepys' wealth, though certainly a 'savings hoard', was assembled over a very short period. It certainly included some old coins – he gave three 'Jacobuses' (gold pieces of James I) to his father-in-law and its random origin and rapid assemblage suggests that it would have been indistinguishable from a 'currency hoard' assembled *ad hoc* in 1667. Indeed, since his surplus increased during 1666 by only £1,800, as against £3,000 in 1665, we might suspect that the dates 1666 and 1667 were relatively slightly represented, i.e. that the hoard ended 'weakly'. The really extensive coinages of guineas lay, in any case, in the future, and we may postulate that Pepys' fortune consisted predominantly of the old 'broad pieces'. Great quantities of these were certainly still available; a poulterer of Gracechurch Street died in November 1662 leaving an unsuspected hoard of 40,000 'Jacobs'. We may conclude that the recovery of a hoard was not necessarily an easy matter, and that there was a significant risk that it would not be recovered intact. The discovery in modern times of a scatter of twenty or thirty broad pieces at Brampton, or between Brampton and London, would give a totally false impression alike of date, of the circumstances of concealment and of the size of the original treasure. It may be objected that the circumstances are unrepresentative, but how are we to know how 'representative' were the circumstances of any find of any date? The coins, with or without a container, will no more tell us this than will the ashes of prehistoric man tell us what language he spoke.

The factors rendering suspect any too facile interpretation of an individual hoard lead naturally to the consideration of significance of maps of hoard distribution. That they have a significance is obvious. Whether we correctly evaluate their evidence, and whether we may generalise from one period to another, is more questionable; for it is noticeable that detailed expositions of this class of evidence are preferred in inverse proportion to the availability of documentary or literary sources. I believe there has been no attempt to explain hoard structure and distribution in the context of a well-documented period. Sixteenth and seventeenth century England offers interesting and promising scope for this exercise, some of the problems of which may here be briefly adumbrated.

A map (Fig. 1) indicates the peace-time distribution of hoards between about 1550 and 1700. Though different in detail, the early and late distributions unite to reveal considerable areas empty of hoards. Hoards deposited in the century preceding the Civil War show concentrations along the Thames valley and in Cheshire and its environs. Although finds of the post-war

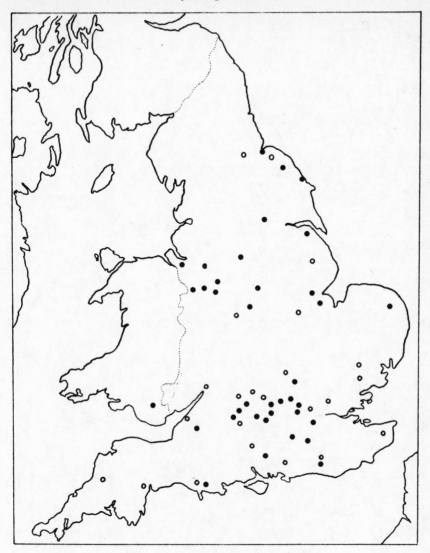

HOARDS DEPOSITED IN ENGLAND

- ● in the century preceding the Civil War
- ○ in the half century following the Civil War

FIG. 1

period have a much wider distribution, it is observable that almost half the peace-time deposits of the period under review fall within a fifty-mile radius of London. However, it is clear that these distributions are not directly related either to the population or wealth of the country, as it is revealed

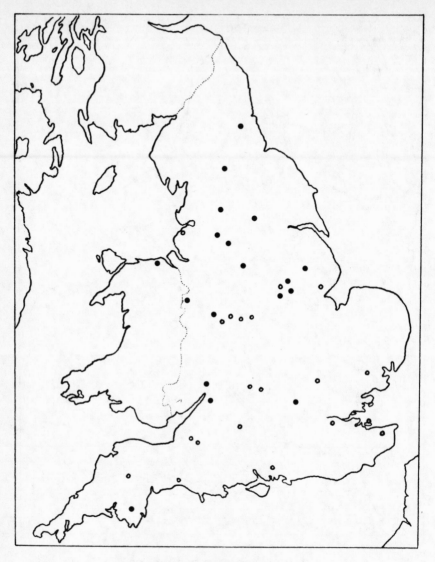

HOARDS DEPOSITED IN ENGLAND

DURING THE CIVIL WAR

● terminating 1641-3

○ terminating 1643-9

FIG. 2

to us by such criteria as the Ship Money Assessment of 1636 or the Hearth Tax Returns of 1690. The importance of London is obvious, but if we can otherwise determine neither the density of the population nor the relative wealth of different areas as viewed by the eminently practical yardstick of taxability, then we must be cautious of how we deduce economic conclusions from distributions of hoards in ill-documented periods.

The pattern of distribution during the Civil War is entirely different (Figure 2), though no easier to understand. The London area is relatively empty of hoards and, indeed, the notable storm-centres of the war, apart from Newark, are scarcely to be discerned. The start of the war seems to have led to the deposit of numerous hoards in the north of England, often in regions where hoarding in the preceding century has left no trace. Perhaps fear of the Scottish army and lack of opportunity for reinvestment stimulated the concealment of newly-acquired wealth in the north to a greater extent than did the sporadic troubles of the south. Throughout the war, it will be observed that the areas securely held by Parliament have produced new finds. In general however, the distribution would be subject to grave risk of misinterpretation if we had not a full historical record. Only in a restricted sense was there a shift in emphasis in the war from the north to the south after 1643, and such important areas as the Oxford–Newbury–London triangle are quite imperceptible. Movements of individual armies stand out not at all. We are left with a very large increase in the deposition of hoards in this period, an accepted symptom of crisis.

The seventeenth-century hoard distributions reveal with startling clarity the impropriety of generalising from such evidence. There are virtually no hoards in Wales because it was poor and thinly populated; there are virtually no hoards along the Cotswolds, in the south Midlands, and East Anglia, where precisely converse conditions prevailed.[11] It might be possible to erect many viable hypotheses to explain why the hinterland of London, so productive of hoards in peace-time, lacks them in time of war; but these would have to be based upon documents, since our *a priori* argumentation would have postulated, quite wrongly, security or depopulation. We have endeavoured to exclude from the war-time map all finds which cannot be said for certain not to have contained the hammered money of Charles II. We must however bear in mind the possibility that some finds of hammered coin, particularly if heavily clipped, belong to the post-war period.

It is not easy to form any reliable estimate of the proportion of coin withdrawn from currency into hoards, or otherwise lost. After the recall of the Commonwealth money in 1660, it was believed that as much as a third of these issues was unaccounted for;[12] presumably, had its currency continued, the proportion unavailable for recall would have increased. Even in these days of ready investment and banking, a significant proportion of current coin is not withdrawn upon demonetization. The recent withdrawals of silver coin of the 925 and 500 standards, followed by the recall of the non-decimal denominations, have given a statistically-based insight into the phenomenon of coin loss which, though evidently not directly applicable to remoter times, has both interest and value. Looking at the first table (Figure 3), we observe that the rate of withdrawal rapidly attains a peak within a few years of its commencement, and thereafter falls dramatically. Expressed as a percentage of the amount of coin potentially available, i.e.

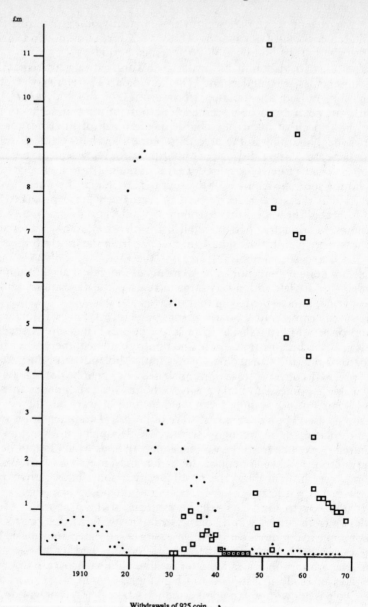

Withdrawals of 925 coin   •

Withdrawals of 500 coin   ▫

FIG. 3

not withdrawn at the moment when large-scale recall was begun (Figure 4), we see that no less than 18 per cent of the total issue of 925 silver subsequent to 1816 remains unaccounted for. Some will doubtless have been exported, some converted into plate; much of it however is likely to have passed into hoards or to have become casual losses. The Central Statistical Office's pamphlet may be usefully consulted on the varying rate of loss of different denominations in recent times. I owe to Mr. B. Koorlander statistics of more than 50,000 half-crowns withdrawn in 1970. Figure 5 expresses these as fractions of the number of coins of each date divided by the number of coins reported to have been struck in that year. Though the habitual use of dies of the preceding year doubtless introduces random disturbances into the resulting distribution, the trend is clear enough. It shows that, given equal numbers in two issues separated by thirty years, the chances of finding a specimen of the earlier date were no greater than one tenth of the likelihood of finding the later coin. The straightness of the main axis of the graph and the absence of systematic withdrawal until 1949 indicates that much of this unavailability of older coin was due to loss or hoarding.

The relatively rapid changes in the age-structure of our currency over the last fifty years owes much to inflation and much to its corollaries, the fall in absolute terms of the purchasing power of each denomination, and the increasing vigour of circulation. Our assessment of the coin evidence of earlier times has to take account of many imponderables, and it is useful to have on record at least one body of material whose behaviour can be documentarily checked.

General conclusions must be approached with caution. In periods when more than one denomination is concurrent, neither hoards nor site-finds can be expected to reflect the true currency situation; it may further be inferred that until comparatively modern times, say after 1800, there was in Britain no such thing as a uniform currency,[13] whether viewed geographically or by social and economic *milieu*. These circumstances do not of course invalidate the following premisses, though they should not be confused with them:

1. In the event of casual loss, small coins and coins of low value are found more commonly relative to numbers issued and in circulation than larger and more valuable pieces.

2. All other things being equal, coins with a long life in currency are found more commonly relative to numbers issued than pieces with a systematically shorter life, e.g. the coinage of Elizabeth I contrasted with the hammered coinage of Charles II.

3. Low denominations have a more vigorous currency than high ones; at any given date the former may be expected to appear much more worn, e.g. Hartford, Huntingdon: Henry VII; half-groats were very much more worn than groats. Newark, Notts: Charles I; groats were very much more worn than sixpences of comparable date.

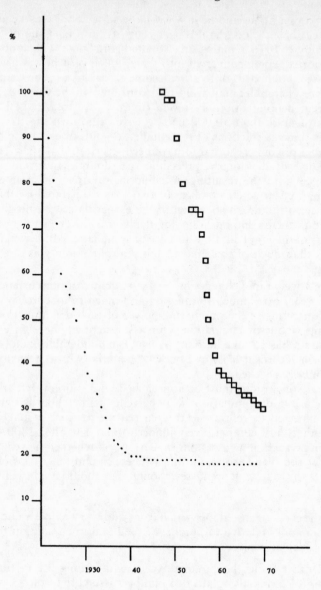

Survival of 925 silver as % of 1920 total •

Survival of 500 silver as % of 1946 total □

FIG. 4

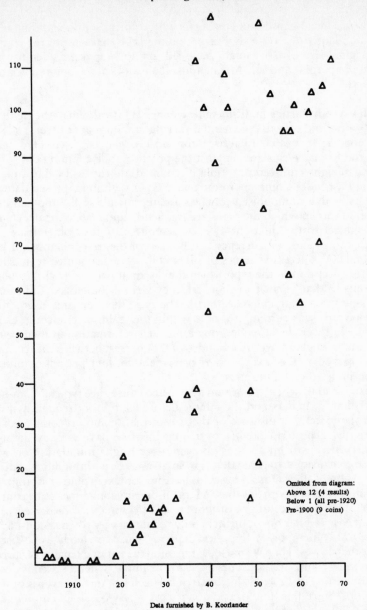

Omitted from diagram:
Above 12 (4 results)
Below 1 (all pre-1920)
Pre-1900 (9 coins)

Data furnished by B. Koorlander

Sample of half-crowns withdrawn in 1970 (52298 Specimens)

No. of coins struck
Millions of coins struck

FIG. 5

4. Coins may be discriminated against by political action and thus appear less abundantly or over a shorter period than the character of the coin and the original size of issue might have led one to suppose, e.g. coins of the Gallic Emperors and of Magnentius; coins of the Commonwealth of England.

5. It was normal in a multi-metallic coinage at least down to the eighteenth century for gold coin to command a varying premium over silver, and silver over copper. It was characteristic for old coins to be discounted against new; the Romans legislated against the practice of discounting old solidi;[14] shroffs in eighteenth-century India discounted old rupees by date and thus led the East India Company to introduce types with immobilised dates.[15] It is probable that immobilised coinages are in principle stable and long-lived, whereas those in which the types are frequently and systematically changed were subject to the discount or even demonetization of older issues. The effect of this factor on currency can be seen in the 'réformations' of Louis XIV and XV. Successive issues of silver coin were discounted from shortly after the inception of the type; when the discount had reduced the value of the coins to that of their mere metal, they were demonetized and restruck with new types at an enhanced tariff. The cycle then repeated itself.[16] Thus only one type was current at a time within the realm of France; in Geneva however, all were legal tender long after their réformation in their country of origin. In England, we are reminded of the contrast between the constantly changing types of the Saxo-Norman penny, and the long periods of immobilization under the Plantagenets.

It is essential, when we are invited to recognise the 'typical' coin-hoard or site-find, to understand the mirage before us; all too frequently it turns out to be merely an instance of the truism that 'common coins are found commonly'. The individuality of a hoard-list we have already discussed. The list of coins from a site is an even more fragile foundation on which to base conclusions. In general, it is so small as to be without much statistical value.[17] Often, all or most of the coins have no context in plan or stratigraphy, or relationship one with another. A large list seems sometimes to be contaminated by the presence of one or more hoards, complete or dispersed, which it is not easy to filter out; a further contaminant is, very often, a considerable number of contemporary forgeries, many of which are likely to be discards rather than losses. Then we must bear in mind the varying lengths of currency of different coins, and ask ourselves, for example, whether a considerably worn sestertius of Trajan is likelier to have been lost under Severus or under Postumus. Since this kind of decision is very rarely possible, I am bound to conclude that a coin list should be interpreted with the utmost reserve. The coin-list of Corstopitum begins with denarii of the Roman Republic, but it would be a rash man who did not recognize in this the limitations of coin-evidence when seemingly opposed to literary statements and the more straightforward testimony of ceramics.

The study of coins is specialised, because it is required at once to be subtle and wide-ranging. It is capable of supplying unique information and of clarifying obscure passages of history. In the hands of insensitive and *a priori* interpreters, it is capable of misleading our archaeological colleagues. But in due course they become disenchanted, and what they cannot rectify by argument they understandably ignore, unless it chances to suit a conclusion already arrived at. To match his unrivalled opportunities for influencing historical thought the numismatist must be ready to eschew the facile and the merely fashionable solution – they will let him and his science down in the end – and be prepared to understand and confess the limitations his material imposes. Mythopoeia may achieve a temporary vogue for its perpetrator, and even perhaps convince him that he has some special faculty for divining truths about coins and history. It is, however, an ignoble art; we must rather strive with all our skill and integrity to avoid making ourselves and others the victims of our own insouciant myth-making.

British Museum
London

Notes

1. See for example Seaby's *Bulletin* 1968.54: 'Incredibly, a degree in classics is still the requisite for a member of the staff of the Coin Department in the British Museum, regardless of what field of numismatics that member of staff may be specializing.' At the time this *canard* was launched the only three members of that staff with classics degrees were the ones specializing in ancient coinage, which seems reasonable.

2. For an exposition of this sort of interpretation, see *The Archaeology of Roman Britain*, 2nd ed. 1969, p. 230; L. R. Laing, *Coins and Archaeology*, 1969, p. 52 contains perhaps the most refined exposé of the "classification" of hoards.

3. R. G. de Glanville, *The Numbers of Coins in Circulation in the United Kingdom*, Studies in Official Statistics, Research Series No. 2, HMSO 1970. See also *Autobiography of William Stout*, ed. J. Harland, London 1851 p. 41, for regional differences in 1695.

4. N. A. Mouchmov, *Le trésor numismatique de Reka-Devnia (Marcianopolis)*, Sofia, 1934.

5. M. Thirion, *Les trésors monétaires gaulois et romains trouvés en Belgique*, Cercle d'Etudes Numismatiques, Travaux 3, Bruxelles 1967.

6. It should however be remarked that as early as the reign of Charles II, the exercise of the royal prerogative over Treasure Trove took account of its historical importance. See *Add. MSS* 32094 f. 266, a letter of Charles II dated 14 August 1672 commanding a find of gold coins or medals at Thakeham, Sussex, to be delivered immediately to Elias Ashmole. For the subject in general, see Sir George Hill, *Treasure Trove in Law and Practice*, Oxford 1936.

7. R. E. M. and T. V. Wheeler, *Report on the Excavation of the Prehistoric, Roman, and Post-Roman Site in Lydney Park, Gloucestershire*, Society of Antiquaries, Research Report No. IX, 1932.

8. See, for example, Whaddon Chase, Bucks, linked with the tribute imposed by Caesar (C. E. Stevens, in *Essays presented to O. G. S. Crawford*, p. 332); Kaiseraugst, Switzerland, linked with the activities of Julian, in spite of the abrupt end of the dated material more than five years before his presence in the area (*Illustrated London News*, 14 and 21 July 1962). Richborough Radiate hoard: 'the coinage of Hengist and Horsa with their Jutes'; ANS. Num. Notes and Mon. no. 80 p. 13.

For a hoard specifically associated with a person and an event, see *AJN* 1912.36; a find of coins in a casket at Bollingen, Württemberg, was accompanied by a paper bearing the following verse:

Der schwedt ist komme,
hat als mitgnomme,
hat auch walle hawe,
i habs vergrabe.
1634 Bozehartt.

9. The association of some coin hoards with the proceeds of robbery is hypothetical, but inherently likely. In the seventeenth and eighteenth centuries considerable sums in cash changed hands by this means, under conditions which might prompt concealment and inhibit recovery. A good example is Sarah Malcolm's hat. When, in 1732/3, this murdress was arrested the hat contained a bag holding 20 moidores, 18 guineas and some broad pieces, interesting evidence for the gold coins available in London on the eve of the demonetization of the gold hammered money. See J. P. C. Kent 'The circulation of Portuguese coins in Great Britain' *Actas do III Congresso Nacional de Numismatica*, Lisboa, 1985, 389–405.

The distribution of Civil War hoards will be dealt with in more and fuller detail by E. M. Besly in a forthcoming British Museum Occasional Paper.

10. Pepys knew the exact *number* of coins; their exact *value* at any time in terms of £.s.d. would depend on the market.

11. These and other factors can most readily be found elucidated in J. Darby, *A Historic Geography of England before 1800*, Cambridge 1969.

12. Pepys, *Diary*, 19 May 1663. The Commonwealth coinage was demonetized by a proclamation dated 7 September 1660, to take effect from 30 November. Pepys remarks that an effective three months' grace was allowed. This demonetized coin was, of course, still protected against forgery and abuse, and Oliver's crowns became an immediate object of interest and collection. Remarkably, a single Commonwealth shilling occurred in the Yearby hoard, deposited at the time of the Recoinage in 1697 (*BNJ*. 1955.294).

13. The provenances of countermarked coins in the early first century AD suggests that in this particular instance a large proportion of the coins ended their current days within a short distance of their presumed place of issue. See C. M. Kraay, in *Essays in Roman Coinage presented to Harold Mattingly*, ed. Carson and Sutherland, Oxford 1956 p. 113.

14. *Cod. Theod.* 9.22.1: 'Omnes solidi . . . uno pretio aestimandi sunt atque vendendi, quanquam diversa formae mensura sit. Nec enim qui maiore habitu faciei extenditur, maieoris est pretii . . . cum pondus idem existat.'

15. Cf. E. Thurston, *History of the Coinage of the Territories of the East India Company in the Indian Peninsula etc.*, Madras 1890, p. 34, citing a document of 1765: 'The annual loss on coinage by the fall of Batta, on the issuing of the new Siccas (rupees), is a very heavy grievance to the country'. Batta is the discount charged by the money-changers.

16. For a succinct account of the process of 'réformation', see A. Engel and R. Serrure, *Numismatique moderne et contemporaine*, I, Paris 1892, p. 25. For the continued currency of old French écus and louis d'ors outside France, see T. Snelling, *Current Coins of Europe*, London 1766, p. 16.

17. For a useful exercise in restrained interpretation, see R. Reece in B. Cunliffe, *Excavations at Fishbourne 1961–1969*, Vol. II. Society of Antiquaries *Reports* no. XXVII. 92.

10
Coins found in Anglo-Saxon burials
S. E. Rigold†

The contexts of these finds are the 'pagan' graves which still provide by far the greater part of the archaeological evidence for the earlier Saxon age. They are 'pagan' in so far as they include grave-goods, which have no use or place in Christian dogma, but they extend into times and places well beyond the official acceptance of Christianity. They occur in Kent a century after the mission of Augustine and in Yorkshire a century after that of Paulinus, and there is no doubt, particularly in these Kentish cases, that the deceased were at least nominally Christian. This date is the terminus for this discussion, but it is not the end of the practice: the difficulty, in England, is to establish many later instances where coins are certainly, not just probably, associated with burials. A late-Saxon cemetery, abandoned in the eleventh century, close to Eynsford Castle, Kent,[1] produced an Aethelred II penny; another, from Bishops Waltham Palace, Hampshire, is not certainly from the cemetery of similar date on the site.[2] The wealth of late-ninth-century Carolingian coins from such Frankish cemeteries as le Martray and le Charnier at Foissy-les-Vézelay, Yonne, some found in sarcophagi and certainly not casual losses, attests the persistence of the practice even in Gaul and there are instances of Anglo-Saxon coins from the earlier eighth century onwards from crowded and over-used churchyards, presumably in continuous use from that time, but with the older burials inevitably disturbed. Among the oldest are the two 'secondary sceattas' from Stourmouth, Kent,[3] while at Richborough, not far away, a number of 'sceattas' and by far the largest assemblage of coins of the age of Offa from any single site are probably to be associated with the burial-ground of the early chapel, which would have lost most of its burial-rights to the parish that absorbed it, rather than to be explained as massive casual losses of offerings.[4] From which it appears that, saving the practice of burying clerics and dignitaries with their insignia, coins are the ultimate and most persistent form of grave goods, commonly, but not always, the only *beigabe* in a relatively late grave. I have argued that the origin of the practice, in the late seventh and eighth-century contexts, beyond which this discussion will be no more concerned, is the propitiation of the dead by a token-payment for the goods that were henceforth reserved for the use of the living.[5] If these later instances are substitutes for general grave-goods, the earlier ones, from Sutton Hoo downwards, are but one kind of commodity among many.

Coins from pagan-type burials may be placed in three categories:

1) Roman coins, *aes* or very occasionally silver, and mainly from the mid-third to the mid-fourth centuries – never late enough and in early enough

contexts to give the slightest colour to the now-exploded notion of a continuity of currency.

2) Gold, or base-gold, coins from any source between the eastern Empire and Visigothic Spain (no Muslim mintages have been found), but predominantly from the Merovingian realm and, at the end of the age, from England itself – the age being that when the western issues were almost exclusively of gold and which coincides exactly with that of pagan or incompletely converted Saxondom, from the mid-fifth century to the third quarter of the seventh.

3) Silver coins, which means, within the termini of this paper, 'sceattas' or small-flan pennies, including those of Frisian, but not, hitherto, Frankish mintage, nor resuscitated, clipped siliquae, though there is one case of an Ancient British coin (Epillus in Kent), close enough in size and weight to have passed as a 'sceatta'.[6]

The sum of these coins, from strictly sepulchral contexts, is perhaps 250 for the first category; at least 40, probably 46 and, it would seem, a large number of unverifiable instances, for the second, out of a total of 137 coins of this class of certain or strongly arguable British and Irish provenance, not counting Sutton Hoo, which provides another 40, nor the Crondall hoard; perhaps 80 certain instances for the third, and many likely but unverifiable.

The Roman coins from Anglo-Saxon cemeteries have been summarily treated by Dr. J. P. C. Kent in the *Festschrift* to Sir Frank Stenton.[7] More instances have come to light, particularly from Miss V. I. Evison's excavation of Long Hill, Dover, but there is little to add or modify in Dr. Kent's general conclusions and the finds are of no chronological significance except by strictly Saxon comparisons. With few exceptions, they are either pierced for mounting, as pendants to the cheaper necklaces or stitched directly onto clothing, or they are ground down to make weights for the small balances that are found with them, another of which came from Long Hill. Those that are intact must either be mere toys or talismans or may perhaps serve the symbolic function of the acceptable coins in graves, in even more token form.

The gold coins, or some of them, have been discussed by Dr. C. H. V. Sutherland but without detailed criticism of his sources,[8] and touched upon in two articles in the Stenton *Festschrift*.[9] Nevertheless, no review of all the finds of gold coinage from this age, apart from Sutton Hoo and Crondall, whether from grave-finds or not, is yet in print. I have made a list that claims to be both critical and as exhaustive as may be, as a contribution to the definitive publication of Sutton Hoo. It would be both unnecessary and premature to recite it here, but the figures, given above, more than double Dr. Sutherland's.

Some general remarks, however, may be made at this stage, for the material is of immense archaeological importance, quite out of proportion to its small numbers, and essentially of the same nature as that from Sutton Hoo,

with all the disputation about the date of striking and the reservation about
the interval before burial. The value of such finds, particularly from graves,
was appreciated nearly forty years ago by Dr. Joachim Werner,[10] whose
further studies have much clarified the significance of its wider distribution.
In fact, there is now almost universal agreement about the lower date of
the content of Sutton Hoo, though less about its (less significant) upper
limit, and a much better assessment of the Visigothic and other material is
now possible than a generation ago, when Dr. J. Allen dated the Sutton
Hoo material nearly two generations later than is now conceded. The interval
between striking and burial remains imponderable, but fortunately the more
significant interval between striking and setting the coins in jewellery is less
difficult, though it appears to be often wide in the earlier sixth century,
when fifth-century coins were still numerous enough to move around, and
very short in the early seventh, when fresh but fugitive coins were quickly
seized upon.

The forty-odd authenticated grave-finds, apart from Sutton Hoo, include
no true hoards, in the sense of numbers of unmounted and potentially
negotiable coins, nor any suspicions of such. The coins may be divided into
unmounted and mounted. The unmounted are hard to reckon: they do not
seem to number more than one or two in normal graves, but they certainly
occur. I am grateful to Mrs. Leslie Webster for showing me a tremissis,
apparently from the beginning of the seventh century, found only this year
in a grave at Broadstairs – a single, fresh coin among other *Beigabe*. It seems
probable that more of the single finds of unmounted coins from such places
as Reculver, where there are known to have been disturbed or eroded
cemeteries are strays from these than are losses from bullion or circulation.
The 'mounted' gold coins, looped or framed, rather than crudely pierced
as are the Roman, are the pendant jewels and have long attracted fame and
attention. They too are commonly in ones and twos, but there are a few
cases of assemblages of larger numbers which have been rated as 'hoards'.
These are simply the appurtenances of more expensive necklaces. Among
these is the famous 'St. Martin's hoard' from Canterbury, originally described as from the 'grounds of St. Augustine's' and perhaps from the prison
between them that was being 'improved' about the time of the discovery.
The greater part is certainly pre-Augustinian, but at least one single pendant
of later date may have become confused with it. Hardly less famous is the
set of four pendant south Gallic solidi from Sarre, Kent, but another, and
earlier set of six mounted tremisses from Faversham had lain without comment in the British Museum for some eighty years, from when it was presented by Sir A. W. Franks until when Mrs. Webster kindly brought it to
my notice. In all the mounted grave-finds total at least 32, probably 38, or
42 if two mounted 'Padas' from Long Hill, Dover, and two, unmounted
from Sarre are included, which are direct successors of base gold tremisses,
though of less than good silver. In general, and where available, solidi were
mounted in preference to tremisses, as broader and more showy, and are
seldom found without signs of mounting. They were not always available:
the sources are fifth or even fourth-century imperial issues, or imitations of

them, eastern issues of the sixth and seventh and, above all, the light issues from Provence that begin in the imperial name *c.* 575 and change to that of the Frankish king, *c.* 615, the best dated and most archetypal of all issues from Gaul.[11] When solidi were not available 'mock solidi' could be manufactured, but towards 575 an alternative was found in the broad, thin tremisses of the Visigoths in Spain. Curiously, none of those bearing the royal name, from Leovigild onwards, has been found, for at this very moment, shortly before Augustine's mission, the main source of gold coin imported into Britain begins to move from Spain and south-west Gaul to west and central Gaul, to settle, after Sutton Hoo, overwhelmingly in Austrasia, with the Provençal mints always accessible. This alone is a cumulative record of economic history, and the steady and even distribution of coins found in small numbers in graves gives the total a statistical significance as a sample that it would not have if disturbed by larger hoards. The value of these coins as relatively firm points in the procession of the finest Kentish and allied jewellery has long been appreciated.

The typical incidence of silver coins in grave-finds begins not with the very earliest 'sceattas', the ultimate 'Padas' and their contemporaries, but with the apparent restoration of coinage in the 'primary sceattas' proper, which, I have claimed, marks the pacification of Kent in the early 690s. Unmounted singles and pairs still occur: there was a single Frisian sceatta[12] found by Miss Evison at Kingston and a pair, not described, from Barham Down near-by. But the distinctive pattern is that of small 'hoards', in at least one case with the remains of a purse, but with few or no other grave-goods, and to a definite tale of pieces – twenty in one instance, possibly in two, eight in three, probably four cases, and in two or three cases five.[13] We may compare the forty from Sutton Hoo, but so many precise dedications in a now relatively small denomination seems to indicate that the whole population was now familiar with sums of money, as distinct from treasure or treasures, and that the same sums were customary not only in Kent and Essex but in Yorkshire. These 'hoards', normally of freshly minted coins in two varieties only, have been enough to establish the *relative* chronology of the primary 'sceattas', to which only one larger, non-sepulchral hoard, from England, is relevant. The final case, from Yorkshire, with more types, falls at the beginning of the 'secondary' phase. Such isolated 'hoards' are, of course, self-referent and of purely numismatic, rather than of wider archaeological relevance. Nevertheless, they assist the internal chronology of the cemeteries and the custom of precise grave-hoards is in itself an important archaeological datum.

The distribution both of mounted gold coins and silver grave-hoards may be set against the overall incidence of gold of the Merovingian period and of 'sceattas', not only in Britain but throughout the marches of the Frankish realm, particularly Frisia and the length of the Rhine. Perhaps the material is too little to decide much, but in England, while there seems to be no contrast of distribution in the gold, the silver hoards are confined to Kent and the Thames estuary, with the outlier in Yorkshire[14] and probably one in Bedfordshire,[15] at a time when 'sceattas' are beginning to show a more than east-coast distribution. This spread is more a feature of the 'secondary' phase and any contrast means little if the 'hoards' are concentrated near the beginning of the 'primary' phase.

It is gratifying that the three means of increasing the relevant material have been pursued so concomitantly: recovery of old and forgotten records, reinterpretation of well-known records and new and well-conducted excavations.

Department of the Environment

Notes

1. Information from Mr. S. R. Harker.

2. of the Confessor: information from Commander R. P. Mack.

3. S. E. Rigold, 'The Two Primary Series of Sceattas', *B.N.J.*, XXX (1960), 52.

4. *Report on the Excavations at . . . Richborough, Kent*, V (1968), 217–223.

5. *op. cit.*, in note 3, 8.

6. *ibid.*, 48.

7. *Anglo-Saxon Coins*, ed. R. H. M. Dolley, London 1961, 18–21 (appendix to 'From Roman Britain to Saxon England').

8. G. H. V. Sutherland, *Anglo-Saxon Coinage in the Light of the Crondall Hoard*, Oxford, 1948, esp. 22–30.

9. *ibid.*, 1–22 (J. P. C. Kent), and 22–38 (P. D. Whitting).

10. J. Werner, *Münzdatierte Austrasische Grabfunde*, Berlin 1935.

11. S. E. Rigold, 'An Imperial Coinage in Southern Gaul in the 6th and 7th Centuries?', *Num. Chron.* 6th ser., XIV (1955), 93–133.

12. *op. cit.* in note 3, 52.

13. *op. cit.* in note 3, *passim*, and 'Addenda and Corrigenda', *B.N.J.*, XXXV (1966), 1–6, which see for the purse.

14. Garton-on-the-Wolds, *op. cit.* in note 3, 49.

15. Sandy, *ibid.* 47.

11
Roman coins from Early Anglo-Saxon contexts
Michael D. King

S. E. Rigold's category (1) of Roman coins found in pagan burials of the Early Anglo-Saxon period may now be quantified on a nation-wide scale, enlarging considerably the sample of finds treated by J. P. C. Kent in the appendix to his article 'From Roman Britain to Anglo-Saxon England' in 1961.[1] In addition, finds of Roman bronze coins on Early Anglo-Saxon settlement sites such as West Stow and Mucking may now shed light upon the usage of such coinage in domestic and craft contexts, rather than merely as grave-goods.

A total of 363 Roman coins have been noted in association with 186 graves from 74 cemeteries and smaller burial sites. A further 67 coins are recorded amongst general finds from Early Anglo-Saxon cemeteries, but are not associated with particular grave-groups.[2] Fifty coin-burials come from Kentish cemeteries, while other concentrations of well-documented finds in graves may be detected in the Upper Thames region and Cambridgeshire (*see* distribution maps, Figures 1 and 2). It should nevertheless be emphasized that in general the deposition of coins in Early Anglo-Saxon graves is minimal and sporadic in all areas, while the above-mentioned regions are particularly rich in excavated cemetery sites.

Roman bronze coins are found in graves dating from the fifth through to the seventh centuries, with the majority of coin-burials dating to the sixth century (*c*. 60 per cent). Only *c*. 14 per cent of early graves with Roman coins may be dated to the fifth century, while the same proportion may be assigned to the seventh century. The remaining 12 per cent of the 186 well-documented graves are not readily datable. Though it is a commonplace that the majority of pagan Anglo-Saxon cemeteries date to the sixth century, these statistics would suggest that the prime usage of Roman coins was in a secondary context at least a century after the arrival of the last recorded issues of Roman bronze coinage in Britain at the beginning of the fifth century.

Though *c*. 40 per cent of the coins located on early cemetery sites have not received (and in most cases do not allow of) identification, it is significant that 72 per cent of those identified represent issues of between AD 260–364. As J. P. C. Kent has observed, issues of the House of Constantine, and to a lesser extent the Gallic emperors, appear most often in the numismatic record from early graves. The general correlation of this record with that from Late Roman town-sites such as Silchester,[3] and the absence of later fourth-century coins in any significant numbers, would suggest that Roman

224

coins were usually quarried from Late Roman sites a considerable time after their original deposition. The one possible exception to this may be the occurrence of a coin of Valens (354–78) in the grave of an apparently Germanic woman at Dorchester-on-Thames (grave III, Minchin Recreation Ground).[4] If this woman represents the suggested early 'federate' presence in Dorchester, it is possible that the coin was current at the time of burial. Three silver coins of the fifth century found in grave II at Chatham Lines in Kent are of prime interest in demonstrating contacts with the continent rather than a surviving system of monetary exchange.[5]

The evidence of early burials suggests that Roman bronze coins were chiefly used for personal ornament, as pendants to necklaces, bracelets and clothing, and dress-accessories kept in workboxes. In most areas coins perforated for suspension account for *c.* 60 per cent of the total coins from well-documented graves. The contrasting situation in Kent, where only 11 per cent of coins are perforated, may be only partially explained by the occurrence of large numbers of unperforated coin-weights accompanying male inhumations with balance-sets. The full explanation may lie in the growth of the practice of coin-dedication in graves, which persisted on a small scale beyond the Early Anglo-Saxon period. Alternatively, coins may have been attached to clothing without being perforated. In general, the presence of Roman coins in early graves reflects both a taste for personal ornament and a taste for all things Roman, as exemplified by the Undley bracteate from Suffolk, displaying the 'Wolf and Twins' motif of *Urbs Roma* issues of Roman coins such as that of *c.* AD 335.

The evidence for the re-use of Roman bronze coins in early settlement contexts comes from a small number of sites including Bishopstone, Sussex (1 coin),[6] Orsett, Essex (1),[7] Sutton Courtenay, Berkshire (3),[8] Heybridge, Essex (5 possibly residual),[9] Chalton, Hampshire (7),[10] and Mucking, Essex (44).[11] The largest number of finds from a single site comes from West Stow in Suffolk, where a total of 289 Roman bronze coins were recorded and listed by P. Curnow.[12] Of these 289 coins, 108 were extracted from the fills of 40 Sunken Featured Buildings, the structures which produce most of the stratified finds on Early Anglo-Saxon settlement sites.

The excavator of West Stow, S. E. West, considers the coins in S. F. B. fills to be contemporary with the use of the structures, which he dates and phases from the fifth to the early seventh century. Of the 98 coins from datable contexts, 65 (66 per cent) come from the fills of 18 sixth-century S.F.B.s, suggesting a similar chronological concentration of finds to the cemetery evidence. P. Curnow has dismissed the possibility of a sub- or post-Roman money economy at West Stow, and has suggested that the source of the large number of fourth-century Roman coins found on the site was the nearby Late Roman town-site of Icklingham.

On the Mucking site, itself neighbouring a Roman villa, only 13 out of the 44 Roman coins found are from layers 5–7 of S.F.B.s, considered by M. U. Jones to be contemporary deposits. Though the 10 Roman coins from the lower levels of S.F.B. 57 were accompanied by 'feminine' objects, none were found to be pierced. At West Stow only 35 pierced coins were

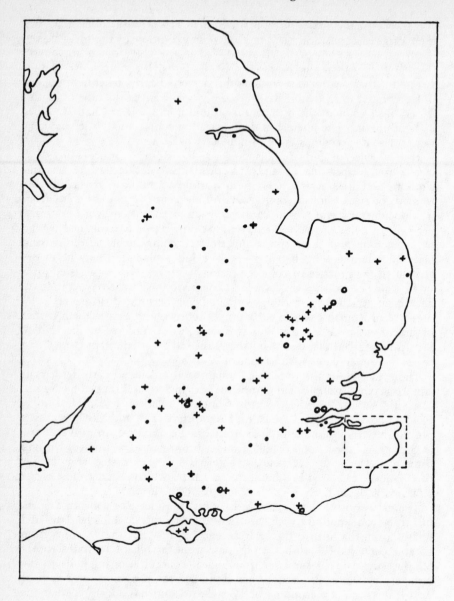

FIG. 1 The distribution of finds of Roman bronze and silver coins on cemetery and settlement sites of the Early Anglo-Saxon period (5th–8th centuries)

Key: + : Well-recorded finds from graves
      ● : Contexts and associations not known
      ○ : Finds from settlements

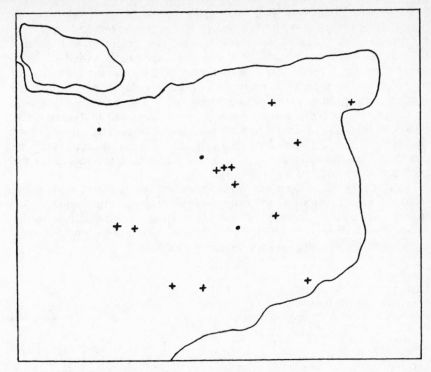

FIG. 2 Find of Roman bronze coins on Kentish cemetery sites of the Early Anglo-Saxon period (5th–7th centuries)

Key: + : Well-recorded finds
    ● : Contexts and associations not known

found on the site, and only 12 of these were in the fills of S.F.B.s. This would suggest that not all recovered Roman coins were put to immediate use as pendants. Altogether, 90 coins from West Stow had undergone some 'post-Roman damage', which included hammering, cutting, chipping and abrading as well as the familiar piercing.

   Such finds of Roman coins on settlement sites may be explained in terms of their use as scrap bronze for remelting. In the absence of evidence to suggest that any of the West Stow coins were used as weights, the use of coin-metal for inlay, brooch-repair and other small-scale metalwork may be suggested.[13] In addition, coins may have been used whole as appliqué ornament. The occurrence of a corroded coin attached to a brooch-fragment in level 7 of S.F.B. 82 at Mucking may suggest a context for other coin-finds on settlement sites.[14] A gilded bronze coin of Nero riveted to part of a bridle-bit in a seventh century grave (83) at Gilton in Kent may be seen to support this suggestion.[15]

The use of Roman coins in small-scale and ornamental metalworking may account for finds on Middle and Late Saxon settlement sites. At Middle Harling in Norfolk five Roman coins, including one fragment, were located near the site of a coin-hoard of Beonna of East Anglia, dated *c.* 760.[16] Excavations at *Hamwih*, near Southampton, have produced 23 Roman bronze coins from eighth-century levels, and it seems highly improbable that they are residual.[17] Finally, the presence of 25 Roman coins (2 pierced) on the site of the tenth-century royal palace at Cheddar in Somerset may be a residue of a much larger number used in metalworking.[18] It was noted that coin no. 16, a *Gloria Exercitus* of *c.* 335–7, was filed down on one side as if possibly intended as a setting for a ring, again suggesting the ornamental potential of coins preserved intact.

Hence the evidence from the Anglo-Saxon settlement sites would appear to complement the information from the early graves in establishing a subsidiary and primarily ornamental function for Roman coins and their bronze content, while definitively laying to rest the concept of a sub- or post-Roman money economy in fifth and sixth-century England.

Department of Archaeology
University of Durham

Notes

1. J. P. C. Kent, 'From Roman Britain to Anglo-Saxon England', *Anglo-Saxon Coins*, ed. R. H. M. Dolley, London 1961, 1–22.

2. M. D. King, *The Distribution and Chronology of Roman Bronze Coin-finds on Early Anglo-Saxon Cemetery and Settlement Sites*, unpublished undergraduate dissertation, Cambridge University 1987.

3. P. J. Casey, *Roman Coinage in Britain*, Aylesbury 1984, 31, fig. 5.

4. J. Kirk, E. T. Leeds, 'Three Early Graves from Dorchester, Oxon.', *Oxoniensia*, 17 (1953), 63–76.

5. M. A. S. Blackburn, 'Three Silver Coins in the Names of Valentinian III (425–55) and Anthemius (467–72) from Chatham Lines, Kent', *Num. Chron.*, 147 (1987).

6. M. G. Welch, 'Anglo-Saxon Sussex', *B. A. R., British Series*, 112 (1983), 24–32.

7. H. S. Toller, 'An Interim Report on the Excavation of the Orsett 'Cock' Enclosure, Essex, 1976–9', *Britannia*, 11 (1980), 35–43.

8. E. T. Leeds, 'A Saxon Village at Sutton Courtenay, Berkshire', *Archaeologia*, 76 (1926), 59–80; *Archaeologia*, 92 (1947), 79–93.

9. N. P. Wickenden, pers. comm.

10. T. C. Champion, 'Chalton', *Current Archaeology*, 59 (1977), 364–9.

11. M. U. Jones, pers. comm.

12. S. E. West, 'West Stow: The Anglo-Saxon Village', *East Anglian Archaeological Report*, 24 (1985), 76–81.

13. See R. F. Jessup, *Anglo-Saxon Jewellery*, 1950, 46; A. Warhurst, 'The Jutish Cemetery at Lyminge', *Archaeologia Cantiana*, 69 (1955), 1–40, 32.

14. J. Woolmer, pers. comm.

15. B. Faussett, *Inventorium Sepulchrale*, ed. C. R. Smith, London 1856, 26–8.

16. M. M. Archibald, 'The Coinage of Beonna in the Light of the Middle Harling Hoard', *B.N.J.*, 55 (1985), 10–54.

17. M. Metcalf, pers. comm.

18. P. Rahtz, 'The Saxon and Medieval Palace at Cheddar', *B.A.R., British Series*, 65 (1979) 288–91.

12

Monetary expansion and recession: interpreting the distribution-patterns of seventh and eighth-century coins

D. M. Metcalf

Conflicting aspects of the numismatic evidence from the second half of the eighth century – on the one hand the restriction of the coinage of King Offa of Mercia (757–96) chiefly to the mints of Canterbury and London, and on the other hand the evidently large quantities in which his coins were struck and their geographical dispersion throughout southern and eastern England, as far as an arc drawn from the Solent to the Wash – gave rise in 1963–4 to a sharp clash of opinions on their appropriate monetary and historical interpretation.[1] This was symptomatic of a more general difference of ideas on how far the economy of early medieval Europe was monetized, and how far based on local self-sufficiency and barter. So far as the reign of Offa is concerned, the debate has now been largely by-passed or rendered obsolete by the recognition that his coinage does not, after all, represent the first stirrings of monetary activity in England: the sceatta currencies of two and three generations earlier were much more copious.

They show a similar 'grain' or pattern to that of Offa's pence, namely a concentration of minting in the mints of the south-east, e.g. Canterbury and London, coupled with circulation over a much wider area. The problem of attributing the sceattas correctly to their mints provoked, incidentally, another intractable controversy in 1966 over a postulated inland mint in the upper Thames valley in the time of King Æthelbald of Mercia (716–57), Offa's great predecessor.[2] The idea of an inland mint remains unwelcome, but new finds have tended to confirm the distinctive distribution-pattern which points to a mint somewhere in the Oxford area.[2a]

A similar pattern of balance between the south-east and the midlands may be discerned a third time over, in the gold coinages from the first three quarters of the seventh century. Here, too, there is scope for different interpretations, but the numbers of provenanced coins are so many fewer that the archaeological evidence is still slender and imprecise.

As is usual in disputes, insights which were true in themselves, but incomplete, were grasped on both sides. What is perhaps unusual is that any reconciling principles proved so hard to find. (The apparent localization of the coins of particular moneyers for Offa was a stumbling-block to which a clue was eventually offered in terms of a Canterbury moneyer who it was suggested had local connections in the West Country.[2b])

It now seems clear, however, that swift fluctuations in the vitality or

230

extent of the English monetary economy during the seventh and eighth centuries hold the key.[3] In this the coinage provides a general lesson in the correct interpretation of archaeological distribution-patterns. The evidence for the geographical extent of monetary circulation at such an early period consists (as has been repeatedly emphasized) of coin-finds from particular places and is thus wholly and inescapably archaeological in character. It indicates a widespread use of coinage in village life throughout southern England; but if there were phases of monetary expansion followed by recession, so that the area occupied by a monetary economy fluctuated, *the overall distribution-pattern of stray finds would tend to define its maximum extent*, at whatever date that may have been, and would obscure the state of affairs at intermediate dates. This is a real problem, because stray losses cannot of course be dated precisely (even if the coins themselves can!) and the boundaries of the area where money was in use may have shifted appreciably over the sort of time span about which there is uncertainty, e.g. one or two decades.

If it is difficult to date single finds of coins closely enough to bring their evidence into conjunction with rapidly shifting patterns of coin use, other classes of archaeological material are probably subject to even wider margins of uncertainty. For them, too, the overall distribution-pattern will inevitably tend to define the maximum area of their diffusion. Archaeologists will on occasion be prudent to interpret their maps with this thought in mind.

The key arguments on which the case for monetary expansion and recession rests are in outline very simple and straightforward. Essentially the same case could be presented three times over in the form of pairs of contrasting distribution maps for the gold coinage of the seventh century, the silver sceatta coinage, and the pennies of Offa. Dating the various phases is unfortunately a good deal more complicated, and relies on arguments which are often inconclusive or tentative. In other words, we can demonstrate the ups and downs, the changes of direction quite easily, but the exact shape of the wave forms, the exact pace of change, is very much more difficult to define. This paper attempts to make the main point, and then to draw attention to the evidence for absolute chronology, providing references to a scattered literature and showing how the various examples that have been adduced are connected with the general argument.

The stock of gold in the Anglo-Saxon kingdoms of the seventh century was fed by the net inflow of precious metal from the Continent. There is no reason to doubt that this arrived chiefly in the form of Merovingian trientes, nor that the monetary wealth of Gaul far outweighed that of Britain. Rigold's inventory of hoards, grave-finds, and single finds of gold coins is the essential source book,[4] in the analysis of which care should be taken to distinguish distribution-patterns of grave-finds and stray losses. The links with Gaul may have received an impetus, from the third quarter of the sixth century onwards, through dynastic and cultural connections between the kingdom of Kent and the Merovingian kingdoms.[5] There are early groups of finds from particular Kentish sites, which may reflect royal interest, e.g. Kings

Field, Faversham. The exceptional concentration of surplus wealth in east Kent spread far beyond the royal household, and is seen in the many finds of gold jewellery.

Together with this should be set the evidence of the Merovingian coins from Sutton Hoo. They are from so many different minor mints that – unless they were a specialist coin collection – they can only be the 'left-overs' from the bottom of a treasure-chest through which a great deal of money had passed.[6] One remembers the various eighth-century grants of remission of tolls on a ship or a share in a ship, at the royal toll stations at Fordwich, Sarre, and London. Ships may have made landfall at earlier dates, and at other ports too: the evidence that has survived obviously reveals only a fraction of the cross-channel trade and the monetary transactions it generated.

The implications need to be explored carefully, since the handling of negative evidence about the date of the small beginnings of any kind of dispersion is bound to be tricky, but the straightforward interpretation seems to involve a substantial growth in the money supply in the late sixth and early seventh centuries, restricted essentially to one or two royal centres in the south-eastern coastlands.[7]

It is curious that the availability of Merovingian gold was not more promptly and fully reflected in the autonomous issues. The Anglo-Saxon gold coinage may have had very small beginnings in Canterbury, and perhaps London, some time in the first two decades of the seventh century, although the dating of London coins to before 616 rests on arguments that should now be abandoned. The interpretation of the 'Eusebius' triens and one or two other coins that may belong to a 'pre-Crondall' phase is inevitably tenuous.[7a] There are virtually no Anglo-Saxon coins in the Crondall hoard of an alloy that is likely to have been used before the time of Dagobert (629–38); the Merovingian coins, which Kent would now date to the 630s, tell the same story: the hoard has a compact age-structure. The question is whether there were any earlier Anglo-Saxon issues about which Crondall is silent, and which have for that reason had an extremely low survival-rate. There were, of course, none at Sutton Hoo (*c.* 625), but that could be a special case for the reason alluded to. One should therefore not be too dogmatic but the straightforward interpretation is that it was not until the 630s and 640s that there was a flowering of the locally-minted coinage.[8] At much the same time there seems to have been an unusual degree of activity in church-building. It is fairly obvious (again from the Crondall hoard) that more than one series of trientes, each distinctive in design, was being issued concurrently, and the implication is that more than one mint was at work. The Crondall find, from the fringes of Bagshot Heath, is itself far removed from the cross-Channel axis of monetary affairs. Canterbury and London still no doubt account for most of the output, but it is the few exceptions that are in a sense the most intriguing – for example, the *Benutigo* runic trientes found at Dorchester in Oxfordshire and at Eastleach Turville in Gloucestershire (and in the Amiens region), or the three puzzling 'York' trientes.[9]

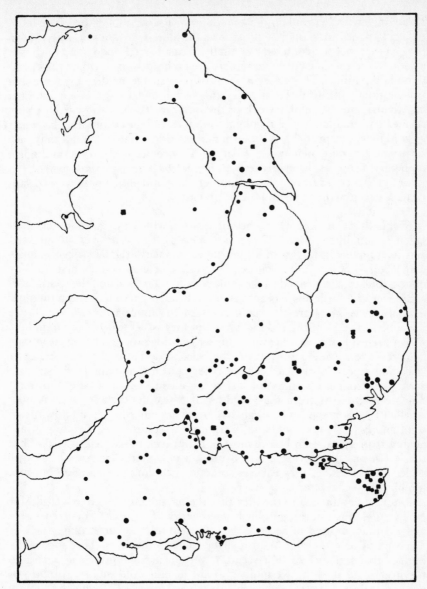

FIG. 1 Finds of sceattas in England. Prolific sites are marked by larger dots. (Source: the check-list of finds printed elsewhere in this volume.)

A recession in the 650s and 660s is evidenced by a contrast in distribution-patterns. The Merovingian coins of the 640s or earlier have a distinctly wider distribution in England than the pale gold issues which followed them. The reader may satisfy himself about the earlier phase by making his own map of

Merovingian and Crondall-phase finds from Rigold's inventory. The later, pale gold issues are shown by squares on the map (*see* Figure 1), where it can be seen that they are confined essentially to east Kent, London and the lower Thames, and the coast of Essex. There are no hoards to elucidate this 'post-Crondall' period.[10] The 'two emperors' type seems to be the only issue that was originally plentiful; 11other designs, such as the 'Crispus' copy found at St Albans, and the similar work of the moneyer *Pada*,[12] are scarce or very scarce. The gradual dwindling of gold supplies and the eventual replacement of gold by silver, probably a little sooner in Britain than in Gaul,[13] may be a sufficient general explanation. What has a more precise bearing on English monetary history is the evidence that, *before the date of its replacement*, the tide of gold receded from much of southern England until it practically disappeared, except in London and the south-east.

It is equally clear that when the trientes (of which the gold content had fallen eventually to around 20 per cent or even 10 per cent) were abandoned and swept away in favour of a pure silver coinage[14] (the denarii or pennies which numismatists call sceattas), those silver coins were at first and for quite a long time restricted to the same region of London and the south-east. Moreover, the earliest issues are very scarce and seem to have been on quite a small scale. They are the runic coins of the moneyer *Pada*, which are presumed to be Kentish, and the contemporary issues signed 'Varimundus', which are evidently East Saxon. Both series bridge the transition from pale gold to silver. They gave way to the eclectic design of Primary Series A (recalling several of the earlier gold types) and the contemporary Series B. Series A is from east Kent, while Series B is a continuation of the 'Varimundus' design, and is from the kingdom of Essex. Its earliest phase is now labelled BX. Series A and B regularly occur together in grave-finds in east Kent and Essex.[15] The *Pada* and 'Varimundus' sceattas had virtually disappeared from circulation before most of the grave-finds were buried. In that sense it seems that Series A and B mark a new start, and are on a larger scale; the preceding, very earliest sceattas, including perhaps BX, are of a 'preliminary' character.

Rigold was attached to the idea that the paymnent of a large wergild for Mul in 694 was a turning-point in the history of the Kentish currency. He saw the inauguration of Series A as a direct result, and accordingly he was disposed to date the first English silver coins to the 680s. This apparently implies that the very earliest sceattas were in use alongside the pale gold thrymsas, and that the wergild was paid in blue gold or in a mixture of gold and silver. He returned to this theme as late as 1977 with the slightly varied suggestion that Series BX was swept away (and therefore does not occur in the grave-finds alongside BI – see above) either in 694 or perhaps for some other similar exaction in the 680s. Rigold's original chronology for the late seventh century was based on the acceptance of a date of *c.* 670 for the Crondall hoard, which would now be widely rejected in favour of a distinctly earlier date, in the 640s. The date he accepted for the Bordeaux hoard has also been undermined.[15a] Numismatists have accommodated the

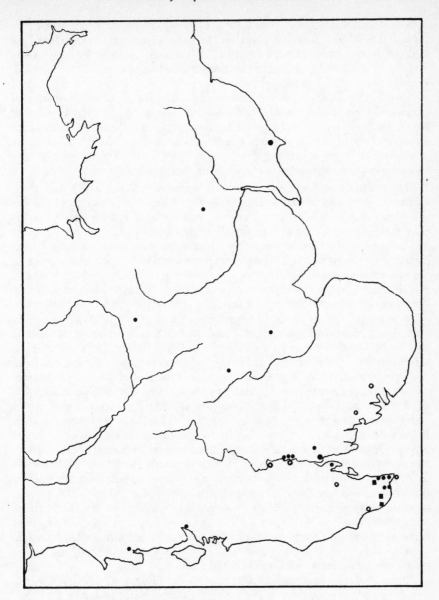

FIG. 2 Finds of sceattas of types belonging to the initial phase (last quarter of the seventh century, approx.), namely Series Pa, Va, BX, and F. (Open circles mark the find-spots of the immediately preceding pale gold thrymsas. Squares mark hoards or grave-finds.)

sceatta chronology to the new dating of Crondall by one or both of two moves. They have called in question the link between the wergild of Mul and the introduction of Series A and B,[16] allowing them to be put earlier; and they have sought to spread the 'preliminary' stage over a longer period. From a purely numismatic or stylistic point of view, one would be inclined to spread the silver issues of *Pada* and 'Varimundus' over a substantial period, say not less than ten years, and to discount somewhat the higher survival-rate of Series A and B. This chronological scheme is hardly firm enough to prove anything independently about the rate of expansion of the new silver coinage: it is the maps, (*see* Figures 1 and 2) that encourage one to detect a slow beginning in the 680s or thereabouts.

The spread of the sceatta coinage over the whole of the English midlands, along the south coast as far as Dorset, and up the east coast as far as Lincolnshire (and even to Whitby and Jarrow)[17] was not accomplished by the diffusion of the Kentish coins of Series A. They never spread far beyond east Kent and Essex, at least in any quantity. Rather, porcupines from the Rhine mouths, and numerous other English types minted locally, gave substance to the monetary expansion. Mints were opened in East Anglia, in Hamwic, and possibly elsewhere too. There were also a good many imitations, presumably the work of enterprising counterfeiters. Even the relative dates of issue of each of these many types are difficult to determine at all certainly. Typological arguments on their own are suspect,[18] and the best guidance lies in the hoards and in the silver contents of the coins. The originally very pure silver of the sceattas declined drastically, until at the end some varieties contained as little as 20 per cent silver. As a general proposition one would not expect sceattas of very different alloy to be circulating concurrently. (But this should not be accepted uncritically, if only because their circulation was to some extent compartmented and under political control.) There is a 'watershed' which Rigold located at a date close to 730: good silver coins are earlier, debased ones are mostly later. Rigold's date, but not his idea, has been overturned by a new study of the Cimiez hoard, which has pushed it back from the late 730s or even the 740s to *c.* 720, by very convincing numismatic arguments. Blackburn has undertaken a consequential revision of all the dates for the sceatta coinages, refining slightly upon Rigold's scheme by speaking of an intermediate as well as of primary and secondary phases. The watershed has become rather more of a plateau, but the secondary (debasement) phase has been moved distinctly earlier, in absolute terms, to begin in *c.* 710, and the introduction of Series A and B to *c.* 680 or 685.

The secondary phase of the sceatta currency in England, characterized by a multiplication of local types and by severe debasement, ended in a ruinous situation, probably in the third quarter of the century.[20] When one comes to survey them, the obviously debased English varieties form a relatively small part of the sceatta series, more restricted in type and origin than a vague impression might have allowed one to assume. Once again, the chronology is extraordinarily difficult to seize. Was there an interval between the disappearance of the sceattas and the origin of the new silver pennies, during which most or all of England was devoid of currency? How can one hope to say when coins fell out of use regionally? Marion Archibald's forthcoming study of the Middle Harling hoard, in which a few of the last of the East Anglian sceattas survive alongside the reformed coins of Beonna, argues for a minimum interval between the debased and the restored coinages.[20a] The chronological pattern may not, of course, have been identical throughout southern England.

What is (again) quite clear is that the new pennies were initially issued on a very small scale and were restricted to east Kent. They were a reformed coinage, of pure silver, and it would be very hard to believe that the debased sceattas were allowed to remain in circulation alongside them – if indeed they had not vanished years previously. The severe debasement is in itself a pointer to a dwindling currency which, one would judge, sank below the point of minimum viability. The question might be answered by saying that in the rest of southern England, outside east Kent, there was almost certainly an interval, of at least two or three decades around the 760s and 770s. It may have begun sooner, and lasted longer. The further one goes into the midlands, no doubt the longer the interval.

Into this monetary vacuum coins of Pepin and Charlemagne were able to penetrate. Normally, foreign coins were rigorously and effectively excluded from circulation. Very few Carolingian coins were able to circulate in England after the 780s,[21] just as very few English pennies were able to escape the melting-pot in Gaul. (But if Offa's pennies survived the journey to Italy, they stood a better chance of gaining currency in north-central or central Italy, where also, it would seem, there was a phase when the local currency was inadequate.[22]) There are finds, for example, from St. Albans, Southampton, and Richborough, and a coin of Tiel which may be an English find.[23] The Pepin from Richborough is a crumb of evidence that even in east Kent the English currency fell into desuetude, in the 760s or thereabouts, although it could be merely a south-coast escaper. Recent additions to the list of pre-reform Carolingian coins found in England are issues of Pepin from near Hod Hill, Dorset and from Repton, Derbyshire, and of Charlemagne from Sancton, North Humberside.[23a] The ratio of coins of Pepin to those of Charlemagne among the finds appears significant.

In Yorkshire, as in East Anglia, there was some sort of continuity throughout the middle years of the century. King Eadberht of Northumbria (737–58) took the altogether unusual step of issuing coins with his name on them. The exact date at which they began to be struck cannot be determined, but as there are seven distinct stylistic groups, as well as the varied issues produced jointly by the king and Archbishop Ecgberht, involving altogether some 400–500 dies, they certainly cannot all be pushed into the closing years of the reign. The best of them seem to have been around 70–80 per cent silver, but their alloy was rather erratic and unreliable.[24] Even at the beginning of Eadberht's reign, the standard of coinage in the southern kingdoms was under pressure, and indeed had probably already been undermined by the number of counterfeits that had been uttered. The Northumbrian royal coinage may have begun in an attempt to maintain, at York, standards of quality and reliability that were being compromised elsewhere. We do

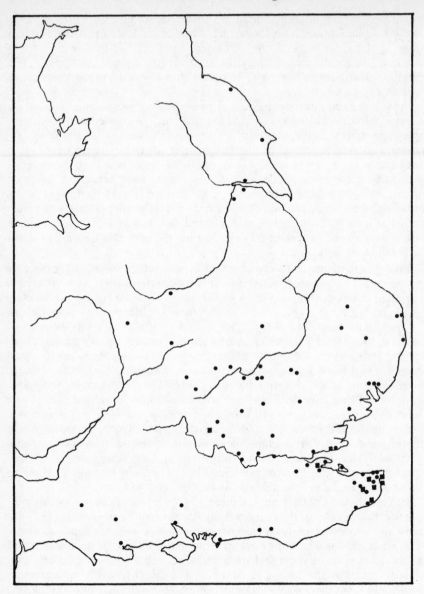

FIG. 3 Finds of sceattas of the remaining types belonging to the primary phase (cf. Fig. 2), (first quarter of the eighth century, approx.), namely Series B, C, D, E, G, X, and *BMC* Types 3b/11, if of good silver.

not know where the silver came from to make this possible. Mining should not be excluded. The coins of Eadberht's successors have had a distinctly lower survival rate, as die estimation has shown, and one would hesitate to see in them any evidence of an early decline in the availability of silver.[24a]

The East Anglian coins of King Beonna were perhaps inspired by the Northumbrian issues. They were until recently extremely scarce, but are now plentiful and well understood as a result of the chance discovery of a very large hoard at Middle Harling, and its thorough study by Miss Archibald.[25]

The question of continuity between sceattas and pennies could perhaps be explored further through the trace-elements in the coins. The early sceattas, for example, have very high gold traces, commonly over 1½ per cent, which one would expect to survive re-minting. The few pennies of Offa and Coenwulf that have been analysed show, by contrast, somewhat lower gold levels – around 0.5 per cent as measured by EMPA, the most reliable method – and so do one or two early Carolingian coins that have been analysed by XRF spectrometry. The implication that the English stock of coinage silver was being diluted or even replaced by metal from a different source deserves further study.[26]

We come, then, to the complicated and intriguing questions of the chronology of Offa's reformed coinage. The picture that will emerge is of a currency launched in east Kent perhaps as early as 765, but which did not gain much momentum until *c.* 786, that is, twenty years later. The bulk of Offa's coins fall into the last ten years of his reign (i.e. 786–96), and only then do they spread swiftly out to become a currency for the English midlands (including southern and eastern Mercia). The main point is once again beyond dispute: Offa's coins have been classified into Group I (early), Group II, and Group III (late), and a pair of distribution-maps of the two categories, Group I and Groups II–III, show a clear difference. The early coins (which again are our only available approximation to early *losses*) are restricted essentially to the south-east and the south coast, while groups II and III have a very much wider distribution north of the Thames, into the midlands and East Anglia. Thus a monetary boom in the years around 790 succeeded a recession that had no doubt perplexed and hampered two of the outstandingly successful figures of eighth-century England, Æthelbald and Offa, from about 750 onwards. It should be mentioned that one student has attempted to make the problem disappear by reversing the previously accepted order of Offa's Groups I and II: the plentiful Group II, including the prestigious portrait coins, is seen as the issue with which the reformed pennies were instituted. The scarce Group I, which seems too miserable a coinage with which to launch a reform, and which is in any case essentially east Kentish, is placed later, and is relegated as almost a 'poor relation' of Group II. On this model, Group I leads directly into Group III, which is demonstrably the work of the Kentish mint in the closing years of Offa's reign.[27] The contrasting maps referred to above are, taken in context, a sufficient refutation of this *ballon d'essai*.

The earliest pennies, on the conventional reading of the evidence, were struck not by Offa, but by two obscure Kentish kings named Heahberht and Ecghberht II, about whom history knows virtually nothing. Even their dates are vague.[28] From charters it is apparent that both were reigning in 765, and it is possible that Ecgberht reigned until *c.* 780 or later.[29] Blunt offered two schemes of dating. The coins of Heahberht might belong to the years 765–75, he suggested, while the earliest of Offa's pence would be from *c.* 775–80. Alternatively, Heahberht's issues may be as late as 775–80, with Offa's first coins following a few years later, say *c.* 784–5. The reason given for preferring the second scheme was that Eoba, Babba, and perhaps Udd (the three men who worked as moneyers for Heahberht or Ecgberht) were still working in the time of Coenwulf, i.e. after 796. The case for Babba is the strongest,[30] but there is nothing impossible about a young man's being a moneyer in 765 and still active in 800. One can point to late Anglo-Saxon moneyers who worked for forty years.

There is one coin of Charlemagne, copied from an English type, which seemed to provide precious evidence that Offa's reform had been launched before *c.* 770. The argument has now been undermined and can no longer be seen as a necessary one, but we should still run over it, if only to conclude that its usefulness is less than it seemed at first. An early coin of Charlemagne, attributed to the mint at Strasbourg, seemed to be imitated from a coin of Ecgberht by the moneyer Babba.[31] It is not the only coin of Charlemagne imitated from an Anglo-Saxon penny.[32] Charlemagne's coinage of the 'experimental' class to which the Strasbourg coin belongs has been dated by Grierson to 768–*c.* 770.[33] The date has been queried, to suggest that the change-over from Charlemagne's Type I to his Type II may in general have been ragged, and may have dragged on at some mints as late as, say, *c.* 772.[34] But in any case, the supposed prototype, that is the coin of Ecgberht II, must be earlier, and can therefore be dated to before *c.* 770, or at the latest 772. The unique Heahberht coin, which is of rather smaller module, may be earlier by a year or two than the more plentiful issues of Ecgberht. And one should remember, at this point, an even smaller, but typologically related, unique sceatta-like coin in the Bibliothèque Nationale.[33] The Strasbourg coin thus seemed to prove an early origin for the reformed pence. But Miss Archibald's study of the Middle Harling hoard has brought forward another possible prototype, in a coin of Beonna by the moneyer Wilred, with the same unusual cruciform design. Proof that Beonna's coins are earlier in origin than *c.* 770 is welcome (as we know only Beonna's *floruit*) but it is not surprising, and it has nothing helpful to add to the chronology of Offa's coins.

The late Sir Frank Stenton's deep and lifelong interest in Offa, and in his coinage, received its final formulation in an address to the British Numismatic Society in 1958, in which, speaking primarily as an historian, Stenton lent the weight of his judgment to an 'early' chronology. Documentary evidence shows that Offa exercised authority in Kent in and after 764, and there is the coin of Heahberht, who was Offa's nominee in *c.* 764 to replace ousted rulers springing from the West Saxon royal house. Ecgberht, initially sub-king of West Kent, may have been Heahberht's son.[35a] The main point which Stenton grasps, however, is that the placing of the king's name on the coins, for the first time in southern England, is likely to stem from a deliberate exercise of will by the ruler, 'emphatically, even flamboyantly, exercising his royal dignity', and that the date of its introduction can be judged by considering Offa's possible motives for such an exercise of will, and the political circumstances in which he might have acted. He was obviously emulating the similar new Frankish royal coinage – introduced, it is generally supposed (though on debateable grounds), in 755,[36] and which Pepin was able to strike in very large quantities.[37] In short, Stenton favoured a date of *c.* 764,[38] in which year Offa was in Canterbury, making grants of land in his own name, but with Heahbehrt's concurrence, and preferred to set the origins of the penny coinage well before the battle of Otford (776), which may possibly have been a setback for Offa, since he cannot be shown to have possessed any authority in Kent in the following nine years.[39] Stenton's suggested date of *c.* 764 remains conjectural, but the evidence for a date earlier than *c.* 770, if it has been correctly argued, substantially narrows the range of historical possibilities.

What, then, is the evidence that the new coinage in east Kent got off to a very slow start, and that the great majority of the surviving coins of Offa (and even more of the original total output, for the earliest varieties have pretty clearly had a higher survival-rate) are to be dated after *c.* 786 – fifteen years or more after the pennies began? It is a matter of complex numismatic judgment, in which one must try to fit into a self-consistent scheme all the 140 or so varieties of Offa's coins; within that context, the question hinges on whether one can correctly attribute coins to Eadberht, bishop of London (772/82–787/89), and how much importance one should attach to two unique varieties both now in the Vatican coin collection and doubtless Italian finds.

The basic point is whether the name 'Eadberht', which occurs on only half-a-dozen out of some 350–400 surviving coins of Offa, is the name of a moneyer (of whom there were at least thirty, some quite active and some much less so) or – quite exceptionally – of a bishop. The strongest argument in favour of the prelate depends on a minute detail: the round m, which as a contraction for *Merciorum* is a standard element of the design, is delicately and wittily altered by the addition of a bar, to make it into a monogram of ep (for *episcopus*); secondly, the dies for the Eadberht coins are almost certainly cut by the same hand as the related coins of the busy moneyer Eoba, who seems to have enjoyed an especially privileged position with the king.[40] The correlation between the moneyer and the workman who actually cut the die is debatable, but in this particular case, if Eoba is the moneyer, it seems very unlikely that 'Eadberht' can be a moneyer's name.

If coins can be assigned to bishop Eadberht, and if it is numismatically unlikely that he himself was exercising the office of moneyer (although Dr. Stewart has argued the case that moneyers in this period were sometimes persons of high status, by no means rude mechanicals), then presumably he had been granted the privilege (and profit) of moneying because the king wished to reward or conciliate him in some particular historical circumstances. As the two coins most directly in question are Italian finds, it is obviously tempting to connect them with the legatine commissions of 786, Offa's 'grateful payments' to the See of St. Peter, and the 'contentious' synod of Chelsea in 787, at which Offa managed to rid himself of the spiritual overlordship of the Kentish archbishop. And the date of issue of these varieties is unlikely to have been significantly earlier than 786–7. It will be clear to the reader that this suggestion belongs in the category of interesting ideas, not proofs positive. But he should not lose sight of the need to create some sort of order out of the 140 varieties of Offa's coins.

In 786 the Pope sent a legate to England – the first such visit since the time of Augustine. Offa welcomed the legatine commission, and saw it as a means of establishing an independent archbishopric for Mercia, which would liberate him from unfriendly Kentish influence in the affairs of his kingdom. He was at odds with archbishop Iænberht. Towards the end of the mission, a general council of the English church was held, and Offa promised to send 365 mancuses each year to Rome for the relief of the poor and the maintenance of lights. This seems to have been essentially a personal offering from Offa to St. Peter's. In 787, at a stormy council at Chelsea, Offa secured the division of the province, and before the end of 788 the bishop of Lichfield received an archbishop's pallium. Eadberht's part in the negotiations is quite unknown, but if he was permitted to strike coins in association with Offa, this was presumably a concession to secure his compliance in 786–87, or to reward him for it. Iænberht, similarly, had been permitted to strike coins jointly with Offa, but presumably at an earlier date, when he was still in favour. Whereas the archbishops of Canterbury continued to enjoy the privilege of minting, Eadberht's name (and this was originally seen as an argument against the attribution) is known only from a small, early group of Offa's coins, one with an Italian provenance. This coin, variety B.36, which is of a distinctive design with a banner, and also a related coin signed by the moneyer Eoba, B.15, are each known from one surviving specimen, and both are in the Vatican Library. It seems highly unlikely that they are earlier than 786.[41] Their relative stylistic position in the series is such that, if they are dated 786–c. 788, the great majority of Offa's coins would seem to be later.

Only a proportion of the surviving coins of Offa are from known findspots. Conclusions based on provenance are therefore liable to margins of error. As far as the evidence goes, however, the early coins were never diffused throughout the southeast of England. Group II mainly fulfilled that role. A relatively high proportion of the provenanced specimens of Group I have been found abroad, and the up-to-date list of English find-spots (for which the writer is indebted to the kind advice of Mr. C. E. Blunt) is as follows:

B7   Between Seaford and Newhaven, Sussex

B8	Winchester
B7/9	Southampton excavations
B17var	Thames foreshore near Wandsworth
B19d.	Richborough excavations, Kent
B-	St Osyth's, Essex
Ecgberht	Stamford Hill, London

By contrast, there are dozens of finds of coins of Groups II and III scattered over the countryside north of the Thames, and south of a line from the Bristol Channel to the Wash.[42] This is the strongest available argument against re-dating Class I. The parallel with Series A of the sceattas will not be lost on the reader.

Offa's East Anglian coinage, which spans Groups II and III, is thought to have begun at a late date – perhaps *c.* 790. Its place of mintage is unknown, but may possibly lie in the Stour valley, towards the east coast. The three known specimens of the 'wolf and twins' coinage of king Æthilberht of East Anglia (whom Offa caused to be murdered in 794) were evidently struck at the same mint. They share an obverse die. One was found at Tivoli, in central Italy.[43] Although the date of origin of the East Anglian mint is too conjectural for its issues to be used in support of the argument of 'slow beginnings', it seems safe to remark that, during a period of at least two decades after the introduction of pennies in Kent, the total output was minimal.

There was a further reform of the coinage by Offa, introducing the larger and marginally heavier Group III coins, with an average weight of roughly 1.3 grammes, compared with roughly 1.2 grammes. The reform was dated by Blunt to Iænberht's lifetime, i.e. before August 792 (but Witney gives the date of his death as 791), again on the evidence of a unique coin, B.132. This has a three-line reverse, like Archbishop Æthelheard's coins and like a number of other Group III coins, and because its weight seemed to him to be on the high side for Group II (1.22 grammes) Blunt suggested that it should be regarded as transitional between Groups II and III. The weight of a single specimen is however inconclusive evidence, as it lies well within normal limits for either group. The three line typology appears equally inconclusive, since one could point, for example, to the precedent of Bishop Eadberht's coins. The obverse design seems to offer a much stronger typological argument, linking the Iænberht coin firmly with a few others naming Heaberht (presumably a moneyer), B.59 and cf B.60, or Pehtwald, B.73, 74, 75. Of this compact little group, B.60 and B.73 have an early look, at least to the writer's eye. Stewart sees Heaberht and Pehtwald as problematic but possibly Mercian moneyers. If we discount the evidence of B.132 for the date of the reform, it may be possible to push the reform forward from 791 to 793,[44] which makes a little more room for the bulk of Group II (mainly at the London mint but probably also at Canterbury?)

The real problem with which the historical context presents the numismatist is to decide whether, in view of the bitter enmity between them from 787 onwards, we can imagine Iænberht and Offa striking coins in their joint

names at all after the synod of Chelsea. B.132 stands quite apart from Iænberht's other coins, B. 125–31, which vary in detail but are essentially of a
single type and form a compact block. We might speculate that B.132 was
minted at London at the time of the legatine mission, or at any rate before the
final rupture at Chelsea. B. 125–31 could be Canterbury coins and earlier
(from 774?). Having reviewed so many inconclusive arguments, we may
think that Iænberht's coinage offers an historical context that is less ambiguous than most. Uncertainties about mint attribution add to the dating difficulties, but the numismatist's instinct, at the end of the day, is that Offa's portrait
coins and related types, which make up a high proportion of the surviving
specimens, are all or virtually all from after *c.* 786.

The volume of output until 786 was, in that case, small. This is the firmest
available evidence, in the midst of a great deal that is suggestive but not independently demonstrable, for severe fluctuations in the extent of the currency
in the second half of the eighth century. If the issue of large quantities of coinage had been available to Offa as a political instrument he would surely have
seized it sooner. Æthelbald, too, cannot have been unaware of the benefits of
a sound currency – of the advantages that King Wihtred of Kent had enjoyed
in an age of more plentiful silver. The lack of bullion frustrated their ambi-
tions; and the currents of trade that brought the precious metals to England's
shores fluctuated in ways that were largely outside their control.

The fluctuations in the geographical extent of the currency into the English
midlands afford the clearest evidence that its use was connected with international trade – even in the seventh century. The coinage does not reflect the
basic regional prosperity of land and men, which remained steady in the
medium term: Gloucestershire and Somerset were without money in the
seventh and eighth centuries not because they were poor or under-exploited
areas, but because they were distant from the currents of cross-Channel trade.

Gaul was far wealthier than Britain. One suspects that its prosperity in
the time of Dagobert 'carried over' to England, and that when peace and
prosperity were sadly cut short by Dagobert's death, there soon followed
an economic recession on this side of the Channel too. Lafaurie discusses
the 'gap' in the Merovingian numismatic evidence, and suggests that the
earliest silver coins are from approximately the time of the death of Clotaire
III (657–73). There was then a political struggle between Neustria and
Austrasia, and it was only after the assassination of Ebroin, mayor of the
Neustrian palace, in 680 or 683, and the battle of Tertry in 687, that Pepin
of Heristal, the Austrasian mayor, was able to re-unite the *Regnum Fran-
corum*. His rule, lasting until 714, was a period of consolidation and, one
may judge, renewed prosperity. Another factor in the revival of the Anglo-
Saxon currency in the first quarter of the eighth century was the subjugation
of Frisia by Pepin in the years around 690 and the conversion of the Frisians
by St. Willibrord's mission from the 690s onwards. Political stability brought
prosperity, and the Frisians were very quick to take advantage of their
improved cultural relations with England; they struck large quantities of
'Porcupine' sceattas.[45] The 'continental runic' sceattas were also produced
in large volume from an early date, as the Aston Rowant hoard illustrates.

Even before this time, the cross-Channel trade to eastern England had, perhaps to a large extent, been in Frisian hands.[46]

The collapse of the sceatta currency, with the dwindling away of the necessary supplies of silver, may be traced to the disruption of the Frisian trade, in its turn the result of Frankish–Frisian conflicts from 734 onwards. The massacre of Boniface and his companions by heathens in east Frisia in 754 marked the end of an age. Meanwhile, west Frisia was subdued by Pepin and by Charlemagne, and drawn into the Frankish orbit.

The revival of English monetary affairs in the time of Charlemagne again has an obvious cultural and political context. Alcuin was at the Frankish court from 782, and was a leading figure in the Carolingian intellectual revival. Relations between Offa and Charlemagne, never easy, were strained from 789 for several years, and the Frankish ports were closed to English traders. In 796 the two rulers patched up their differences, and concluded what has been described as 'the first commercial treaty in English history'.[47] The chronology of the English coinage in the 780s and 790s helps to set this well-known document in its context.

The chronological arguments as they have been summarised here may seem rather technical: for the present, they are the best arguments we have. The picture that has been sketched is as follows:

From *c*. 550	Inflow of continental gold coins, which are plentiful only in a few royal centres in the south-east, e.g. Faversham.
c. 625	Sutton Hoo treasure of Merovingian tremisses (left-overs?)
630s, 640s	Merovingian tremisses spread more widely into English midlands. English mints begin to strike tremisses, mainly at Canterbury and London but probably also elsewhere.
c. 645	Crondall hoard (mixed Merovingian and English coins).
650s, 660s	Further debasement of the tremisses. Recession, contraction of currency area.
670×675?	Debased gold swept away, silver denarii ('sceattas') replace them. Small scale minting of *Pada*, 'Varimundus', and perhaps BX types.
680×685 onwards	Primary phase of sceattas, still somewhat restricted
690s onwards	Pepin brings renewed prosperity to the *Regnum Francorum,* and subdues Frisia. St Willibrord's mission.
694	Kent pays Essex a large wergild for Mul.
c. 700 onwards	Frisian trade with England increases. Intermediate phase of sceattas.
c. 720	Cimiez hoard.

c. 720 onwards	Secondary phase of sceattas. Growth of regional currencies and local minting more widely through England.
734 onwards	Frisian/Frankish conflict.
c. 740 onwards	Independent 'restored' issues in Northumbria.
754	Martyrdom of Boniface.
c. 750–*c.* 765?	Collapse of sceatta currencies in most English regions.
760s	Carolingian coins penetrate the English currency.
c. 765 onwards?	Reformed pennies of good silver struck in minimal quantities at Canterbury for Haeberht, Ecgberht, Iænberht, and Offa.
776	Battle of Otford.
776–85	Minimal Mercian influence in Kent.
786	Legatine commission.
787	Council of Chelsea.
c. 786	Offa's coinage minted in larger quantities and used much more widely north of the Thames.
c. 793	Monetary reform introduces heavier pennies of Group III.
796	Commercial treaty between Offa and Charlemagne.

Notes

1. A thorough survey of Offa's coinage, which is still the basic reference, is C. E. Blunt, 'The coinage of Offa', *Anglo-Saxon Coins* (ed. R. H. M. Dolley), 1961, pp. 39–62. It should be supplemented by reference to I. Stewart, 'The London mint and the coinage of Offa', in *Anglo-Saxon Monetary History*, ed. M. A. S. Blackburn, Leicester, 1986, pp. 27–43. Blunt's attribution of all but a handful of the coins to Canterbury prompted a critique, D. M. Metcalf, 'Offa's pence reconsidered', *Cunobelin* 9 (1963), 37–52. One of the themes discussed there, namely the scale of the coinage, provoked a vigorous debate, which came to be concerned with where the coins were used: P. Grierson, 'Mint output in the time of Offa', *The Numismatic Circular* 71 (1963), 114–15; D. M. Metcalf, 'English monetary history in the time of Offa: a reply', *ibid.*, 165–67; Grierson, 'Some aspects of the coinage of Offa', *ibid.*, 223–25; Metcalf, 'Evidence relating to die-output in the time of Offa', *ibid.*, 72 (1964), 23; P. Spufford, 'Die-output', *ibid.*, 79; C. S. S. Lyon, 'The estimation of the number of dies employed in a coinage', *ibid.*, 73 (1965), 180–81; Grierson, 'Variations in die-output', *ibid.*, 76 (1968), 298–99. Other studies on medieval die output, by Stewart and Mate, in the *Numismatic Chronicle* for 1963, 1964, and 1969, have thrown light on the Offa debate, and have demonstrated surprisingly large average figures for die output in the fourteenth century, and these have since been confirmed by J. D. Brand in *Mints, Dies, and Currency* (ed. R. A. G. Carson). The original debate meanwhile moved on, and became more generalized, in the pages of the *Economic History Review*: Metcalf, 'How large was the Anglo-Saxon currency?', *ibid.* 2nd. Ser., 18 (1965), 475–82; Grierson, 'The volume of the Anglo-Saxon coinage', *ibid.* 2nd. Ser., 20 (1967), 153–60; Metcalf, 'The prosperity of north-western Europe in the eighth and ninth centuries', *ibid.*, 344–57. Supplementary comments on other aspects of Offa's coinage will be found in articles cited below.

2. A brilliant paper, which transformed the sceatta problem, and which has been the essential bias for subsequent work, is S. E. Rigold, 'The two primary series of sceattas', *British Numismatic Journal* 30 (1960–61), 6–53. A critique of some of the details of Rigold's classification was presented in D. M. Metcalf, 'A coinage for Mercia under Aethelbald', *Cunobelin* 12 (1966), 26–39. This was largely repudiated in Rigold, 'The two primary series of sceattas: addenda and corrigenda', *British Numismatic Journal* 35 (1966), 1–6. Similar revisions are urged again in Metcalf, 'The "Bird and Branch" sceattas in the light of a find from Abingdon', *Oxoniensia* 37 (1972), 51–65.

2a. The 'bird and branch' coins in the 'upper Thames valley' style have been found at Abingdon, Dorchester, and Moulsford (closely grouped), and at Southampton.

2b. D. M. Metcalf, 'The ninth-century moneyer Werheard and the problem of local connections', *Wiltshire Archaeological Magazine* 72/73 (1977–8), 195–8.

3. The idea of a fluctuating monetary economy was put forward in D. M. Metcalf,

J. M. Merrick, and L. K. Hamblin, *Studies in the Composition of Early Medieval Coins* (Minerva Numismatic Handbooks, 3), 1968, at pp. 8f. It was taken up again in Metcalf, 'An early Carolingian mint in the Low Countries: BONA = Tiel', *Revue Belge de Numismatique* 116 (1970), 141–52.

4. S. E. Rigold, 'The Sutton Hoo coins in the light of the contemporary background of coinage in England', in R. Bruce-Mitford, *The Sutton Hoo Ship Burial*, vol. 1, 1975, pp. 653–77, when there is a list of 138 finds with two addenda. A few more coins can now be added, of which the latest include a tremissis of Rouen from Knighton, near Uffington, Oxon.; a *Madelinus* tremissis of Dorestad from Caistor St. Edmunds, near Norwich; a triens found in 1979 at Skipton, Yorks; and a tremissis of Quentovic from Barham, Suffolk.

5. The historical background to the resumed flow of continental coinage to Britain is carefully discussed (with maps) in C. H. V. Sutherland, *Anglo-Saxon Gold Coinage*, 1948, at pp. 22–30, where he points to the marriage of Bertha, daughter of Charibert I, to king Æthelberht of Kent. For the date see F. M. Stenton, *Anglo-Saxon England*, 3rd edn., 1971, p. 105, where the marriage is placed 'before 588', and cf. Sutherland, p. 29, n. 1, relying on Bede's testimony for an earlier date.

6. It has been an unresolved puzzle why the forty coins and coin-blanks should have been so miscellaneous, and it has been unfashionable to think that there could have been a 'normal' money economy in East Anglia in the 620s; but one should consider whether the royal treasury may not have accumulated a store of wealth, for example by levying a toll on ships from the continent. Merchants no doubt preferred to put together coins of a kind, and outpayments may have been made from the royal treasury selectively – in coins of Dorestad or Quentovic or Marseilles, for example – the active mints, whose products were widely known and acceptable. For an interesting commentary on the Sutton Hoo coins, see E. G. Stanley, 'The date of Beowulf: some doubts and no conclusions', in *The Dating of Beowulf*, ed. C. Chase, Toronto, 1981, pp. 197–211 at pp. 203–5.

7. There may have been an initial period when, for example, there were accumulations of wealth in Canterbury and its ports that had not spilled over even into the restricted area of east Kent. For a note on the grants of remission, see D. Whitelock, *English Historical Documents*, *c.* 500–1042, 1955, p. 451.

7a. For the Anglo-Saxon gold coinage, Sutherland's standard work (note 5 above) must now be supplemented by I. Stewart, 'Anglo-Saxon gold coins', in *Scripta Nummaria Romana*, ed. R. A. G. Carson and C. M. Kraay, 1978, pp. 143–72.

8. Sutherland, *op. cit.*, pp. 52f., 95, etc. Assuming that the Audvarld coins stand at the head of one series, the attribution to king Eadbald of Kent (616–40) imposes a later date of origin than might otherwise have been canvassed. The gold contents of the Crondall specimen, previously estimated at about 80 per cent are shown by Oddy's careful S. G. measurement to be only 66.8 per cent – in line with the best Anglo-Saxon coins in the hoard, but not higher. This argues for a late dating. See W. A. Oddy, 'The analysis of four hoards of Merovingian gold coins', *Methods of Chemical and Metallurgical Investigation*

of Ancient Coinage, ed. E. T. Hall and D. M. Metcalf, 1972, pp. 111–25. The argument from the 'pagan interlude' at London (*c.* 616–675) and a coinage 'certainly Christian in character' in the Crondall hoard, which has been taken to require a pre-616 date for the coins in question (Sutherland, *op. cit.*, pp. 41f.) and to support their attribution to the episcopacy of Mellitus, hinges on the 'ecclesiastical character' of the obverse type, and should in the writer's view be treated with the greatest reserve. The gold contents of these coins average only 64.1 per cent (Oddy, *op. cit.*). All previous arguments should now be reconsidered in the light of J. P. C. Kent, 'Gold standards of the Merovingian coinage, A.D. 580–700', in *Methods of Chemical and Metallurgical Investigation*, pp. 69–74.

9. Sutherland, *op. cit.*, pp. 35, 50f., etc. (but the reading 'Beartigo' is no longer found acceptable by runologists. See R. I. Page, *An Introduction to English Runes*, 1973, esp. at pp. 119–33. For the coin purchased in Amiens, see I. Stewart, *loc. cit.* (note 7a above). The authenticity of the York thrymsas has been disputed – see P. Grierson in *British Numismatic Journal* 31 (1962), 8–10. One of the York coins has since been analysed, and found to contain 46 per cent gold, 52 per cent silver, and 2 per cent copper, with substantially higher figures for gold at the surface: see S. C. Hawkes, J. M. Merrick, and D. M. Metcalf, 'X-ray fluorescent analysis of some dark-age coins and jewellery', *Archaeometry* 9 (1966), 98–138, at pp. 128 and 137. The figures favour its authenticity.

10. The 'post-Crondall' phase was identified and discussed in Rigold, *op. cit.* (1960–61) at 11 ff. and (particularly) *id.* (1966), 2f.

11. Important new thoughts are offered on the chronology of the 'post-Crondall' phase in Rigold, *op. cit.* (1966), and it is proposed to redate it to between the later 660s and the early 680s. This is on the basis of continental hoard-evidence and of what would seem to be still a rather late date for Crondall ('around, or soon after, 650').

12. Sutherland, *op. cit.* pp. 78ff., and Rigold, *op. cit.* (1960–61), 11ff.

13. For England, Rigold suggested 686–7, while Metcalf, Merrick, and Hamblin, *op. cit.* (1968), pp. 18f., have argued for a slightly earlier date, in the reign of Hlothere (674–86). A valuable survey of the difficult continental evidence has been published in J. Lafaurie, 'Monnaies d'argent mérovingiennes des VIIe et VIIIe siècles', *Revue Numismatique* 6th Ser., 11 (1969), 98–219. His conclusions are, briefly, that dwindling issues of gold continued to at least *c.* 675/80 in Gaul generally (cf. the Bordeaux hoard) and perhaps to *c.* 700 at Marseilles. The earliest silver coins appear to be *c.* 670, but the following fifteen years were politically very unsettled. For a better assessment of the Bordeaux hoard than that on which Rigold relied, see J. Lafaurie in C. Higounet, *Histoire de Bordeaux*, vol. 2 for a list of the Merovingian coins. The latest Visigothic coins were after 695 (Egica with Wittiza).

14. Metal analyses in Metcalf, Merrick and Hamblin, *op. cit.*, showing 96–98 per cent 'silver' (silver plus gold traces). The figures await confirmation by EPMA.

15. Rigold, *loc. cit* (1960–61, 1966), with the attributions for Series B as modified in Metcalf, *Cunobelin* 12 (1966).

15a. See note 13.

16. The wergild paid for the death of Mul is unlikely to have been as large, in comparison with the scale of the currency, as to exhaust it (Metcalf, Merrick, and Hamblin, *op. cit.*, p. 18). This raises once again the question of average die output in the seventh century. Cf. note 1.

17. Figures 1–3, representing the very early, the primary, and the secondary phase distribution-patterns, are taken from D. M. Metcalf, 'Monetary circulation in southern England in the first half of the eighth century', in *Sceattas in England and on the Continent*, ed. D. Hill and D. M. Metcalf, Oxford, 1984, pp. 27–69.

18. M. Morehart, 'Some dangers of dating sceattas by typological sequences', *British Numismatic Journal* 39 (1970), 1–5. The general conclusions of this article, however, can only be regarded as shooting at clay pigeons.

19. M. Blackburn, 'A chronology for the sceattas', in *Sceattas in England and on the Continent*, ed. D. Hill and D. M. Metcalf, Oxford, 1984, pp. 165–74.

20. J. P. C. Kent, 'From Roman Britain to Saxon England', *Anglo-Saxon Coins*, pp. 1–22, discusses the question of 'gaps' in the dark-age currency. He argues, in connection with the late-seventh century coinage, that 'when either typological or metallic degeneration occurred, its progress was rapid'; and (accepting a date of 737 for the Cimiez hoard) that 'it is difficult to protract this (sceatta) coinage beyond 750, if so late a date is possible, and just as a large gap looms between the Roman and the Anglo-Saxon coinage, so a shorter one seems to intervene between "sceatta" and penny . . .'. A much later terminal date and a shorter gap are argued by M. M. Archibald in her article on the coinage of Beonna.

20a. In *BNJ* 56 (1986), forthcoming.

21. This is cautiously yet forcefully argued in R. H. M. Dolley and K. F. Morrison, 'Finds of Carolingian coins from Great Britain and Ireland', *British Numismatic Journal* 32 (1963), 75–87. See further P. V. Addyman and D. H. Hill, 'Saxon Southampton: a review of the evidence, I', *Proceedings of the Hampshire Field Club* 25 (1968), 61–93, at 80f.

22. C. E. Blunt and R. H. M. Dolley, 'The Anglo-Saxon coins in the Vatican Library', *British Numismatic Journal* 28 (1955–57), 449–58; R. Dura and G. Sambon, *Museo Bartolomeo Borghesi* (sale cat. of 24 April 1880), Rome; H. H. Völckers, *Karolingische Münzfunde der Frühzeit (751–800)*, Göttingen, 1965, for coins of Offa in the Ilanz hoard.

23. Dolley and Morrison, *op. cit.*; D. M. Metcalf, 'A coin of Pepin from Richborough, Kent, struck at (?) Utrecht', *Hamburger Beiträge zur Numismatik* 20 (1966), 384–87.

23a. *Proc. Dorset Nat. Hist. Arch. Soc.*, 105 (1983), 151; *Anglo-Saxon Monetary*

History, ed. M. A. S. Blackburn, p. 30; *Numismatic Chronicle*, 143 (1983), 141.

24. The standard work on the early Northumbrian coinage is J. Booth, 'Sceattas in Northumbria', in *Sceattas in England and on the Continent* (see note 17), pp. 71–111. Analyses of silver content are included in Booth's catalogue. Further unpublished analyses undertaken in the British Museum Research Laboratory round out the picture considerably. For the quantities in which the coins were struck, see D. M. Metcalf, 'Estimation of the volume of the Northumbrian coinage, *c.* 738–88', in *Sceattas in England and on the Continent*, pp. 113–16.

24a. Metcalf, *loc. cit.*

25. H. E. Pagan, 'A new type for Beonna', *British Numismatic Journal* 37 (1968), 10–15 argues that the hybrid nature of the coins of Beonna must lie in the fact that the area where they circulated was one where the effect of reform elsewhere was being felt but where the principles of that reform had not yet been applied. He was therefore inclined to date them *c.* 770 or later. There is, however, no obvious stylistic link between the first pennies and the coins of Beonna, and it seems preferable because of their alloy to regard them as sub-Northumbrian, whatever their date. The connections with Maastricht are very suggestive for economic history, as are the two Low Countries provenances for the East Anglian coins. One specimen of Beonna was 70–80 per cent silver: Metcalf, Merrick, and Hamblin, *op. cit.*, pp. 39f. and 57. For the stylistically related Maastricht 'sceatta' coinage, one specimen of which is as low as 33–35 per cent silver, see an analysis in D. M. Metcalf and L. K. Hamblin, 'The composition of some Frisian sceattas', *Jaarboek voor Munt- en Penningkunde* 55 (1968), 28–45, no. 0.126.

26. Much more evidence from the reign of Offa – and also from coins of Pepin and Charlemagne – will be needed before any firm conclusions can be drawn. One would, of course, also be interested to see whether Group II coins yield a different pattern of gold traces from Group I. For the scientific context, references to individual analyses, and other examples of differences in general levels of gold traces, see D. M. Metcalf, 'Analyses of the metal contents of medieval coins', *Methods of Chemical and Metallurgical Investigation*, pp. 383–434, at pp. 403–6, 408, and 420. Unpublished analyses by Dr. J. P. Northover of sceattas and of pennies of Offa in the Cardiff collection have been taken into consideration here.

27. C. S. S. Lyon, 'Historical problems of Anglo-Saxon coinage – (1)', *British Numismatic Journal* 36 (1967), 215–21.

28. Stenton, *op. cit.*, pp. 35f., 206–9, 216n., 222n.

29. C. E. Blunt, 'The coinage of Offa', *Anglo-Saxon Coins*, pp. 39–62, at pp. 53f.

30. It is possible, though this is special pleading, that two men of the same name were moneyers. This might help to unravel the complexities of the coins of Eoba (by detaching Group III). Udd and Dud may well be different men. Dud is something of a special case – it seems that he was 'a dud' at portraits, and had to borrow por-

trait dies from a variety of other moneyers – Metcalf, in *Cunobelin* 9 (1963), at 48.

31. D. M. Metcalf, 'Fiufar or Arfiuf = Strasbourg', *Hamburger Beiträge zur Numismatik* 20 (1966), 380–84.

32. C. E. Blunt, 'Four Italian coins imitating Anglo-Saxon types', *British Numismatic Journal* 25 (1945–48), 282–85; D. M. Metcalf, 'Italian and other imitations of the coins of Offa', *Hamburger Beiträge zur Numismatik* 20 (1966), 387–92.

33. P. Grierson, 'Money and coinage under Charlemagne', in *Karl der Grosse*, vol. 1, Dusseldorf, 1965, pp. 501–36.

34. Metcalf in *Hamburger Beiträge zur Numismatik* 20 (1966), at 381f.

35. C. E. Blunt, 'A coin of Heaberht, king of Kent: Lord Grantley's attribution vindicated', *British Numismatic Journal* 27 (1952–54), 52–54. The coin of Heahberht was acquired in Rome.

35a. K. P. Witney, *The Kingdom of Kent*, 1982, pp. 198–205 attempt a reconstruction of the dynastic struggles of these years.

36. The nature of the reform of 755 is examined in D. M. Metcalf and H. A. Miskimin, 'The Carolingian pound: a discussion', *Numismatic Circular* 76 (1968), 296–98, 333–34.

37. There are virtually no die-links among the surviving coins of Pepin: D. M. Metcalf, 'The prosperity of north-western Europe in the eighth and ninth centuries', *Economic History Review* 2nd Ser., 20 (1967), 344–57.

38. See F. M. Stenton, *Preparatory to Anglo-Saxon England* pp. 371–82, and H. E. Pagan in *Numismatic Chronicle* 7th Ser., 72 (1972), 335–7.

39. Witney, *The Kingdom of Kent*, p. 205 puts it more strongly: 'for nine years ... the charters show that first Egbert and then Ealhmund reigned in complete independence of (Offa). The vindictive hatred which he later expressed for Iænberht and the Cantware no doubt sprang from the humiliation of this defeat.'

40. The dies of the London and Ilanz specimens of Blunt var. 10, and B.34 and Lockett 362 are surely all by the same hand. Note, on the Eadbehrt coin, B.34, the elongated bar of the F; the titulus (unusually) above it; the two dots vertically to the left of the F; the long, leaning M for Merciorum with a contraction-mark across it; and the elegant seriffing. Locket 362 (also variety B.34) is even closer in general style to the London coin. For further stylistic commentary, see *Hamburger Beiträge zur Numismatik* 20 (1966), 387–88.

41. D. M. Metcalf, 'A note on chronology', *Numismatic Circular* 71 (1963), at 167.

42. How far was the geographical expansion of Offa's coinage achieved by local minting (in a way analogous with the expansion of the sceattas)? The parallel is certainly inexact. Although the topic has remained, unfortunately, an embattled

one, the historian should note that the consensus has moved some way from the position of ten or twelve years ago, when there would have been general acceptance of the idea that the great bulk of Offa's coins were struck at Canterbury, with only one small group coming from another mint, in East Anglia. The suggestions made by Metcalf in *Cunobelin* 9 (1963) – which never gained entry to the consensus, but which may deserve re-examination in light of the topographical analysis in *Oxoniensia* 37 (1972) – were (i) that Eoba, Ibba, Ealraed, and Eadhun were a group of moneyers who operated separately in Group II; 'coins of the four moneyers account for a good half of the finds from north of the Thames and west of the fenlands. They seem, in a word, to belong to Mercia'; (ii) that of Alhumund, who was the only moneyer to use the formula OFRA (for *Rex Anglorum*), belonged similarly to middle Anglia or the fenlands; (iii) that the Offa/Iænberht coins had an essentially west Saxon rather than a Kentish distribution, and that the Ethelnoth die-link does not tie them firmly to Canterbury. Of these three, (i) at least looks no worse for wear, and a small addition can be made to the provenances on which it was based: D. M. Metcalf, 'A coin of Offa from Deddington Castle, Oxon.', *British Numismatic Journal* 40 (1971), 171–72. Meanwhile, new insights have been gained by a study of mint organisation in C. E. Blunt, C. S. S. Lyon, and B. H. I. H. Stewart, 'The coinage of southern England, 796–840', *British Numismatic Journal* 32 (1963), 1–74. For Offa, this adds a Mercian mint at (?) London (moneyers Ludoman, Wilhun), and another undetermined mint (Ciolhard, Ibba, Eama). Canterbury, of course, remains the major mint, with a normal complement (in the 1820s) of six moneyers. For the attribution of moneyers to the London mint, see now I. Stewart, *loc. cit.* (note 1 above).

43. The East Anglian coinage has been carefully discussed by Blunt, *op. cit.* See also Blunt, Lyon, and Stewart, *op. cit.* For the Tivoli coin, see the sale-catalogue of the Lockett collection, lot 323; and for die-duplication see the comment in Metcalf, *Cunobelin* 9 (1963), at 45, n. 29. The range of issues at the East Anglian mint is of marginal consideration in judging Lyon's II–I–III sequence.

44. P. Grierson, 'Money and coinage under Charlemagne', in *Karl der Grosse*, vol. 1, at pp. 510f.; D. M. Metcalf, 'The date of Charlemagne's reform', *Numismatic Circular* 76 (1968), 153–54.

45. Much of Series B.II could also be Frisian.

46. Stenton, *op. cit.*, p. 221: Bede refers to a Frisian merchant in London in 679.

47. *Ibid.*, p. 221.

13

Some thoughts on the manner of publication of coins found in the course or archaeological excavations

Michael Dolley†

Since coins were first invented, there have been instances of their accidental loss – and of their being found. Had it not been so, Scripture would have been the poorer by at least one parable. The law of treasure trove, too, might have been very different. In the course of this paper there will be discussed some aspects of the problem of exactly how coins recovered in an archaeological excavation may best be recorded for the benefit of posterity. The first point to be made, and it is one too often forgotten, is that the archaeologist is not the only nor even the prime beneficiary from his discoveries. Granted that there are many cases when the principal importance of what may be a very common coin is its stratification, and the light that it sheds on the chronology of a particular context, there is always the possibility that the coin may turn out to be a variety hitherto unknown to the numismatist. A good example of this is a tenth-century coin of Anlaf Sihtricsson occurring in Mr. A. B. Ó'Ríordáin's recent excavations at the High Street site in Dublin. It is only the fourth coin of its particular issue to have come to light in modern times, while the name of the moneyer – Bleseret – is one that has not previously been recorded. In other words, any worthwhile report on the coin will have to satisfy the legitimate curiosity alike of numismatists and of students of Viking-age personal names. The former will expect some reference at least to the other three coins, one in an English private cabinet and two in Continental museums, while the latter will expect awareness, if not comprehension, of their highly specialized concern. In the background lurks the historian as such. If the coin is in fact of Anlaf Sihtricsson, and if the mint really is York – questions that only a numismatist can answer – the newly-discovered coin will be another crumb of evidence for those who are attempting to estimate the interdependence of Dublin and York in the early 940s. It seems scarcely necessary to add that there are at least two classes of specialist historians hanging on the answer; Irish historians concerned with the story of the absorption of Dublin into Ireland, and English historians no less concerned with the how and why of York's reabsorption into England.

It follows from this that a numismatic report on coins found in excavations is a matter for a specialist. The person who writes the report must be at, or near to, the centre of things numismatic, and this means that the number of potential reporters is limited, and also that they will have numerous other calls upon their time. It is arguable, indeed, if there are in these islands even a dozen students who are both technically equipped and temperamentally suited to produce adequate reports on long runs of coins from sustained excavation at major urban sites. In particular, archaeologists who are seeking numismatic reporters should be on their guard against narrow specialisms. There ought to be the same attention paid to Roman coins occurring in mediaeval contexts as to mediaeval coins appropriately stratified, and in the same way there must be an end of the practice of not submitting for report post-mediaeval coins from the levels overlying the structures formally under investigation.

Some recent examples will illustrate the importance of this insistence on the inclusion of the apparently irrelevant. At Dublin and at Southampton, Roman coins have occurred in mediaeval levels. In the case of Dublin, it has been possible to suggest deliberate import in Viking times as scrap copper, and in post-Viking times accidental occurrence in ballast brought over by ships exporting corn to England. There was also the consideration that the reporter happened, at that very time, to be sponsoring a student's Academy monograph on Roman material brought over to Ireland, so that both he and his student were vitally interested in – and peculiarly qualified to assess – evidence that not all Roman coins found in Ireland need have arrived there either in antiquity or else in modern times. The labourer is indeed worthy of his hire, and it seems not inappropriate that the reporter who may well spend weeks preparing a report on only a dozen coins should be rewarded by the occasional windfall of this kind. At Southampton, the nature of the Roman coins found by Dr. Colin Platt in fact proved extremely relevant to the source of the rubble used when one particular stretch of twelfth-century wall was thrown up to meet a specific emergency, while the nature of the mutilation of one of them prompted not unuseful speculation on the possibility of *damnatio memoriae* in the ancient world, and of confusion of orichalcum with gold by mediaeval finders with consequent distortion of the record. As regards more modern coins found in overlying levels, there are still mediaeval specialists who would go to the stake for the principle:

Numismatista sum et numismatici nil a me alienum puto

and it is well to remember that one of a mediaeval numismatist's few checks on his inferences from coins unsupported by archives is his observation of the behaviour of coins where documentation in fact exists. Recently, one Irish archaeologist seemed just a little taken aback by his chosen reporter's insistence that the post-mediaeval coins also should be produced. He might have been less surprised had he known that the numismatist in question had with the editor of the county journal a prosopographical note on some seventeenth-century tokens of the adjacent area, a note breaking entirely new ground where the particular series was concerned. In any case, and particularly where there has been disturbance of the site, the numismatist is, or should be, anxious to know whether coins that usually bear dates do, in fact, occur in the anticipated sequence. Not all mediaeval coins are closely dated, and the numismatic reporter may be encouraged, in certain circumstances, to argue for a date from context provided only he can be satisfied that the apparent stratification of the site is reasonably secure.

From this there arises another very important consideration. Ideally the archaeologist should have lined up his numismatic reporter before a single sod is lifted or a spit turned. Even at this stage co-operation is useful. The numismatist can suggest to the archaeologist the types of coin for which he should be looking, and even give him some idea of the quantity in which they are likely to occur. Different coins, too, survive in different soils in a very wide spectrum of condition. In most Irish contexts, for example, the base bracteates of the twelfth century can hope to be recovered only by the exercise of great care and even then only under the most favourable of conditions. It may even be necessary, too, for the numismatist to indicate to the archaeologist that he should be on his guard against giving access to his site to a particular local collector, while the best check on the integrity of individual diggers is if the numismatist is alerted to the fact that a particular excavation is producing a particular type of coin with a particular type of patination. It is little use to scholarship if it is only months, if not years, after the event that the numismatist realises that there had come onto the market coins with the identical 'colour' at precisely the time that honest workmen and volunteers – and one hastens to add that the vast majority of helpers (and coin-collectors) are honest – must have been handing in to their supervisors material of the same description.

To be commended on other grounds is the increasingly widespread practice of the archaeologist reporting to his numismatic specialist the coins as and when they come to light. This does not dispense him from the obligation of himself provisionally identifying each coin the moment it is brought to the find-table. Coins often survive in a very precarious condition, and can begin to deteriorate as soon as exposed to the air. Even where this happens, though, a good photograph or a good drawing – or preferably both – is a record for which the reporter may be very grateful. There is also the consideration that coins may disappear as the result of purely human agencies. Site-huts are not always secure, and occasionally coins may have to be sent through the post. Much more important, though, is the desirability of the numismatist pondering his material over as long a period as possible. Again, the Dublin excavations provide a case in point. As a result of Mr. Ó'Ríordáin's discoveries, numismatists are now having to re-think completely the Irish bracteates. These fragile and exceptional coins come at the very end of the Hiberno-Norse series, and are completely without legends. Before the excavations, the debased series now associated with the Dublin mint had been known from fewer than half-a-dozen specimens, all deriving from one virtually undated early nineteenth-century context. Now, however, more than a score of examples have come to light at the High Street site alone, and the exact archaeological contexts have to be studied with the closest attention if there is to be any hope of achieving a dating within the decade rather than the half-century. As a result, the excavators themselves are on their toes exactly to note and to record the last scrap of evidence which may establish the date of loss. Not the least fortunate and happy aspect of the Dublin excavations is the *rapport* that has been established between excavator and numismatic reporter, but again it should be stressed that Mr. Ó'Ríordáin's own provisional identifications have proved without exception to be correct, so that his reporter's frequent hurried trips to Dublin to inspect the latest discovery never once have been the occasion of disappointment. The archaeologist, it should be emphasized, must be on his guard against the local pundit. The letters FRNS can embrace a terrifyingly broad band of *expertise*, and only last year, one young Belfast graduate found himself correcting one such pseudo-savant's identifications which were out in some cases by more than a century.

In the course of any protracted excavation, then, the numismatic reporter may hope to have been shown his material when and as it has come to light. In some cases, there will have had to be taken a decision to clean, and again one would urge submission where possible of all such coins to the numismatist before dispatch to the laboratory. Coins have been known to disintergrate under cleaning, and there are occasions when the fleeting impression of the coin on its corrosion products may reveal more to the experienced numismatist's eye than the end-product of the cleaning process. This is not to criticise the scientists. Stabilisation and conservation are critical, and it will be little use to posterity if a little heap of oxides is all that is available should, years later, somebody wonder if, perhaps, this or that expert was nodding, and identified as Anglo-Saxon a fragment that in the light of re-examination of some associated pottery is more likely to have been Plantagenet. At this stage, too, a decision may well have to be taken on whether or not a particular coin should be the subject of separate publication.

Here every case has to be judged on its own merits, and excavator and numismatist each may have his own reasons for desiring publication prior to the definitive report on the coins as an entity. Increasingly, archaeology is becoming a matter of public relations, and an excavator may well wish to maintain interest in, and support for, a particular excavation by selective publication of the sum of the highlights of each season's work. The very last coin to be found on the High Street site at Dublin is a case in point. It is a London penny of Ælfred the Great struck almost certainly in 886, and as such with its portrait and London monogram is immediately intelligible as a find of the greatest significance even by a lay audience. Equally, the numismatist may feel that a particular coin deserves early publication to focus informed opinion on a particular problem. For example, a decade ago no mediaeval Norwegian coin was known with a find-spot from these islands. The tally now stands at three, and the story of their discovery is salutary. The first was sent to the writer by Mr. R. B. K. Stevenson who was going through unpublished material from the excavations between the wars at Jarlshof. The second was submitted to him by Mr. Iain Crawford who had recovered it in the course of his current excavations at the Udal on North Uist. Both coins had to be referred to a Norwegian colleague, and he in turn flushed a third with an unrecorded Scottish provenance in the trays of the Royal Coin Collection at Copenhagen. Here early numismatic publication has proved in the best interests of all concerned, but the writer hastens to add that it is his personal conviction that such cases should be the exception and the rule. It is not to the long-term advantage of numismatics, let alone of archaeology, that numismatists should be spared the labour of reading through proper reports on the totality of the numismatic material recovered from a particular site. In twentieth-century numismatics the suet may well prove to be at least as important as the plums, and if the latter have been unduly culled there is a real danger that the numismatic report on the coins as a whole may be put on the long finger and never in fact completed. This said, though, the excavator himself may have sound academic reasons as opposed to propagandist reasons for desiring early publication of individual coins found in a particular context. A good example is afforded by the Anglo-Saxon pennies of the tenth century discovered by Dr. George Eogan in the primary silt of a souterrain dug into the prehistoric mound at Knowth. The discovery raised questions so fundamental for the interpretation of the site, and of others like it, that publication of the two coins in advance of the final report seems entirely justified. As ever, though, an element of *rapport* between excavator and numismatist is essential if there is not to be conflict, and both need to have a very real understanding of the problems of each of the disciplines involved.

We come now to the preparation of the final report; the description and discussion of all the coins found which will be printed as an appendix to the excavator's report on the excavations as a whole. Inevitably, it will be of a length proportionate to the number and importance of the coins in question, and it is the submission of this paper that it should be in a form enabling it to be read as a consecutive entity. Particularly suspect should be undue tabularization, and an increasingly questionable practice may be thought the citation of coins by mixed alphabetical and numerical symbols referring to standard works when these are not accompanied by brief descriptions of the coins. It is too easy with such algebraic formulae for printer's errors to creep in undetected in a way impossible when even a few words of text are involved. In a Roman coin's description, for example, ORTENS AVG is a palpable misprint for ORIENS AVG, but *RIC* 732 for *RIC* 723 is a slip as easy to make as difficult to detect when once overlooked by the proof-reader. Some thought, too, should be given to the ultimate destination of the coins. In most cases it is likely that they will end up in a local museum, but in the nature of things the institutions are few where they can hope to command the constant surveillance of a trained numismatist. Over the years some at least will inevitably become parted from their envelopes, and it is essential that the descriptions printed in the excavation report should be detailed enough to allow of the actual specimens being identified by a subsequent generation of researchers. If only for this reason, full details should be given of weight and patination, even in the case of fragmentary coins, while illustration should be on a scale as generous as the circumstances of the case permit. Fortunately excavators themselves are beginning to appreciate the attractions of illustration, and where the number of coins is relatively small, as with Mr. Thomas Fanning's highly instructive series from Clontuskert Priory, photographic reproduction of the totality need not present undue difficulty. In the same way, it should be normal practice for brackets to indicate those letters in legends which are wanting or illegible, and a note of die-axis, where appropriate, is a courtesy for which a future student may evince gratitude out of all proportion to the labour involved. No less desirable are systematic references to a selection of the standard works involved, and here the numismatic reporter should remember that it is not every public, let alone private, library that can boast a run of British Museum catalogues and of their Continental counterparts. It certainly is not beneath the dignity of a report of this kind to give references, where appropriate, to one or more of the more easily available handbooks of the type put out by B. A. Seaby Ltd. and Spink & Son, and especially when some of the more enlightened excavators will be found including copies of such works in their on-site libraries.

A special problem is posed by the discovery of coin-hoards. This has happened in the writer's own experience at Mellifont, at Winchester, at Southampton and at Dublin. Here there do seem to be arguments for separate publication, though the form of the publication may vary very considerably. At Mellifont, the early thirteenth-century hoard was the only numismatic material recovered, and was so integral to discussion of the problem of the church's rebuilding that the excavation-report was, in fact, the only possible vehicle of publication. At Winchester, though, the later thirteenth-century hoard found by Mr. Martin Biddle was one of a well-known type, and, questions of treasure trove practice apart, a good case could be made for immediate publication in one of the numismatic journals where coin-hoards normally figure. At Southampton, on the other hand, the eleventh-century hoard was completely atypical, and involved coins from a foreign series not normally found in an English context. Here the best solution has seemed to be publication as an appendix to the numismatic report. The Dublin discovery again presented special problems. The number of coins – or more strictly of tokens – was very large, 2,061 to be precise, and the series was one to which more recent scholarship had given a totally aberrant date. To have included the hoard in the main report would have been completely to distort the picture of the pattern of coin-use which is one of the most valuable contributions which arhcaeological excavation can make to numismatics, while relegation of the hoard to an appendix would have produced a ludicrous imbalance inasmuch as any adequate discussion just of the context would have occupied more space than the description and discussion of all the other coins from the site. The circumstances of the loss of this hoard, moreover, have proved extremely relevant to other disciplines, and in this case separate publication of the cess-pit and of its contents in monograph form has seemed the best solution. There will also be, of course, the fullest of cross-referencing between this monograph and the coin-report as such, and since each element is of sufficient importance to stand on its own feet, there is no real danger of either being neglected or, when published, overlooked.

To the report's exact description and identification of each and every coin there should be attached an estimate, as close as possible, of the date at which the particular piece is likely to have been lost. Something that it is very difficult for the numismatist to convey to the archaeologist is the very uneven lifespan of mediaeval coins. There are Anglo-Saxon pennies where we can be morally certain that they were demonetized — and effectively so — within months of their issue. In these cases the *termini post* and *ante quos* of manufacture and loss so closely correspond that the non-numismatist may have difficulty in grasping that *c.* 997, for example, may mean in certain circumstances 'after June 997 and before March 998'. One is careful to qualify this statement because a coin of that particular variety found in Ireland as opposed to England might well have *terminus ante quem* for loss as opposed to striking nearer the year 1000, though it would still have been struck before September 997 and probably not been removed from England after March 998. At the other end of the scale there were some later mediaeval English pennies where the lifespan could be as long as two hundred years and more. Worn pennies of Edward I still were passing as coin as late as the reign of Henry VIII, and it is here that the numismatist out of his experience has to deploy all his resources if the archaeologist is not to be misled. Merely to state 'Penny of Edward I, Fox class IV' is not enough. Even if the archaeologist does not look up a standard work of reference and find there an indication of date of striking which in reality is no more than a *terminus post quem*, the probability is that he will think in terms of a *terminus ante quem* of 1307, or even of *c.* 1300, although, in fact, it is not until the middle of the fourteenth century that an Edward I penny still in reasonably sharp condition ceases to be acceptable as a perfectly plausible single-find. In many cases, too, it is the numismatist's task to estimate the extent to which loss of weight may be due to wear or to deliberate clipping or to the leaching out of one or more of the constituent metals as a result of exposure to particular types of soil, and in practice a very considerable amount of expertise is necessary if there is to be drawn with confidence any firm line between wear and corrosion.

The sensational later Hiberno-Norse penny of *Agnus Dei* type, found at the end of February 1973 on the Christ Church Place site at Dublin, is a case in point. The coin may look to the untrained eye a pretty worn and battered thing, but in point of fact the apparent wear is attributable very largely to corrosion and to double-striking which last affects the reverse in particular, so that it is unlikely to have been lost all that long after it was struck. It affords, too, yet another illustration of the desirability of coins from continuing excavations being shown to the reporter as and when they occur. It is significant that this coin seems to be only the second specimen known today of a type which first came to light in 1639, even more suggestive that the coin should be a die-duplicate of that in the Ulster Museum, but too easily forgotten that to establish even so much involved the reporter in visits to two museums a hundred miles apart and in the consultation of quite a body of literature outside his own rather extensive notes. Firmly to place the new coin in its exact place in the Hiberno-Norse series will necessitate a study of the Danish issues which seem to provide the immediate models for both the obverse and the reverse types, and this, involving as it will a visit to Copenhagen, is something that one can imagine that most reporters would prefer not to have sprung on them against a deadline of a few months if not weeks. Of course it may be objected that all this is work that should have been done years ago, but so to protest is to ignore the realities of numismatics. Not the least important consequence of the discovery of long runs of coins from excavations is the pressure they exert towards a more searching probe of areas of relative neglect, and the absence of this type from the collections at Dublin and London unquestionably lies at the root of failure, hitherto, to attach due importance to a quite unexpected as well as unprecedented instance of a Danish coin influencing one from Ireland. It was only this same spring, though, that there has appeared the first paper to recognize parallel Hiberno-Norse influence on the Danish coinage approximately a generation earlier.

As already remarked, there are certain mediaeval series where reasonably close datings for particular issues have still to be achieved. There are also areas where the numismatist still has none too clear an idea of how long an individual denomination may have remained in general currency. There seems, then, much to be said for the format which was recently devised for the publication of Dr. Platt's coins from Southampton. Appended to the description of each coin is a summary account of its archaeological context, so that the reader is given an immediate impression of the associated material. Not all numismatists are ignorant of or uninterested in archaeological methods, while it is not only numismatists who have found it difficult on occasion to pick up a reference to an individual coin in the main body of an archaeologist's report. Nor should it be assumed that numismatic interest is confined to chronology. Increasingly students are concerned with coin-use, and the circumstances of discovery may well afford a clue as to whether a particular coin is a casual loss out of circulation or a stray from a dispersed hoard. In the same way, that a gold coin of the early fourteenth century comes from the sump of a privy is no argument that such pieces passed freely from hand to hand in day-to-day commerce, whereas the loser of a galley-halfpenny of the same period might well have accepted, if he even noticed, his loss rather than prise up floor-boards or paving-stones. It was, moreover, the minute description of exactly how the thirteenth-century pennies occurred in Mr. Liam de Paor's excavations of the abbey church of Mellifont which was decisive that they represented a small personal cache and not the scatter of a major treasure imperfectly recovered in the course of a major conflagration which has passed unnoticed in the historical record, and here there are implications for the historian inasmuch as the hypothesis of the major treasure would not have accorded with the theory that Mellifont may have been burned in the Bruce war.

It is to be hoped that the numismatic appendixes to excavation-reports will be used increasingly by numismatists as an important source of information supplemental to that afforded by coin-hoards. For this reason it is desirable that different series should be clearly distinguished, and there is something to be said for an overall chronological arrangement with Roman coins preceding mediaeval, and mediaeval modern, and the different series distinguished by an index letter preceding the number. Coin R.2, then, can be immediately identifiable as Roman, E.5 as English, S.1 as Scottish

and C.4 as Continental. It is very desirable, too, that included should be
not only coins as such, but such paranumismatica as jettons or reckoning-
counters and coin-weights. The simple occurrence of these can provide a
useful pointer to the degree to which the excavator has been able to recover
numismatic material which by its nature is easily overlooked, and especially
under adverse conditions of weather or of soil. At Exeter, for example, the
apparent absence of certain series struck in silver could have been dismissed
as without particular significance had not Mr. John Collis recovered a surprising proportion of counters and of other objects in base metal. What
seems to have occurred is that, down the centuries, erosion of an unstable
site has resulted in differential recovery of precious metal coins, and hence
the desirability of a report on coins found always including some discussion
of the particular problems of the site where these are relevant to what may
or may not have come to light. This is not to say that all numismatic reports
should conform to a single model. Overstandardization is one of the banes
of modern scholarship as well as of modern living, and the present writer
with half-a-dozen reports in progress has no desire to become a prisoner of
his own uniformity. If, though, a report is to be read as an intelligible entity,
it probably will follow a general pattern, and more and more it would seem
desirable that there should always be one or two final paragraphs where
the numismatist, as such, attempts to interpret the material as a whole
against the background of existing knowledge. It is curious, for example,
that different sites at Southampton should have produced such very different
runs of coins, and it would appear that some excavators have been digging
'Hamwih', and others the mediaeval town which may have overlapped –
but which certainly did not coincide with – the earlier settlement. Even
more interesting is the contrast between the totality of the coins found over
the last century in the Southampton area and those recovered by Mr. Biddle
at Winchester, and it is worth recalling that only very recent recognition
that 'Hamwih' and not Winchester was the mint of the earliest pennies of
Wessex stemmed directly from the coincidence that Mr. Biddle and Dr. Platt
should have chosen to use the same individual to report on their numismatic
material.

All of which brings this paper back to where it began. The archaeologist,
it was observed, is by no means the only beneficiary from his discoveries
and, if there can once be established a tradition of detailed reporting of the
coin-material from archaeological excavations, numismatics in these islands
seem set fair to achieve a new dimension. In this connection, too, we do
well to remember that changed circumstances have put a new onus on the
excavator. In the old days, the navvy with his pick and shovel and the
ploughman following his share were responsible for the recovery of many
critical coins which today, with the general employment of the bulldozer
and tractor, would go totally unremarked. One trembles to think what has
been irretrievably lost with the construction of multi-storey office-blocks
and of motorways, and what with penalty-clauses for non-fulfilment of
contracts by given dates with consequent deliberate suppression of all
archaeological material unearthed in the course of the work, systematic

excavation by trained archaeologists alone can tell us what coins, in fact, were the staple of currency in the principal cities and towns of mediaeval England and Ireland.

A few words in conclusion. It is undoubtedly true that proper numismatic reports are going to be longer than they were in the past, and this in an age when printing-costs are mounting very steeply. It will, perhaps, help to reconcile archaeologists to this expense if they reflect that the preparation of adequate comment on the coins may well have involved the reporter in quite literally weeks of work over and above the years of study that he will have spent in acquiring the necessary *expertise*. Instant identification is rarely possible, and instant comment likely to be jejune where not completely erroneous. Proper numismatic appendixes, too, should ensure that excavation-reports are purchased by numismatic libraries and by numismatists on an ever-increasing scale. There is the further consideration that more than one excavator has exhibited of recent years a not unwelcome realization of the expense to which his numismatic reporter may have been put when preparing the coins for publication. This is not to hint that numismatists should be paid, nor even that their expenses need be met, but the notional amount might be at the back of the archaeologist's mind when he is costing his report, and used mentally to offset part at least of the printing bills. Nor should it be forgotten that the numismatic reporter will wish to see his work in print in a form that will not prejudice acceptance of the theories advanced let alone his own often hard-won reputation. If any interval of more than a few months should elapse between the receipt of a typescript and its dispatch to the printer, it may seem prudent as well as courteous for the archaeologist to enquire whether there are any modifications that the numismatist might like to make in the light of his subject's inevitable progress over the intervening period. The numismatist, too, might be allowed to correct his proofs. The present writer was just a little surprised to open one journal and find one report appearing nearly a decade after its composition, and can only congratulate himself that it did not 'date' more than it did. On another occasion, he was frankly startled to be told by one excavator who had enlisted his services that if he wanted a copy of the printed report he would have himself to apply to the Ministry concerned. He believes this particular report has still to appear, again after more than a decade, but hastens to add that the particular interlude is one as atypical as infelicitous. One of the more rewarding of his experiences over the last couple of decades has been the chance of working in close harmony with a number of very distinguished archaeologists who might otherwise have remained 'names', and it is on this note that the present paper can very fittingly terminate.

14
English medieval coins as dating evidence
Marion M. Archibald

The English Medieval coinage was struck almost exclusively in the noble metals: with the solitary exception of the 'stycas' issued in Northumbria during the first half of the ninth century, no really base, let alone copper or bronze coins, were produced. After a brief and rapidly debased series of gold coins at its inception in the second quarter of the seventh century, the English medieval coinage remained, with one short-lived gold series under Henry III, exclusively silver until the re-introduction of gold as part of the normal currency in 1344. Thereafter, until the end of the medieval period, gold and silver continued together as the only coinage metals. Again, with relatively few, and for the most part early, exceptions the two metals were consistently of high quality and the weight standard, where it is known or can be deduced with reasonable certainty, was accurate within the acceptable tolerances.[1] All medieval coins were therefore individually valuable[2] and this fact had an outstanding influence on every aspect of their behaviour in circulation. Their value for one thing meant that fewer of them were likely to be casually lost, and so it is not surprising to find that they are much less common as site finds than Roman coins which were drawn from a currency including at all periods a large output of low denominations in base metal.[3] Paradoxically, however, their very scarcity ensures that more is expected of medieval coins as dating evidence, not less. It would be hard to over-state the difficulties placed in the way of interpreting medieval site finds by this lack of numbers for it is axiomatic that, hoards apart, the value of coins as dating evidence rises in geometric progression with their increase in numbers. Moreover, unjustifiably precise and even erroneous deductions from the meagre coin evidence produced by most medieval excavations are the more likely to pass unchallenged, since this period generally lacks the closely datable pottery series which can, hopefully, be relied upon to temper any sanguine conclusions based on the fuller coin lists from Roman sites. It is all the more important, therefore, that the medieval coin evidence should not be pushed beyond what it can reasonably sustain.

Throughout this paper it is assumed that the coins being discussed have come from excavations conducted to the highest possible standard and that there is no doubt about their stratigraphical context. One aspect of archaeological interpretation does, however, require to be mentioned specifically. Many competent excavators who are fully alive to the potential presence of residual pottery are often curiously blind to the fact that, in this respect, coins can behave in precisely the same way as sherds. The regularity with which coins are found in the spoil heaps of even the best-regulated excavations should demonstrate the ease with which they can be overlooked and redeposited in a later level. Once again, the more equivocal dating of most medieval pottery means that it is less likely to alert the excavator to the presence of residual material. On the other hand, the likelihood of an intrusive coin from a disturbed earlier layer should not be exaggerated. The high metal value of medieval coins made them worth retrieving at any time and so, no doubt, their residual-survival rate is lower *pro rata* than that of the small base-metal Roman coins whose low intrinsic value would have rendered them virtually worthless – other than in large quantities – after they had been economically superseded or politically outdated. Equally, if a level of independently established date contains a coin known to have been struck at a considerably earlier period it should not be assumed on this evidence alone that residual material from an earlier level is present. To do so might easily lead to wrong conclusions about the status and date of some of the associated pottery. The relative longevity of different series of medieval coins will be discussed later. Suffice it here to contrast two successive examples: in normal circumstances a penny of 1250 found in a level of 1300 is certainly residual, but a penny of 1300 from a level of 1350 could very well be a contemporaneous loss as the coins of 1300 were among the commonest of those in circulation fifty years later. From now on it is assumed, unless otherwise stated, that the coins being discussed are primary losses in the layers from which they have been excavated.

In order to use a coin as dating evidence the archaeologist requires to know within the narrowest possible limits the date of its deposition. The precision with which this can be estimated – and it must be remembered that it is, at best, only an estimate – is dependent upon the extent to which it is possible to answer the following questions:

(1) When was this coin struck?
(2) How long afterwards was it deposited?

It may seem hardly necessary to dwell upon the first of these questions but it is important to recognize that the issue dates of many medieval coins are not so certain as is sometimes supposed. The archaeologist may to some extent have only himself to blame if he derives a false impression of finality from the bold type in dealers' catalogues and popular handbooks, useful as the best of these undoubtedly are. Numismatists themselves however must bear some responsibility for this situation. The confident way in which they have often asserted their views has left the impression that near-certainty exists in the current ordering and absolute dating of some series and it tends to be forgotten that their results of necessity depend to a very considerable extent upon numismatic hypothesis rather than upon demonstrable historical fact.[4] What *caveats* do remain in the original scholarly papers are naturally less likely to find a place in the distillations presented in the short general works in the hands of the non-specialist. As the terminal dates over which medieval numismatists are agonizing are often a matter of only a year or two either way, this may scarcely seem relevant in the context of field archaeology where the dating limits for all other classes of excavated material are so much wider. This is in fact very far from the case, however, since there is a danger that the aura of finality and precision which surrounds the dating of some medieval coins may spread to encompass the dating of others where no such extravagant claims to narrow dating have ever been made and for which they would be inappropriate and misleading. Unfortunately for the archaeologist, it is often with the commonest coins that there is greatest difficulty in providing a closely defined date.

On the question of duration in circulation, the virtual absence of any other evidence in the earlier medieval period, and very little of it on this score even after documentation of the coinage begins to become more plentiful in the twelfth century, obliges us to make use of the hoards.[5] In his paper, Dr. Kent has already pointed out the dangers of equating the coins actually current with the content of contemporary hoards. Most of his strictures are as valid for the middle ages as they are for periods before and after, and so to save reiterating them at every turn in this discussion it is assumed that they will be mentally read into all that follows. Provided that we make these allowances for possible distortion, and appreciate that we may still not be making enough allowances, hoards can be a reasonably reliable guide to the broad-outline content of currency. The proportions of coins of different reigns and types present in particular hoards are of course expressable as precise figures. These figures provide a very important guide to the relative commonness of these groups but they must not be taken as evidence of the presence of precisely those proportions among the coins in circulation unless this is borne out by a considerable body of homogeneous hoard evidence. The political, economic, geographical and personal factors influencing the content of both hoards and currency make such generalizations inapplicable. Once again the results are valid; it is only in pushing them towards unjustified precision that the danger lies. To do so only weakens credibility in those matters where certainty is in fact possible.

Here as elsewhere, individual longevity of isolated coins[6] as demonstrated by hoards is of little archaeological significance except as a warning that such survivals, especially of common coins, do occur and should be remembered. It is however a principle of paramount importance in estimating the likely duration of circulation that, between recoinages and other things being equal, common coins survive longer than rare ones. In other words, coins from long reigns and from types produced in large numbers remain in circulation in proportionally larger numbers than coins from short reigns and from types issued in small quantities. The different manifestations of this phenomenon will be best discussed in their appropriate chronological position in the latter part of this paper. Let us close the subject here by noting that the coins found by the archaeologist are of course most likely to be just such common coins.

Another factor which must be taken into consideration in assessing duration of circulation is wear. First of all it is necessary to distinguish wear, i.e. abrasion of the surface of the coin through circulation, from poor appearance resulting from other causes (e.g. weak or faulty striking technique), the use of worn or corroded dies or the corrosion of the surface of the coin by chemicals in the soil after its deposition. Once again it must be borne in mind that geographical and personal circumstances which we have no possible way of assessing will have influenced the condition of the coin which we are considering. Coins circulating in out-of-the-way places may have been in worse condition than those available to persons of comparable position in one of the major commercial centres, and a person of some standing in a remote district may well have been able to insist upon payments in coin of a better standard that that normally current among his immediate neighbours.[7] Most important of all, the condition of the isolated site-find may not have been typical of the state of the currency from which it was lost. There is of course no way of telling by looking at a coin whether it was in abnormally good or bad condition compared with its fellows. If there are two or more coins to consider it becomes increasingly possible to form an opinion on this point and so it is again desirable for the archaeologist to tell his coin expert how his coins are stratigraphically associated.

Differential rates of wear can be distinguished between coins of the same denomination circulating at different periods and among the various denominations struck at any one time and circulating together: the later the period, the greater the wear; the higher the denomination, the less the wear. Pennies surviving from the Anglo-Saxon and Norman periods generally show little sign of wear. This is partly because their life in circulation was often comparatively short, but principally because coins did not then circulate from hand to hand to the extent that they did in the later middle ages. As the actual use of coin intensified and, at a later date, inflation caused the relative value of money to decline, the increased circulation of coins caused them to wear at a faster rate. In addition, the introduction of the immobilized types after 1158 afforded coins a much longer potential life in circulation and so, certainly from the middle of the Short-Cross period onwards, wear becomes a factor of considerable importance in assessing the duration of circulation. Even so, hoards show that Short-Cross and Long-Cross pennies required to have been in circulation for a fairly long period before they begin to show appreciable signs of wear. Although we must allow for discrimination in favour of coins in better condition in these hoards their evidence is valid since the contrast in condition with equally long-lived pennies in later hoards is striking. By the later fourteenth century pennies begin to show wear within a shorter period, while half-groats and groats are in relatively unworn condition after the same length of time in circulation. By the mid-fifteenth century the rate of wear on all denominations has increased, the half-groats now being noticeably more worn than comparable coins in earlier hoards. Groats still exhibit surprisingly little wear after even twenty years in circulation. (It is important to note that we are still speaking of wear through surface abrasion and not loss of weight by clipping which will be considered later.)

Despite being struck in much softer metal, medieval gold coins are rarely found in really worn condition. Their high individual value ensured that they did not circulate to the same extent as silver coins, although here also the denomination rule applies: half-nobles are more worn than nobles of the same issue date in any hoard and quarter-nobles are always in the worst condition of the three.

It is clear, therefore, that the number of variable factors potentially present make wear an unreliable guide to the duration in circulation of an isolated site-find. This does not mean, however, that the evidence of wear should be disregarded. While it is improper to suggest a precise number of years of currency for a particular coin, it is unnecessarily cautious, for example, to leave the *termini* of a very worn penny of Short-Cross type Ia at 1180–1250, the limits of currency of the type itself. It is quite legitimate for someone with experience in dealing with both hoards and site-finds to offer an informed opinion, qualified by the usual *caveats* about possible abnormalities, on the broad margins within which a coin is likely to have been lost. This is much more helpful to the archaeologist than either pretended precision unsupportable on the evidence or unduly wide margins based upon exaggerated allowances for atypical conditions. As we have said before, it is the common and the typical which are most likely to turn up.

A word may also be said in general terms about halfpennies. Halfpennies are much commoner as site finds than their incidence in hoards would suggest. The reason for this was that people normally preferred to hoard their wealth in the highest denomination available to them unless an acute emergency forced them to bury their cash-in-hand without the possibility of pre-selection. Hoards which do contain appreciably larger quantities of low denominations in general and halfpennies in particular are more commonly found in the remote and generally less prosperous parts of the British Isles.[8] The Saxon round halfpennies from Alfred to Edgar are so rare that little is known about their currency pattern. It is noticeable that the cut-halfpennies in hoards of the period until the reintroduction of the round halfpenny in 1279 sometimes include a greater proportion of earlier coins than the rest of the hoard.[9] In the later sterling-penny period there is documentary evidence that inadequate supplies of halfpennies were being produced and that base Scottish and foreign coins had perforce to be used instead. This is borne out by what little hoard evidence we have on the subject.[10] It is also suggested that a greater proportion of older halfpennies may well have been kept in circulation, although there is not enough evidence to test this hypothesis satisfactorily. Throughout the whole of the medieval period, therefore, the archaeologist must be on his guard against the possibility that a halfpenny from his site may have been in circulation for longer than could be expected of a penny struck at the same time. (The question of weight comes into this question, especially in the sterling period, and these halfpennies will be discussed again later along with the other contemporary denominations.)

The rest of this paper is devoted to a discussion of how far it is possible to date the issue and duration in circulation of individual examples of the different series of the English medieval coinage. Points of general validity are made in the sections where a particularly apt example arises. It will be readily appreciated that this task involves a high degree of compression and simplification which is bound to leave many points inadequately considered.

The reader is referred in the footnotes to the principal papers where questions of dating are discussed, but even here space permits only the basic sources to be mentioned. A more complete picture of the current state of numismatic research, though it is not of course specifically geared to the question of dating, is to be found in the critical essays which make up the English medieval section in the quinquennial surveys of the International Numismatic Commission.[11]

Finally a word about the choice of a date at which to close this discussion. It would be possible to choose many different dates at which the 'medieval coinage' came to an end depending upon which departure from the earlier norm is considered to be of greatest significance. For the writer this comes with the first conscious debasement of the fine metal standard which had been the keystone of the English medieval coinage system, by order of Henry VIII in 1542.

The 'thrymsa' and 'sceattas' coinage

The largely anepigraphic thrymsa and sceatta coinage demonstrates right away how apparently well-established dating can be overturned and revised not in terms of just a year or two but of decades. The work by Dr. Kent on the Merovingian coinage[12] has made it necessary to push back the beginnings of the gold thrymsa coinage from the third to the second quarter of the seventh century. It is unlikely that the English issues maintained a high gold content for long, if at all, after the Merovingian standard had collapsed, between 640 and 650. We do not know the exact date of the introduction of the silver sceatta, but it is likely to have been some time during the last quarter of the seventh century. The latest discussion of the question dates the introduction of the sceatta to about 680.[13] A fixed point is provided by the introduction of the broad denier in Merovingian Gaul by Pepin in 755. How long it was before the English coinage followed suit it is impossible to say. On analogy with the rapidity with which Offa later adopted the reformed standard of Charlemagne, it might well have been sooner than the date of *c.* 775 usually suggested for this event. Sir Frank Stenton, for example, found no historical reason why Offa's Canterbury coinage should not have begun in *c.* 764.[14] Some support for an earlier start for the broad penny in English coinage is provided by the recent discovery of sceattas of Beorna, of E. Anglia, struck about 757, by a moneyer, Wilfred, who is also known to have produced broad penny coins for Offa. It is uncertain how closely the Offa coins followed those of Beorna, but it is unlikely to have been very long.[15]

Another material question in discussing a terminal date for the sceattas is whether or not they were being struck right up to the introduction of new pennies. The problems of the detailed dating of sceattas remain formidable. Recent work by Rigold, Metcalf and Sutherland have done much to establish the broad outlines of the chronological sequence and to work out in detail the devolution of particular groups.[16] The precise chronological relationship between these groups and absolute dates for their issue remain elusive. While hoards can often raise more problems than they solve they do at least provide certainly associated groups of material which can be related to continental finds containing coins whose dates are more securely established. For instance, the Aston Rowant (Oxon.) hoard includes both English and Continental coins which, when fully published, will provide important evidence on the chronological relationships of these series.[17]

Site finds, especially from large-scale excavations, can also be valuable in this context and it is thus particularly important that the excavator should work closely with his coin expert to make clear which coins can be stratigraphically associated. Another important development in recent years has been the information about metal detector finds which is allowing more meaningful distribution maps to be built up for the various categories of sceattas. Particularly important have been groups of scattered finds from Anglo-Saxon market sites, such as Barham outside Ipswich and a site near Royston (Herts.) where the Iknield Way intersects Watling Street.

We have similarly very little hard evidence on which to base an estimate of the relative longevity of different groups of sceattas. Few hoards of any statistically viable size have come to light in England and the continental ones, while helpful, raise internal problems of their own. *Prima facie*, however, the evidence from other coinages suggests that earlier finer or heavier coins do not generally remain current for long after the standard of similar coins actually being struck has fallen, (although they may of course be deliberately sought out for hoarding). Since the deterioration in the metal of the English coins demonstrably did not cease when the stage of a fine silver coinage was reached and since differing weight standards can be distinguished, further progress along these lines may be expected as metrological investigations are more systematically undertaken. Such hoards and groups of related finds as do exist show, however, that some sceattas did in fact circulate long enough to display slight signs of wear and that different weight standards can be present in the one find. Nevertheless it appears that the coins did not generally have a very long life in circulation. Taking all these things into account and with rare exceptions the archaeologist cannot expect to have the deposition of a single sceatta from most of the major groups dated with any degree of confidence within a narrower margin than twenty years.

The Early Saxon penny from Offa to Edgar

The arrival of the broad penny removes many of the worst dating problems since henceforth coins generally bear the name of the issuing authority. There is for example no overt reason to believe that any coinages of this particular period were ever issued posthumously, except in the special case of the memorial issues in the name of St. Edmund of East Anglia. In most cases, therefore, the known dates of accession and deposition or death provide absolute and certain *termini* for the issue of the coins. In addition, recent work has enabled the major issues of the eighth and ninth centuries to be broken down within shorter dating periods, particularly important being the subdivision of the long reigns of the leading Mercian and West Saxon Kings.[18] It should again be emphasized, however, that while a fortunate historical chance makes the beginning or end of some of these internal groups tolerably certain, the terminal dates of others are more open to question. These sub-divisions of the coinage should not be regarded as fixed chronological compartments but as periods of coinage whose start and finish fall within a band of time, longer or shorter depending upon the context and the strength of the evidence. It should also be borne in mind that in the period under immediate review there is still little evidence on which to base an estimate of how continuous the striking of coins actually was. Was it in the nature of an uninterrupted flow, or was it instead a series of sporadic bursts of high or indeed at times, low, output interspersed with periods of inactivity? The latter is often the impression given by the coins although one must be wary of the false picture that can be presented if most of the known coins could have come from a limited number of large hoards. Some evidence on this score for the ninth century is provided by the mint of Canterbury, where coins of the same type were struck for two and sometimes three different authorities by moneyers of the same name. It would be a reasonable hypothesis that the issues for each authority were made in turn rather than concurrently and surviving coins offer some support for this view. However, if numismatists are right in equating the role of the moneyer in the ninth century with that of a contractor rather than an operative, as indeed is proved for his later medieval successors, then there is of course no reason, other than deductions made from the coins themselves, to suggest that issues for several authorities were not produced concurrently.

To return to specific dating questions, it should be noted that while the main sequence of Alfred's types[19] is clear, there is still great uncertainty about the dating of the, at present, rare types associated with his middle period, and also about the inception of the so-called 'Guthrum' type which was undoubtedly the type in issue at the close of the reign. The prolific St. Edmund Memorial coinage continues to present considerable problems of absolute dating. The dates of its beginning and end are not known for certain, although the relative sequence of the major groupings within it – in particular the pre- and post-Cuerdale phases (*c.* 903) – has been convincingly demonstrated by Mr. Blunt in his recent survey.[20] All numismatists who have considered the coinage of Northumbria agree that the traditional arrangement requires emendation and the groundwork for a revised chronology was published by Mr. Lyon.[21] More recently Mr. Pagan[22] has proposed a radial re-dating for the ninth-century coinage of Northumbria which involves fairly drastic changes in the king-list. In principle, numismatists should be very chary of rejecting written historical evidence on the basis of their own hypotheses about the coins, since these so often involve interdependent judgments about metal content, duration and intensity of production and longevity of dies for which there is rarely sufficient evidence to enable unequivocal conclusions to be drawn. Miss E. Pirie has published several studies of the Northumberland stycca series based on hoards, archaeological and casual finds which give a new basis for the re-appraisal of this coinage.[23]

The progress made in the internal dating of the eighth and ninth-century coinages has not been matched by comparable advances in the tenth-century series before the reform of Eadgar, but this will shortly be remedied by the appearance of a volume of studies of the tenth-century coinage.[24] Here again, however, we can expect a more refined relative chronology but precise dates for the different groupings will be difficult to establish within narrow limits.

We have hardly any evidence on which to base conclusions about how the circulation medium was affected by the internal changes made in Offa's coinage, in particular by the increase in the weight standard shortly after 790. This is because no hoard buried in Offa's reign has come to light since the scientific recording of hoards began about the middle of the eighteenth century. Earlier listings of prominent collections and sale catalogues give us glimpses of hoards in the late seventeenth and early eighteenth centuries which were the sources of the coins now in modern cabinets, and it is to be hoped that the detective work now being undertaken on the manuscript sources of early antiquaries will yield fruitful results. Again, because we have no hoards before about 830, we are also unable to say how long it was before the seemingly plentiful issues of Offa were superseded by those of Coenwulf and whether this was by process of natural wastage and casual restriking or whether it was by a deliberate recoinage. The Mercian element in the Delgany hoard[25] shows that Offa's coins had been reduced to a very low percentage of the currency by *c.* 830 if not before. By the date of the deposition of the Middle Temple hoard[26] *c.* 841–2, including representatives of the coinage of Wiglaf, Offa's issues had lost ground still further. (The numbers of coins forming the populations of these hoards are of course statistically low, with the usual dangers of distortion which this implies, but it is counterbalanced to some extent by the fact that we have two hoards which appear to tell the same story.) The archaeologist looking for a *terminus ante quem* for the Offa penny found on his site can be sure, abnormal survivals apart, that it was deposited before 830 and on the basis of the very high proportion of coins of Coenwulf, can be reasonably, if less certainly, assured that the effective *terminus* can be pushed back to *c.* 820.

These two hoards also illustrate the general point made earlier that coins from long reigns can dominate the coinage for many years. In Delgany, Coenwulf accounts for more than 70 per cent of the Mercian element in a hoard buried ten years after his death. To put it another way, a coin lost while these hoards were being counted out and found on a modern excavation has an almost four-to-one chance of having been struck before 821 in a level of *c.* 830 and a three-to-one chance of having been struck before 821 in a level of 841–2. As an example of the way this currency pattern can affect dating, let us consider the case of a hypothetical archaeologist digging in the Middle Temple who, incredibly, comes upon intact levels which he can date on the basis of the artefacts they contain to the ninth century in general terms. He has found a very thick devastation layer which extends to widespread parts of his site and he wonders if it might be possible to tie it to one of the documented raids of the Danes upon London. By great good fortune he finds a coin in this layer, but it turns out to be a penny of Coenwulf of Mercia whom he knows died in 821, fourteen years before the first major descent of the Danes is recorded anywhere in England and twenty-one years before the Anglo-Saxon Chronicle mentions that the Danes did great slaughter in London. Scrupulously following his training not to expect all fires, even if extensive, to be documented ones, he dates his level to Mercian London about twenty years before the arrival of the Danes. He could well be right in so doing, for the coins of Coenwulf would certainly have been commoner at the end of his own reign than twenty years later, but the important point to remember is that a coin of Coenwulf does not *rule out* a date of twenty years later and that the level of the Danish raid of 842 might well have contained a coin of this reign. This demonstrates that just as it is possible for an over narrow interpretation of the evidence of a single coin to lead to an erroneous equation with an historical event, so too it can, on occasion, cause the complete rejection of just such an association for which the coin evidence is quite compatible.

The uneven incidence of adequately published hoards of statistically viable size means that, even if space permitted, this survey could not be comprehensive. There is for example neither a sizeable hoard found in Mercia nor a find with a large Mercian element contained within it discovered elsewhere which would enable us to assess the later currency of the issues of Coenwulf relative to those of his successors before Burgred. In the small find from Sevington (Wilts.)[27] however buried *c.* 850 there were still four coins of Coenwulf out of a total Mercian element of fourteen coins. The large hoard from this generation is also from the West Saxon kingdom: the great Dorking hoard[28] found in 1817. This hoard closes with a large number of coins of the first type of Aethelberht and is usually dated to *c.* 861. Unless there was a substantial savings element present, it would be legitimate to look at the pattern of the contents as evidence for the relative commonness of the various issues of Aethelwulf. Using the periods established by Blunt and Dolley in their study of the issues of Aethelwulf[29] we have the following result:

Period 1	839–*c.*843	13 per cent
Period 2	*c.* 843–*c.* 848	33 per cent
Period 3	*c.* 848/51–*c.* 855	15 per cent
Period 4	*c.* 855–859	39 per cent

Towards the end of the reign of Aethelwulf it appears, therefore, that about half the coins of his reign in currency were those struck ten years or more earlier. Again, no general validity is claimed for these figures. They are quoted as an example of how apparently differential rates of production at particular periods during a long reign can affect the proportions of early and late coins surviving in circulation after its close.

Very much more work will be required before it is possible to assess the currency pattern of this period in any detail, but the main divisions are clear. A terminus is reached in the mid-870s when the earlier coins of high silver content were swept away by the large issues of baser coins of the later groups of the 'lunette' type produced towards the end of the reign of Burgred and by the parallel issues of his brothers-in-law, Aethelred I and Alfred of Wessex. This is demonstrated by the contents of the hoards buried during the early years of Alfred's reign, in the period 871–*c*. 875. In hoards which only just reach into Alfred's reign, such as Trewhiddle[30] and Gravesend,[31] there is still a significant number of the earlier issues, but in the hoards presumptively a little later in date, since they now include substantial numbers of Alfred's first type such as Beeston Tor[32] and Croydon,[33] the earlier coins have virtually disappeared. The archaeologist may therefore assume with reasonable confidence that, the usual abnormal survivals apart, the issues of Aethelwulf and his Mercian contemporaries and of Aethelberht, not to mention the last survivors of earlier coinages, have an absolute terminus of *c*. 875.

Once again the dearth of hoards from the middle period of Alfred's reign makes it difficult to say precisely when these common lunette coins ceased to play a significant part in the currency. Certainly none of them appeared in the huge Cuerdale hoard buried *c*. 905. Allowing for discrimination against them in later hoards when coins of better metal content were available, the archaeologist may safely place a terminus to their circulation at the end of Alfred's reign with the likelihood that they had been effectively superseded about a decade later.

The later issues of Alfred were replaced virtually completely by those of his son and grandson, Edward the Elder and Aethelstan, and their issues remained in circulation in proportionally decreasing numbers until the coinage was the subject of a major reform towards the end of the reign of Eadgar. Although there is a rich crop of hoards buried just before the reform,[34] few are large enough or published in sufficient detail to be useful here, and even the evidence of large and well-published hoards about the composition of the currency at this date is inconclusive. The 1950 Chester hoard[35] buried *c*. 970 showed 73 per cent of the English element struck before 959 and 51 per cent struck before 955. The 1945 Tetney hoard[36] also of *c*. 970 showed only 39 per cent struck before 959 and 12 per cent struck before 965. The difference is explained by the fact that in Tetney the coins of Eadgar are much more heavily represented and coins earlier than Eadred are entirely absent, while in Chester there are substantial numbers of coins of both Eadmund and Aethelstan as well as a few of Edward the Elder and even one stray of Alfred. This demonstrates how the easily-explained variation in the representation of the latest pieces in a hoard can influence the proportions and also the danger of relying on the unsupported evidence of a single hoard. It does not alter the fact, however, that on one occasion at least, a coin lost in *c*. 970 could have had an evens chance of having been struck fifteen years or more before the date of its deposition. The smaller finds from Chester (East Gate)[37] and Douglas[38] suggest that the Tetney figures – or perhaps even somewhat lower ones – would be more likely to represent the 'normal' presence of earlier issues in the currency just before Eadgar's reform. It must, however, be borne in mind that the regional and personal factors influencing the composition of hoards and currency would have been more marked at this period than during the later middle ages when coins were in more normal and active circulation. On one point, however, the evidence of the hoards is clear: the reform of Eadgar brought about a rapid and complete recoinage which provides the archaeologist with the absolute *terminus ante quem* of 973–6 for all these earlier issues.

The reform of Eadgar to Stephen

The last century of the Anglo-Saxon penny has attracted enormous scholarly attention[39] during the past twenty five years and the results achieved by Dolley and other students have illuminated many different aspects of the coinage and its organization of great importance to those engaged in related disciplines. From the point of view of dating, the order of the types has been revised and now seems well-established. Sub-division of many of those types by numismatic and metrological techniques has provided a soundly based and highly detailed relative chronology.

The question of the absolute dating for coins of this period brings us to the famous 'sexennial cycle' and its lineal descendant, the 'triennial cycle'. The basic thesis as proposed by Dolley and Metcalf[40] was that the types of the late Saxon and early Norman penny were changed regularly on Michael-mas Day, at six-year intervals from Eadgar's reform which is dated by them to 973 and, after a period of transition, generally at three-year intervals from the middle of the reign of Edward the Confessor until the system was brought to an end by the anarchy under Stephen. The periodic nature of the changes in type has long been part of the English numismatic canon but the new theory, which insists upon absolute regularity in the duration of the types from the very start and upon the precision in their dating, is not universally accepted and indeed is currently the subject of much discussion.[41] Even the date of Michaelmas 973 proposed for the Reform itself is a hypothesis put forward principally on the grounds that the date of 975 given in the one late written text to mention the event, is not consistent with this particular interpretation of the numismatic evidence. A key diffi-culty which some critics have in accepting the rigid sexennial cycle is that it demands two full six-year periods for the 'Hand' coins.[42] It is not possible within the scope of this paper to air the complex arguments adduced for and against particular aspects of this hypothesis. It is necessary, however, for the archaeologist to be aware that numismatic opinion is not unanimous and that absolute dates for the issue of the types of the late Saxon penny have yet to be finally established. The fact that the absolute dates proposed for the types are indeed still open to revision is demonstrated by Dolley's more recent proposal to extend the suggested currency of the Last Small Cross type of Aethelred II and so to push forward the start of Cnut's Pointed Helmet type from 1023 to 1024, with the consequent change from 1029 to 1030 for the introduction of the Short-Cross type.[43] Once again the actual lengths of time involved are, for the most part, comparatively short from the archaeological point of view, but it is clear that if too great reliance is placed by the archaeologist upon a precise date for a site-find, a dangerous circular argument could arise: a coin found on a site mentioned in a documentary source and being of approximately the right date is held to prove the connection between the level in which it was found and the event recorded in the written text; the discovery of this coin in a 'historically dated' level is then held to prove the essential rightness of the proposed precise dating for the type to which it belongs. When stated thus baldly the illogicality of this is manifest at once, but it is not too far removed from the sort of reasoning that can go on if both numismatist and archaeologist are not extra-careful to avoid pushing their evidence beyond the limits of what it will actually prove.

Perhaps even more important to the question of archaeological dating than the exactness or otherwise of the limiting dates of issue of the various types are the implications of the second contention of the hard-line supporters of the sexennial cycle theory. This is that the introduction of a new type both theoretically and in practice always demonetized the previous one along the lines of a continental *renovatio monetae* and that the whole operation was completed within a very short space of time. Obviously if this could be accepted it would be of immense value to the archaeologist who could then be assured – the usual abnormal survivals apart – that only one type was around to be lost except during the short period of transition at the beginning of each type and that 'there is a broad coincidence between currency and period of issue'.[44] Can he in fact be sure of this throughout the entire period under review? The archaeologist is concerned not so much with what theoretically *ought* to have happened but with what actually *did* happen in practice. Since large-scale excavation of extensive late Saxon levels is even nowadays, alas, rare we are still forced to turn to the hoard evidence, equivocal as it is, in attempting to assess the validity of this proposition at different periods within the last century of the Anglo-Saxon penny.

Mr. Dolley and Dr. Metcalf point out that of the thirteen hoards known to them buried in England between 973 and 1042, eight were of one type only, five were of two types only and no hoards contained more than two types.[45] Although the number of these hoards is statistically small and the particular circumstances of the time could go some way at least towards explaining the preponderance of one-type hoards, the total absence of multiple-type hoards except in areas outside the jurisdiction of the English monarchy is none the less impressive. It suggests that during the reign of Aethelred II each type was in fact effectively replaced by its successor. How rapidly this was accomplished is very difficult to assess on the present evidence. Unless we can accept that a much higher proportion of hoards was likely to have been deposited, without the possibility of selection, during the proposed very short transitional period following the introduction of a new type than during all the remaining years of its currency, then the five-to-eight ratio of two-type to one-type hoards suggests that the change-over may not necessarily have been quite so expeditious as is sometimes postulated. The archaeologist can however be reasonably confident that an Aethelred II penny from his site in England did not normally outlast the type which followed its own and that an effective terminus is likely to have been within three years or so of the introduction of the new type.

The much higher proportion of multiple-type hoards buried during the period 1042–66 led Dolley and Metcalf to suggest that 'a breakdown was threatening the system of regular renewal of the coinage.'[46] There is evidence of this even earlier. The Wedmore hoard,[47] which closes with the first type of Edward the Confessor and is dated *c.* 1043, contained substantial numbers of coins of all the major types from Cnut's first type onwards. The later Milton Street hoard,[48] buried *c.* 1055, which closes in Helmet, the sixth type of Edward the Confessor, includes representatives from most of the types back again to the first type of Cnut. Since, however, we have at least three hoards of one or two types only buried during the period 1017–42, it is not possible to say how general the circulation of earlier types actually was during those years. The evidence is, however, strong enough to urge caution on the archaeologist who might otherwise be tempted to set very narrow limits to the currency of one of these coins found on his site.

The evidence of the larger number of multiple-type hoards from the reign of Edward the Confessor demonstrates that even more care must be taken in using one of his coins for dating purposes. From the first part of the reign, the Milton Street hoard already mentioned shows that 34 per cent of the coins available to, and chosen for concealment by the hoarder, were of the type currently in issue at the date of the deposition in *c.* 1055 but that 22 per cent were of the first type of the reign and 30 per cent were struck during the reigns of Cnut and his sons. The contents of the multiple-type hoards buried at the close of the reign show that by then the bulk of the coins current did not stretch back beyond the type in issue when the weight of the penny was increased following the abolition of the *heregeld* in 1051, i.e. the Expanding Cross type. The Seddlescombe[49] and Gracechurch Street[50] hoards which close with the second-last type of the reign include only the types from Helmet onwards. The large find from Chancton[51] buried in 1066 in fact goes back to the Expanding Cross type itself. Although the types heavily represented in the apparently even larger find from Walbrook[52] are also from Expanding Cross onwards, 10 per cent of the coins were struck before the accession of Edward the Confessor. How soon the first four types of the reign and also the last survivors of the earlier issues ceased to be an appreciable part of the available currency is difficult to say. The owner of the Milton Street hoard, for example, still had proportionally large numbers of them although his hoard was concealed in the Helmet type. Once again it is fortunate, given the equivocal nature of the evidence, that our present purpose does not require us to come to any decision about the precise extent to which the generality of currency was multiple-type. It would, however, be going against this evidence to deny that large numbers of coins were still available to be included in hoards long after their types had ceased to be struck, and that hoarders apparently saw no reason to discriminate against them or were not in a position to do so. In the view of the writer it would therefore be unjustified for the archaeologist to assume that the currency of a penny of Edward the Confessor found on his site can be equated with the period of issue to which it belongs.

In the Norman period, the sequence of the types of William I and William II proposed by Brooke[53] more than fifty years ago still stands, but his ordering of the types of Henry I has not proved altogether satisfactory. Dolley has shown that BMC type XI should precede BMC type X[54] and recently it has been suggested that further emendation may still be required in the middle period of the reign.[55]

In attempting to provide absolute dates for the issue of the types of William I and William II, the numismatist must fit thirteen types into a period of thirty four years. In 1963, Mr. North was able to postulate a triennial cycle by attributing only one year's duration to the last type of both William I and William II.[56] In 1966, Dolley found this arrangement unsatisfactory since it required all the Paxs coins to be produced within a year and he proposed to substitute a system of two-year types at the beginning of the reign of William I followed by three-year types from BMC type V onwards.[57] As an example of the variation in dating which arises from the application of these theories, a penny of BMC type V of William I would, according to the first, be dated 1077–1080 and, according to the second, to ?1074–1077. It is of course quite proper for the numismatist to try to establish absolute dates for these successive types, but it is important for the archaeologist to understand that there is in fact no incontrovertible evidence to prove the uniformity in the duration of the types far less the correctness of the precise dates proposed for their issue based upon these hypothetical divisions of the coinage. On the question of the duration of the types in circulation, one-type hoards are in the majority and suggest a theoretical intention of regular renewal of the coinage which was being fairly systematically carried out. Once again, however, there are a number of multiple-type hoards such as St. Mary Hill[58] and Tamworth[59] which show that it would be unwise to assume that the currency dates of a site-find can always be virtually equated with the issue dates of the type to which it belongs.

The dating problem is even greater with Henry I, who struck fifteen types in a reign of thirty five years and whose issues are even less amenable to the imposition of a triennial cycle. Dolley was able to propose a succession of three-year issues by suggesting that change of issue and change of type did not coincide on two occasions during the reign, i.e. that the type introduced after each of the two major recorded inquisitions into the coinage lasted only for the unexpired time of the three year 'issue' which had begun with its predecessor.[60] There are in the writer's view serious difficulties to accepting such an arrangement of the coinage. For example, Dolley suggests that type X was introduced after the inquisition which took place at Christmas 1124 and that the succeeding type was introduced during 1125, presumably *ex hypothesi* at Michaelmas. On this basis type X lasted for only nine months or, if Michaelmas is abandoned, certainly for less than a year. Type X was, however, a prolific type whose dies display a large number of variant forms. Coins of type X outnumber most if not all of the other types of Henry I before type XIII in modern cabinets and are second in commonness only to type XV, the last type of the reign, as strays in later hoards. It was, as noted above, on the basis of similar arguments that Dolley himself rejected the suggestion that the Paxs type of William I had run for only one year, although in the writer's opinion the variations in type X of Henry I are of a more obviously chronological character than those in the Paxs type. Although, therefore, the main outlines of the arrangement of the coins of Henry I is clear, numismatics cannot so far offer the archaeologist the agreed sequence of closely dated types which would provide a narrow chronology for the issue-dates of his site-finds.[61]

An assessment of the duration of the types in currency is made difficult by the fact that until recently the hoard evidence for the issues of Henry I was concentrated almost exclusively at the end of the reign. The hoard of some 744 coins and additional fragments found in Lincoln in 1971–2 is therefore of outstanding importance, for although it was deposited during the currency of type XV it also included substantial numbers of types VII, X, XIII and XIV.[62] The proportions of individual types in the hoard prior to type XV are very broadly similar to those in modern cabinets and suggest that these variations in representation reflect to some degree different levels of output and/or inequalities in the duration of their respective life at issue, rather than the presence of a substantial savings element in the hoard or of concealed bias in systematic collections due to the accident of hoard discovery. It must be admitted, however, that the few other large hoards buried at the end of the reign of Henry I and during the earlier years of Stephen are substantially one or two-type and contain no more than the odd stray from issues before type XIV. It is possible that towards the end of the reign an effort was made to eliminate from circulation the coins of the middle period, of miscellaneous size and generally lower weight, but the Lincoln hoard shows that even then large numbers of long-superseded types were still accessible to the hoarder. It also demonstrates how a major new hoard can provide a startlingly different view of the currency of a particular period from that which could have been legitimately deduced from the previously available evidence. This should warn us of the dangers inherent in accepting too readily the universal validity in practice of a complete and inflexible system of renewal of the coinage at periods for which the hoard evidence, even if fairly prolific, is uneven or of equivocal character. One-type hoards are, after all, less difficult to explain away in a multiple-type period than multiple-type hoards in a period when a rigid cyclical system is alleged to be in operation. To sum up then for Henry I, the hoard evidence is really too slight to enable us to draw any firm conclusions, but it would appear that during the middle period of the reign the system of complete renewal of the coinage – if such were in fact envisaged – had ceased to be fully operative, although it seems that issues then being produced did not survive the end of the reign. Hoards from the beginning of Stephen's reign suggest that the large and prolonged issue of his type I soon reduced the surviving coins of Henry I to a small proportion of the currency and so an effective terminus for their circulation may be placed *c.* 1140.

The reign of Stephen itself presents even greater problems. However debatable the effect of the Civil War on other aspects of administration, a hitherto unprecedented situation was brought about in the coinage. The royal monopoly, which had never been seriously challenged since the earliest times, was now broken and surviving coins support the statements of contemporary chroniclers that the barons were issuing their own coins. Hoards show that fairly large numbers of irregular coins circulated alongside the king's money. The proportion of hoard-contents represented by such coins is likely to be a minimum figure for those in general circulation – and hence among site-finds – since any element of selection would have been to their disadvantage. Most of these pieces are, however, so idiosyncratic in style that it is rarely possible to date them other than within the broad limits provided by their official prototypes or by the regular issues associated with them in hoards. Their numbers should not be exaggerated, however, for, even allowing for discrimination against them, they are far outnumbered in large hoards by Stephen's regular issues.

Dating even those official issues is still fraught with difficulty. Brooke divided the coinage of Stephen into seven types but of these only types I, II and VII are now universally accepted as substantive. Type VI is sometimes accorded this status but types III, IV and V are generally classified as local issues of the East Midlands. Since, however, so few of these coins are known, the possibility of 'new' mints coming to light cannot be completely ruled out. In a famous paper,[63] Elmore Jones outlined the immense difficulties in dating Stephen's types and more recently Mack has surveyed in detail the evidence for dating the official and irregular issues of the period.[64] Mr. R. J. Seaman has recently proposed that Stephen Type I was issued beyond the period of Stephen's captivity in 1142 and its currency extended into the early 1150s. This view has not been accepted by the author or G. C. Boon, who prefer to follow Brooke's earlier dating.[65] The suggestions that the inception of type II followed the release of Stephen from captivity in 1142 and that the issue of type VII followed the Treaty of Winchester in 1153 have much to recommend them but problems remain and there is no positive proof of the necessity for these particular dates.

There is similarly little evidence for the currency pattern in Stephen's reign. We do not know whether or not there was an attempt to replace type I and all its many imitations when type II was introduced: the Linton hoard,[66] virtually our only evidence on this point, contained nearly equal numbers of types I and II. From this evidence it could be argued *either* that types I and II circulated freely together *or* that the hoard had been buried during the period of transition before the issues of type II had fully replaced those of type I. It is just not possible to say which of these possibilities is the more likely to be correct, although the previous pattern of the English coinage would tend to make the replacement of the one type by the other the more attractive proposition. The Awbridge hoard[67] concealed *c.* 1165 contained only three irregular strays prior to type VII so it is possible that some attempt was made at the end of the reign to rid the currency of the issues of the Civil War period. On such pitifully meagre evidence the numismatist is reluctant to propose *termini* for the currency of the various issues of Stephen. Very tentatively it might be suggested that type I was probably replaced by type II during the middle 1140s and, with more conviction, that both types I and II had disappeared before the end of the reign. Type VII certainly remained current until the *renovatio monetae* of 1158 when the Tealby type was introduced. On analogy with later recoinages, it is likely that the coins of Stephen ceased to be an appreciable part of the currency within about three years of the introduction of the new type, giving an effective *terminus* of *c.* 1161. The fact that coins of Stephen still accounted for 25 per cent of the Awbridge hoard buried as late as 1165 shows, however, that the replacement of all the old coins may not have been as universally expeditious as was apparently the case at later recoinages.

Tealby, Short-Cross and Long-Cross pennies

The reorganization of the coinage by Henry II in 1158 marks the beginning of the next major phase of the English medieval coinage. It comprises the Tealby type, 1158–80,[68] the Short-Cross type, 1180–1247,[69] and the Long-Cross type, 1247–79.[70] The short-lived periodic types of the late Saxon and Norman series were abandoned in favour of an immobilised type of indefinite duration. The coins no longer necessarily bear the name of the contemporary monarch: the Short-Cross coins read HENRICVS REX unchanged throughout the reigns of Henry II, Richard I, John and Henry III and the Long-Cross coins bear the name and numeral of Henry III until the end of the issue seven years after the accession of Edward I. Fortunately, the reverses were not immobilized and continued to show the name of the moneyer and mint. The terminal dates of each of these three types are established by documentary references and, allowing for the short time-lag between the issue of an order and its execution, the dates of the beginning and end of each of these coinages is certain.

It is important to appreciate that the 'classes' into which these coinages are divided are of quite a different character from the 'types' of the late Saxon and Norman series. The latter were of contemporary significance, deliberately brought about as a means of differentiating issues for administrative purposes. The classes of the later coinages are, however, sub-divisions distinguished for their own convenience by modern numismatists. Some of the mutations utilized for this purpose were of contemporary significance when the coins were produced, but most of them were the result of practical workshop necessity rather than deliberate administrative decision. Because they were not intentional marks of differentiation at the time, the features on which these modern classifications are based are not always mutually exclusive and so the various groupings tend to merge into one another. The classes of these immobilized coinages did not replace or demonetize their predecessors in the type. Coins from the earliest class in each case theoretically could, and allowing for natural wastage did in fact, remain current until the type itself was superseded at the end of the coinage. English numismatists have worked out a very detailed chronology for these types, which must be the envy of archaeologists on the Continent where many of the more completely immobilized types have yet to be broken down into an acceptable relative chronology, far less into a closely dated sequence.

For absolute dating, we are fortunate to have an increasing volume of documentary references to the coinage itself as well as to the careers of the individual moneyers. Towards the end of the Short-Cross period precise figures for the amounts of bullion struck at the principal mints of London and Canterbury also become available[71] and these can be used in conjunction with the incidence of the various classes in hoards to provide a check on the dates deduced for them from other sources. The documentary evidence is, however, rather uneven and so while it is possible to date the issue of some coins very precisely, most can still be dated only within wide margins. Indeed, the main classes into which these three coinages have been divided cover, for the most part, comparatively long periods of time and their *termini* are often not known with any real certainty. In the earlier classes in each case, where there was a high output by many moneyers at a large number of mints, it is generally easier to provide narrower dating than it is in the longer-lived later classes struck by a smaller number of moneyers at a reduced number of mints. Sub-groups too can usually be assigned with confidence to a period early or late within the class but it is hardly ever possible to put a narrow date upon the issue. The precision with which an individual example of one of these coinages can be dated depends upon the luck of a documentary reference to the moneyer of the coin itself or to those of other coins which can be numismatically related to it. This is, however, a field where new information is regularly coming to light as the great series of public records are more systematically explored from the point of view of the coinage, and therefore it is very much in the archaeologist's interest to show his coin to an expert who may be able to provide him with a much narrower issue-date than he himself would have been able to deduce from the tables in the standard hand-books. It would, however, be as well for him to face the fact that the issue-date margins will generally be fairly wide and, except for the early coins, somewhere in the region of five years with up to ten years possible in some cases.

If the *termini post quem* of different groups of these coins are not always determinable within narrow limits, the absolute *termini ante quem* are more certain. The evidence of hoards suggests that the recoinages of 1180, 1247 and 1279 were carried out quickly and comprehensively. However, the evidence of hoards buried early in a recoinage period is particularly open to bias. There is likely to have been a greater element of selection in their composition since the hoarder would naturally discriminate against the coins which were being demonetized in favour of the new issues whenever his circumstances enabled him to do so. The case for a rapid change-over would appear to be supported however by the fact that such references as we have to prosecutions for recirculating the old coins are all within a few years of the start of the recoinage. Even more telling, the early closure of the provincial recoinage mints shows that the large-scale restriking of the previous issue had been completed within a short time. The recoinage of the three types under discussion would, on this basis, appear to have been accomplished within about three years. Bearing in mind the earlier remarks about the possibility of abnormal survivals, the *terminus* for the circulation of a Tealby penny would be *c.* 1183, for a Short-Cross penny, *c.* 1250, and for a Long-Cross penny, *c.* 1282. Recently Dr. Mate has shown from documentary sources that considerable quantities of Long-Cross coins were still being restruck up to seven years after the start of the recoinage.[72] This is reflected in the high level of production which continues in class IV of the sterling coinage after the closure of the provincial recoinage mints. This suggests that the similar fairly high output which was maintained after the closure of the recoinage mints in 1250 may also have included substantial numbers of restruck coins of the previous Short-Cross type. It could be, therefore, that we are over-estimating the speed with which the old issues totally disappeared after the introduction of the succeeding type. On the other hand we should be careful not to exaggerate the amount of this residue of earlier coins. The number of old coins in circulation would have become less and less statistically significant as the recoinage progressed, so that the chance of a lost coin being of the previous type would have diminished rapidly and well before the last of them had been restruck. In addition, the level of production could also have been affected by economic or political circumstances unconnected with the recoinage.

The factors influencing the issue-dates and terminal-dates of the various groups of these three coinages are sufficiently alike to allow them to have been usefully considered together, but the same treatment is not practicable in a discussion of their behaviour in circulation. While the currency patterns still have some features in common they are, in detail, quite distinct.

The Tealby coinage, struck from 1158 to 1180, conforms to the characteristic pattern of immobilized types. There was a period of high output at the beginning of the issue while the old pennies of Stephen were being recoined, followed by relatively low output during the remaining years of the coinage although production was on a slightly increased scale towards its close. This pattern is particularly important from the point of view of dating since a penny struck at any time during the Tealby coinage could legally have remained current until the end. Even allowing for natural wastage by loss, export and hoarding, coins of the first prolific class A struck during the first three years of the issue continue to account for a sizeable proportion of the currency medium until the last decade of the coinage. In the Larkhill[73] hoard buried early in the 1170s, 38 per cent of the coins were of class A struck between 1158 and 1161. By the time of the concealment of the Ampthill[74] and the Leicester[75] hoards buried at the end of the coinage just before 1180, the proportion of class A had fallen to 17 per cent and 16 per cent respectively. We cannot unfortunately distinguish the numbers of specific middle-period classes in the original nineteenth-century accounts of the Ampthill find, but in the case of Leicester as many as 64 per cent of the coins present had been struck before 1170, ten years prior to the deposition date. Once again, no claim is being made for the general validity of the precise proportions derived from a few isolated hoards, but the figures demonstrate that for an excavated coin a deposit-date ten or even twenty years after its issue-date remains a statistically significant possibility. It is therefore easy to see how, without careful evaluation, a Tealby penny of class A found in the destruction level of an undocumented motte-and-bailey castle might seriously mislead the archaeologist about the date at which the slighting had taken place.

The Short-Cross coinage was struck over a much longer period of time, from 1180 to 1247, and on a much more massive scale. Hoards buried during its currency are relatively abundant but unfortunately few of those large enough to be statistically viable have been adequately published. Records of early finds are often incomplete, listing only a selection of the coins which may not be typical of the hoard as a whole. On the one hand, the bias could be against the issues of poor style produced under Richard I and early John in favour of later coins of more prepossessing appearance or in better condition. Alternatively, the surviving parcel could be merely the dregs of a hoard after the more attractive-looking coins had been abstracted and disposed of by an earlier owner. While it is sometimes possible to recognize that bias is present, its precise extent is not always calculable. The work of reassessing Short-Cross hoards inadequately published in the past is being energetically pursued by Mr. Brand and other students. The problems they face are, however, particularly intractable since the criteria now recognized as significant for the detailed sub-division of the Short-Cross coinage are not those likely to have been mentioned by early antiquaries. If the names of the moneyers were recorded, classification according to modern typology is made easier but the precise information essential for statistical work on currency behaviour is often lacking.

This is particularly regrettable for the hoards might otherwise have provided evidence of the effect upon the currency of the reform of the coinage which is recorded by the chroniclers as having taken place in 1205. The sudden improvement in the style of the coins in class Va, which is demonstrably part of the same drive towards reform, can however be shown to have begun in 1204.[76] It is important to appreciate that this was not a *renovatio monetae* in the continental sense of demonetizing and restriking all previous issues. It obviously could not have been so intended for it is inconceivable that no greater differentiation would then have been made between the old and unacceptable coins and the new ones than the change in style between what modern numismatists know as classes I–IV and class V. Indeed, what appears in essence to have happened was that any surviving coins struck before the introduction of the Short-Cross type were finally demonetized and all Short-Cross coins which had lost an eighth of their weight or more were similarly required to be withdrawn from circulation and recoined. Unfortunately we do not have consecutive bullion figures for the output of the London and Canterbury mints until the last thirteen years of the type and so it is not possible to make the direct comparisons between the output of these earlier classes and that of the later issues which would assist us in estimating how extensive the recoinage of classes I–IV actually was. That coins of classes I–IV could and did survive in currency after

1204–5 is demonstrated by the fact that 15 per cent of the coins present in the great 1902 Colchester hoard[77] were of those classes struck nearly forty years before its deposition date. There is little that can be said as yet about the statistical proportions of classes V, VI, VII and VIII in circulation at different periods. A great deal more detailed analysis of early hoard-publications requires to be done before this can be attempted and a correlation of the various classes and sub-groups of the coins with the recently published bullion figures for the output of the London and Canterbury mints has yet to appear in print. Two small parcels from the large Eccles hoard of 1864[78] which came to light fairly recently do, however, offer some indication of the likely proportions of the different classes in the find as a whole although of course it must be borne in mind that the two samples are certainly not random ones and are likely to be biased in the ways suggested above. The larger of the groups from this hoard shows the following proportions if provincial mints are excluded: class V, 20 per cent; class VI, 26 per cent; class VII, 54 per cent. This particular parcel included no coins prior to class V although the other, smaller, parcel included one penny of class IV, thus showing that earlier coins were indeed present in this find also. As we have seen, the Colchester hoard buried about the same time contained 15 per cent of these earlier coins so it seems that the 6 per cent figure for the early classes in the smaller parcel from Eccles should be accepted as a guide to the minimum representation of the early coins in the hoard as a whole. On this basis we find that in a hoard buried *c.* 1240 about a quarter of the coins were struck before 1210 and about half the coins were struck before *c.* 1218. From the archaeological point of view this means that a Short-Cross penny in a level of 1240 might have a one-in-four chance of having been struck thirty years earlier and an evens chance of having been struck twenty years earlier. While once again not claiming general validity for such figures derived from a few ill-published hoards, the possibility of very long survival is a factor which must be considered in assessing the value of a Short-Cross penny as dating evidence. It is therefore particularly necessary that, despite the difficulties, an informed judgement on the question of wear should be attempted as discussed above.

The Long-Cross coinage was comparatively short-lived, lasting only thirty two years from 1247 to 1279. Its internal currency pattern reverts to one more closely allied to the classic form of immobilized coinages noted in the Tealby period: a high initial output, this time maintained at a lower but still fairly intensive level during the middle period of the issue and then falling sharply to a low level in the last decade. In the first part of the huge 1969 Colchester[79] hoard abstracted from currency in 1256, 51 per cent of the English coins present were of the recoinage classes struck before 1250. Although the hoard evidence for the currency pattern at the end of the Long-Cross period is inadequate, the bullion figures allow us to deduce that since comparatively fewer coins were then being produced, the currency would still be denominated by the earlier issues struck at least ten years previously. If, therefore, an archaeologist finds a penny of class Vc struck in 1256, the level from which it came might in fact be of ten or even twenty

years later. Indeed, given the difficulties in attempting to estimate the duration in circulation from the slight signs of wear which these coins normally
display – the time-scale being shorter than in the case of the Short-Cross
coins – the archaeologist is likely to find his coin expert unwilling to commit
himself to a definite *terminus ante quem* before the end of the currency of
the type.

The sterling coinage, Edward I to Henry VIII

The recoinage instituted by Edward I in 1279 marks the beginning of the
long final phase of the English medieval coinage. Although this period of
over two hundred and fifty years can be sub-divided on the basis of individual
reigns, the advent of new denominations, new letter forms and new styles
of portraiture as well as, more importantly, successive reductions in the
standard issue weights, it still constitutes what is essentially a single currency
period. A coin struck at the start could theoretically have remained current
throughout and in fact no general *renovatio monetae* took place again until
the Great Recoinage of 1695. Not surprisingly therefore remarkable
examples of individual longevity can be found in hoards buried late in the
period under review. For example, no fewer than eleven out of the 1,008
coins in the Hartford (Hunts.) hoard buried in *c.* 1509 were from issues
struck for Edward III some 150 years before.[80] Although the basic designs
of both gold and silver denominations remained virtually unaltered throughout the period this is not just another of the immobilized coinages. With
one late exception just beyond the end of our period[81] the name of the
contemporary monarch always appears on the coins and a deliberate and
increasingly elaborate system of initial and privy-marking was developed.
These marks were devised for purposes of internal mint control and did not
in any way limit the circulation of the coins, but they have enabled a detailed
relative chronology of the coinage to be established for the late medieval
period.

  From the point of view of absolute dating, the major events affecting the
coinage are increasingly well-documented and provide fixed points within
some reigns. There are, however, counterbalancing disadvantages in the
new system. The admirable practice begun by Henry III of adding the king's
numeral to his title was abandoned and not resumed until the last coinage
of Henry VII, so that we are once again confronted with the problem of
dividing issues between homonymous kings whose reigns followed one
another. The main outlines have been securely established for many years
now but several inconvenient grey areas remain. It is still not possible, for
example, to draw a precise line between sub-groups of the common type X
sterling pennies which should be attributed to Edward I and which to Edward
II within the limiting dates of the type of 1302–10. The recoinage of 1279
also saw the disappearance of the moneyers' names from the reverse of the
coins just at the time when the increasing survival of both state and private
papers might have made narrow dating easier. In this period we must rely

to a great extent upon the comings and goings of the holders of the ecclesiastical privilege mints to provide fixed points within the regal framework. Even this useful aid to dating can fail us as in the reign of Henry V where both the relevant ecclesiastics[82] had been consecrated before the king's accession and disobligingly outlived him. Thus, although the relative chronology of the coins of Henry V is clear it is not yet possible to put precise dates upon their issue. This sort of problem recurs right up to the end of the period under review and indeed beyond. The internal chronology of the Second Coinage of Henry VIII, struck between 1526 and 1544, has yet to be fully worked out. The archaeological implications of this particular difficulty are considerable, for an excavator might hope to use one of these coins found on his site to associate a particular level with some local event during the dissolution of the monasteries only to find his coin expert unable to put a precise date upon its issue. The bullion figures which were such a useful check on the dating of the Long-Cross series are less useful in the sterling period. Here we have a full range of multiples and sub-multiples in silver and later in gold and rarely do the surviving bullion accounts record the exact proportions of each denomination struck from the total amount of metal used. It is therefore only in the most general terms that the bullion figures assist in dating the different issues of coins.

It is not possible to discuss in detail here the dating of all the many groups within the later medieval coinage and the reader is referred to the principle monographs most conveniently listed in North's second volume.[83] Once again the archaeologist cannot be expected to investigate all the complexities of numismatic dating for himself but he should be aware of its present limitations. The issue of some later medieval coins can be dated with absolute certainty to within a period of a few months, but these are generally the rarer types which he will be particularly lucky to see. Some common coins, especially those struck at the beginning of a particular reign or issue, can also be dated with considerable precision, but most site-finds will belong to the category of coins which depend for their dating to a very considerable extent upon the informed but none the less subjective judgment of the numismatist. Such results are inevitably open to revision and as an example of this we may take the dating of the introduction of class V in the sterling-penny coinage. Brooke dated this event to 1284[84] and that was still the accepted date when North's handbook appeared in 1960.[85] By 1968, however, opinion had altered and the date given in North's most useful booklet[86] on sterling pennies was *c.* 1290, now generally agreed to be more acceptable. Such changes affect not only the coins immediately concerned but have wide ramifications in other coinages whose types have been dated by analogy or by association in finds. Hoards and levels in earlier excavations which were provided with *termini* on the basis of an outmoded and now forgotten chronology can all too easily be 'contrasted' with more recent hoards and levels containing precisely similar coins but differently dated by current numismatic opinion. Numismatists themselves can fall into this trap and archaeologists should be especially careful to bear such possible revisions in mind when comparing their own with earlier results.

If the issues of the sterling coins can generally be dated within what are, from the archaeological point of view at least, fairly narrow limits, the estimation of their probable duration in circulation presents even greater problems than it did at earlier periods. There are no further complete recoinages to provide watertight chronological compartments for the currency of the various groups of coins which make up the later medieval series. The reductions in the standard weight of the different denominations, to be discussed later, are useful reference points within the series but it is important to appreciate that they are in no way absolute *termini* for the currency of all earlier issues as were the formal recoinages of 1180, 1247 and 1279. There was no legal bar to the continued circulation of a coin merely on grounds of age, and in consequence, to a greater extent than ever before, common coins from large issues remained a proportionally dominant element in the currency long after they were struck. The forces which eventually drove out of circulation in turn all but a few stray survivors of each group of earlier coins were practical and economic rather than purely administrative, although of course all of these influences interacted upon one another. Some coins were lost to circulation by loss, export and hoarding and others no doubt disappeared at each successive reduction in the standard weight as some profitably heavy coins were taken to the mint to be recoined. In the end, although the weight of old coins still in circulation may still have been, on average, within the currently acceptable tolerances, their demise must have been hastened by the fact that their dreadfully worn and clipped appearance made them less acceptable in commercial transactions when there were enough new coins available to enable these to be insisted upon as the medium of payment. Since any bias in the selection of coins for hoarding is likely to have been to the exclusion of older pieces, the number of such coins present in hoards may safely be regarded as a minimum figure for those available to their owners at the time of deposition. This is not to imply that the figure is universally valid for the currency pattern all over the country, for once again geographical position and individual circumstances would have had their effect upon composition. If selection *did* play a significant part in the hoards we are to consider then we may yet be underestimating the amount of early worn coins in everyday use at this time. Nevertheless, although in the sterling period the incidence of hoards is still uneven and the number of large and well-published ones, as always, less than could be desired, there are at this time more frequent occasions when a greater number of nearly contemporaneous hoards permit more securely based assessments to be made about the broad-outline content of the generality of English currency.[87] It will be easier to discuss this changing pattern if the pennies, the groats and the gold issues are considered in turn, leaving aspects of currency which are peculiar to any of the sub-multiples of these denominations to be mentioned in passing.

The common recoinage issues of 1279–82 still account for around 50 per cent of the pennies present in several hoards buried *c.* 1290 and the even larger output of the years 1300–10 mean that again about 50 per cent of all pennies in hoards of the 1320s were produced at that time. Even after the prolific issues of Edward III's pennies struck from 1351 onwards began to find their way into hoards in quantity, the coins of Edward I and Edward II continued to play an important part in the currency. This is clearly illustrated by two hoards buried in the early 1360s. In Durham,[88] *c.* 1361, 40 per cent of the pennies had been struck before the death of Edward II in 1327 and in Coventry,[89] *c.* 1363, about 38 per cent were from the same period. When it is recalled that the bulk of these coins would have been produced during the two periods of heaviest output before 1310, the dominance of really early coins is all the more striking. As late as the early 1420s coins of Edward I and Edward II still account for about a quarter of the pennies present.[90] It was not until the large issues of pennies produced in the later years of Henry V and in the earlier part of the reign of Henry VI reached their full representation in circulation in the late 1420s that the pennies of Edward I and Edward II dwindled to a small minority of those present and they do not appear to have been finally swept away – apart from stray survivors – until the appearance of the coins of Edward IV's Light Coinage struck after the reduction of the standard weight in 1464.

In their turn the common pennies of Edward III, especially coins from the huge issues of the pre-Treaty period, 1351–60, eventually overtook the coins of the first two Edwards as the dominant element among pennies in circulation. They constitute around 60 per cent of the pennies in hoards buried in the early 1360s and sixty years later the coins of Edward III still account for about 50 per cent of the pennies in hoards of the early 1420s. Adding to these the earlier Edwardian sterlings still around, we find that in the early 1420s about 75 per cent of the pennies in circulation had been struck at least forty years before. In the Brentwood find[91] the representation of these coins in a hoard probably buried shortly before 1420 reaches a startling 95 per cent. Although there are enough other hoards to show that such a high figure is unusual it demonstrates the danger of facile generalisations on the basis of what is considered to be 'normal'. As the largest denomination available is generally preferred for hoarding, there is a decrease in hoards composed entirely of pennies or including statistically useful numbers of them as groats became increasingly available and inflation brought them within reach of a wider sector of the community. The lack of a sufficient number of suitable hoards therefore makes it difficult to discuss with any confidence the currency pattern in the later fifteenth century for the penny denomination. Among the small number of pennies present in the Wyre Piddle hoard[92] buried *c.* 1467 Edward I and Edward II accounted for 5 per cent of those present, Edward III for 17 per cent, Henry V and Henry VI for 66 per cent and Edward IV for just 2½ per cent. Unfortunately there are no large hoards of pennies of this period which would allow us to assess how typical this pattern was. We have for example virtually no information about the speed with which newly struck coin became incorporated into the currency of different areas. This is a material point where pennies are concerned since after the reintroduction of the groat in 1351 the striking of pennies was increasingly left to the mints of York and Durham just as, from the Light Coinage of Edward IV onwards, the halfgroats became predominantly the preserve of the Canterbury mint and, in the reign of Henry VII, of the York mint in addition. At the end of our period it is clear from hoards such as that recently found at Little Wymondley that the massive issues of Henry VII's sovereign type pennies ousted virtually all of the earlier pennies from circulation.[93]

During the fourteenth and fifteenth centuries there are frequent complaints about the shortage of halfpennies and farthings. The latter were naturally rarely chosen for inclusion in hoards and so we have no evidence about their currency pattern. Halfpennies also occur only infrequently in large numbers in hoards. The find from Attenborough of c. 1420 suggests, however, that halfpennies in circulation outside the main commercial centres may well have included fewer of the latest issues. Although it was concealed towards the end of the reign of Henry V this hoard contained none of his comparatively common halfpennies although several of the much rarer coins of his father were present.

The groats of Edward III, and especially the pre-Treaty issues struck between 1351 and 1360, dominated the currency of this denomination until the appearance of the massive issues of Henry VI's first, Annulet, type produced from 1422–27. In the Reigate hoard of c. 1450–55 Edward III accounted for only 8 per cent of the total number of groats present, Henry VI Annulet for 48 per cent and the remaining issues of Henry VI struck between 1427 and the date of deposition for 37 per cent. In other words, 63 per cent of the total were struck more than twenty years before the coins were abstracted from circulation and although some of these earlier coins were badly clipped, most of the Annulet issue show little sign of actual wear and it would be an impossible task to suggest within narrow limits the years of wear on any individual specimen if it had been found in isolation. In the Wyre Piddle hoard, which as we have noted may possibly have included an unusually high number of earlier coins, Edward III still accounted for 13 per cent, Henry VI, Annulet, for 30 per cent and later Henry VI for 20 per cent of the total number of groats present. The common issues of Edward IV's Light Coinage which had already been in intensive production for three years before the deposition of the hoard amounted to only 23 per cent. In aggregate 49 per cent of the groats were at least fifty years old at the date of deposition. It is clear, however, that when the Light Coinage groats of Edward IV and Henry VI Restored eventually reached their full representation in the coinage they ousted all but a few stray survivors of the earlier heavy coinages. The Light Coinage groats of Edward IV, especially those of the huge issues struck immediately after the reduction in the standard weight had taken place in 1464, dominated the currency until they in turn were superseded by the large issues produced for Henry VII from his Second Coinage onwards. In the hoard from an unknown location[94] buried in c. 1485 the figures were, Edward IV First Reign, 62 per cent; Henry VI Restored and Edward IV Second Reign, 35 per cent; Richard III, 3 per cent. In the Hounslow hoard[95] of about ten years later only 16 per cent is yet of Henry VII but at the end of the reign his groats account for 55 per cent of that denomination present in the Hartford hoard[96] of c. 1509. The issues of

Henry VII continue to dominate the currency during the years of comparatively low output of groats during Henry VIII's First Coinage. After 1526
however the prolific issues of the Second Coinage of reduced-weight groats
ousted the earlier heavy coins, as is shown by the contents of another
unprovenanced hoard[97] where 4 per cent were groats of Edward IV, 17 per
cent of Henry VII, 1 per cent of Henry VIII's First Coinage and 77 per cent
of his Second Coinage. The momentous decision to reduce the fineness of
the metal of the silver coinage taken in 1542 and certainly put into operation
in 1544 brought Gresham's Law into play and the new bad money drove
out the last of the medieval silver coinage.

Although there are fewer large and well-documented hoards of gold coins
on which to base an assessment of their currency pattern, those which have
been recorded suggest that it was broadly similar to that already charted
for the groats. In view of this and also since the archaeologist is less likely
to meet gold coins on his excavation, they are dealt with more briefly here
than were the silver issues. The large issues of Edward III and Henry VI
dominated the currency in turn. In the large hoard of gold coins found at
Fishpool[98] no less than 85 per cent of the coins had been struck before
1427, thirty seven years before the hoard was buried, most of the group
being coins of the very common Annulet issue. The transition between the
noble coinage produced before 1465 and the ryal and angel coinage struck
thereafter is unfortunately ill-documented by hoards. The ryal enjoyed a
brief heyday and then the angel, which had got off to a slow start, took
over and emerged as the late-medieval English gold coin *par excellence*. The
hoard from Park Street[99] near St. Albans, illustrates the possible range of
coins current in *c.* 1520: ryals of Edward IV, 14 per cent, angels of Henry
VI Restored and Edward IV, 23 per cent, angels of Henry VII, 44 per cent
and angels of Henry VIII, First Coinage, 19 per cent. One divergence from
the silver pattern is the commonness of these First Coinage angels of Henry
VIII in contrast to the silver coins of that issue which are scarce. The
introduction in 1526 of the Crown series of gold coins of reduced metal
fineness to correspond with the contemporary French issues was not really
a departure from the medieval standards in quite the same way as the later
debasement of the silver coinage for fine gold coins continued to be struck
in quantity and the two circulated, appropriately valued, side by side until
beyond the end of our period.

No apology is made for this recital of the longevity of the components
of the English sterling coinage since the archaeologist has tended to under-
estimate greatly the probable age of site-finds at their date of deposition. If
then the individual coins of all denominations could and did survive in
quantity for very long periods how far is it possible to estimate the probable
duration in circulation of a single excavation coin?

Some guidance is provided by the progressive reductions in the standard
weights of English medieval coins caused by inflation. The following table
gives the more important of these[100] for the larger gold and silver denominations. The sub-multiples followed *pari passu*. For the gold issues and for
the groats these reductions in weight provide a fairly reliable method of

determining the currency period in which site-finds were last in circulation. The vast majority of these two denominations circulating at any one time conformed to the weight standard then in operation regardless of the weight at which they had been originally struck. Their weight had been reduced to a small extent by wear – very much less for the gold than for the silver of course – but principally by clipping. As always there are the odd stray survivors of heavy weight and a few older coins circulated at a little above the new standard, as indeed did some of those only recently struck. As they are rarely appreciably above the current standard, however, there is usually little doubt to which period they belong. In the same way a coin could be abnormally clipped at any period, but once again although the exceptions must be borne in mind they do not alter the broad general rule. For example, in the Reigate hoard of *c.* 1450–55 buried during the 60 grain period, fifteen out of 374 Annulet groats weighed 48 grains or less, i.e. the weight of groats current after 1464. Nevertheless, 80 per cent of them were between 56 and 60 grains and 3 per cent were above 60 grains, so clearly the rule is generally valid in this case. The groats of Edward III present in this same hoard although struck at 72 grains are, with only the odd exception, all cut down to below the new standard of 60 grains. In the Fishpool hoard of 1464 the forty gold coins struck prior to the reduction in the standard weight in 1412 had, with one exception, been clipped down within the acceptable range for 108 grain nobles, although they had themselves been struck in the 120 grain period. It should be mentioned however that we do not know how long the generality of coinage took to adapt itself to these changes in standard weight. The hoard evidence for periods immediately following them is minimal. The Wyre Piddle hoard of *c.* 1467 is a case in point but we have already had reasons to suggest that it may have been rather behind-hand. For what it is worth, eighty four out of the ninety six groats in this hoard struck before 1464 weigh more than the new standard weight of 48 grains and fifty nine of them weigh more than 54 grains, half-way between the old and the new standards. Thus even for the large denominations the picture is not entirely clear.

WEIGHTS OF THE ENGLISH MEDIEVAL COINAGE

	Silver			Gold	
1279	penny	22¼ gr	1351	noble	120 gr
1351	groat	72 gr	1412	"	108 gr
1412	"	60 gr	1465	ryal	120 gr
1464	"	48 gr		angel	80 gr
1526	"	42⅔ gr			

It is, however, the pennies which the archaeologist is more likely to find and with them the above criteria are unfortunately of more limited use. The hoard evidence suggests that all earlier pennies irrespective of issue peak on the current issue weight and are not, as in the case of the gold and the groats, cut down *below* it. A clear demonstration of the currency pattern of pennies is given in the histograms of coins in the Attenborough hoard of *c.* 1420. Here we see that all the pennies struck before the reduction in the standard weight in 1412 peak on the new standard of 15 grains with almost as many coins above it as below it although only the rare exception is above 18 grains, the previous standard weight. On grounds of weight alone therefore we are not able to say, for example, whether a penny of Edward I weighing 16½ grains was an underweight coin lost during the 15 grain standard. Thus, whereas we are on fairly safe ground in confining the possible duration of currency of a groat within one standard-weight period, we are unable to attribute an isolated penny even within those wide limits on the basis of weight alone.

Given the number of potential variables, no mathematical formula based on a fixed – or even sliding – scale of annual loss of weight through wear can possibly provide a precise date for the deposition of an isolated coin. It is here that the figures from hoards can help by providing a yard-stick of the possible statistical likelihood of a certain type of coin being around in quantity at different periods. This would enable us to say, for example, that our penny of Edward I weighing 16½ grains was in fact very much less likely to have been around after the pennies of Henry VI reached a dominant position in the currency in the later 1420s, although of course a later survival cannot be ruled out. Statistically too a date in the 18 grain period before 1412 is much more likely. In the last resort, however, any attempt to narrow the dating margins involves considering the superficial appearance of the coin. Wear is of course a very fallible guide but it is legitimate for someone with wide experience of both hoards and site-finds to express an opinion about the possible period of currency of the coin in question. Even so, the margins finally suggested are likely to be wide ones and the archaeologist should not be surprised if they are sometimes thirty or forty years.

This paper has been a plea for a realistic view of medieval English coins as dating evidence. Archaeologists want dating evidence which is certain and precise and when they find a coin they all too readily assume that they have got it. They rarely have.

Notes

1. For references to be published analyses of English medieval coins see E. T. Hall and D. M. Metcalf (Ed.), 'Methods of chemical and metallurgical investigation of ancient coinage', *Royal Numismatic Society*, Special Publication Number 8, London, 1972. For a discussion of the issue weight of a group of die-linked sterling pennies see Marion M. Archibald, 'The Mayfield (Sussex) 1968 hoard of English pence and French gros, *c.* 1307', in R. A. G. Carson (Ed.), *Mints dies and currency, Essays dedicated to the memory of Albert Baldwin*, London, 1971, 151–9.

2. It is notoriously difficult to suggest present-day equivalent values for medieval coins but an acceptable rule of thumb is that an Anglo-Saxon penny was worth about what £10 is to us. By the fifteenth century a penny was equivalent of about £4. The lowest denomination then current, the farthing, was therefore worth about £1.

3. This remark refers to Roman coins as a whole: Roman *silver* coins are similarly rare as site-finds. Medieval pewter tokens of the mid-thirteenth century (see M. Dolley and W. A. Seaby, *NCirc* Vol. 79 No. 12 (Dec. 1971), 446–8.) and the bronze jettons produced from the late-thirteenth century onwards (see F. P. Barnard, *The Casting-Counter and the Counting Board*, Oxford, 1916 (Reprinted 1984) are outside the scope of this paper. This series has now been dealt with in a series of papers by M. Mitchiner and A. Skinner, principally:
English tokens, *c.* 1200 to 1425, *BNJ*, 1983, 29–78.
English tokens, *c.* 1425 to 1672, *BNJ*, 1985, 86–163.
The fact that reckoning counters are found on sites where it is unlikely that formal accounting was done suggests that these pieces to some extent, and in an informal way, supplied the need for lower denominations not met by the regal coinage. Despite the advances in the dating of bronze jettons, largely the result of the work of the late S. E. Rigold and M. Mitchiner, chronological problems still remain. The common French and early Nuremburg tokens found on British sites cannot yet be closely dated. In this case numismatists look to their archaeological colleagues to supply them with evidence of jettons from levels of independently established date which may be used to build up a securely based chronology for these common pieces.

4. For a historian's view of this and related problems see Professor P. Grierson's Presidential Addresses to the Royal Numismatic Society, *NC* 1965, I–XIII and *NC* 1966, I–XV.

5. Hoards mentioned in this paper as *Inventory* followed by a number will be found listed with references to the primary publications in J. D. A. Thompson, 'Inventory of British coin hoards, AD 600–1500', *Royal Numismatic Society*, Special Publication No. 1, London, 1956.

6. For example, the penny of Archbishop Ceolnoth, 833–870, found in the Cuerdale hoard buried in *c.* 903 (*Inventory* 112). Longevity is particularly to be expected in the immobilized sterling coinage and even more spectacular examples

occur, e.g. the penny of Edward I struck in 1280 found in the Wyre Piddle hoard buried in *c.* 1467 (Marion M. Archibald, 'The Wyre Piddle (Worcs.) 1967 hoard of fifteenth-century silver coins', *NC* 1970, 133–62).

7. In Border ballads certain sums are required to be paid in 'white money', i.e. not in the base Scottish coins which formed the bulk of the normal currency but in English coins of full silver content. For example,
   And he has paid the rescue shot
   Baith wi' gowd and white monie
'Jamie Telfer of the Fair Dodhead', No. 111 in *Oxford Book of Ballads*, 1969, 556. Even in England when the currency contained many very worn and clipped coins or foreign copies in base metal, people tried, where they could, to specify that payment should be made in 'good money'. (Mavis Mate, 'Monetary policies in England, 1272–1307', *BNJ* XLI 1972, 41.)

8. Hoards from Ireland for example include on average a greater number of half-pennies than English hoards of the same scale and period.

9. The earliest coin in the 1972 Prestwich hoard of 1,065 coins of the period of Stephen was a cut-halfpenny of the first type of Henry I struck shortly after his accession in 1100. The earliest pennies in the hoard were however 65 of his last type struck in the years immediately prior to his death in 1135.

10. P. Spufford, 'Continental coins in late medieval England', *BNJ* XXXII, 1963, 133. There were seven Scottish *halfpennies* out of a total of 66 of this denomination in the Attenborough hoard compared with only nine Scottish *pennies* out of a total of 965 of that denomination. (Marion M. Archibald, 'The Attenborough (Notts.) 1966 hoard', *BNJ* XXXVIII, 1969, 58.)

11. The latest volume in this series is *A survey of numismatic research, 1978–84*.

12. J. P. C. Kent, 'Problems of chronology in the 7th century Merovingian coinage', *Cunobelin* No. 13 1967, 24–30.

13. P. Grierson and M. Blackburn, *Medieval European Coinage* Vol. 1, Cambridge, 1968. An important survey of this problem is contained in Mr. C. S. S. Lyon's Presidential Address to the British Numismatic Society, *BNJ*, XXXVI, 1967, 218–21.

14. F. M. Stenton, 'The Anglo-Saxon coinage and the historian' in D. M. Stenton (Ed.), *Preparatory to Anglo-Saxon England. Being the collected papers of Frank Merry Stenton*, Oxford, 1970, 371–82.

15. M. Archibald, 'The coinage of Beorna in the light of the Middle Harling hoard', *BNJ*, LV, 1985.

16. S. E. Rigold, 'The two primary series of sceattas', *BNJ* XXX, 1960–61, 6–53; 'Addenda and Corrigenda', *BNJ* XXXV, 1966, 1–6.
    D. M. Metcalf, 'A stylistic analysis of the 'Porcupine sceattas', *NC* 1966, 179–205; 'A coinage for Mercia under Aethelbald', *Cunobelin* No. 12 1966, 26–39; 'The "Wolf" sceattas', *BNJ* XXXVI, 1967, 11–28.

C. H. V. Sutherland, *Anglo-Saxon gold in relation to the Crondall find*, Oxford, 1948. Written twenty five years ago, this work inevitably requires revision in detail and especially in dating if Dr. Kent's view of the chronology is accepted but is most useful as the only comprehensive survey of the gold series.
D. Hill and D. M. Metcalf (eds.), *Sceattas in England and on the Continent*, Oxford, 1984.

17. *Coin hoards I.* No. 347 (1975).

18. *Offa*: C. E. Blunt, 'The coinage of Offa' in R. H. M. Dolley (Ed.), *Anglo-Saxon Coins* (henceforth referred to as *ASC*), 39–62. *Period 796–840*: C. E. Blunt, C. S. S. Lyon and B. H. I. H. Stewart, 'The coinage of southern England, 796–840', *BNJ*, 1–74. *Aethelwulf*: R. H. M. Dolley and K. Skaare, 'The coinage of Aethelwulf, king of the West Saxons, 839–58', *ASC*, 63–94. *Vikings*: C. S. S. Lyon and B. H. I. H. Stewart, 'The Northumbrian Viking coins in the Cuerdale hoard', *ASC*, 98–121. *Burgred*: H. E. Pagan, 'Coinage in the age of Burgred', *BNJ*, XXXIV, 1965, 11–27. *Alfred*: R. H. M. Dolley and C. E. Blunt, 'The chronology of the coins of Aelfred the Great', *ASC*, 77–95. *St. Edmund Memorial*: C. E. Blunt, 'The St. Edmund Memorial coinage', *Proc. Suffolk Inst. Arch.* Vol. 31, 1969, 234–225.
The complex historical and numismatic problems of the origins of the issue of the broad penny are not yet completely resolved:
Ian Stewart: 'The London mint and the coinage of Offa', in M. A. S. Blackburn (Ed.) *Anglo-Saxon monetary history: essays in memory of Michael Dolley.* Leicester, 1986.

19. See reference in note 18 above.

20. See reference in note 18 above.

21. C. S. S. Lyon, 'A reappraisal of the sceatta and styca coinage of Northumbria', *BNJ* XXVIII, 1956, 227–42.
Mr. Dolley and Dr. Metcalf did however consider the order of the types of Eadgar before his Reform in their paper on the latter subject. *ASC* 136–168.

22. H. E. Pagan, 'Northumbrian numismatic chronology in the ninth century', *BNJ* XXXVIII, 1969, 1–15.

23. E. J. E. Pirie, *A catalogue of early Northumbrian coins in the Museum of Antiquities, Newcastle upon Tyne.* (Newcastle, 1982). 'Finds of "sceattas" and "stycas" in Northumbria in Blackburn' (Ed.), *Anglo-Saxon Monetary History.* (Hereafter *ASMH*.) 'Post Roman coins from the York excavations, 1971–81' *The archaeology of York*, Vol. 18. York, 1986.

24. C. E. Blunt, C. S. S. Lyon and I. H. Stewart *Coinage in 10th century England*, forthcoming.

25. *Inventory* 117.

26. *Inventory* 366 but see *ASC*, 64.

27. *Inventory* 328 but see C. E. Blunt, 'The Sevington hoard of 1834', *BNJ* XLI, 1972, 7–20.

28. *Inventory* 123 but see *ASC* 65–7 and *BNJ* XLI, 179–80.

29. See reference in note 18 above.

30. *Inventory* 362 but see C. E. Blunt and D. M. Wilson, 'The Trewhiddle hoard', *Archaeologia* XCVIII, 1961, 75–122.

31. *Inventory* 176.

32. *Inventory* 40.

33. N. P. Brooks and J. A. Graham-Campbell, 'Reflections on the Viking-age silver hoard from Croydon, Surrey', in Blackburn (Ed.) *A-S MH*.
    Inventory 111 but see *ASC*, 65. For all hoards containing coins of Alfred see C. E. Blunt and R. H. M. Dolley, 'The hoard evidence for the coins of Alfred', *BNJ* XXXIX, 1968–9, 220–47.

34. A listing of hoards of the Viking age, *c*. 795–1105, essential to a full assessment of the hoard evidence is given in R. H. M. Dolley, *Sylloge of Coins of the British Isles, The Hiberno-Norse coins in the British Musuem*, London, 1966, 47–54.
    M. Blackburn and H. Pagan, 'A revised check-list of coin hoards from the British Isles, *c*. 500–1100', in Blackburn (Ed.) *A-S MH*.
    Since this paper was written the important hoard from Morley St. Peter (Norfolk), closing with a single coin of Athelstan, *c*. 925, has been published. T. H. McK. Clough, *Sylloge of the Coins of the British Isles*, Vol. 26.

35. *Inventory* 86.

36. *Inventory* 355.

37. *Inventory* 84.

38. *Inventory* 127.

39. The contributions of Mr. Dolley and other students to this series are scattered in many books and journals both British and foreign. They can best be traced by referring to the bibliography in another major contribution to the study of the late Saxon coinage, H. Bertil A. Petersson, *Anglo-Saxon currency*, Lund, 1969. (It should be noted that Petersson's hypothesis of a septennial cycle for the issues of Aethelred II has not found support among other students.) For papers published since the compilation of Petersson, see the Anglo-Saxon and Hiberno-Norse section in 'A survey of numismatic research 1966–1971', II, *International Numismatic Commission*, New York, 1973.
    For a complete listing of the works of Dolley see now R. H. Thompson, 'The published writings of Michael Dolley, 1944–83', in *A-S MH*. An important study of the coinage of Edward the Confessor with implications for the earlier and later issues with particular reference to the groupings of mints and the movements of moneyers is:
    A. Freeman, *The moneyer and mint in the reign of Edward the Confessor, 1042–1066*. (Oxford, 1985.)

40. R. H. M. Dolley and D. M. Metcalf, 'The reform of the English coinage under Eadgar', in *ASC*, 136–168. Many of Mr. Dolley's later papers deal with the implications of this theory and may be found by reference to the bibliographical sources quoted in note 39 above.

41. Professor Grierson put forward the historian's view of the matter in his first Presidential Address to the Royal Numismatic Society, *NC* 1962, I–XIV. Dolley defended his view of the date of the reform in 'Roger of Wendover's date for Eadgar's coin reform' *BNJ*, XLIX, 1979.
    An important review of the evidence which opposes Dolley's views will be found in J. Brand, *Periodic change of type in the Anglo-Saxon and Anglo-Norman periods*, Rochester, 1984.

42. See especially J. D. Brand, 'Meretricious metrology', *NCirc* 1967, 63–5 and 'The "Reform" of Eadgar in 973', *NCirc* 1967, 94. Petersson also considers this problem, *op. cit.*, 104–7 and 148–52.

43. M. Dolley, 'A further die-link in the Scandinavian imitative series', in *Fornvannen*, 1968, 116–19.

44. M. Dolley, 'Medieval British and Irish coins as dating evidence for the archaeologist', *World Archaeology*, Vol. I, No. 2, 204.
    The number of hoards known to have been buried in the period has increased since the publication of this paper and they have been conveniently gathered together by Mr. Dolley in his listing of the Viking age hoards mentioned in note 34. Few of the additions which have for the most part been derived from early accounts are however recorded fully enough to be useful evidence on the present problem.

45. Dolley and Metcalf, *op. cit.*, 158.

46. *Inventory* 374, but see the list of coins from this hoard in the British Museum given in R. H. M. Dolley and Mrs. J. S. Strudwick, 'The provenances of the Anglo-Saxon coins recorded in the two volumes of the British Museum Catalogue', *BNJ* XXVIII, 1955–57, 51–4.

47. *Inventory* 270.

48. *Inventory* 327.

49. *Inventory* 244.

50. *Inventory* 81 and 345.

51. *Inventory* 81 and 345.

52. *Inventory* 255. Mr. Dolley and Dr. Metcalf suggest, *op. cit.*, 158, that the Sedlescombe hoard should perhaps be considered as part of the bullion reserve of the Hastings mint at the time of the Conquest, and that we cannot be certain that the great treasures from Chancton and Walbrook were not likewise official stocks of bullion. If this were so then their evidential value as multiple-type

hoards would of course be less convincing. These hoards are indeed large but in the opinion of the writer they are not so enormous as to demand an official source in the absence of other compelling reasons why this must be so. They are treated as non-official in this paper.

53. G. C. Brooke, *British Museum Catalogue, The Norman Kings*, London, 1916.

54. M. Dolley, *The Norman Conquest and the English coinage*, London, 1966, 23–5.

55. M. Archibald, 'Coins' in G. Zarnecki *et al.* (eds.), *English Romanesque art, 1066–1200*. (1984). D. Walker, 'A possible monetary crisis in the early 1100s', *Seaby Coin and Medal Bulletin*, 1984, 284–6.

56. J. J. North, *English hammered coinage*, Vol. I. London, 1963, 140–1.

57. Dolley, *op. cit.*, note 54, 15–18.

58. *Inventory* 250. It is particularly unfortunate that our knowledge of the contents of this important hoard largely depends upon those coins from it which passed through the hands of John White the notorious forger and 'improver' of coins.

59. *Inventory* 350.

60. Dolley, *op. cit.*, note 54, 21–8.

61. The writer has suggested, *op. cit.*, note 55, that the reform type that followed the castration of the moneyers in December 1124 was Type XIII not Type X as hitherto believed.

62. The types of the 744 hitherto identifiable coins are:
    type VI   1   type X   186   type XIV   305
    type VII   30   type XII   1   type XV   54
    type XI   5   type XIII 162

63. F. Elmore James, 'Stephen type VII', *BNJ* XXVIII, 1957, 537–54.

64. R. P. Mack, 'Stephen and the anarchy 1135–54', *BNJ* XXXV, 1966, 38–112. Also the author in Zarnecki (ed.), *English Romanesque Art, op. cit.*, note 55.

65. G. C. Boon. *Welsh hoards, 1979–81*. (Cardiff, 1986) for the Coed-y-Wenallt hoard of coins of Stephen and Matilda.

66. *Inventory* 235.

67. *Inventory* 16.

68. D. F. Allen, *British Museum Catalogue, The Cross-and-Crosslets ('Tealby') type of Henry II*, London, 1951.

69. The standard paper on this series is still L. A. Lawrence, 'The Short-Cross

coinage', *BNJ* XI, 1914, 59–100. This should be read in conjunction with the important papers by Mr. J. D. Brand principally, 'Some Short-Cross questions', *BNJ* XXXIII, 1964, 57–69. The most convenient place to find examples of his sub-divisions of the types is the arrangement of the Short-Cross pennies in D. M. Metcalf, *Sylloge of the coins of the British Isles, Ashmolean Museum, Oxford, Part 2: English coins 1066–1279*. London, 1969.

70. L. A. Lawrence, 'The Long-Cross coinage', *BNJ* IX, 1912, 145–79; X, 1913, 69–93; XI, 1914, 101–19.

71. C. E. Blunt and J. D. Brand, 'Mint output of Henry III', *BNJ* XXXIX, 1970, 61–6.

72. M. Mate, 'Monetary policies in England, 1272–1307', *BNJ* XLI, 1972, 34–79, and in this context especially table 1, p. 75.

73. *Inventory* 381.

74. *Inventory* 7.

75. *Inventory* 231.

76. J. D. Brand, 'Some Short-Cross questions', *BNJ* XXXIII, 1964, 65.

77. *Inventory* 94.

78. *Inventory* 152. See also J. D. Brand, 'Another small parcel from the great find at Eccles', *BNJ* XXXIII, 172–3.

79. A report on this hoard will appear in a future volume of *BNJ*.

80. A summary of the contents of this hoard appears in *NC*, 1974.

81. The coinage of Edward VI in the name of Henry, 1547–50.

82. Archbishop Bowet of York, 1407–23 and Bishop Langley of Durham, 1406–1437.

83. J. J. North, *English hammered coinage*, Vol. 2, Edward I to Charles II, 1272–1662, London, 1960.

84. G. C. Brooke, *English coins*, London, 1932, 123. A revised edition was published in 1950.

85. North *op. cit.*, note 79, 22.

86. J. J. North, *The coinages of Edward I & II*, London, 1968, 20. Several important hoards have been published since 1974 which confirm the conclusions outlined in this paper. References to these publications can be found in *A Survey of Numismatic Research*, 1978–84. *op. cit.*, note 11.

87. Hoards deposited after 1500 are referred to by the letter and number code employed in I. D. Brown and Michael Dolley, *A bibliography of coin hoards of Great Britain and Ireland 1500–1969*, Royal Numismatic Society and Spink & Son Limited, Special Publication No. 6, London, 1971.

88. *Inventory* 149.

89. Publication by the writer in *BNJ* 1974.

90. For a general discussion of this question and for tables comparing the content of later medieval English hoards of pennies see Marion M. Archibald, 'The Attenborough, (Notts.), 1966 Hoard', *NC* 1967, 133–46.

91. Publication by the writer in *BNJ* 1974.

92. Marion M. Archibald, 'The Wyre Piddle (Worcs.) 1967 hoard of fifteenth century silver coins', *NC* 1970, 133–62.

93. There are three remarkable features of this coinage: first, its obverse design which is a complete departure from that of previous issues; second, the fact that the London mint plays a major part in the striking of pennies for the first time in many years; third, the very much larger output of pennies than for a long time. Could it be that we have here a more deliberate attempt to get rid of the surviving dregs of the older issues by striking a very large new coinage of distinctive design? The condition of old pennies was of course much worse than that of groats of comparable age. This may perhaps offer an explanation why this elaborate design was used for the pennies and not for any of the regular issues of larger silver coins.

94. Found in 1972; being studied in the British Museum for publication by the writer.

95. *Inventory* 369.

96. *Inventory* 195.

97. Summary list in *NC* 1974.

98. Marion M. Archibald, 'Fishpool, Blidworth (Notts.), 1966 hoard', *NC* 1967, 133–46.

99. *Bibliography* EL12.

100. A complete list may be found in J. J. North, *English hammered coinage*, Vol. 2, London, 1960, 173.

Index

Abergele (Wales) hoard, 86 ff.
aes, asses, 103
   of Caligula, demonetised, 119
   Minerva, 120
   of Nero, 123
Alcester (Warks.) hoard, 94
Anglo-Saxons
   burials, 210ff., 224
   Eadberht of Northumbria, 237
   Edgar, reformed coinage of, 275ff.
   Edward the Confessor, coinage
      of, 277
   gold, 231
   money supply, 230ff.
   see also Offa; Saxons
annona militaris, 41, 52, 53
army pay, 106–7, 118–19, 123, 155n(71)
asses *see aes*

Baldock (Herts.), 63, 65
Bamburgh (Northumb.) hoard, 95
barbarous radiates *see* radiates
Belgic coinage, 1
Bermondsey hoard, 97
Besley, E. M., 130, 148n(4), 152n(57)
Birdoswald hoard, 16
Boon, T. M., 148n(19)
Bourton (Glos.) hoard, 13
Boxmoor (Herts.), 68
bracteates, Irish, 256
Braughing, 7ff.
Brickstock, J., 172n(215)
Brindle hoard, 97
Bristol (Glos.) hoard, 86ff.
Britain, Roman coinage in, 73ff.
Brown, R. A., 153n(57)

Cabum, 5ff.
Caerleon (Gwent), 106, 108, 110, 117,
   124, 126, 131, 137
Caernarvon (Segontium), 125, 126, 138
Caerwent, 41, 43, 110, 124, 143, 145
Caligula, *aes* of, demonetised, 119
Camulodunum *see* Colchester
Canterbury (Kent) hoards, 97, 220
Carausius, 132ff.

'Carausius II' *see* Domino group
Carolingian coins in England, 237
Carrawburgh hoard, 86ff.
Casey, P. J., 127
circulation patterns, 194ff.
circulation wear, 266
Cirencester (Glos.) hoard, 96
Civil War hoards, 206ff.
Claudian copies, 118ff.
   all without 'P.P.', 119
   background, 118–19
   distribution, 121
   end of, 123–4
   grades, Sutherland's, 116, 120
   mostly Minerva asses, 120
   origin, 119
   proportion to orthodox, 121
   stages of production, 121–2
   unofficial character, 122–3
clipped siliquae, 145
coin(s)
   clusters, 73ff.
   loss historiograms, 41ff., 60, 61
   moulds, table of localities, 127
   reports, 258ff.
   withdrawal, 209
   see also counterfeits; hoards
Colchester (Camulodunum), 4, 116, 119,
   120, 121, 127
Coleraine hoard, 21, 34
Commonwealth coinage, 209
   Civil War hoards, 206ff.
Corbridge (Northumb.), 40, 44
counterfeits and counterfeiting
   barbarous execution, 113–14
   cast, 107–10, 112, 124–7, 135–7
      passim
   cliché, 112
   confusion of design, 110, 128, 134, 137
   decline in size, 114–15
   epidemic and endemic, 102, 113
      end of, 115–16
   law of, 102–3
   'lightweights', 108, 124–5
   modern parallels, 117–18, 143
   moulds, list of, 127

plated, 106, 111–13, 124, 144
profit motive in, 114
status of, 116–17
struck, 110–11 and *passim*
see also Claudian copies; radiates,
    barbarous; 'falling horsemen'
countermarks, 106–7, 119, 121
Crawford, M. H., 111, 157n(85)
Cunetio hoard, 38
Cunobelin, gold coinage of, 5

Dark Age coinage, absence of, 116, 145
dating
    deposit, 195ff.
    Norman coinage, 278ff.
    radiates, barbarous, 126–8
Davies, J. A., 128, 130
Dawson, G. J., 152n(43)
defaced coins, 106–7
Delgany hoard, 272
denarius, Republican, 91ff.
deposit dating, 195ff.
dies, false, 110
dispersed hoards, 204ff.
'Domino group', 142–3
Dorchester (Dorset) hoard, 38
Dorchester on Thames (Oxon.) hoards,
    97, 225
Dorking hoard, 273
Dublin coin finds, 254

Eadberht of Northumbria, 237
Edgar, reformed coinage of, 275ff.
Edlington (Yorks.) hoard, 38
Edward the Confessor, longevity of
    coinage, 277
emergency hoards, 15
English mediaeval coin weights, 292
Exeter, 106, 122

'falling horsemen', 140ff.
    'minimissimi', 141–2
    site of production, 141
false coins *see* counterfeits
Farringford (I.o.W.) hoard, 13
Filey (Yorks.) hoard, 96
forgeries *see* counterfeits
fourth century hoards, 96ff.
France, Roman coinage in, 74ff.

Gadebridge villa, 58, 66
Gare (Cornwall) hoard, 94
Germany (Rhineland), 106, 124, 139
Giard, J.-B., 114, 116, 120, 121, 130,
    149n(24), 153n(54), 154n(64)
gold coinage
    Anglo-Saxon, 231

of Cunobelin, 5
mediaeval, 291
Merovingian, 222
Gosbecks (Essex) hoard, 38
Great Burstead (Essex) hoard, 13
Great Casterton, 59
Great Weldon, 65ff.
Greek imperial coins, 19
Grondall hoard, 232

Hall, J., 125
Ham Hill (Som.) hoard, 94
Hammerson, M. J., 123
Hamwih (Hants.), 228, 262
Handley (Dors.) hoard, 86ff.
Hengistbury Head, 3
hoards, coin, 13ff.
    Civil War, 206ff.
    composition, 17
    containers, 23, 24, 25
    content diversity, 202ff.
    contexts, 13
    dispersed, 204ff.
    emergency, 15
    fourth century, 96ff.
    location, 26, 27
    mediaeval, 203
    multi-container, 204
    Pepys's, 205ff.
    post-mediaeval, 203
    Roman bronze, 94ff.
    Romano-British, 13ff., 86ff.
    Severan, 86ff.
    see also individual hoards, e.g. Abergele;
        Dorchester
Housesteads, 50

Icklingham (Suff.) hoard, 96
Ilchester (Som.) hoard, 94
Irish bracteates, 256
Italy, Roman coinage in, 73ff.

Johns, C. M., 155n(67)

Kent, J. P. C., 116, 138, 143
    quoted, 175n(241)
Kenyon, R., 106, 116, 118, 121, 149n(24,
    28), 152n(48)
Kiddington (Oxon.) hoard, 96
King Harry Lane (Verulamium), 61
Kraay, C. M., 107

Langton (Yorks.), 69
Laxton hoard, 97
Leeds (Yorks.) hoard, 14
Leysdown (Kent) hoard, 94
'Limesfalsa' *see* counterfeits, 'lightweights'

Little Langford hoard, 96
Llanbethery (S. Glam.), 113, 137
London, 111, 125, 127
long-cross pennies, 281ff.
Lydney (Glos.), 114, 115, 120, 126, 138,
    140, 141, 142

Malton (Yorks.), 59, 69
market centres, 2ff.
Mattingley, H. B., 128, 130
mediaeval
    coin losses, 264
    coin weights, English, 292
    gold coinage, 291
    hoards, 203
Merovingian coinage, 231ff.
    gold, 222ff.
    silver, 244
Middle Harling (Norf.), 228, 237
Middle Temple hoard, 272
Mildenhall (Wilts) (Cunetio) hoard, 38
military site coin deposits, 50ff.
minims, 114–15, 129–30, 138–9, 140–2
    absent from Carausian copies, 128, 133
    radiates, barbarous, 128–9
Minnit, S., 143
Minster (Kent) hoard, 13
Mitard, P.-H., 110, 128, 130, 154n(64)
money supply
    Anglo-Saxon, 230ff.
    feebleness of, 103
moulds, coin, table of localities, 127
    see also counterfeits, cast
mucking, 225
multi-container hoards, 204

Nero, *aes* of, 123
Norman coinage
    dating, 278ff.
    of Stephen, order of coin issues, 280
Northallerton (Yorks) hoard, 14
Northants hoard, 96
Northover, J. P., 146n(4), 151n(41)
nummularii, 103–4

Offa, coinage of
    chronology, 239ff., 269ff.
    distribution, 230ff.
    mints, 230
Okehampton (Devon) hoard, 13
O'Neil, B. H. St.J., 116, 141, 156n(80)
overstrikes, 119, 133–5, 140
Owslebury, 1
Owston Ferry (Lincs.) hoard, 86ff.

Penard, 111, 130, 134

pennies
    long and short cross, 281ff.
    Saxon, 270ff.
    Tealby, 281ff.
Pepys's hoard, 205ff.
Peterborough (N'hants.) hoard, 95
Piercebridge (Durham), 55
Portmoak (Scotland) hoard, 86ff.
post mediaeval hoards, 203
Potin coinage, 1, 2ff.
    in Gaul, 8
pre-Claudian types, copies of, 120
publication standards, 254ff.

radiates, barbarous, 21, 22, 126ff.
    date, 126–8
    distribution, 130–2
    fantastic types, 128–9
    minims, 128–9
    sites of production, 102
Ramsgate (Kent) hoard, 95
Redenhall hoard, 97
renovatio monetae, 276
Republican denarius, withdrawal, 91ff.
residuality, 19, 20, 92ff., 194, 260, 265
Rhineland, 106, 124, 139
Rhodes, siege of, 15
Richborough (Kent), 39, 116, 121, 130,
    141
river finds, 116, 120, 157n(83)
Rochester, 4
Rogers, G. B., 164n(144)
Romano-British hoards, 13ff., 86ff.
Romans
    army pay, 106–7, 118–19, 123,
        155n(71)
    bronze hoards, 94ff.
    coinage, 73ff.
    coins in Saxon sites and graves, 218,
        224ff.
    denarius, Republican, 91ff.
    see also aes; Claudian copies

St. Alban's (Verulamium), 4, 59, 61ff.,
    110, 116, 120, 128, 132
St. Martin's hoard, Canterbury, 220
sampling bias, 190
Saxons
    coin circulation life, 273ff.
    grave goods, 218ff., 225
    penny coinage, 270ff.
    Roman coins on sites and in graves, 218,
        224ff.
Scarborough (Yorks) hoard, 96
sceattas, 218, 221, 234ff., 269ff.
Seaby, P. J., 152n(49)
Segontium *see* Caernarvon

Severan coin hoards, 86ff.
sexennial cycle theory, 275
Shiel, N., 135, 170n(187)
short-cross pennies, 281ff.
Silchester, 41, 42, 112, 119, 141, 143
    hoard, 86ff.
siliquae, clipped, 145
site finds, 39ff.
small site coin lists, 57ff.
Stephen, order of coin issues, 280
sterling coinage, 286ff.
stipendia *see* army pay
Sutherland, C. H. V., 116, 120, 121, 122,
    123
Sutton Hoo, 220

Tealby pennies, 281ff.
Theodosian copies, 145
Thomgrafton hoard, 20
Traprain hoard, 34

Usk (Gwent), 120, 121, 122, 123, 140

Valentinianic copies, 144
Verulamium *see* St. Alban's
Viking coinage, 254ff.

Wales, forts in, 115, 123
Warle hoard, 97
West Stow, 225
Weymouth (Dorset) hoard, 96
Wheeler, T. V., 140
Whitchurch (Avon), 125, 126, 127, 130,
    131
White Woman's Hole (Som.), 102, 114,
    123, 129, 138
Wingfield (Suffolk) hoard, 13
Wiveliscombe hoard, 97
Woodbridge hoard, 97
Wroxall hoard, 97
Wroxeter (Salop.), 110, 115, 127

Yatton (Som.) hoard, 14

Ziegler, R., 130